20天

背完考研英语（一）

核心词汇

新东方考试研究中心 / 编著

浙江教育出版社·杭州

P前言
Preface

　　词汇是英语学习的基础，提高英语水平，词汇是要攻克的第一道难关。对于考研的学生来说，词汇不过关，就意味着"读不懂、译不通、写不出"，进而导致总体成绩达不到要求。背单词是复习考研英语要做的第一件事，有了好的词汇基础，才能为提高个人的语言水平以及应试能力做好铺垫。

　　但背单词这件事，很多考生容易虎头蛇尾：一方面是大多数考生的备考时间有限，另一方面是一些考生背单词没有计划，背了忘，忘了再背，如此一来，最终收效甚微。无奈的是，英语是考研的必考科目之一。针对这些情况，在考量了考生的真实需求后，我们专门为备考考研英语（一）的学生编写了这本融合学习计划和词汇精华的词汇书，它是一本非常适合考研英语（一）考生应急备考的书籍。本书的首要目标是帮助考生达到一定的分数要求，故在内容上我们做了减法，剔除一些非重点、非必要的内容，没有冗赘陈述，没有将背单词这种简单的问题复杂化，从而帮考生实现短期备考。本书的具体特点如下：

　　1. 内容精准。编者精心研究历年考研英语（一）真题，结合考试大纲，统计各词汇的考频，据此确定其中2000个核心单词收入本书，每个单词下只收录考试常考的释义、搭配、例句以及易错单词的辨析，让考生有的放矢，了解重点，对症下药。同时，在有限的时间内，获取重点内容，使备考更高效。

　　2. 目标导向。本书规划了20天的学习计划，浓缩了备考考研英语（一）词汇的精华内容，特别是真题例句比例达到了70%，是考生应急背单词、快速了解真题难度的有效复习资料。另外，本书在每一天的开始设置了Previous Check栏目，供考生背单词前自测、筛出已知和未知的词汇，以便合理分配复习时间，有针对性地选取个人所需的内容学习，而不是把所有单词全部纳入学习计划。同时，在每一天的后面设置了Review栏目，以便于考生在每天的学习后进行自测，检查学习效果，也可在若干天的学习后，循环复习，巩固之前的单词记忆。

3. 多方巩固。全书为所有的词汇配套了词汇拼写音频，精确到字母的朗读，方便考生随时听音记单词，做听写练习或检测和巩固记忆效果，结合本书配套的背单词小程序，学习效果更好。

4. 全面贴心。本书内含字帖范例，可供考生临摹，帮助考生提高书写美观程度，进而提高分数。另外，本书还提供了书写区，考生不必随身携带其他笔记本，方便涂写，贴心备考。

有了好的单词书，再利用适当的记忆技巧，背单词就会事半功倍。为此，我们推荐考生：

❶ 循环记忆，反复背诵。要想记牢单词是要下一番功夫的，单纯注重当时的记忆效果，而忽视了后期复习、巩固，同样是达不到良好效果的，所以一定要通过反复背诵，巩固、加强记忆效果。

❷ 选择有利于记忆的时间段背单词。据生理学家数据分析得知，在上午 6:00-7:30、8:00-10:00、下午 4:00-5:00、晚上 8:00-10:00 这四个时间段，人的记忆力较好。

真心希望本书能帮助广大考研考生取得满意的成绩。由于时间有限，本书错误之处在所难免，恳请广大考生能给我们提出宝贵意见，以便我们不断改善。

新东方考试研究中心

目录
Contents

- confer
- boot
- increase
- tempt
- realistic
- compound
- forth
- failure
- plaster
- guide
- assign
- develop
- scrutiny
- participant
- peculiar
- congress
- subscribe
- sake
- balance
- academic
- wander
- defer
- clip
- encourage
- cautious
- relevant
- combine
- status
- penalty
- operate
- believe

- fuss
- institution
- bonus
- alternative
- accept
- strength
- appeal
- engage
- domain
- instruct
- stress
- inferior
- premise
- graduate
- master
- obsession
- benefit
- device
- degree
- indicate
- particular
- transplant
- awake
- supreme
- challenge
- predict
- burn
- private
- oriental
- convert
- deliver

- respond
- naval
- migrate
- composition
- initiate
- extraordinary
- diffuse
- inner
- invite
- scholar
- fetch
- wage
- mammal
- structure
- guess
- chance
- precious
- compensate
- query
- tragic
- skip
- decade
- prudent
- variation
- elaborate
- restraint
- cheat
- spray
- drastic
- stare
- mandate

- admission
- manner
- file
- upset
- thesis
- phrase
- explicit

Writing Models ◎ ············

confer

boot

increase

tempt

realistic

compound

forth

failure

plaster

guide

assign

develop

confer / kən'fɜː(r) /
- 释 v. 商讨, 协商; 赋予, 授予
- 搭 confer sth. on/upon sb. 授予某人某物
- 例 You would **confer** a great favor upon me by coming with me. 你和我一起来对我来说是莫大的帮助。
- 派 conference / 'kɒnfərəns / n. 会议; 讨论 ‖ conferment / kən'fɜːmənt / n. 给予; 商量

boot / buːt /
- 释 n. 靴子; (汽车后部的) 行李箱; 猛踢 v. 启动 (计算机); 猛踢; 装入操作系统
- 搭 get the boot 被解雇; 被抛弃 ‖ lick sb.'s boots 阿谀奉承; 拍马屁
- 例 All I have to do is to go to my CD shelf, or **boot** up my computer and download still more recorded music from iTunes. 我所要做的就是去翻我的CD架, 或者启动我的电脑, 依旧从iTunes下载更多录制好的音乐。(2011年)

increase
- 释 / ɪn'kriːs / v. 增加; (使) 增长 / 'ɪŋkriːs / n. 增加; 增长
- 例 From the 10th century onwards, as merchant and travel routes became more developed, the construction of caravanserais **increased** and they served as a safe place for people to rest at night. 从10世纪起, 随着商路和旅行路线的日益发达, 商队客店的建设也随之增加, 它们成为人们夜间休息的安全场所。(2023年)
- 近 soar / sɔː(r) / v. 急剧增加, 飙升; 高飞
- 反 decrease / dɪ'kriːs / v. 减少; 下降 / 'diːkriːs / n. 减少; 下降 ‖ reduce / rɪ'djuːs / v. 减少

tempt / tempt /
- 释 v. 吸引; 引诱
- 例 You might even be **tempted** to assume that humanity has little future to look forward to. 你甚至可能会忍不住认为, 人类几乎没有未来可言。(2013年)
- 派 temptation / temp'teɪʃn / n. 诱惑
- 近 attract / ə'trækt / v. 吸引

realistic / ˌriːə'lɪstɪk /
- 释 adj. 现实的; 务实的; 现实主义的
- 例 They tend to keep a tighter hold on their purse and consider eating at home a **realistic** alternative. 他们往往把钱包括得紧紧的, 认为在家吃饭是一种务实的选择。(2010年)

compound / 'kɒmpaʊnd /
- 释 n. 化合物; 复合词
- 例 Scientists say the **compound** is likely to cause cancer but have no hard scientific proof. 科学家们说, 这种化合物可能致癌, 但没有确凿的科学证据。(2020年)

forth / fɔːθ / 　007

释 *adv.* 向前; 向某处

搭 and so forth 等等 ‖ back and forth 来来回回地

例 It was the purpose and responsibility of great minds to go **forth** and seek out the truth, which they believed to be founded in knowledge. 伟大思想家的目的和责任就是去传播和探求真理, 他们相信真理是建立在知识之上的。(2020年)

近 forwards / 'fɔːwədz / *adv.* 向前; 今后 ‖ onwards / 'ɒnwədz / *adv.* 向前; 前往

failure / 'feɪljə(r) / 　008

释 *n.* 失败; 失败的事

搭 academic failure 学业上的失败

例 The difference between C-grade and A-grade managers may very well be the difference between business success or **failure**. C级经理人和A级经理人之间的差别很可能就是企业成败的差别。(2022年)

plaster / 'plɑːstə(r) / 　009

释 *n.* 灰泥; 石膏; 膏药

例 Almost all of the interior detail is of cast iron or **plaster**; the use of wood was minimized to insure fire safety. 几乎所有的内部细节都是铸铁或石膏; 为了确保消防安全, 尽量减少了木材的使用。(2018年)

guide / 'gaɪd / 　010

释 *v.* 指导; 给某人领路 *n.* 指南; 指导者; 导游

例 The rough **guide** to marketing success used to be that you got what you paid for. 曾经, 营销成功的大致指南是"一分钱一分货"。(2011年)

assign / ə'saɪn / 　011

释 *v.* 分配, 委派; 指定时间、地点等

搭 assign sth. to sb. 把某物分配给某人

例 The student union of your university has **assigned** you to inform the international students about an upcoming singing contest. 你所在大学的学生会指派你向留学生们告知即将举行的歌唱比赛。(2020年)

派 assignment / ə'saɪnmənt / *n.* 分配; 任务; (课外)作业

近 allot / ə'lɒt / *v.* 分配 ‖ allocate / 'æləkeɪt / *v.* 分配

develop / dɪ'veləp / 　012

释 *v.* 发展; 开发; 出现(问题); (使)成长; 患(病); 修建

例 Sophisticated technologies **develop** from small inventions. 尖端技术是由小发明发展而来的。(2024年)

Writing Models ◎

scrutiny

participant

peculiar

congress

subscribe

sake

balance

academic

wander

defer

scrutiny / ˈskruːtəni /　　　　　　　　　　013

释 *n.* 仔细检查；认真彻底的审查

例 Manuscript will be flagged up for additional **scrutiny** by the journal's internal editors, or by its existing Board of Reviewing Editors or by outside peer reviewers. 稿件将由期刊的内部编辑、现有的审稿编辑委员会或外部的同行评审员进行额外审查。（2015年）

近 inspection / ɪnˈspekʃn / *n.* 检查；视察 ‖ investigation / ɪnˌvestɪˈɡeɪʃn / *n.* 调查；侦察

participant / pɑːˈtɪsɪpənt /　　　　　　　014

释 *n.* 参与者

例 The reach of art-science tie-ups needs to go beyond the necessary purpose of research communication, and **participants** must not fall into the trap of stereotyping each other. 艺术与科学结合的范围要超越研究交流的必要目的，参与者不能陷入对彼此的刻板印象的陷阱。（2022年）

peculiar / pɪˈkjuːliə(r) /　　　　　　　　015

释 *adj.* 奇怪的；独特的；专门的；特殊的

例 The **peculiar** part is that the journal that the editor is supposedly working for is not profiting at all—it is just providing citations to other journals. 奇怪的点在于，据说编辑为之工作的期刊根本没有获利，只是为其他期刊提供引文。（2023年）

近 distinctive / dɪˈstɪŋktɪv / *adj.* 有特色的，与众不同的 ‖ particular / pəˈtɪkjələ(r) / *adj.* 独有的；特别的

congress / ˈkɒŋɡres /　　　　　　　　　　016

释 *n.* 国会；议会；代表大会

例 The bill proved largely popular and sailed through **Congress** with large majorities in favor. 事实证明，该法案大受欢迎，并在国会以绝大多数赞成票顺利通过。（2023年）

派 congressman / ˈkɒŋɡrəsmən / *n.* 国会议员

近 parliament / ˈpɑːləmənt / *n.* 议会，国会

辨 parliament指英国或加拿大等国的议会，通常首字母大写；congress指美国等国的国会，也可指代表大会。

subscribe / səbˈskraɪb /　　　　　　　　017

释 *v.* 订阅；认购（股份）；定期捐款

例 Copyright rested with the journal publisher, and researchers seeking knowledge of the results would have to **subscribe** to the journal. 论文版权归期刊出版商所有，想了解实验结果的研究者不得不订阅该期刊。（2008年）

派 subscriber / səbˈskraɪbə(r) / *n.*（报刊等的）订阅人 ‖ subscription / səbˈskrɪpʃn / *n.*（报刊等的）订阅

sake / seɪk /   `078`

释 *n.* 目的；利益；理由；日本清酒

搭 for the sake of 为了……起见；因……的缘故；为获得（或保持）某物

例 The Romans buried the nails probably for the **sake** of hiding them from the locals. 罗马人埋葬这些钉子可能是为了不让当地人找到它们。（2024年）

balance / 'bæləns /   `079`

释 *v.* 平衡；均衡 *n.* 平衡；余额

例 It has restored the **balance** among neighboring jurisdictions. 它恢复了相邻辖区之间的平衡。（2024年）

反 imbalance / ɪm'bæləns / *n.* 不平衡

academic / ˌækə'demɪk /   `020`

释 *adj.* 学业的；教学的；学术的；学院的；学业优秀的 *n.* 高等院校教师；高校科研人员

例 The solution is to change the mindset of the **academic** community, and what it considers to be its main goal. 解决的办法是改变学术界的思维模式以及学术界所认为的主要目标。（2013年）

wander / 'wɒndə(r) /   `021`

释 *v.* 漫游；闲逛；徘徊；流浪；漂泊；走失；离散；走神；蜿蜒 *n.* 游荡；溜达；闲逛；徘徊

例 What about the son or daughter who is grown but seems to be struggling and **wandering** aimlessly through early adulthood? 那些已经长大成人，但似乎还在成年早期漫无目的地挣扎和徘徊的儿子或女儿该怎么办？（2007年）

defer / dɪ'fɜː(r) /   `022`

释 *v.* 推迟；延期；服从

搭 defer to 听从，服从

例 This is why repeated attempts at reform legislation have failed in recent years, leaving the Postal Service unable to pay its bills except by **deferring** vital modernization. 这就是为什么近年来改革立法的多次尝试都以失败告终，导致邮政局无力支付账单，只能推迟重要的现代化进程。（2018年）

近 postpone / pə'spəʊn / *v.* 延迟；延期；暂缓 ‖ prolong / prə'lɒŋ / *v.* 延长

辨 delay、postpone、prolong和defer四个词均有"延期"的意思。delay为普通用词，多指因外界原因推迟或耽误；postpone多指有安排的延期，常指明延期到什么时间；prolong指把时间延长至超过正常或通常的限度；defer语气强于postpone，多指故意拖延。

Writing Models ◎

clip

encourage

cautious

relevant

combine

status

penalty

operate

believe

fuss

institution

bonus

clip / klɪp / `0 2 3`

释 *v.* 删减，缩短；剪（掉）；修剪；夹住 *n.* 夹，钳；回形针；（视频的）片段

例 Your pages will be easier to keep track of that way, and, if you have to **clip** a paragraph to place it elsewhere, you will not lose any writing on the other side. 这样，你的页面将更容易记录，而且，如果你不得不剪切一个段落并将其放在其他地方，你也不会丢失另一侧的任何文字。（2008年）

近 prune / pruːn / *v.* 修剪 ‖ shear / ʃɪə(r) / *v.* 剪，修剪

encourage / ɪnˈkʌrɪdʒ / `0 2 4`

释 *v.* 支持；鼓励；激励；促进；助长；鼓动，怂恿

例 If we are serious about ensuring that our science is both meaningful and reproducible, we must ensure that our institutions **encourage** that kind of science. 如果我们真的要确保我们的科学既有意义又可复制，我们就必须确保我们的机构鼓励这种科学。（2019年）

派 encouragement / ɪnˈkʌrɪdʒmənt / *n.* 鼓励；鼓舞

反 discourage / dɪsˈkʌrɪdʒ / *v.* 阻止；使灰心

cautious / ˈkɔːʃəs / `0 2 5`

释 *adj.* 谨慎的，小心的

例 Because employment protection laws make it costlier to fire an employee, employers are more **cautious** about hiring new staff. 由于就业保护法提高了解雇员工的成本，雇主在招聘新员工时更加谨慎了。（2022年）

relevant / ˈreləvənt / `0 2 6`

释 *adj.* 相关的；有意义的；有价值的；切题的

例 If you're doing research, you can have AI go out and look for **relevant** sources and information that otherwise you just wouldn't have time for. 如果你正在做研究，你可以让人工智能去寻找相关的资料来源和信息，不这样的话，你根本没有时间去做这些事。（2021年）

combine `0 2 7`

释 / kəmˈbaɪn / *v.* （使）结合；联合；混合；兼有；兼备；兼做；协力
/ ˈkɒmbaɪn / *n.* 集团；联合企业

例 In previous eras of drastic technological change, entrepreneurs smoothed the transition by dreaming up ways to **combine** labor and machines. 在以往技术急剧变革的时代，企业家们通过想象出劳动力和机器结合的方法实现了平稳过渡。（2018年）

status / ˈsteɪtəs / `0 2 8`

释 *n.* 地位；身份；职位；（进展的）状况，情形

例 His father was a clerk in the British Navy pay office—a respectable position, but with little social **status**. 他的父亲是英国海军饷处的一名职员，这种职位体面，但社会地位不高。（2017年）

penalty / ˈpenəlti /

释 *n.* 处罚，惩罚；罚款；（体育运动对犯规者的）判罚；点球

例 The current state of affairs may have been encouraged—though not justified—by the lack of legal **penalty** (in America, but not Europe) for data leakage. 目前的状况可能是由于（在美国，而非欧洲）对数据泄露行为缺乏法律惩罚所促成的，尽管这并不合理。（2017年）

030

operate / ˈɒpəreɪt /

释 *v.* 操作，使运行；工作；控制；经营，营业；动手术

例 The Government has pledged to change the law to introduce a minimum service requirement so that, even when strikes occur, services can continue to **operate**. 政府已经承诺修改法律，引入最低服务要求，以便即使发生罢工，服务也能继续运行。（2021年）

031

believe / bɪˈliːv /

释 *v.* 相信；认为；对……有信心；信任

搭 believe in 信任；相信某人（或事物）的存在

例 Dr Annie Swanepoel, a child psychiatrist, **believes** that there are ways to incorporate them into western life. 儿童精神病学家安妮·斯瓦内普尔博士认为，有办法让它们（这些做法）融入西方生活。（2024年）

032

fuss / fʌs /

释 *n.* 忙乱；大惊小怪；紧张不安 *v.* 过分关心（枝节小事）；（为小事）烦恼；（对……）关爱备至

搭 make a fuss of/over sb. 对某人过分体贴；大惊小怪

例 The point of a style upgrade isn't to become more vain or to spend more time **fussing** over what to wear. （穿衣）风格升级并不是为了变得更虚荣，也不是为了花更多的时间在穿什么上纠结。（2016年）

033

institution / ˌɪnstɪˈtjuːʃn /

释 *n.* 机构；体制；社会福利机构

搭 financial institution 金融机构

例 Simply, there are people in Nigeria who cannot travel to the Smithsonian **Institution** to see that part of their history and culture represented by the Benin Bronzes. 确实，在尼日利亚也有人无法前往史密森学会参观贝宁青铜器所代表的他们那部分历史和文化。（2024年）

派 institutional / ˌɪnstɪˈtjuːʃənl / *adj.* 机构的；慈善机构的

034

bonus / ˈbəʊnəs /

释 *n.* 奖金；意外收获

例 Starting next year, any guaranteed **bonus** of top executives could be delayed 10 years if their banks are under investigation for wrongdoing. 从明年起，如果高管所在的银行因不法行为而被调查，那么他们的任何固定奖金都可能被推迟十年发放。（2019年）

Writing Models ◎

alternative

accept

strength

appeal

engage

domain

instruct

stress

inferior

premise

graduate

master

alternative / ɔːl'tɜːnətɪv / 035

释 *adj.* 另类的；非传统的；可供替代的 *n.* 可供选择的事物

例 For wild animals that cannot be returned to their natural habitats, zoos offer the best **alternative**. 对于无法返回自然栖息地的野生动物来说，动物园提供了最好的替代选择。（2022年）

accept / ək'sept / 036

释 *v.* 接受；认可；接纳（为成员等）

例 Humility requires you to recognize weaknesses in your own arguments and sometimes also to **accept** reasons on the opposite side. 谦虚要求你认识到自己论点中的不足，有时还要接受反方的理由。（2019年）

派 acceptance / ək'septəns / *n.* 接受 ‖ acceptable / ək'septəbl / *adj.* 可接受的

strength / streŋθ / 037

释 *n.* 力量；强度；实力；优势；强烈程度

例 I believe it is precisely this permanent coexistence of metaphysical message through physical means that is the **strength** of music. 我相信，正是这种通过物理手段传递形而上信息的永久共存，才是音乐的力量所在。（2014年）

appeal / ə'piːl / 038

释 *v.* 吸引，引起兴趣；上诉；呼吁 *n.* 吸引力；上诉；呼吁

例 Lower-income jobs like gardening or day care don't **appeal** to robots. 园艺或日托等较低收入的工作对机器人没有吸引力。（2018年）

近 fascinate / 'fæsɪneɪt / *v.* 吸引；使着迷

engage / ɪn'geɪdʒ / 039

释 *v.* 从事；吸引住（注意力、兴趣）；使加入；使融入；聘请

搭 engage in sth.（使）从事，参加 ‖ engage with 与……建立密切关系；尽力理解

例 "There is one and only one social responsibility of business," wrote Milton Friedman, a Nobel prize-winning economist, "That is, to use its resources and **engage** in activities designed to increase its profits." 诺贝尔经济学奖得主米尔顿·弗里德曼写道："企业的社会责任有且只有一个，那就是利用其资源，从事旨在增加利润的活动。"（2016年）

domain / dəʊ'meɪn / 040

释 *n.*（知识、活动的）领域，范围，范畴；领土，领地；势力范围；域

例 One suggestion is that AI models could be trained on images in the public **domain**, and AI companies could forge partnerships with museums and artists, Ortiz says. 奥尔蒂斯说，一个建议是，人工智能模型可以用公有领域的图像进行训练，而且人工智能公司可以与博物馆和艺术家建立合作关系。（2024年）

instruct / ɪn'strʌkt /

释 v. 指示；吩咐；教；告知，通知

例 I can't think of a single search I've done where a board has not **instructed** me to look at sitting CEOs first. 我想不出在我做猎头寻找候选人时，有任何一次董事会没有指示我首先查看（其他公司的）现任的首席执行官们。（2011年）

stress / stres /

释 n. 精神压力；压力；强调 v. 强调；着重

例 Chaudhary said that parents now had less childcare support from family and social networks than during most of humans' evolutionary history, but introducing additional caregivers could reduce **stress** and maternal depression, which could have a "knock-on" benefit to a child's wellbeing. 乔杜里说，与人类进化史中的大部分时期相比，现在的父母从家庭和社会网络中获得的育儿支持更少，但引入额外的照顾者可以减轻压力和产妇抑郁，这可能会对孩子的健康产生"连锁"影响。（2024年）

派 stressful / 'stresfl / adj. 压力大的；紧张的

inferior / ɪn'fɪəriə(r) /

释 adj. 劣等的，次的；级别低的 n. 下级，下属

搭 inferior to 比……差；低于……的

例 They are often **inferior** to live concerts in quality. 它们（录音文件）的品质往往不如现场音乐会。（2011年）

反 superior / suː'pɪəriə(r) / adj. 上好的；上级的 n. 上级

premise / 'premɪs /

释 n. 前提；假设

例 The **premise** was that the common law of contract lacked sufficient safeguards for workers against arbitrary conduct by management. 其前提是，普通合同法没有为工人提供足够的保障，使其免受管理层的专制行为的侵害。（2022年）

graduate

释 / 'ɡrædʒuət / n. （大学）毕业生 / 'ɡrædʒueɪt / v. 毕业

例 Today, 28 per cent of **graduates** in the UK are in non-**graduate** roles, a percentage which is double the average among OECD countries. 如今，英国有28%的大学毕业生从事不需要文凭的工作，这一比例是经合组织国家平均水平的两倍。（2022年）

派 graduation / ˌɡrædʒu'eɪʃn / n. 毕业；毕业典礼

master / 'mɑːstə(r) /

释 v. 掌握；精通 n. 主人；雇主；老板；专家；高手；（局势的）控制者；硕士学位 adj. 原始拷贝的，母盘的

例 Retailers that **master** the intricacies of wholesaling in Europe may well expect to rake in substantial profits thereby. 零售商如果掌握了在欧洲批发的复杂技巧，很可能会因此获得可观的利润。（2010年）

047

obsession / əbˈseʃn /

释 *n.* 痴迷; 困扰; [心理]强迫观念
例 These **obsessions** made Tom nervous and irritable. 这些困扰使汤姆神经紧张, 急躁易怒。

048

benefit / ˈbenɪfɪt /

释 *n.* 利益, 好处; 救济金 *v.* 对……有益; 得益
搭 benefit from 得益于……
例 Both the wildlife park and zoo claimed to be operating for the **benefit** of the animals and for conservation purposes. 野生动物园和动物园都声称是为了动物的利益, 以及出于保护的目的而运营的。(2022年)

049

device / dɪˈvaɪs /

释 *n.* 装置; 设备; 手段, 策略
例 Using tracking **devices**, researchers have shown that they have "remarkable spatial acuity." 利用跟踪装置, 研究人员证明它们 (大象) 具有 "非凡的空间敏锐度"。(2024年)

050

degree / dɪˈɡriː /

释 *n.* 程度; 学位; 级别
搭 bachelor's degree 学士学位 ‖ doctoral degree 博士学位
例 Their sons or daughters would never say such a thing; it's as if they already know that their **degree** won't define them in the same way. 他们的儿子或女儿永远不会说这样的话; 他们似乎已经知道, 他们的学位不会以同样的方式定义他们。(2022年)

051

indicate / ˈɪndɪkeɪt /

释 *v.* 表明, 暗示; 指示, 指出; 象征, 代表
例 Our findings **indicate** that people do not only feel different when they are the centre of attention but that their brain reactions also differ. 我们的研究结果表明, 当人们成为注意力的中心时, 他们不仅感受不同, 而且大脑的反应也不同。(2020年)

052

particular / pəˈtɪkjələ(r) /

释 *adj.* 专指的; 独特的; 非同寻常的
搭 in particular 特别
例 The volatile chemicals produced by plants can be carried a long way, and they are very characteristic: Each plant or tree has its own **particular** odor signature. 植物产生的挥发性化学物质可以被扩散至很远, 而且它们非常有特点: 每种植物或树木都有自己独特的气味特征。(2024年)

053

transplant

释 / trænsˈplænt / *v.* 移植 (器官), 使迁移 / ˈtrænsplænt / *n.* (器官) 移植
例 His only chance of survival was a heart **transplant**. 只有进行心脏移植, 他才有望活下去。

awake / əˈweɪk /

释 v. （使）醒来；（被）唤起 adj. 醒着的
例 The brain is as active during REM (rapid eye movement) sleep—when most vivid dreams occur—as it is when fully **awake**, says Dr. Eric Nofzinger at the University of Pittsburgh. 匹兹堡大学的埃里克·诺夫辛格博士说，大脑在快速眼动睡眠期间（最生动的梦境发生时）与完全清醒时一样活跃。（2005年）

054

supreme / suˈpriːm /

释 adj. 最高的，至高无上的；极大的，极度的
例 All this was put at great risk late last month, when the U.S. **Supreme** Court issued a ruling in an Idaho case that provides the U.S. Environmental Protection Agency (EPA) far less authority to regulate wetlands and waterways. 上个月底，美国最高法院在爱达荷州的一起案件中做出裁决，使得美国环境保护局（EPA）对湿地和水道的管理权限大大降低，所有这一切就变得岌岌可危了。（2024年）

055

challenge / ˈtʃælɪndʒ /

释 v. 向……挑战 n. 挑战；盘问
例 The non-intrusive delivery of the marketing messages in a way that is sensitive to the needs of the target customer is one of the critical **challenges** to the digital marketer. 以一种理解目标客户需求的方式、非侵入式地传递营销信息是数字营销者面临的关键挑战之一。（2023年）

056

predict / prɪˈdɪkt /

释 v. 预测；预报；预言；预告
例 You want to **predict** if something needs attention now and point to where it's useful for employees to go to. 你要预测某些事情现在是否需要关注，并指出员工要关注的对其有用的地方。（2021年）

057

burn / bɜːn /

释 v. 燃烧；烧伤；烧毁 n. 灼伤
搭 burn out 烧坏 ‖ burn down 烧毁 ‖ burn off 烧尽
例 The idea that one might **burn** down an entire house just to reclaim the nails underlines how scarce, costly and valuable the simple-seeming technology was. 一个人可能仅仅为了回收钉子而烧毁整栋房子，这凸显了这项看似简单的技术是多么稀缺、昂贵以及有价值。（2024年）

058

private / ˈpraɪvət /

释 adj. 私有的；个人的；私人的；私下的；民营的 n. 二等兵，列兵
搭 in private 私下地
例 In New Zealand, a 2016 **private** members' Bill tried to permit firms and high-income employees to contract out of the unjustified dismissal regime. 在新西兰，2016年的一项民营成员法案试图允许公司和高收入雇员签约退出不合理解雇制度。（2022年）

059

Writing Models

oriental

convert

deliver

respond

naval

migrate

composition

initiate

extraordinary

diffuse

inner

invite

oriental / ˌɔːriˈentl / 060

释 *adj.* 东方的; 东方人的

例 His dad has **oriental** blood in his veins. 他的爸爸有东方人的血统。

convert 061

释 / kənˈvɜːt / *v.* (使) 转变, 转换, 转化; 可转变为 / ˈkɒnvɜːt / *n.* 改变宗教 (或信仰、观点) 的人; 皈依者

例 A recent annual study of countries and their ability to **convert** growth into well-being sheds some light on that question. 最近一项有关各国及其将增长转化为福祉的能力的年度研究为这一问题提供了一些启示。(2017年)

deliver / dɪˈlɪvə(r) / 062

释 *v.* 发表 (讲话); 传送; 交付

搭 deliver lessons 讲课

例 Not only can AI help to create the marketing content, but it can also provide a non-intrusive way of **delivering** the content to the target customers. 人工智能不仅可以帮助创建营销内容, 还能提供一种非侵入式的方式将内容传递给目标客户。(2023年)

派 delivery / dɪˈlɪvəri / *n.* 递送

respond / rɪˈspɒnd / 063

释 *v.* 回应, 应对

例 Specific brain regions that **respond** during direct gaze are being explored by other researches, using advanced methods of brain scanning. 其他研究人员正在利用先进的脑部扫描方法, 对直接注视时产生反应的特定脑部区域进行探索。(2020年)

naval / ˈneɪvl / 064

释 *adj.* 海军的; 军舰的

例 The rates of pulmonary disease and heart disease were similar between **naval** and army personnel. 海军和陆军人员的肺病和心脏病发病率相似。

migrate / maɪˈɡreɪt / 065

释 *v.* 迁移; 移居; 移动

例 Large numbers of people **migrated** from California, mostly to other parts of the West. 大量人口迁出了加利福尼亚州, 其中大部分流向了西部的其他地区。

composition / ˌkɒmpəˈzɪʃn / 066

释 *n.* 成分, 构成; 作品, 作曲; 作文

例 Beethoven's importance in music has been principally defined by the revolutionary nature of his **compositions**. 贝多芬在音乐界的重要性主要体现在其作品的革新性上。(2014年)

initiate

067

释 / ɪ'nɪʃieɪt / *v.* 开始; 启动, 发起; 初步了解; 让……加入 / ɪ'nɪʃiət / *n.* 新加入者

例 The most famous of these efforts was **initiated** by Noam Chomsky, who suggested that humans are born with an innate language-acquisition capacity that dictates a universal grammar. 这些尝试中最著名的是由诺姆·乔姆斯基发起的, 他认为人类与生俱来就具有语言习得能力, 这种能力决定了一种通用语法。(2012年)

extraordinary / ɪk'strɔ:dnri /

068

释 *adj.* 非凡的; 特别的

例 Shakespeare's lifetime was coincident with a period of **extraordinary** activity and achievement in the drama. 莎士比亚生时正逢戏剧活动异常活跃、成就非凡的时期。(2018年)

派 extraordinarily / ɪk'strɔ:dnrəli / *adv.* 极其地

diffuse / dɪ'fju:s /

069

释 *adj.* 扩散的; 漫射的; 不清楚的; 冗长的; 难解的; 啰唆的 *v.* 减弱, 平息 (不良情绪或局面); 扩散, 渗透, 弥漫; 使 (观点或信息) 传播, 散布

例 And third, through a more **diffuse** "halo effect," whereby its good deeds earn it greater consideration from consumers and others. 第三, 通过更广泛的"光环效应", 使其善举赢得更多消费者和其他人的青睐。(2016年)

inner / 'ɪnə(r) /

070

释 *adj.* 内部的, 里面的; 内心的

例 Mental health has commonly been called conscience, instinct, wisdom, common sense, or the **inner** voice. 心理健康通常被描述成良知、本能、明智、常识或内心的声音。(2016年)

近 interior / ɪn'tɪəriə(r) / *adj.* 内部的; 里面的 *n.* 内部; 内陆; (国家的) 内政, 内务

反 outer / 'aʊtə(r) / *adj.* 外部的, 外面的

辨 inner含义广泛, 指事物的中心或接近中心的部位, 也可指内心隐秘的活动; interior指某物的内部, 尤指某物的内侧, 也可指内地的或国内的。

invite / ɪn'vaɪt /

071

释 *v.* 邀请 *n.* 邀请; 请柬

搭 invite sb. to do sth. 邀请某人做某事

例 You infer information you feel the writer has **invited** you to grasp by presenting you with specific evidence and clues. 你通过感受作者向你展示的具体证据和线索来推断作者想让你掌握的信息。(2015年)

派 invitation / ˌɪnvɪ'teɪʃn / *n.* 邀请

scholar / ˈskɒlə(r) /

釋 *n.* 学者

例 **Scholars** have long debated whether there is ever such a thing as a truly selfless act. 长期以来，学者们一直在争论是否存在真正无私的行为。

派 scholarship / ˈskɒləʃɪp / *n.* 学问；学术；奖学金

072

fetch / fetʃ /

釋 *v.* 售得，卖得（某价）；（去）拿来；（去）请来

例 These rules say they must value some assets at the price a third party would pay, not the price managers and regulators would like them to **fetch**. 这些准则规定，它们必须按照第三方愿意支付的价格对某些资产进行估值，而不是按照管理机构和监管机构期望售卖的价格。（2010年）

073

wage / weɪdʒ /

釋 *n.* （通常指按周领的）工资，工钱

例 With more hires available, businesses haven't had to raise **wages** as much to fill jobs, thereby easing the pressure on those businesses to raise their prices. 有了更多的招聘机会，企业不必提高过多工资来填补工作空缺，从而减轻了这些企业提高薪资的压力。

近 salary / ˈsæləri / *n.* 薪金，薪水 ‖ income / ˈɪnkʌm / *n.* 收入；收益 ‖ earnings / ˈɜːnɪŋz / *n.* 薪水；工资；收入

辨 wage或wages通常指在工厂等工作的雇员按周领取的工钱；salary通常指办公室工作人员、教师、医生等专业人员按月领取的薪水；income一般看作是可靠的固定收入；earnings泛指工作所得的报酬，不包括非劳动所得。

074

mammal / ˈmæml /

釋 *n.* 哺乳动物

例 A parallel situation exists in respect of predatory **mammals** and fish-eating birds. 食肉哺乳动物和食鱼鸟类也存在类似的情况。（2010年）

075

structure / ˈstrʌktʃə(r) /

釋 *n.* 结构；构造；建筑物；精心组织；周密安排；体系 *v.* 使形成体系；系统安排；精心组织

例 You are now not wanted; you are now excluded from the work environment that offers purpose and **structure** in your life. 你现在不被需要了，你现在被排除在为你的生活提供目标和周密安排的工作环境之外。（2014年）

076

guess / ges /

釋 *v.* 猜测；估计；猜到；想，以为 *n.* 猜测；猜想

搭 have/make a guess (at sth.)（对某事）做猜测 ‖ take a guess 猜测

例 Whether this research translates elsewhere is anybody's **guess**. 至于这项研究是否适用于其他地方，谁也说不准。（2021年）

077

chance / tʃɑːns / 078

释 *n.*（尤指希望发生的事的）可能性；机会；冒险；偶然

搭 by any chance 或许，可能 ‖ by chance 偶然；碰巧；意外 ‖ take a chance 冒险；碰运气

例 Since plants don't have nervous systems, the **chances** that they have consciousness are effectively zero. 由于植物没有神经系统，它们具有意识的可能性实际上为零。（2022年）

precious / 'preʃəs / 079

释 *adj.* 宝贵的；珍贵的；珍奇的

例 Ancient Greek philosopher Aristotle viewed laughter as "a bodily exercise **precious** to health." 古希腊哲学家亚里士多德认为笑是"一种对健康来说很宝贵的身体锻炼"。（2011年）

近 valuable / 'væljuəbl / *adj.* 贵重的；宝贵的

compensate / 'kɒmpenseɪt / 080

释 *v.* 补偿；弥补；给……赔偿（或赔款）

搭 compensate for 弥补（过失）；抵消

例 Many comics were first motivated to be funny to **compensate** for not being popular in life. 许多喜剧演员最初都是为了弥补在生活中不受欢迎而开始搞笑的。

派 compensation / ,kɒmpen'seɪʃn / *n.* 补偿；赔偿 ‖ compensatory / ,kɒmpen'seɪtəri / *adj.* 补偿的；赔偿的；补偿性质的；赔偿性质的

query / 'kwɪəri / 081

释 *n.* 疑问；询问；问号 *v.* 怀疑；表示疑虑；询问

例 They conducted a survey in which several hundred people were **queried** about their dietary habits. 他们进行了一项调查，在调查中，对数百人的饮食习惯进行了询问。

tragic / 'trædʒɪk / 082

释 *adj.* 悲惨的；可悲的；悲剧的 *n.* 悲剧

例 Since then, he was known to both throw the hat to the floor in fits of anger and carry it valiantlly into battle, and the hat has become the embodiment of the **tragic** hero. 从那以后，人们知道他会在愤怒时把帽子扔到地上，也会戴着帽子勇敢地上战场，这顶帽子就成了这位悲剧英雄的化身。

派 tragically / 'trædʒɪkli / *adv.* 悲惨地，不幸地

skip / skɪp / 083

释 *v.* 跳过；略过；不做；悄悄溜走

搭 skip off/out 溜走；突然离去 ‖ skip over 匆匆翻阅；略过

例 Anyone who has toiled through the exam will testify that test-taking skill matters, whether it's knowing when to guess or what questions to **skip**. 任何辛苦准备过考试的人都会证明，考试技巧很重要，无论是知道什么时候该猜测，还是知道什么问题该跳过。

Writing Models ◎

decade

prudent

variation

elaborate

restraint

cheat

spray

drastic

stare

mandate

admission

0 8 4
decade / ˈdekeɪd /

释 *n.* 十年，十年期（尤指一个年代）

例 During the **decade** before the economic crisis, spending on legal services in America grew twice as fast as inflation. 在经济危机前的十年里，美国法律服务支出的增长速度是通货膨胀速度的两倍。（2014年）

0 8 5
prudent / ˈpruːdnt /

释 *adj.* 谨慎的；慎重的；精明的

例 Public-sector unions are **prudent** in taking actions. 公共部门工会在采取行动时十分谨慎。

派 prudence / ˈpruːdns / *n.* 谨慎

反 imprudent / ɪmˈpruːdnt / *adj.* 不理智的；不深思熟虑的

0 8 6
variation / ˌveəriˈeɪʃn /

释 *n.* 变化；变体

例 Despite **variations** in detail, wholesale markets in the countries that have been closely examined—France, Germany, Italy, and Spain—are made out of the same building blocks. 尽管在细节上有所不同，仔细研究后发现，法国、德国、意大利和西班牙这些国家的批发市场在组建方式上是相同的。（2010年）

0 8 7
elaborate / ɪˈlæbərət /

释 *adj.* 复杂的；（有时过于）周密的；精心制作的

例 The Navy Department moved into the east wing in 1879, where **elaborate** wall and ceiling stenciling and marquetry floors decorated the office of the Secretary. 海军部于1879年搬进了东翼楼，在那里，部长办公室有着精心设计的墙壁、镂花式天花板和镶嵌式地板。（2018年）

派 elaboration / ɪˌlæbəˈreɪʃn / *n.* 详尽阐述，细化；精心完成的东西

0 8 8
restraint / rɪˈstreɪnt /

释 *n.* 克制；约束；限制；控制；制约因素；管制措施

例 The government has acted with **restraint** in dealing with this crisis. 政府在处理这场危机时采取了克制的行动。

0 8 9
cheat / tʃiːt /

释 *v.* 欺骗；蒙骗；作弊

搭 cheat sb. (out) of sth. （尤指用不诚实或不正当的手段）阻止某人得到某物

例 Such co-operation is likely to be stable only when each animal feels it is not being **cheated**. 只有当每只动物都觉得自己没有被欺骗时，这种合作才可能稳定。（2005年）

近 deceive / dɪˈsiːv / *v.* 欺骗；蒙骗；误导 ‖ fool / fuːl / *v.* 欺骗；愚弄

辨 cheat指为得到钱财或其他东西而欺骗；deceive尤指利用别人的信任欺骗；fool指蒙骗、愚弄。

◎ Study Notes

spray / spreɪ /

090

释 *v.* 喷，喷出；（使）溅出；扫射 *n.* 水雾；喷剂

例 In a Swiss study, researchers **sprayed** oxytocin into the noses of half the subjects; those subjects were ready to lend significantly higher amounts of money to strangers than were their counterparts who inhaled something else. 在瑞士的一项研究中，研究人员向一半受试者的鼻子中喷洒了催产素；与吸入其他物质的受试者相比，这些受试者更愿意把相当高数额的钱借给陌生人。（2018年）

drastic / 'dræstɪk /

091

释 *adj.* 极端的；剧烈的

例 The most **drastic**, and thoroughly illegal, reaction has been the emergence of Sci-Hub, a kind of global photocopier for scientific papers, set up in 2012, which now claims to offer access to every paywalled article published since 2015. 最极端且完全非法的变化是Sci-Hub的出现，它就像是一台全球科学论文复印机，成立于2012年，现在声称可以访问自2015年以来发表的所有付费文章。（2020年）

派 drastically / 'dræstɪkli / *adv.* 剧烈地；大幅度地

stare / steə(r) /

092

释 *v.* 盯着看；凝视；注视 *n.* 盯；凝视；注视

搭 stare at 盯着看；凝视；注视

例 People barely looked at each other or smiled, and appeared to take pains to **stare** straight ahead after entering the church. 人们几乎不看对方，也不笑，似乎在进入教堂后都会竭力目视前方。

近 gaze / geɪz / *v.* 凝视；注视；盯着 ‖ peer / pɪə(r) / *v.* 仔细看；端详

辨 stare尤指不友善或吃惊地盯着、凝视、注视；gaze指凝视、注视；peer尤指看不清楚时仔细看、端详。

mandate / 'mændeɪt /

093

释 *n.* 授权；授权令；任期 *v.* 授权；强制执行；委托办理

例 But are such government **mandates** even necessary? 但这样的政府授权其实有必要吗？（2020年）

派 mandated / 'mændeɪtɪd / *adj.* 获得授权的 ‖ mandatory / 'mændətəri / *adj.* 强制的；法定的；义务的

admission / əd'mɪʃn /

094

释 *n.* （机构、组织等的）准许加入，加入权，进入权；承认，招认；入场费；门票费

例 He studied the results of 9,323 MBA interviews conducted by 31 **admissions** officers. 他研究了31名招生官进行的9 323次MBA面试结果。（2013年）

manner

file

upset

thesis

phrase

explicit

manner / ˈmænə(r) / 　　　　　　　　　　095

释 n. 方式; 方法; 举止; 态度; [pl.]礼貌; 规矩; 习俗

搭 in a ... manner 以……的方式

例 On the other, it links these concepts to everyday realities in a **manner** which is parallel to the links journalists forge on a daily basis as they cover and comment on the news. 另一方面, 它(法律)将这些概念与日常现实联系起来, 其方式与记者每天在报道和评论新闻时建立的联系相似。(2007年)

file / faɪl / 　　　　　　　　　　096

释 n. 文件; 文件夹; 档案 v. 把……归档; 提起(诉讼); 提出(申请)

例 Later, more established companies raced to add such patents to their **files**, if only as a defensive move against rivals that might beat them to the punch. 后来, 更多的老牌公司争先恐后地在自己的档案中加入这类专利, 哪怕只是作为一种防御措施, 以抵御可能击败它们的对手。(2011年)

upset 　　　　　　　　　　097

释 / ˌʌpˈset / *adj.* 难过的; 沮丧的; 不舒服的 　/ ˌʌpˈset / *v.* 使烦恼; 使生气; 打乱; 使不适 　/ ˈʌpset / *n.* 烦恼; 失望; 混乱; 麻烦

搭 be/get upset about 为……感到难过

例 "Figuring out a way to accelerate that transition would make sense for them," he said, "but if you discontinue it, you're going to have your most loyal customers really **upset** with you." 他说: "找出加速转型的方法对他们而言是可行的, 但如果你终止(印刷), 将真的会令那些最忠实的客户对你感到失望。"(2016年)

派 upsetting / ʌpˈsetɪŋ / *adj.* 令人烦恼的; 使人不高兴的

近 distress / drˈstres / *v.* 使苦恼; 使忧虑; 使悲伤 *n.* 忧虑; 悲伤; 困苦

thesis / ˈθiːsɪs / 　　　　　　　　　　098

释 n. 论文; 毕业论文; 学位论文; 命题; 论题

例 So, at the end of a decade of **thesis**-writing, many humanities students leave the profession to do something for which they have not been trained. 因此, 在写了十年论文之后, 许多人文学科的学生放弃了本专业, 转而从事他们未接受过专业训练的工作。(2011年)

phrase / freɪz / 　　　　　　　　　　099

释 v. 用言语表达 n. 短语, 词组; 习语; 警句

例 Having not received a response, Young wrote a second letter the following day that was more harshly **phrased**. 由于没有收到回复, 杨第二天又写了第二封信, 措辞更加严厉。

explicit / ɪk'splɪsɪt /

100

🔵 *adj.* 清楚明白的；易于理解的；直截了当的

🔵 The law is very **explicit** about how these measures should be enacted. 法律对如何实施这些措施有非常明确的规定。

🔵 explicitly / ɪk'splɪsɪtli / *adv.* 明确地；直截了当地 ‖ explicitness / ɪk'splɪsɪtnəs / *n.* 直言不讳；明确性

☐ ☐ academic
☐ ☐ accept
☐ ☐ admission
☐ ☐ alternative
☐ ☐ appeal
☐ ☐ assign
☐ ☐ awake
☐ ☐ balance
☐ ☐ believe
☐ ☐ benefit
☐ ☐ bonus
☐ ☐ boot
☐ ☐ burn
☐ ☐ cautious
☐ ☐ challenge
☐ ☐ chance
☐ ☐ cheat
☐ ☐ clip
☐ ☐ combine
☐ ☐ compensate
☐ ☐ composition
☐ ☐ compound
☐ ☐ confer
☐ ☐ congress
☐ ☐ convert
☐ ☐ decade
☐ ☐ defer
☐ ☐ degree
☐ ☐ deliver
☐ ☐ develop
☐ ☐ device

☐ ☐ diffuse
☐ ☐ domain
☐ ☐ drastic
☐ ☐ elaborate
☐ ☐ encourage
☐ ☐ engage
☐ ☐ explicit
☐ ☐ extraordinary
☐ ☐ failure
☐ ☐ fetch
☐ ☐ file
☐ ☐ forth
☐ ☐ fuss
☐ ☐ graduate
☐ ☐ guess
☐ ☐ guide
☐ ☐ increase
☐ ☐ indicate
☐ ☐ inferior
☐ ☐ initiate
☐ ☐ inner
☐ ☐ institution
☐ ☐ instruct
☐ ☐ invite
☐ ☐ mammal
☐ ☐ mandate
☐ ☐ manner
☐ ☐ master
☐ ☐ migrate
☐ ☐ naval
☐ ☐ obsession

☐ ☐ operate
☐ ☐ oriental
☐ ☐ participant
☐ ☐ particular
☐ ☐ peculiar
☐ ☐ penalty
☐ ☐ phrase
☐ ☐ plaster
☐ ☐ precious
☐ ☐ predict
☐ ☐ premise
☐ ☐ private
☐ ☐ prudent
☐ ☐ query
☐ ☐ realistic
☐ ☐ relevant
☐ ☐ respond
☐ ☐ restraint
☐ ☐ sake
☐ ☐ scholar
☐ ☐ scrutiny
☐ ☐ skip
☐ ☐ spray
☐ ☐ stare
☐ ☐ status
☐ ☐ strength
☐ ☐ stress
☐ ☐ structure
☐ ☐ subscribe
☐ ☐ supreme
☐ ☐ tempt

☐ ☐ thesis
☐ ☐ tragic
☐ ☐ transplant
☐ ☐ upset
☐ ☐ variation
☐ ☐ wage
☐ ☐ wander

音频

Previous Check

- [ ] unfold
- [ ] stake
- [ ] division
- [ ] abide
- [ ] approve
- [ ] valuable
- [ ] evolve
- [ ] pessimistic
- [ ] search
- [ ] previous
- [ ] magnetic
- [ ] demand
- [ ] deter
- [ ] integrity
- [ ] criticism
- [ ] requirement
- [ ] contrary
- [ ] entire
- [ ] constrain
- [ ] contact
- [ ] neglect
- [ ] profound
- [ ] classical
- [ ] constitute
- [ ] conceal
- [ ] case
- [ ] inference
- [ ] wreck
- [ ] massive
- [ ] matter
- [ ] competent

- [ ] estimate
- [ ] tuition
- [ ] misery
- [ ] tide
- [ ] client
- [ ] overturn
- [ ] surround
- [ ] respect
- [ ] focus
- [ ] creative
- [ ] budget
- [ ] column
- [ ] multiple
- [ ] despite
- [ ] uniform
- [ ] trend
- [ ] unanimous
- [ ] hold
- [ ] numerical
- [ ] technical
- [ ] choose
- [ ] invalid
- [ ] priority
- [ ] emerge
- [ ] council
- [ ] abound
- [ ] manifest
- [ ] show
- [ ] contest
- [ ] historical
- [ ] bar

- [ ] chronic
- [ ] component
- [ ] mind
- [ ] primary
- [ ] prominent
- [ ] distribute
- [ ] scholarship
- [ ] immune
- [ ] permission
- [ ] spark
- [ ] exercise
- [ ] vast
- [ ] date
- [ ] poetry
- [ ] slight
- [ ] waste
- [ ] reality
- [ ] rapid
- [ ] overcome
- [ ] carve
- [ ] soil
- [ ] entry
- [ ] span
- [ ] safety
- [ ] regular
- [ ] highly
- [ ] frequent
- [ ] wonder
- [ ] range
- [ ] sketch
- [ ] flash

- [ ] bless
- [ ] fantasy
- [ ] greet
- [ ] wave
- [ ] panic
- [ ] sincere
- [ ] naive

unfold / ʌnˈfəʊld / 001

释 v. 展开; 展现; 逐渐明朗; 使 (事情等) 传开

例 A few generative rules are then sufficient to **unfold** the entire fundamental structure of a language, which is why children can learn it so quickly. 这样，几条生成规则就足以让一门语言的整个基本结构展现出来，这就是儿童可以如此快速地学习一门语言的原因。(2012年)

近 open / ˈəʊpən / v. 开; 打开 ‖ reveal / rɪˈviːl / v. 揭示; 揭露

stake / steɪk / 002

释 v. 以……打赌, 拿……冒险 n. 桩; 重大利益; 赌注

搭 stake (out) a claim (to/for/on sth.) 声称对……有所有权

例 And so we would call on state lawmakers from Richmond to Albany to consider reviewing their own wetlands protections and see for themselves the enormous **stakes** involved. 因此，我们呼吁从里士满到奥尔巴尼的州立法者考虑重新审视本州的湿地保护措施，并亲自了解其中涉及的巨大利害关系。(2024年)

division / dɪˈvɪʒn / 003

释 n. 分配; 分割; [数]除法; 部门

例 After learning multiplication, the students were taught **division**. 学习了乘法之后，学生们又学了除法。

abide / əˈbaɪd / 004

释 v. 遵守; 接受, 遵照 (规则, 决定, 劝告); 逗留, 停留

搭 abide by 遵守

例 The company, a major energy supplier in New England, provoked justified outrage in Vermont last week when it announced it was reneging on a longstanding commitment to **abide** by the state's strict nuclear regulations. 该公司是新英格兰地区的一家主要能源供应商，上周，当它宣布放弃长期承诺遵守佛蒙特州的严格核法规时，激起了该州人们的义愤。(2012年)

approve / əˈpruːv / 005

释 v. 认可; 赞同; 同意; 批准

搭 approve of 同意; 赞同

例 The state has **approved** the building plans, so work on the new school can begin immediately. 该州已经批准了这项建筑计划，因此建新学校的工作可以立即开始。

valuable / ˈvæljuəbl / 006

释 adj. 有价值的; 宝贵的; 很重要的; 贵重的; 很有用的

例 This was an attempt to recover the **valuable** nails, which could be reused after sifting the ashes. 这是为了回收宝贵的钉子而做的尝试，这些钉子在筛掉灰烬后可以重新使用。(2024年)

evolve / ɪ'vɒlv /

007

释 *v.* 发展，进展；进化；逐步形成

例 "For consciousness to **evolve**, a brain with a threshold level of complexity and capacity is required," he added. 他补充道："为了让意识进化，需要一个复杂性和容量达到临界值的大脑。"（2022年）

近 progress / prəʊ'gres / *v.* 进展 ‖ advance / əd'vɑːns / *v.* 推进，进展

辨 evolve在作"发展"讲时，强调符合自然规律，循序渐进；progress指按某一既定目标前进，取得发展，目的性很明确，强调稳定地前进；advance主要用于具体的人或物，也可指科学技术和运动等。

pessimistic / ˌpesɪ'mɪstɪk /

008

释 *adj.* 悲观（主义）的；厌世的

搭 be pessimistic about 对……感到悲观的

例 This long perspective makes the **pessimistic** view of our prospects seem more likely to be a passing fad. 这种长远的视角使我们对前景的悲观看法看起来更有可能成为一种过眼云烟。（2013年）

近 depressed / dɪ'prest / *adj.* 沮丧的

反 optimistic / ˌɒptɪ'mɪstɪk / *adj.* 乐观的

search / sɜːtʃ /

009

释 *v./n.* 搜寻；搜查；（在计算机上）搜索

例 Then he tried **searching** for his name to see if a piece he had worked on had been published. The online search brought back work that had his name attached to it but wasn't his. 然后，他试着搜索自己的名字，看看自己参与创作的作品是否已经发表。网上搜索的结果是，有他名字的作品却不是他的。（2024年）

近 hunt / hʌnt / *v./n.* 搜寻；打猎；追捕

previous / 'priːviəs /

010

释 *adj.* 以前的，之前的

搭 previous to 在……之前

例 One **previous** study looked at the Efé people of the Democratic Republic of Congo. 之前的一项研究调查了刚果民主共和国的埃菲人。（2024年）

magnetic / mæg'netɪk /

011

释 *adj.* 磁的；有磁性的；富有吸引力的；有魅力的

例 Archaeologists also may locate buried remains by using such technologies as ground radar, **magnetic**-field recording, and metal detectors. 考古学家还可能会利用地面雷达、磁场记录和金属探测器等技术定位被掩埋的遗骸。（2014年）

demand / dɪˈmɑːnd /

01 2

释 v. 强烈需求；需要 n. 要求；需求；所需之物
搭 in demand 需求大 ‖ on demand 一经要求
例 And the **demand** that rose in those societies for entry to higher education extended to groups and social classes that had not thought of attending a university before the war. 这些社会中，人们对高等教育的需求不断增长，已经扩展至战前从未想过要上大学的群体和社会阶层中。（2021年）

deter / dɪˈtɜː(r) /

01 3

释 v. 制止；阻止；威慑；使不敢
例 However, none of these requirements should **deter** large retailers (and even some large food producers and existing wholesalers) from trying their hand, for those that master the intricacies of wholesaling in Europe stand to reap considerable gains. 然而，这些要求都不应该阻止大型零售商（甚至是一些大型食品生产商和现有批发商）跃跃欲试，因为那些掌握了欧洲批发业错综复杂规律的企业将获得可观的收益。（2010年）

integrity / ɪnˈtegrəti /

01 4

释 n. 诚实，正直；完整，完好
例 **Integrity** had collapsed, she argued, because of a collective acceptance that the only "sorting mechanism" in society should be profit and the market. 她认为，诚信之所以崩溃，是因为大家都认为社会中唯一的"分类机制"应该是利润和市场。（2015年）

criticism / ˈkrɪtɪsɪzəm /

01 5

释 n. 评论文章，评论；指责，批评
例 Zoos, which spare no effort to take care of animals, should not be subjected to unfair **criticism**. 动物园不遗余力地照顾动物，不应受到不公正的批评。（2022年）
近 comment / ˈkɒment / n. 评论；闲话 ‖ critique / krɪˈtiːk / n. 评论；批评

requirement / rɪˈkwaɪəmənt /

01 6

释 n. 要求（或必要条件）；所需的（或所要的）东西
例 Many too are seeing the advantages of scrapping a degree **requirement** for certain roles. 许多人也看到了取消某些职位的学位要求的好处。（2022年）

contrary / ˈkɒntrəri /

01 7

释 adj. 相对立的；相反的；逆反的；犟的 n. 相反的事实（或事情、情况）
搭 on the contrary 与此相反；恰恰相反 ‖ to the contrary 相反的（地）
例 **Contrary** to the descriptions on record, no systematic implication was found that levels of productivity were related to changes in lighting. 与记录中描述的相反，没有发现生产力水平与照明变化有关的系统暗示。（2010年）

entire / ɪn'taɪə(r) /   018

释 *adj.* 全部的；整个的；完全的

例 To realize how great was the dramatic activity, we must remember further that hosts of plays have been lost, and that probably there is no author of note whose **entire** work has survived. 要想了解戏剧活动的规模有多大，我们必须谨记，大量戏剧已经失传，而且可能没有任何著名作家的全部作品得以流传下来。（2018年）

constrain / kən'streɪn /   019

释 *v.* 限制，约束；强迫，强制

例 If not placing jobs at risk, to the extent employment protection laws **constrain** business owners from dismissing underperforming managers, those laws act as a constraint on firm productivity and therefore on workers' wages. 在某种程度上，就业保护法限制企业主解雇表现不佳的经理，但如果不将（工人的）工作置于风险之中，那么这些法律就会限制公司的生产力，从而影响工人的工资。（2022年）

派 constraint / kən'streɪnt / *n.* 约束；限制

近 restrict / rɪ'strɪkt / *v.* 约束；限定 ‖ limit / 'lɪmɪt / *v.* 限制；限定

contact / 'kɒntækt /   020

释 *n.* 联系；接触；联络人 *v.* （使）联系 *adj.* 接触性的

搭 in contact with 与……有联系 ‖ make contact with 联系……

例 The publishing industry talks about diversity in terms of authors and staff but it also needs a plurality of ways of delivering intellectual **contact**, choice and different voices. 出版业谈论的是作者们和全体员工的多样性，但它也需要多种方式来提供知识联系、选择和不同的声音。（2023年）

neglect / nɪ'glekt /   021

释 *v.* 忽视；疏忽；疏于照管 *n.* 忽略，忽视

搭 neglect to do sth. 忘记做某事 ‖ the neglect of 忽视……

例 This seems a justification for **neglect** of those in need, and a rationalization of exploitation, of the superiority of those at the top and the inferiority of those at the bottom. 这似乎是忽视那些需要帮助的人的正当理由，也是剥削、上等人的优越感和下等人的劣等感的合理化。（2018年）

近 ignore / ɪg'nɔː(r) / *v.* 不理睬，忽视 ‖ disregard / ˌdɪsrɪ'ɡɑːd / *v.* 不顾；忽视

profound / prə'faʊnd /   022

释 *adj.* 深刻的，意义深远的；深厚的

例 This aversion to arguments is common, but it depends on a mistaken view of arguments that causes **profound** problems for our personal and social lives—and in many ways misses the point of arguing in the first place. 这种对争论的厌恶很常见，但它依赖于一种对争论的错误认知，它给我们的个人生活和社会生活带来了深远的问题，而且在很多方面，它首先就忽略了争论的意义。（2019年）

Writing Models ◎

classical

constitute

conceal

case

inference

wreck

massive

matter

competent

estimate

tuition

classical / 'klæsɪkl /   `023`

释 *adj.* 古典的；经典的；传统的

例 A Polish digital artist who uses **classical** painting styles to create dreamy fantasy landscapes, Greg Rutkowski has made illustrations for games such as Dungeons & Dragons and Magic: The Gathering. 格雷格·鲁特科夫斯基是一位波兰数字艺术家，他用古典绘画风格创造出梦幻般的奇幻景观，他曾为《龙与地下城》和《魔法：收集》等游戏创作图解。（2024年）

constitute / 'kɒnstɪtjuːt /   `024`

释 *v.* 组成，构思；设立；被算作

例 Correct grammar and sentence structure do not in themselves **constitute** good writing. 正确的语法和句子结构本身并不能被算作好的写作。

近 compose / kəm'pəʊz / *v.* 构成；创作，作曲 ‖ comprise / kəm'praɪz / *v.* 包括，由……组成；构成

conceal / kən'siːl /   `025`

释 *v.* 隐藏；掩盖；隐瞒（信息）；掩饰（情感）；遮盖

搭 conceal sth. from sb. 向某人隐瞒某事

例 His paternal grandparents, a steward and a housekeeper, possessed even less status, having been servants, and Dickens later **concealed** their background. 他的祖父母是管家和杂务主管，地位甚至更低，一直是仆人，狄更斯后来隐瞒了他们的背景。（2017年）

case / keɪs /   `026`

释 *n.* 容器；箱；盒；事例；具体情况；事实；诉讼；调查的案件；病例；病人；论据，理由

搭 (just) in case 以防；以防万一 ‖ in any case 无论如何

例 In many **cases** the experts have a hard time agreeing on what is the real object and what is a forgery. 在许多情况下，专家们很难就哪些是真品、哪些是赝品达成一致意见。（2024年）

近 instance / 'ɪnstəns / *n.* 实例

inference / 'ɪnfərəns /   `027`

释 *n.* 推理，推断，推论

例 You make further **inferences**, for instance, about how the text may be significant to you, or about its validity—**inferences** that form the basis of a personal response for which the author will inevitably be far less responsible. 例如，你会进一步推断文本对你的意义或其有效性——这些推断构成了个人反应的基础，而作者对这些反应的责任必然要少得多。（2015年）

wreck / rek /   `028`

释 *n.* （轮船、汽车、飞机失事后的）残骸 *v.* 摧毁

例 The moment the rescue crew located the **wreck**, they fired a signal gun. 搜救人员一找到残骸就发射了信号弹。

massive / ˈmæsɪv /

029

释 *adj.*（尺寸、数量、规模）巨大的；非常严重的

例 The notion is that people have failed to detect the **massive** changes which have happened in the ocean because they have been looking back only a relatively short time into the past. 这种观点认为，人们之所以未能发现海洋发生的巨大变化，是因为他们一直都只回顾相对较短的时间内的过去。（2006年）

matter / ˈmætə(r) /

030

释 *v.* 要紧；有重大影响；事关紧要 *n.* 问题；（统称）物质；事情；（某种）东西，物品；关乎……的事情

搭 as a matter of fact 事实上；其实；说真的

例 Again, the story an exhibit is trying to tell is what **matters**. The monetary value of the objects on display is a distant second place in importance. 同样，展览要讲述的故事才是重要的。展品的货币价值在重要性上远居次位。（2024年）

competent / ˈkɒmpɪtənt /

031

释 *adj.* 有能力的，能胜任的；能干的，称职的

搭 be competent to do sth. 有能力做某事

例 In fact, it is difficult to see how journalists who do not have a clear grasp of the basic features of the Canadian Constitution can do a **competent** job on political stories. 事实上，很难想象对加拿大宪法基本特征都没有清晰了解的记者是如何胜任政治报道工作的。（2007年）

estimate

032

释 / ˈestɪmət / *n.* 估计；估价；估计的成本；判断 / ˈestɪmeɪt / *v.* 估计，估算；评估

例 In December of 1869, Congress appointed a commission to select a site and prepare plans and cost **estimates** for a new State Department Building. 1869年12月，国会任命了一个委员会，负责为新的国务院大楼选址、制订计划和估算费用。（2018年）

派 underestimate / ˌʌndərˈestɪmeɪt / *v.* 低估 / ˌʌndərˈestɪmət / *n.* 低估

tuition / tjuˈɪʃn /

033

释 *n.*（尤指对个人或小组的）讲授，教学，指导；（尤指大专院校的）学费

搭 tuition waiver 免除学费

例 We are thus led to distinguish, within the broad educational process which we have been so far considering, a more formal kind of education—that of direct **tuition** or schooling. 因此，在我们目前所考虑的广泛的教育过程中，我们被引导要区分出一种更为正式的教育，即直接的个人辅导或学校教育。（2009年）

近 tutorship / ˈtjuːtəʃɪp / *n.* 辅导

01　02　03　04　05　06　07　08　09　10

misery

tide

client

overturn

surround

respect

focus

creative

budget

column

multiple

despite

misery / ˈmɪzəri / ⓪③④

释 *n.* 痛苦, 悲惨, 不幸; 贫穷

例 You could argue that art became more skeptical of happiness because modern times have seen so much **misery**. 你可以说, 艺术对幸福越来越持怀疑态度是因为现代人经历了太多的不幸。（2006年）

派 miserable / ˈmɪzrəbl / *adj.* 痛苦的, 悲惨的

近 anguish / ˈæŋɡwɪʃ / *n.* 痛苦, 苦恼

反 pleasure / ˈpleʒə(r) / *n.* 愉快, 快乐

tide / taɪd / ⓪③⑤

释 *n.* 潮流, 趋势; 潮汐, 海浪

搭 turn the tide 转变运气; 改变形势

例 A badly run "year of culture" washes in and out of a place like the **tide**, bringing prominence for a spell but leaving no lasting benefits to the community. 办得不好的"文化年"会像潮汐一样冲进冲出一个地方, 带来一时的显赫, 但不会给社区带来持久的好处。（2020年）

client / ˈklaɪənt / ⓪③⑥

释 *n.* 客户; 委托人, 当事人

例 When the bottles were released in 1986, they were offered only to some top **clients**, and they were not made available to the public for purchase. 1986年这些酒上市时, 只提供给一些顶级客户, 并不向公众出售。

overturn / ˌəʊvəˈtɜːn / ⓪③⑦

释 *v.* 改变; 推翻; 颠倒

搭 overturn a decision 撤销决议

例 In a rare unanimous ruling, the U.S. Supreme Court has **overturned** the corruption conviction of a former Virginia governor, Robert McDonnell. 在一次罕见的无异议裁决中, 美国最高法院推翻了对弗吉尼亚州前州长罗伯特·麦克唐奈尔的腐败定罪。（2017年）

近 overthrow / ˌəʊvəˈθrəʊ / *v.* 推翻 ‖ revoke / rɪˈvəʊk / *v.* 撤销; 废除

surround / səˈraʊnd / ⓪③⑧

释 *v.* 围绕, 包围 *n.* 环绕物

例 It allows us to see the beauty that **surrounds** us each moment in nature, in culture, in the flow of our daily lives. 它让我们在大自然、文化和日常生活的流动中, 看到每时每刻围绕在我们身边的美。（2016年）

respect / rɪˈspekt / ⓪③⑨

释 *v.* 尊敬; 尊重; 仰慕; 慎重对待; 遵从 *n.* 尊敬; 尊重; 方面, 细节

例 The reality is that water, and the pollutants that so often come with it, don't **respect** state boundaries. 现实情况是, 水以及通常随水而来的污染物往往不分州界。（2024年）

focus / 'fəʊkəs /
040

释 *v.* 集中（注意力、精力或光束于）；聚焦（于）；（使）调节焦距 *n.* 中心点；焦距，调焦

例 The founders deliberately **focused** their projects around light—hence the "visual studies" in the name. 创始人们特意将其项目的重点放在光线上——因此名称中有"视觉研究"。（2022年）

creative / kri'eɪtɪv /
041

释 *adj.* 创造性的；有创造力的

例 Mental health is the source of **creativity** for solving problems, resolving conflict, making our surroundings more beautiful, managing our home life, or coming up with a creative business idea or invention to make our lives easier. 心理健康是创造力的源泉，它能帮助我们解决问题、化解矛盾、让周围环境更美、管理好家庭生活，或者想出一个有创意的商业点子或发明，让我们的生活更轻松。（2016年）

反 conventional / kən'venʃənl / *adj.* 常规的，因循守旧的

budget / 'bʌdʒɪt /
042

释 *n.* 预算；财政收支状况 *v.* 安排开支；编制预算 *adj.* 价格低廉的

例 An old saying has it that half of all advertising **budgets** are wasted—the trouble is, no one knows which half. 俗话说，一半的广告预算都被浪费了——问题是，没人知道是哪一半。（2013年）

column / 'kɒləm /
043

释 *n.* （报刊的）专栏，栏目；（书、报纸印刷页的）栏，页

例 For the past several years, the Sunday newspaper supplement *Parade* has featured a **column** called "Ask Marilyn." 在过去的几年里，周日报纸副刊《旅行》一直有一个名为"问玛丽莲"的专栏。（2007年）

派 columnist / 'kɒləmnɪst / *n.* 专栏作家

multiple / 'mʌltɪpl /
044

释 *n.* 倍数 *adj.* 多样的，多重的

搭 multiple choice 多项选择

例 The company has since landed 230 rockets, which is many **multiples** of the number of rockets launched by all other U.S. companies in the eight years since. 此后，该公司共发射了230枚火箭，是此后八年中所有其他美国公司发射火箭数量的许多倍。

despite / dɪ'spaɪt /
045

释 *prep.* 不管；尽管

例 We are not boycotting PRH titles but we are doing our utmost to ensure that availability for customers remains good **despite** the lower overall levels of stock. 我们并没有抵制企鹅兰登的书籍，尽管库存整体水平偏低，我们会尽最大努力确保为客户提供良好的供应。（2023年）

uniform

trend

unanimous

hold

numerical

technical

choose

invalid

priority

emerge

---

uniform / ˈjuːnɪfɔːm / ⓪④⑥

㊉ *n.* 制服；校服 *adj.* 一致的；统一的；一律的

例 Does that mean the writing is on the wall for all European royals, with their magnificent **uniforms** and majestic lifestyles? 这是否意味着，所有穿着华丽制服、过着奢华生活的欧洲王室成员的命运都已注定？（2015年）

trend / trend / ⓪④⑦

㊉ *n.* 趋势；趋向；动态；动向；规范；风尚，时尚 *v.* 倾向

例 *Nature*'s poll findings suggest that this **trend** is as strong as ever, but, to make a collaboration work, both sides need to invest time, and embrace surprise and challenge.《自然》杂志的民意调查结果表明，该趋势一如既往地强劲，但要使合作奏效，双方都需要投入时间，并接受惊喜和挑战。（2022年）

unanimous / juˈnænɪməs / ⓪④⑧

㊉ *adj.* 全体一致的，一致同意的

搭 be unanimous in sth. 对某事一致同意

例 The young man was elected chairman by a **unanimous** vote. 那个年轻人以全票当选主席。

hold / həʊld / ⓪④⑨

㊉ *v.* 拿着；抓住；抱住；托住；按住；保持不变；召开，举行；使保持（在某位置）；容纳，包含；控制；顶住，坚持住；存贮；拥有，持有；赢得；持有（信念、意见）；认为；（打电话时）等待，不挂断 *n.* 抓，握，拿；影响；控制

搭 hold on 坚持住，挺住；（电话用语）别挂断，等一下 ‖ hold up 举起；支撑

例 Ancient art that is displayed in foreign countries by all means should be returned to the original country. The foreign countries have no right to **hold** back returning the items. 在外国展出的古代艺术品无论如何都应归还原属国。外国无权阻止归还这些物品。（2024年）

派 holder / ˈhəʊldə(r) / *n.* 持有者；支托物 ‖ uphold / ʌpˈhəʊld / *v.* 维持（原判、裁决等）；维护（法律、正义等）

近 grasp / ɡrɑːsp / *v.* 理解；毫不犹豫地抓住（机会）；抓紧 *n.* 理解（力）；抓紧

numerical / njuːˈmerɪkl / ⓪⑤⓪

㊉ *adj.* 数字的；用数字表示的；数值的

例 IQ tests ask you to complete verbal and visual analogies, to envision paper after it has been folded and cut, and to deduce **numerical** sequences, among other similar tasks. 智商测试要求你完成语言和视觉类比，设想纸张折叠和裁剪后的效果，推断数字顺序，以及其他类似任务。（2007年）

⊙ Study Notes

technical / 'teknɪkl /

🔵 *adj.* 技术的; 技巧的

🟠 technical upgrading 技术升级 ‖ technical innovativeness 技术创新

🔵 "Setting the proper investment level for security, redundancy, and recovery is a management issue, not a **technical** one," he says. 他说: "为(数据的)安全、备份和恢复设定适当的投资水平是一个管理问题, 而不是技术问题。"(2007年)

051

choose / tʃuːz /

🔵 *v.* 选择; 挑选; 选取; 宁愿; 情愿; 决定

🟠 pick and choose 挑拣; 精挑细选

🔵 When finding their way to waterholes, they headed off in exactly the right direction, on one occasion from a distance of roughly thirty miles. What is more, they almost always seem to **choose** the nearest waterhole. 在寻找水坑时, 它们(大象)的走向非常精确, 有一次它们从大约30英里外的地方出发。而且, 它们看起来几乎总是选择最近的水坑。(2024年)

🟣 select / sɪ'lekt / *v.* 选择 ‖ pick / pɪk / *v.* 选择

052

invalid

🔵 / ɪn'vælɪd / *adj.* 无效的, 作废的; 无根据的; 病弱的 / 'ɪnvəlɪd / *n.* 病人; 伤残者; 退役军人

🔵 Now the company is suddenly claiming that the 2002 agreement is **invalid** because of the 2006 legislation, and that only the federal government has regulatory power over nuclear issues. 现在, 该公司突然声称: 由于2006年的立法, 所以2002年的协议无效, 而且只有联邦政府才有权监管核问题。(2012年)

🟤 invalidate / ɪn'vælɪdeɪt / *v.* 使无效或作废 ‖ invalidity / ˌɪnvə'lɪdəti / *n.* 无效; 伤残

🔴 valid / 'vælɪd / *adj.* 有效的; 有根据的

053

priority / praɪ'ɒrəti /

🔵 *n.* 优先; 优先权; 首要事情, 优先事项

🔵 The Conservatives' planning reform explicitly gives rural development **priority** over conservation, even authorizing "off-plan" building where local people might object. 保守党的规划改革明确将农村发展置于保护之上, 甚至在当地人可能反对的情况下授权进行 "计划外" 建设。(2016年)

054

emerge / ɪ'mɜːdʒ /

🔵 *v.* 出现, 浮现, 露出; 露头; 形成; 兴起;(事实、意见等)露出真相, 被知晓

🔵 Self-sliding doors began to **emerge** as a commercial product in 1960 after being invented six years previously by Americans Dee Horton and Lew Hewitt. 自六年前由美国人迪·霍顿和卢·休伊特发明后, 滑动门于1960年开始作为商业产品出现。(2024年)

055

Writing Models ◎

council

abound

manifest

show

contest

historical

bar

chronic

component

mind

primary

---

council / ˈkaʊnsl /

释 *n.* 委员会；理事会；议会

例 Labour likewise wants to discontinue local planning where **councils** oppose development. 工党同样希望在议会反对发展的地方停止地方规划。（2016年）

近 commission / kəˈmɪʃn / *n.* 委员会 ‖ committee / kəˈmɪti / *n.* 委员会

056

abound / əˈbaʊnd /

释 *v.* 富于，大量存在

搭 abound in 富于，大量存在

例 Opportunities for misinterpretation, error, and self-deception **abound**. 曲解、错误和自欺欺人的机会比比皆是。（2012年）

057

manifest / ˈmænɪfest /

释 *v.* 表明，清楚显示（尤指情感、态度或品质）；使人注意到 *adj.* 明显的，显现出的

搭 manifest sth. in sth. 在某事物中表现出来某事物

例 The growth of higher education **manifests** itself in at least three quite different ways, and these in turn have given rise to different sets of problems. 高等教育的发展至少以三种截然不同的方式显示出来，而这些方式反过来又引发了不同的问题集。（2021年）

派 manifestation / ˌmænɪfeˈsteɪʃn / *n.* 显示；表现

058

show / ʃəʊ /

释 *v.* 表明；（图画、图表、文章等）表示；表现；显示出（品质、特征）；展示 *n.*（电视或广播）节目；演出

例 The experiment **showed** that elephants may well use smell to identify patches of trees that are good to eat, and secondly to assess the quality of the trees within each patch. 实验结果表明，大象很可能利用气味来识别适合食用的树丛，其次还可以利用气味来评估每片树丛中树木的品质。（2024年）

近 display / dɪˈspleɪ / *v.* 表现；陈列 *n.* 展示；表演；陈列 ‖ exhibit / ɪɡˈzɪbɪt / *v.* 表现；展览 *n.* 展览品

059

contest

释 / kənˈtest / *v.* 竞争；争夺；辩驳 / ˈkɒntest / *n.* 竞赛；争夺；竞争

例 The election was so one-sided that it was really no **contest**. 选举如此一边倒，实际上毫无竞争可言。

派 contestant / kənˈtestənt / *n.* 竞争者，参加竞赛者

近 competition / ˌkɒmpəˈtɪʃn / *n.* 竞争者

060

historical / hɪˈstɒrɪkl /

释 *adj.* 有关历史研究的；历史的；历史题材的

例 **Historical** particularism, which emphasized the uniqueness of all cultures, gave new direction to anthropology. 历史特殊论强调所有文化的独特性，为人类学指明了新的方向。（2009年）

061

bar / bɑː(r) / ⓪⑥②

🄡 *n.* 酒吧；柜台；律师职业；（专售某类饮食的）小吃店；条；块；带 *v.* 封；堵；禁止，阻止（某人做某事）

🄣 behind bars 蹲班房；被监禁 ‖ the bar exam 律师资格考试

🄔 It needs to give the commission explicit authority once and for all to **bar** broadband providers from meddling in the traffic on their network and to create clear rules protecting openness and innovation online. 它需要一劳永逸地赋予委员会明确的权力，禁止宽带提供商干涉其网络上的流量，并制定明确的规则保护网络的开放性和创新性。（2021年）

chronic / ˈkrɒnɪk / ⓪⑥③

🄡 *adj.* 慢性的；长期的；习惯性的；严重的

🄔 Not everyone experiences the kinds of severe **chronic** stresses Alvarez describes. 并非每个人都经历过阿尔瓦雷斯所描述的那种长期的严重压力。（2008年）

component / kəmˈpəʊnənt / ⓪⑥④

🄡 *n.* 组成部分 *adj.* 组成的

🄔 Together, they make up the reading **component** of your overall literacy, or relationship to your surrounding textual environment. 它们（不同类型的阅读方式）共同构成了你整体读写能力中的阅读部分，或者说是你与周围文本环境的关系。（2015年）

mind / maɪnd / ⓪⑥⑤

🄡 *n.* 思考能力；智慧；思维方式；头脑；大脑；富有才智的人 *v.* 介意；当心

🄣 keep sb./sth. in mind 将……记在心中；记起；考虑 ‖ come to mind 突然记起（或想到）

🄔 During the Renaissance, the great **minds** of Nicolaus Copernicus, Johannes Kepler and Galileo Galilei demonstrated the power of scientific study and discovery. 文艺复兴时期，尼古拉斯·哥白尼、约翰尼斯·开普勒和伽利略·伽利雷的伟大思想展示了科学研究和发现的力量。（2020年）

🄟 mindset / ˈmaɪndset / *n.* 心态；思维模式

primary / ˈpraɪməri / ⓪⑥⑥

🄡 *adj.* 主要的；最重要的；最初的 *n.*（美国）初选

🄔 The growth of the use of English as the world's **primary** language for international communication has obviously been continuing for several decades. 英语作为世界上主要的国际交流语言，其使用量的增长显然已持续了几十年。（2017年）

🄢 main / meɪn / *adj.* 主要的；最重要的 ‖ major / ˈmeɪdʒə(r) / *adj.* 主要的；重要的

Writing Models ◎

prominent

distribute

scholarship

immune

permission

spark

exercise

vast

date

poetry

slight

waste

prominent / ˈprɒmɪnənt /

067

释 *adj.* 突出的，显著的；杰出的

搭 play a prominent part/role 扮演举足轻重的角色

例 It is also less **prominent** in many social studies courses. 它在许多社会研究课程中也不太突出。（2023年）

近 outstanding / aʊtˈstændɪŋ / *adj.* 突出的；杰出的

distribute / dɪˈstrɪbjuːt /

068

释 *v.* 分发；分配；分销；使分散；使分布

例 The African savanna elephant, also known as the African bush elephant, is **distributed** across 37 African countries. 非洲草原象，又被称为非洲灌木象，分布在37个非洲国家。（2024年）

scholarship / ˈskɒləʃɪp /

069

释 *n.* 奖学金；学术；学问；学术研究

例 Our foundation will seek to award **scholarships** to students and to contribute to the local community. 我们的基金会将设法为学生提供奖学金，并为当地社区做出贡献。

immune / ɪˈmjuːn /

070

释 *adj.* 不受影响的；免疫的；免除的

搭 immune system 免疫系统

例 Nor are highly paid managers themselves **immune** from the harm caused by the ERA's unjustified dismissal procedures. 高薪管理人员本身也不能不受《雇佣关系法》的无理解雇程序所造成的危害的影响。（2022年）

近 exempt / ɪgˈzempt / *adj.* 免除（规则、职责、义务等）的

permission / pəˈmɪʃn /

071

释 *n.* 准许；许可

例 As a condition of receiving state approval for the sale, the company agreed to seek **permission** from state regulators to operate past 2012. 作为获得州政府批准出售的条件之一，该公司同意寻求州监管机构的许可，以便在2012年以后继续运营。（2012年）

spark / spɑːk /

072

释 *v.* 引发；出发；冒火花 *n.* 火花；火星；诱因

搭 spark up 激起，突然引发（争论等）

例 But it has already **sparked** significant controversy, with the United States trade representative opening an investigation into whether the tax discriminates against American companies, which in turn could lead to trade sanctions against France. 但它已经引发了巨大的争议，美国贸易代表开启了一项调查看看这项税收是否歧视美国公司，这反过来可能导致对法国的贸易制裁。（2020年）

exercise / ˈeksəsaɪz / ⓄⓈⓈ

🟡 *n.* 锻炼, 运动; 行驶; 运用; 练习; 演习 *v.* 行驶; 运用; 锻炼

🔵 No matter how you "enhance" enclosures, they do not allow for freedom, a natural diet or adequate **exercise**. 无论你如何 "改善" 圈地，它们都没有将自由、天然的饮食或是充分的运动考虑在内。(2022年)

vast / vɑːst / ⓄⓊⒶ

🟡 *adj.* 巨大的; 大量的; 辽阔的

🔵 Zoos are, in that sense, similar to natural history and archaeology museums, serving to satisfy our need for contact with these living creatures while leaving the **vast** majority undisturbed in their natural environments. 从这个意义上来说，动物园类似于自然历史和考古博物馆，满足我们与这些生物接触的需要，同时又让绝大多数动物不受干扰地生活在它们的自然环境中。(2022年)

🟣 vastness / ˈvɑːstnəs / *n.* 巨大; 广大; 广漠

date / deɪt / ⓄⓊⒻ

🟡 *n.* 日期; 约会; 约会对象; 时期 *v.* 注明日期; 与 (某人) 谈恋爱; 过时

🟢 to date 迄今; 到目前为止 ‖ date back (to...) 追溯到; 始于

🔵 This means the mileage cost can vary depending on demand, route, and travel **date**. 这意味着里程费用会因需求、路线和旅行日期的不同而变化。

poetry / ˈpəʊətri / ⓄⓊⒻ

🟡 *n.* 诗集; 诗歌; 诗作

🔵 Up to the age of thirty or beyond it **poetry** of many kinds gave him great pleasure. 到三十岁或三十岁以后，各种各样的诗歌给他带来了极大的乐趣。(2008年)

slight / slaɪt / ⓄⓊⒻ

🟡 *adj.* 轻微的, 略微的; 细小的; 瘦小的; 不足道的 *n.* 冷落; 轻视

🔵 By Wednesday, Los Angeles will begin to feel some **slight** cooling through the rest of the week as a new blast of cold air moves down the coast. 到周三，随着一股新的冷空气沿着海岸向下移动，在本周接下来的几天洛杉矶的温度会略微有些下降。

🟣 slightly / ˈslaɪtli / *adv.* 轻微地; 稍微

waste / weɪst / ⓄⓊⒻ

🟡 *v.* 浪费; 滥用 *n.* 浪费; 滥用; 废物; 垃圾; 荒原

🔵 Peretti says the *Times* shouldn't **waste** time getting out of the print business, but only if they go about doing it the right way. 佩雷蒂说，除非以正确的方式着手，否则《纽约时报》不应该浪费时间在摆脱印刷出版行业上面。(2016年)

🟣 wasteful / ˈweɪstfl / *adj.* 浪费的; 挥霍的

Writing Models ◎

reality

rapid

overcome

carve

soil

entry

span

safety

regular

highly

frequent

wonder

---

reality / ri'æləti /   079

释 *n.* 现实; 实际情况; 事实; 实际经历

搭 in reality 实际上, 事实上

例 "Each year the physical presence rule becomes further removed from economic **reality** and results in significant revenue losses to the states," he wrote in an opinion joined by four other justices. 他在与其他四位大法官共同发表的意见书中写道: "每年, 实际存在的规则都在进一步脱离经济现实, 给各州造成了巨大的收入损失。"(2019年)

---

rapid / 'ræpɪd /   080

释 *adj.* 迅速的; 快速的; 瞬间的

例 These demands resulted in a very **rapid** expansion of the systems of higher education, beginning in the 1960s and developing very rapidly (though unevenly) during the 1970s and 1980s. 这些需求导致了高等教育体系的迅速扩张, 从20世纪60年代开始, 并在20世纪70年代和80年代发展得非常迅速 (尽管不均衡)。(2021年)

派 rapidly / 'ræpɪdli / *adv.* 快速地 ‖ rapidity / rə'pɪdəti / *n.* 迅速

---

overcome / ˌəʊvə'kʌm /   081

释 *v.* 克服; 解决; 战胜

例 Washington, who had begun to believe that all men were created equal after observing the bravery of the black soldiers during the Revolutionary War, **overcame** the strong opposition of his relatives to grant his slaves their freedom in his will. 在独立战争中看到黑人士兵的英勇表现之后, 华盛顿开始相信人人生而平等, 他克服亲属的强烈反对, 在遗嘱中赋予了他的奴隶们以自由。(2008年)

---

carve / kɑːv /   082

释 *v.* 雕刻; 刻上; 切; 奋斗取得

例 For example, even in dense forest, you should be able to spot gaps in the tree line due to roads, train tracks, and other paths people **carve** through the woods. 例如, 即使在茂密的森林中, 你也应该能够发现由于道路、火车轨道和人们在树林中开辟的其他路径而形成的林木线缺口。(2019年)

---

soil / sɔɪl /   083

释 *n.* 土壤

例 Moreover, some have been found to have a valuable function in building up **soil** fertility. 此外, 有些已被发现在提高土壤肥力方面具有重要作用。(2010年)

---

entry / 'entri /   084

释 *n.* 进入; 参与, 加入; 参赛

例 Travelers who want to watch the lighting in person must enter from specific spectator **entry** points on Fifth Avenue. 想要亲自观看灯光秀的游客必须从第五大道的特定观众入口进入。

11　12　13　14　15　16　17　18　19　20

span / spæn /   085

释 *n.* 时间段；（注意力的）持续时间；持续

例 In addition, new digital technologies have allowed more rapid trading of equities, quicker use of information, and thus shorter attention **spans** in financial markets. 此外, 新的数字技术使股票交易和信息的使用更加迅速, 从而缩短了金融市场的注意力持续时间。（2019年）

safety / 'seɪfti /   086

释 *n.* 安全；安危；安全性；安全场所

例 Americans are willing to tolerate time-consuming security procedures in return for increased **safety**. 美国人愿意忍受耗时的安检程序, 以换取更高的安全性。（2017年）

regular / 'regjələ(r) /   087

释 *adj.* 有规律的；定时的；频繁的；惯常的；普通的

例 In 2007, Indonesia started phasing in a program that gives money to its poorest residents under certain conditions, such as requiring people to keep kids in school or get **regular** medical care. 2007年, 印尼开始分阶段实施一项计划, 即在一定条件下向最贫困的居民提供资金, 比如要求他们让孩子上学或接受定期医疗。（2021年）

反 irregular / ɪ'regjələ(r) / *adj.* 无规律的；参差不齐的

highly / 'haɪli /   088

释 *adv.* 很；非常；高标准地；赞赏地

例 But these provisions create difficulties for businesses when applied to **highly** paid managers and executives. 但当这些条款被用在高薪的经理和管理人员身上时, 就给企业带来了难题。（2022年）

frequent / 'friːkwənt /   089

释 *adj.* 频繁的；经常发生的

例 Even among those who got a cold, the ones who felt greater social support and received more **frequent** hugs had less severe symptoms. 即使在感冒患者中, 那些感受到更多社会支持、得到更频繁拥抱的人的感冒症状也没有那么严重。（2017年）

派 frequency / 'friːkwənsi / *n.* 频率；频繁

wonder / 'wʌndə(r) /   090

释 *v.* 想知道；想弄明白；琢磨；对……感到诧异

例 When our ancestors were hunters and gatherers 10,000 years ago, they didn't have time to **wonder** much about anything besides finding food. 一万年前, 当我们的祖先还是狩猎者和采集者时, 他们除了寻找食物, 没有时间去琢磨太多的事情。（2009年）

Writing Models ◎

range

sketch

flash

bless

fantasy

greet

wave

panic

sincere

naive

---

range / reɪndʒ / 091

释 *v.* 包括（从……到……）之间的各类事物；变化，变动；排列，排序 *n.* 一系列；范围，界限；射程

搭 a range of 一系列 ‖ range over 涉及；包括

例 Despite these challenges, Jackson captured dozens of striking photos, **ranging** from majestic images like his now-famous snapshot of Old Faithful, to casual portraits of expedition members at the camp. 尽管有这些挑战，杰克逊还是拍下了数十张令人震撼的照片，从他现在著名的"老忠实"绝美快照，到探险队成员在营地的随意肖像照，不一而足。（2023年）

sketch / sketʃ / 092

释 *n.* 素描，速写；幽默短剧；短篇文学作品；简报；概述 *v.* 画素描；概述；简述

例 The first published **sketch**, "A Dinner at Poplar Walk" brought tears to Dickens's eyes when he discovered it in the pages of *The Monthly Magazine*. 当狄更斯在《月刊》上发现其第一篇发表的短篇小说《杨树小径上的晚餐》时，不禁热泪盈眶。（2017年）

flash / flæʃ / 093

释 *v.* （使）闪光；（使）闪现；（快速地）出示 *n.* 闪光；闪亮；闪现

搭 in/like a flash 转瞬间；立即

例 When the monologues ended, pictures of their sons **flashed** on the screen. 当独白结束时，屏幕上闪现出他们儿子的多幅照片。

bless / bles / 094

释 *v.* 求上帝降福于；祝福

搭 be blessed with 赋有（能力等）；享有（幸福等）

例 We are **blessed** to be surrounded by incredible friends and families who support us each step of the way. 我们很幸运，身边有无与伦比的朋友和家人，他们支持我们行进道路上的每一步。

派 blessing / 'blesɪŋ / *n.* 上帝的恩宠；祝福；好事

fantasy / 'fæntəsi / 095

释 *n.* 幻想；想象；想象产物；幻想作品

例 On display here are various **fantasy** elements whose reference, at some basic level, seems to be the natural world. 展示中有各种各样的幻想元素，在某种基本层面上，它们的参照物似乎是自然界。（2013年）

greet / griːt / 096

释 *v.* 向……问好；迎接；对……做出反应

例 People have streamed out of houses to **greet** and congratulate them. 人们纷纷走出家门，向他们表示欢迎和祝贺。

wave / weɪv /

释 *n.* 海浪；波涛；心潮；风潮；挥手；波 *v.* 挥手；挥舞

例 The single is making **waves** in the pop sector, holding at No. 1 for a second week on Pop Airplay with a 28% swell in weekly plays. 这首单曲在流行音乐领域掀起风潮，在流行音乐播放榜上连续两周占据第一位，周播放量上升了28%。

panic / 'pænɪk /

释 *n.* 惊恐；恐慌局面 *v.* 使惊慌；惊慌

搭 in panic 处于极度恐慌或紧张的状态

例 "There are as many scientists working against all the **panic** of global climate change as there are those who are pushing it," she claims. 她说："反对全球气候变化恐慌的科学家和推动全球气候变化恐慌的科学家一样多。"（2023年）

sincere / sɪn'sɪə(r) /

释 *adj.* 真诚的；诚挚的

例 The aim is to create **sincere** expressions of gratitude that acknowledge their individual contributions and reinforce a positive team atmosphere. 这样做的目的是真诚地表达感激之情，承认他们的个人贡献，营造积极的团队氛围。

派 sincerity / sɪn'serəti / *n.* 真诚，真挚 ‖ sincerely / sɪn'sɪəli / *adv.* 真诚地；诚实地

naive / naɪ'iːv /

释 *adj.* 天真的；幼稚的；缺乏经验的

例 They should exhibit strong interest and respect for whatever currently interests their fledgling adult (as **naive** or ill-conceived as it may seem) while becoming a partner in exploring options for the future. 他们应该对孩子目前感兴趣的任何事情（尽管可能看起来很幼稚或不切实际）表现出强烈的兴趣和尊重，同时成为孩子探索未来选择的伙伴。（2007年）

- ☐ ☐ abide
- ☐ ☐ abound
- ☐ ☐ approve
- ☐ ☐ bar
- ☐ ☐ bless
- ☐ ☐ budget
- ☐ ☐ carve
- ☐ ☐ case
- ☐ ☐ choose
- ☐ ☐ chronic
- ☐ ☐ classical
- ☐ ☐ client
- ☐ ☐ column
- ☐ ☐ compete
- ☐ ☐ component
- ☐ ☐ conceal
- ☐ ☐ constitute
- ☐ ☐ constrain
- ☐ ☐ contact
- ☐ ☐ contest
- ☐ ☐ contrary
- ☐ ☐ council
- ☐ ☐ creative
- ☐ ☐ criticism
- ☐ ☐ date
- ☐ ☐ demand
- ☐ ☐ despite
- ☐ ☐ deter
- ☐ ☐ distribute
- ☐ ☐ division
- ☐ ☐ emerge

- ☐ ☐ entire
- ☐ ☐ entry
- ☐ ☐ estimate
- ☐ ☐ evolve
- ☐ ☐ exercise
- ☐ ☐ fantasy
- ☐ ☐ flash
- ☐ ☐ focus
- ☐ ☐ frequent
- ☐ ☐ greet
- ☐ ☐ highly
- ☐ ☐ historical
- ☐ ☐ hold
- ☐ ☐ immune
- ☐ ☐ inference
- ☐ ☐ integrity
- ☐ ☐ invalid
- ☐ ☐ magnetic
- ☐ ☐ manifest
- ☐ ☐ massive
- ☐ ☐ matter
- ☐ ☐ mind
- ☐ ☐ misery
- ☐ ☐ multiple
- ☐ ☐ naive
- ☐ ☐ neglect
- ☐ ☐ numerical
- ☐ ☐ overcome
- ☐ ☐ overturn
- ☐ ☐ panic
- ☐ ☐ permission

- ☐ ☐ pessimistic
- ☐ ☐ poetry
- ☐ ☐ previous
- ☐ ☐ primary
- ☐ ☐ priority
- ☐ ☐ profound
- ☐ ☐ prominent
- ☐ ☐ range
- ☐ ☐ rapid
- ☐ ☐ reality
- ☐ ☐ regular
- ☐ ☐ requirement
- ☐ ☐ respect
- ☐ ☐ safety
- ☐ ☐ scholarship
- ☐ ☐ search
- ☐ ☐ show
- ☐ ☐ sincere
- ☐ ☐ sketch
- ☐ ☐ slight
- ☐ ☐ soil
- ☐ ☐ span
- ☐ ☐ spark
- ☐ ☐ stake
- ☐ ☐ surround
- ☐ ☐ technical
- ☐ ☐ tide
- ☐ ☐ trend
- ☐ ☐ tuition
- ☐ ☐ unanimous
- ☐ ☐ unfold

- ☐ ☐ uniform
- ☐ ☐ valuable
- ☐ ☐ vast
- ☐ ☐ waste
- ☐ ☐ wave
- ☐ ☐ wonder
- ☐ ☐ wreck

音频

Previous Check

- [ ] incorporate
- [ ] apologize/-ise
- [ ] seek
- [ ] considerable
- [ ] define
- [ ] upgrade
- [ ] adverse
- [ ] cease
- [ ] consent
- [ ] question
- [ ] tactic
- [ ] burden
- [ ] declare
- [ ] virtue
- [ ] conservative
- [ ] dedicate
- [ ] inspect
- [ ] fail
- [ ] satire
- [ ] authentic
- [ ] release
- [ ] interact
- [ ] conscious
- [ ] alliance
- [ ] stern
- [ ] complicated
- [ ] indispensable
- [ ] arrange
- [ ] compact
- [ ] combination
- [ ] destiny

- [ ] surpass
- [ ] legislation
- [ ] innovation
- [ ] trigger
- [ ] glare
- [ ] shortage
- [ ] career
- [ ] sphere
- [ ] view
- [ ] display
- [ ] recognition
- [ ] quote
- [ ] obscure
- [ ] dramatic
- [ ] confine
- [ ] humanity
- [ ] supply
- [ ] accord
- [ ] observe
- [ ] correspond
- [ ] erroneous
- [ ] obvious
- [ ] gamble
- [ ] external
- [ ] appearance
- [ ] suggest
- [ ] safeguard
- [ ] grieve
- [ ] tissue
- [ ] board
- [ ] advise

- [ ] humble
- [ ] minimize/-ise
- [ ] ethic
- [ ] majority
- [ ] union
- [ ] acquisition
- [ ] assumption
- [ ] addict
- [ ] religion
- [ ] indeed
- [ ] scream
- [ ] outline
- [ ] illuminate
- [ ] fragment
- [ ] legacy
- [ ] oral
- [ ] shade
- [ ] add
- [ ] clue
- [ ] match
- [ ] crew
- [ ] ambiguous
- [ ] bid
- [ ] purse
- [ ] conception
- [ ] lock
- [ ] analogy
- [ ] intelligence
- [ ] seize
- [ ] casualty
- [ ] panel

- [ ] alcohol
- [ ] envelope
- [ ] humiliate
- [ ] relax
- [ ] variable
- [ ] panorama
- [ ] spontaneous

incorporate / ɪnˈkɔːpəreɪt /

🟢 *v.* 将……包括在内；包含；吸收；使并入；注册成立

🟠 Attempts have been made to curb this tendency, for example, by trying to **incorporate** some measure of quality as well as quantity into the assessment of an applicant's papers. 为了遏制这种趋势已经采取了一些尝试，例如，试图将一些衡量质量和数量的标准纳入申请人论文的评估中。（2019年）

apologize/-ise / əˈpɒlədʒaɪz /

🟢 *v.* 道歉；谢罪

🟠 apologize to sb. 向某人道歉 ‖ apologize for sth. 为某事道歉

🟠 You should **apologize** to the others for your lateness. 你应该为迟到而向其他人道歉。

seek / siːk /

🟢 *v.* 寻求；寻找；请求（帮忙）；力图

🟠 seek sb./sth. out 寻找到，挑选出；物色

🟠 Scientists are increasingly **seeking** out visual artists to help them communicate their work to new audiences. 科学家们越来越频繁地找视觉艺术家来帮助他们，将他们的工作传达给新的观众。（2022年）

considerable / kənˈsɪdərəbl /

🟢 *adj.* 相当多（或大、重要等）的

🟠 Brain reprogramming is not a revolutionary approach as there once were many pain clinics that used such techniques with **considerable** success. 大脑重编程并不是一种革命性的方法，因为曾经有许多疼痛诊所使用过这种技术取得了相当大的成功。

🟣 substantial / səbˈstænʃl / *adj.* 大量的，可观的

define / dɪˈfaɪn /

🟢 *v.* 给……定义；解释；阐明，明确，界定；确定……的界限

🟠 Technology **defines** people's understanding of the world. 技术界定了人们对世界的理解。（2024年）

🟣 definition / ˌdefɪˈnɪʃn / *n.* 定义；清晰度

upgrade

🟢 / ˌʌpˈgreɪd / *v.* 提升，改进；（使）升级；提高（飞机乘客、旅馆住客等的）待遇 / ˈʌpgreɪd / *n.* 升级

🟠 As an executive coach, I've seen image **upgrades** be particularly helpful during transitions—when looking for a new job, stepping into a new or more public role, or changing work environments. 作为一名高管教练，我看到形象升级在转型期特别有用——在寻找新工作、进入一个新角色或更有公众性的角色，或工作环境改变时。（2016年）

adverse / əd'vɜːs /　007

释 *adj.* 不利的，有害的
搭 be adverse to 跟……相反；不利于；反对
例 Nicotine has **adverse** effects on human beings. 尼古丁对人体有害。

cease / siːs /　008

释 *v.* 停止，终止，结束
例 There will eventually come a day when *The New York Times* **ceases** to publish stories on newsprint. 终有一天，《纽约时报》将不再用新闻纸发表报道。（2016年）
近 terminate / 'tɜːmɪneɪt / *v.* 终止，结束
辨 cease和terminate都有"结束"的意思。cease为正式用语，用于表示状态的"停止，终止"；terminate在书面语中出现较多，常用来表示某一过程由于某种原因而结束或终止。

consent / kən'sent /　009

释 *n.* 同意，准许；赞同 *v.* 同意，准许
搭 consent to 同意……
例 There are lessons about informed patient **consent** to learn. 在病人知情同意方面，我们需要吸取教训。（2018年）
近 approval / ə'pruːvl / *n.* 同意；赞成 ‖ assent / ə'sent / *n.* 同意；允许

question / 'kwestʃən /　010

释 *n.* 问题；询问；试题 *v.* 询问；怀疑
搭 in question 正被提及的；有关的 ‖ out of the question 完全不可能的
例 It would be absurd to try to track the changing price of sports cars since 1695, but to ask the same **question** of nails makes perfect sense. 试图追踪跑车自1695年以来的价格变化是荒谬的，但对钉子提出同样的问题却非常合理。（2024年）

tactic / 'tæktɪk /　011

释 *n.* 手段，策略；战术
例 This is a **tactic** vendors of all sizes can employ to make returns somewhat more predictable. 各种规模的供应商都可以采用这种策略，使回报稍微更可预测。

burden / 'bɜːdn /　012

释 *n.* 重担，负担 *v.* （使）担负（沉重或艰难的任务、职责等）；负重
例 And firms pay staff less because firms carry the **burden** of the employment arrangement going wrong. 而且，企业支付给员工的薪水也会变少，因为企业要承担雇佣安排出错的责任。（2022年）

declare / dɪ'kleə(r) /　013

释 *v.* 公布，宣布，宣告；表明；宣称；断言；申报（收益、应纳税物品）
搭 declare against/for 声明反对/支持
例 The order also **declared** that state and local governments couldn't regulate broadband providers either. 该命令还宣布州政府和地方政府也不能监管宽带供应商。（2021年）

Writing Models ◎

virtue / ˈvɜːtʃuː /

014

释 *n.* 高尚的道德；正直的品性；美德；优秀品质；良好习惯；优点；长处

搭 by/in virtue of 凭借；依靠；由于；因为

例 But all too often such policies are an insincere form of **virtue**-signaling that benefits only the most privileged and does little to help average people. 但是，这些政策往往是一种体现美德的虚假形式，只有利于最有特权的人，对普通人没有什么帮助。(2020年)

conservative / kənˈsɜːvətɪv /

015

释 *adj.* 保守的；[C-]（英国）保守党的 *n.* 保守者；[C-]（英国）保守党党员，保守党支持者；保守者

例 Yet that demand has been almost impossible to fill—in part because of pushback from broadband providers, anti-regulatory **conservatives** and the courts. 然而，这一需求几乎无法满足，部分原因是宽带供应商、反监管的保守人士和法院的阻挠。(2021年)

dedicate / ˈdedɪkeɪt /

016

释 *v.* 致力；题献

搭 dedicate oneself to sth. 致力于某事；献身于某事

例 That's one reason why we have launched *Arc*, a new publication **dedicated** to the near future. 这也是我们推出《弧线》的原因之一，这是一本致力于研究近期未来的新刊物。(2013年)

派 dedication / ˌdedɪˈkeɪʃn / *n.* 奉献；献词 ‖ dedicated / ˈdedɪkeɪtɪd / *adj.* 献身的；一心一意的

近 devote / dɪˈvəʊt / *v.* 致力于；奉献 ‖ contribute / kənˈtrɪbjuːt / *v.* 贡献

inspect / ɪnˈspekt /

017

释 *v.* 检查；查看；视察

例 A number of companies, particularly in energy and transportation, use AI image processing technology to **inspect** infrastructure and prevent equipment failure or leaks before they happen. 许多公司，尤其是能源和交通领域的公司，都在使用人工智能图像处理技术来检查基础设施，并在设备故障或泄漏发生之前加以预防。(2021年)

fail / feɪl /

018

释 *v.* 失败；未能（做到）；出故障；使失望；不及格

例 In other words, they all share a view that the international tax system has **failed** to keep up with the current economy. 换句话说，他们都认为国际税收制度未能跟上当前经济的发展。(2020年)

派 failure / ˈfeɪljə(r) / *n.* 失败；失败的事

satire / ˈsætaɪə(r) /

019

释 *n.* 讽刺；讽刺作品

例 The writer's **satire** on thieves is popular. 那位作家描写小偷的讽刺作品很受欢迎。

virtue

conservative

dedicate

inspect

fail

satire

authentic

release

interact

conscious

alliance

stern

authentic / ɔː'θentɪk / 020

释 *adj.* 真实的; 真正的; 真品的; 逼真的

例 Reproductions, even if perfectly made, cannot take the place of the **authentic** objects. 复制品即使制作得再完美，也无法取代真品的地位。（2024年）

release / rɪ'liːs / 021

释 *v.* 发布; 发行; 发放; 解除; 释放 *n.* 释放; 解除; 发行物

例 Soon after his father's **release** from prison, Dickens got a better job as errand boy in law offices. 父亲出狱后不久，狄更斯找到了一份更好的工作——在律师事务所当跑腿小弟。（2017年）

近 deliver / dɪ'lɪvə(r) / *v.* 释放

interact / ˌɪntər'ækt / 022

释 *v.* 相互影响，相互作用; 交流，沟通

搭 interact with 与……相互作用/影响

例 Algorithms used to simulate human interactions are creating many of these concerns, especially as no-one is quite sure what the outcomes of using AI to **interact** with customers will be. 用于模拟人类互动的算法正在引发许多这样的担忧，尤其是没有人能够完全确定使用人工智能与客户互动会产生什么样的结果。（2023年）

conscious / 'kɒnʃəs / 023

释 *adj.* 意识到的，有意的; 自觉的

搭 conscious of (doing) sth. 意识到（做）某事

例 This forces users to be more **conscious** of their role in passing along information. 这迫使用户更加意识到自己在传递信息方面的作用。（2018年）

alliance / ə'laɪəns / 024

释 *n.* 联盟; 结盟

例 A native literary drama had been created, its **alliance** with the public playhouses established, and at least some of its great traditions had been begun. 本土的文学戏剧艺术已经产生了，其与公众剧院的联盟关系也得以确立，至少，它的一些优秀传统已经初具雏形。（2018年）

stern / stɜːn / 025

释 *adj.* 严厉的，苛刻的; 严峻的; 难对付的 *n.* 船尾

例 If the bar exam is truly a **stern** enough test for a would-be lawyer, those who can sit it earlier should be allowed to do so. 如果律师资格考试对有意成为律师的人确实是一个足够严格的考验，那么就应该允许那些能够提前参加考试的人参加。（2014年）

近 strict / strɪkt / *adj.* 严厉的，严格的 ‖ severe / sɪ'vɪə(r) / *adj.* 严厉的; 严峻的; 严重的

complicated / ˈkɒmplɪkeɪtɪd /   026

释 *adj.* 复杂的; 难懂的

例 But in the everyday practice of science, discovery frequently follows an ambiguous and **complicated** route. 但在日常科学实践中, 发现往往遵循一条模糊且复杂的路线。(2012年)

indispensable / ˌɪndɪˈspensəbl /   027

释 *adj.* 必需的, 不可或缺的

例 Marris distorts our findings, which actually prove that zoos serve as an **indispensable** link between man and nature. 马里斯歪曲了我们的发现, 这些发现实际上证明了动物园充当了人与自然之间不可或缺的纽带的作用。(2022年)

arrange / əˈreɪndʒ /   028

释 *v.* 安排; 排列; 整理

例 This would be reasonable if it were not for the fact that scientists can easily **arrange** to cite themselves in their future publications, or get associates to do so for them in return for similar favours. 如果不是因为科学家们可以很容易地在他们的未来出版物中安排引用自己的话, 或者让同事为他们这样做以换取类似的好处, 这是合理的。(2019年)

近 organize / ˈɔːɡənaɪz / *v.* 安排; 组织

辨 arrange和organize都有 "使有条理, 安排" 的意思。arrange指按计划、秩序和需要等进行安排, organize指按计划或需要把人或物安排组织成一个整体。

compact   029

释 / kəmˈpækt / *v.* 压紧; 简化 / ˈkɒmpækt / *n.* 约定; 契约; 合同 *adj.* 紧密的; 简洁的; 结实的

例 "The basic **compact** underlying representative government", wrote Chief Justice John Roberts for the court, "assumes that public officials will hear from their constituents and act on their concerns". 首席大法官约翰·罗伯茨代表法院写道, "代议制政府的基本契约假设公职人员会听取选民的意见, 并会根据他们的担忧采取行动"。(2017年)

combination / ˌkɒmbɪˈneɪʃn /   030

释 *n.* 结合, 联合; 结合体; 混合物; (用于开密码锁的)字码组合

搭 in combination with 联合

例 The word "caravanserai" is a **combination** of the Persian words "kārvān", which means a group of travellers or a caravan, and "sarāy", a palace or enclosed building. "caravanserai" 一词由波斯语 "kārvān" 和 "sarāy" 结合而成。"kārvān" 意为一群旅行者或大篷车, "sarāy" 意为宫殿或封闭式建筑。(2023年)

近 association / əˌsəʊsiˈeɪʃn / *n.* 联合 ‖ coalition / ˌkəʊəˈlɪʃn / *n.* 联合; 合并

destiny / 'destəni /
031

释 *n.* 命运，天命，定数

例 This movement, driven by powerful and diverse motivations, built a nation out of a wilderness and, by its nature, shaped the character and **destiny** of an uncharted continent. 这场运动由强大而多样的动机驱动，在荒野中建立了一个国家，并从本质上塑造了一个未知大陆的特征和命运。（2015年）

surpass / sə'pɑːs /
032

释 *v.* 超过；胜过

例 The beauty of the lake **surpassed** all my expectations. 这个湖的美超出了我的预料。

近 exceed / ɪk'siːd / *v.* 超过

legislation / ˌledʒɪs'leɪʃn /
033

释 *n.* 法律；立法，制定法律

例 In quick succession, the Senate and House passed **legislation** protecting Yellowstone in early 1872. 1872年初，参议院和众议院快速相继通过了保护黄石公园的立法。（2023年）

近 regulation / ˌregju'leɪʃn / *n.* 规章；条例 ‖ rule / ruːl / *n.* 规则；条例

innovation / ˌɪnə'veɪʃn /
034

释 *n.* 创新，革新

例 Technological **innovation** is integral to economic success. 技术创新是经济成功不可或缺的因素。（2024年）

trigger / 'trɪɡə(r) /
035

释 *n.* 扳机 *v.* 引发，导致

例 Though plants lack brains, the firing of electrical signals in their stems and leaves nonetheless **triggered** responses that hinted at consciousness, researchers previously reported. 此前研究人员报告说，虽然植物没有大脑，但其茎叶中的电信号发射却引发了暗示意识的反应。（2022年）

glare / gleə(r) /
036

释 *v.* 怒目而视 *n.* 刺眼的光；（长久地）怒视，瞪眼

搭 glare at 怒目而视

例 The question draws an immediate reaction, as the young man turns sharply, **glaring** at the camera with contempt. 这个问题立即引起了他的反应，那位年轻人猛地转过身来，蔑视地盯着镜头。

shortage / 'ʃɔːtɪdʒ /
037

释 *n.* 不足，缺少

例 Food **shortages** often occur in time of war. 在战争期间常常发生粮食短缺的情形。

career

sphere

view

display

recognition

quote

obscure

dramatic

confine

humanity

supply

accord

career / kəˈrɪə(r) / 038

释 n. 职业生涯; 职业 adj. 就业的 v. (尤指失控地)猛冲, 疾驰, 飞奔

例 Education, and not just knowledge gained on campus, will be a core part of Generation Z's **career** trajectory. 教育，而不仅仅是在校园里获得的知识，将成为 Z 世代职业生涯轨迹的核心部分。（2022年）

sphere / sfɪə(r) / 039

释 n. (活动、兴趣等的)范围, 领域; 阶层, 圈子; 球体

例 In certain areas of mathematics, a **sphere** attached to a **sphere** is still a **sphere**, though perhaps a bigger or lumpier one. 在数学的某些领域，一个球体连着一个球体仍然是一个球体，尽管可能是一个更大或更笨重的球体。

view / vjuː / 040

释 n. (个人的)看法; 态度; (理解或思维的)方法; 视野; 风景 v. 把……视为; 以……看待; 观看; 查看

例 Before each of their revelations, many thinkers at the time had sustained more ancient ways of thinking, including the geo-centric **view** that the Earth was at the centre of our universe. 在每一个真相被公之于众之前，当时的很多思想家都固守着更为陈旧的思维方式，包括地球是我们宇宙的中心的地心说。（2020年）

派 viewpoint / ˈvjuːpɔɪnt / n. 观点; 角度

display / dɪˈspleɪ / 041

释 n. 展出, 陈列, 表演, 表露; (屏幕)显示内容 v. 显示, 显露(某种情感、态度或特质); 展示, 陈列

例 What intrinsic factors make the West a suitable home for these artifacts but preclude them from being preserved and **displayed** by their countries of origin? 是什么内在因素使西方成为适合这些文物的家园，而让它们无法在原属国得到保存和展出？（2024年）

recognition / ˌrekəɡˈnɪʃn / 042

释 n. 认可, 承认; (国际上的)正式承认; 认出, 识别; 赞赏

搭 in recognition of sth. 作为对……的奖赏, 用以肯定

例 His status in Lord Wellington's headquarters and the **recognition** given to him for his work were bound up with the class politics of the Army at the time. 他在威灵顿勋爵司令部中的地位以及对他工作的认可与当时军队的阶级政治息息相关。（2022年）

quote / kwəʊt / 043

释 v. 引用, 引述; 举证; 报价 n. 引用; 引语

例 Quite a lot, according to a handful of scientists **quoted** in the *News Feature*. 《新闻特写》引述了几位科学家的观点，（他们认为不可取之处）有很多。（2014年）

obscure / əbˈskjʊə(r) / 0**4**4

释 *adj.* 鲜为人知的；复杂难懂的 *v.* 使模糊；使费解

例 Factors such as the place and period in which we are reading, our gender, ethnicity, age and social class will encourage us towards certain interpretations but at the same time **obscure** or even close off others. 诸如我们阅读的地点和时代、我们的性别、种族、年龄和社会阶级等因素会促使我们做出某些解读，但同时也会模糊甚至封锁其他解读。（2015年）

近 ambiguous / æmˈbɪgjuəs / *adj.* 不清楚的 ‖ vague / veɪg / *adj.* 含糊的，不明确的

dramatic / drəˈmætɪk / 0**4**5

释 *adj.* 戏剧的；戏剧般的；突然的；激动人心的；巨大的；令人吃惊的

例 In a competitive news environment, pollsters often highlight their most negative or **dramatic** findings in order to get coverage. 在竞争激烈的新闻环境中，民调机构为了获得报道，往往会突出最负面或最令人吃惊的调查结果。

confine / kənˈfaɪn / 0**4**6

释 *v.* 监禁；禁闭；限制；限定；使离不开（或受困于床、轮椅等）

搭 be confined in prison 被囚禁在监狱里

例 Cooper and her colleagues argue that the success of the crown for Hull, where it brought in £220m of investment and an avalanche of arts, ought not to be **confined** to cities. 库珀和她的同事们认为，"皇冠"为赫尔市带来了2.2亿英镑的投资和大量艺术作品，其成功不应局限于城市。（2020年）

humanity / hjuːˈmænəti / 0**4**7

释 *n.* 人类；人道；仁慈；人性

例 The purpose of editing the *News of the World* was not to promote reader understanding, to be fair in what was written or to betray any common **humanity**. 编辑《世界新闻报》的目的不是促进读者的理解，也不是在报道中保持公正或背叛任何普遍的人性。（2015年）

supply / səˈplaɪ / 0**4**8

释 *v.* （尤指大量）供应，供给，提供 *n.* 供应；供给；提供；储备；补给

例 Scientists need journals in which to publish their research, so they will **supply** the articles without monetary reward. 科学家们需要期刊来发表他们的研究成果，因此他们会在没有金钱回报的情况下提供这些文章。（2020年）

accord / əˈkɔːd / 0**4**9

释 *n.* 协议；条约 *v.* 给予；授予；（与……）一致；符合；配合

搭 in accord with 与……一致（或相符合）

例 The country that resisted joining the **accords** at the time has been the biggest winner ever since. 那个当时抵制加入该协议的国家自那以后成了该协议的最大赢家。

Writing Models ◎ ┄┄┄┄┄

observe

correspond

erroneous

obvious

gamble

external

appearance

suggest

safeguard

grieve

tissue

board

---

observe / əbˈzɜːv / 050

释 *v.* 看到；注意到；观察；注视；监视

例 And it carries "significant repercussions for water quality and flood control throughout the United States," as Justice Brett Kavanaugh **observed**. 正如大法官布雷特·卡瓦诺所看到的那样，它"对整个美国的水质和防洪都有重大影响"。（2024年）

---

correspond / ˌkɒrəˈspɒnd / 051

释 *v.* 相一致；相当于；通信

例 In the end, credibility "happens" to a discovery claim—a process that **corresponds** to what philosopher Annette Baier has described as the commons of the mind. 最终，可信度"发生"在一个发现主张上——这个过程恰与哲学家安妮特·拜尔所描述的"思想的共性"一致。（2012年）

---

erroneous / ɪˈrəʊniəs / 052

释 *adj.* 错误的，不正确的

例 Allen's contribution was to take an assumption we all share—that because we are not robots we therefore control our thoughts—and reveal its **erroneous** nature. 艾伦的贡献在于抓住了一个我们公认的假设——因为我们不是机器人，所以我们可以控制自己的思想——并揭示了其错误本质。（2011年）

---

obvious / ˈɒbviəs / 053

释 *adj.* 明显的；显然的；易理解的；公认的；当然的；因显而易见而不必要的

例 It is not yet clear how much more effective airline security has become—but the lines are **obvious**. 目前还不清楚航空公司的安全措施有多有效，但安检队伍明显变长了。（2017年）

---

gamble / ˈɡæmbl / 054

释 *v.* 赌博 *n.* 投机；冒险；赌博

搭 gamble on 冒……的风险；碰……的运气

例 He had never **gambled** before the casino sent him a coupon for $20 worth of gambling. 在赌场寄给他价值20美元的赌博优惠券之前，他从未赌博过。（2006年）

近 bet / bet / *v.* 打赌；赌博 ‖ wager / ˈweɪdʒə(r) / *v.* 下赌注

---

external / ɪkˈstɜːnl / 055

释 *adj.* 外部的，外面的；表面的

例 At first glance this might seem like a strength that grants the ability to make judgments which are unbiased by **external** factors. 乍一看，这似乎是一种力量，赋予了人们做出不受外部因素影响的判断的能力。（2013年）

反 internal / ɪnˈtɜːnl / *adj.* 内部的；内在的

appearance / ə'pɪərəns / `056`

释 *n.* 露面, 出现; 外观, 外貌; 表象; 问世

例 Some academics went further, calling the **appearance** of many food deserts nothing but a mirage—and not the real problem. 一些学者做了更进一步的说明, 他们认为很多食品荒漠的出现只不过是妄想, 而且也并不是真正的问题。

派 disappearance / ˌdɪsə'pɪərəns / *n.* 不见, 消失

suggest / sə'dʒest / `057`

释 *v.* 建议; 提议; 推荐; 暗示; 表明

例 New research **suggests** that smell is a crucial factor in guiding elephants—and probably other herbivores—to the best food resources. 新的研究表明, 气味是引导大象——可能还有其他食草动物——找到最佳食物资源的关键因素。(2024年)

safeguard / 'seɪfgɑːd / `058`

释 *n.* 防护装置; 预防措施 *v.* 保护; 护卫

例 Keeping clean is a **safeguard** against disease. 保持清洁是一种预防疾病的措施。

grieve / griːv / `059`

释 *v.* (使)悲伤, (使)伤心; (使)悲痛

搭 grieve over/for 因……悲伤

例 This service honors loved ones who died and provides a time of reflection and peace with words of comfort, music and prayers for anyone **grieving**. 这一仪式是为了纪念逝去的亲人, 并通过安慰的话语、音乐和祈祷为悲伤的人们提供一个回忆和平静的时刻。

派 grievous / 'griːvəs / *adj.* 使人痛苦的; 令人伤心的

反 delight / dɪ'laɪt / *v.* 使高兴; 使欣喜

tissue / 'tɪʃuː / `060`

释 *n.* (动植物的)组织; 面巾纸

例 Growth, which rarely continues beyond the age of 20, demands calories and nutrients—notably, protein—to feed expanding **tissues**. 生长很少持续到20岁以后, 它需要热量和营养物质——尤其是蛋白质——供应身体组织的生长。(2008年)

board / bɔːd / `061`

释 *n.* 板; 木板; 董事会, 委员会, 理事会; 膳食 *v.* 登上(火车、船或飞机); (在学校)寄宿

搭 on board 在(火车、轮船或飞机)上

例 Glenn Branch, the centre's deputy director, cautions that setting state-level science standards is only one limited benchmark in a country that decentralises decisions to local school **boards**. 该中心副主任格伦·布兰奇警告说, 在一个将决策权下放给地方学校委员会的国家, 制定州级科学标准只是一个有限的基准。(2023年)

advise / əd'vaɪz / 062

释 *v.* 劝告；忠告；提出建议；提供咨询；通知；正式告知

例 According to Ortiz, AI companies are **advised** to adopt a different strategy for AI model training. 据奥尔蒂斯所说，人工智能公司被建议采取不同的人工智能模型训练策略。（2024年）

humble / 'hʌmbl / 063

释 *adj.* 谦逊的；低下的，卑微的；普通的 *v.* 贬低；使感到卑微

搭 in my humble opinion 以我拙见

例 He fought many hard battles and achieved notable merits, but he remains **humble**. 他参加过许多激烈的战役，立下了汗马功劳，但他仍然很谦逊。

minimize/-ise / 'mɪnɪmaɪz / 064

释 *v.* 使减到最少；使降到最低；贬低……的重要性

例 The TMT site was chosen to **minimize** the telescope's visibility around the island and to avoid archaeological and environmental impact. 30米望远镜的选址是为了尽量减少望远镜在岛上的能见度，并避免对考古和环境造成影响。（2017年）

ethic / 'eθɪk / 065

释 *n.* 道德；行为准则

例 As a result, they are raising tricky questions about **ethics** and copyright. 因此，它们引起了有关道德和版权方面的棘手问题。（2024年）

majority / mə'dʒɒrəti / 066

释 *n.* 大部分；大多数；多数票

例 Among the children who had not been tricked, the **majority** were willing to cooperate with the tester in learning a new skill, demonstrating that they trusted his leadership. 在没有上当受骗的孩子中，大多数都愿意与测试者合作学习一种新技能，这表明他们信任测试者的领导能力。（2018年）

union / 'juːniən / 067

释 *n.* 工会；联盟；协会

例 The responsibility for the latest wave of strikes rests on the **unions**. 工会对最近的罢工浪潮负有责任。（2021年）

acquisition / ˌækwɪ'zɪʃn / 068

释 *n.* 获得；（知识、技能等的）习得；收购

搭 language-acquisition capacity 语言习得能力

例 Much more could be done to encourage "long-termism," such as changes in the tax code and quicker disclosure of stock **acquisitions**. 还可以做更多的事情来鼓励"长期主义"，比如修改税法和更快地披露股票收购信息。（2019年）

assumption / əˈsʌmpʃn /
069

释 n. 假设；（责任的）承担

例 Such behaviour is regarded as "all too human", with the underlying **assumption** that other animals would not be capable of this finely developed sense of grievance. 这种行为被看作是"人类独有的"，其潜在的假设是，其他动物不会有这种高度进化的不满意识。（2005年）

addict / ˈædɪkt /
070

释 n. （吸毒）上瘾者；对……入迷的人

例 Nevertheless, Williams's suit charges that the casino, knowing he was "helplessly **addicted** to gambling," intentionally worked to "lure" him to "engage in conduct against his will." 然而，威廉姆斯的诉讼指控赌场明知他"不可救药地沉迷于赌博"，却故意"引诱"他"违背其意愿行事"。（2006年）

religion / rɪˈlɪdʒən /
071

释 n. 宗教；宗教信仰；特别的兴趣

例 This kind of thinking is why so many people try to avoid arguments, especially about politics and **religion**. 这种想法就是很多人尽量避免争论的原因，尤其是关于政治和宗教的争论。（2019年）

indeed / ɪnˈdiːd /
072

释 adv. 确实；其实；实际上；真正地

例 **Indeed**, it was frequently the first stop for merchants looking to sell their wares and stock up on supplies for their own journeys. 实际上，这里经常是商人们出售商品和为自己的旅程储备物资的第一站。（2023年）

scream / skriːm /
073

释 v. 尖叫；高声喊；尖声说

例 Of course, the pharmaceutical companies will **scream**. 当然，医药公司会尖声抗议。（2005年）

outline / ˈaʊtlaɪn /
074

释 n. 概述；梗概；轮廓 v. 概述；显示……的轮廓

例 Your **outline** should smoothly conduct you from one point to the next, but do not permit it to railroad you. 你的概述应该能够引导你流畅地从一个论点过渡到下一个论点，而不是让你仓促地得出结论。（2008年）

illuminate / ɪˈluːmɪneɪt /
075

释 v. 照明；照亮；阐明；解释

例 Yet its report may well set back reform by obscuring the depth and breadth of the challenge that Congress asked it to **illuminate**. 然而，其报告很可能会因为没有弄清国会要求其阐明的挑战的深度和广度而阻碍改革。（2014年）

fragment / ˈfræɡmənt / 　　　　　076

🔴 *n.* 碎片 *v.* （使）碎裂，破裂，分裂

🔵 Most ground surveys involve a lot of walking, looking for surface clues such as small **fragments** of pottery. 大多数地面勘测都需要大量步行，寻找地面上的线索，比如陶器的小碎片。（2014年）

🟠 fragmentation / ˌfræɡmenˈteɪʃn / *n.* 破碎；碎片化 ‖ fragmented / fræɡˈmentɪd / *adj.* 支离破碎的

legacy / ˈleɡəsi / 　　　　　077

🔴 *n.* 遗留；遗留问题；遗产；遗赠财物

🔵 "I wouldn't pick a year to end print," he said. "I would raise prices and make it into more of a **legacy** product." "我不会选择要在哪一年结束印刷，"他说。"我会提高报纸的价格，让它更像一款传统产品。"（2016年）

🟣 inheritance / ɪnˈherɪtəns / *n.* 继承物；遗产；遗产继承

oral / ˈɔːrəl / 　　　　　078

🔴 *adj.* 口头的；与口有关的

🔵 In both **oral** and written English, talking is triumphing over speaking, spontaneity over craft. 在口头英语和书面英语中，"说"都战胜了"讲"，"自发性"战胜了"技巧性"。（2005年）

shade / ʃeɪd / 　　　　　079

🔴 *n.* 阴凉处；（树）荫；阴影部分 *v.* 遮蔽

🔵 The sparkling swimming pool is privately watched over and **shaded** by trees. 波光粼粼的游泳池被私人看管，并被树木遮蔽。

🟠 shady / ˈʃeɪdi / *adj.* 阴凉的；背阴的；可疑的；不法的

add / æd / 　　　　　080

🔴 *v.* 增加；添加；加；补充说

🟢 add ... in 把……加进去；包括 ‖ add ... to ... 增添……至…… ‖ add up 把……加起来 ‖ add up to 总共是，总计为

🔵 And for authors who wish to steer clear of citation cartel activities: when an editor, a reviewer, or a support service asks you to **add** inappropriate references, do not oblige and do report the request to the journal. 对于那些希望避开引文卡特尔活动的作者：当编辑、审稿人或支持服务人员要求你添加不适当的参考文献时，不要帮他们的忙，一定要向该期刊报告他们这个请求。（2023年）

🟠 addition / əˈdɪʃn / *n.* 增加；添加

🔴 subtract / səbˈtrækt / *v.* 减；减去

clue / kluː / 　　　　　081

🔴 *n.* 线索，迹象；提示

🟢 not have a clue 一无所知；不知怎么做

🔵 If you are unfamiliar with words or idioms, you guess at their meaning, using **clues** presented in the context. 如果你不熟悉单词或习语，你可以利用上下文中提供的线索来猜测它们的意思。（2015年）

match / mætʃ / 082

釋 *v.* 般配; 与……相匹敌 *n.* 比赛; 相配的人（或物）; 火柴

例 On a cold winter's day, few culinary pleasures can **match** it. 在一个寒冷的冬日, 鲜有其他的烹饪乐趣能与之媲美。（2020年）

crew / kruː / 083

釋 *n.* 全体船员; 全体乘务员; 专业团队; 一群（或一帮、一伙）人

例 Following in the footsteps of U.S. guilds, French TV **crew** members are poised to go on strike amid a battle with producers over minimum wages. 继美国行业协会之后, 法国电视台的工作人员也准备举行罢工, 与制片人就最低工资展开斗争。

ambiguous / æmˈbɪɡjuəs / 084

釋 *adj.* 模棱两可的; 不明确的

例 Of all expressions, about 45 percent were categorized as friendly, 37 percent were aggressive and 18 percent were **ambiguous**, writes Susan. 苏珊写道, 在所有表情中, 约有45%被归类为友好的, 37%是有攻击性的, 18%是模棱两可的。

反 unambiguous / ˌʌnæmˈbɪɡjuəs / *adj.* 意思清楚的; 无歧义的

bid / bɪd / 085

釋 *n.* 出价; 投标; 叫牌; 努力尝试; 努力争取 *v.* 出价; 投标; 努力争取

搭 bid for sth. 出价; 努力争取, 力求获得

例 Britain's towns, it is true, are not prevented from applying, but they generally lack the resources to put together a **bid** to beat their bigger competitors. 诚然, 英国的城镇并没有被禁止申请（这个称号）, 但它们一般都缺乏资源, 无法在竞标中击败更大的竞争对手。（2020年）

purse / pɜːs / 086

釋 *n.* 钱包, 皮夹子（尤指女用的）

例 They should start by discarding California's lame argument that exploring the contents of a smart phone—a vast storehouse of digital information—is similar to, say, going through a suspect's **purse**. 他们应该先摒弃加州的蹩脚论点: 搜索智能手机的内容——一个巨大的数字信息仓库——就像翻查嫌疑人的钱包。（2015年）

近 wallet / ˈwɒlɪt / *n.* 钱包, 皮夹子

conception / kənˈsepʃn / 087

釋 *n.* 概念; 理解; 构思, 构想

例 This top-down **conception** of the fashion business couldn't be more out of date or at odds with the feverish world described in Elizabeth Cline's *Overdresse*. 这种自上而下的时尚商业概念已经过时, 与伊丽莎白·克莱恩《过度着装》一书中描述的狂热世界格格不入。

近 concept / ˈkɒnsept / *n.* 概念; 观念

Writing Models ◎

lock

analogy

intelligence

seize

casualty

panel

alcohol

envelope

humiliate

relax

variable

panorama

spontaneous

lock / lɒk / 　088

释 *v.* 锁上；把……锁起来 *n.* 锁

例 Museums **locked** some of them away in the dark. 博物馆把它们中的一部分锁在了暗处。（2022年）

反 unlock / ʌn'lɒk / *v.* 开锁；发现；揭开

analogy / ə'nælədʒi / 　089

释 *n.* 类比；比喻；类推

例 To borrow an **analogy** from a prominent physician turned investor—Venrock's Bob Kocher—becoming a founder is kind of like having a child. 借用一位著名医生出身的投资者、文洛克创投的鲍勃·科赫的类比：成为一名创始人有点像有了一个孩子。

intelligence / ɪn'telɪdʒəns / 　090

释 *n.* 智能；聪明；情报

例 There has been some exploration around the use of artificial **intelligence** (AI) in digital marketing. 围绕人工智能（AI）在数字营销中的应用，人们进行了一些探索。（2023年）

派 intelligent / ɪn'telɪdʒənt / *adj.* 智能的；有才智的

seize / siːz / 　091

释 *v.* 抓住，把握（机会、时机、主动等）；捉住；攻占，夺取；没收；逮捕

搭 seize on/upon 突然大为关注，抓住（可利用的事物）

例 However, Blunt and Krasinski **seized** the opportunity and realized their dreams. 然而，布朗特和卡拉辛斯基抓住了这个机会，并实现了他们的梦想。

casualty / 'kæʒuəlti / 　092

释 *n.* 伤员；遇难者；受害者，受害方

例 We shall see whether that plurality is a **casualty** of the current need among publishers to be big enough to take on all-comers. 这种多元化是否会成为当前出版商追求足够大的规模以应对所有竞争者的受害者，我们将拭目以待。（2023年）

近 victim / 'vɪktɪm / *n.* 受害者；牺牲品

panel / 'pænl / 　093

释 *n.* 专门小组；讨论小组；控制板，仪表盘

例 The Federal Circuit issued an unusual order stating that the case would be heard by all 12 of the court's judges, rather than a typical **panel** of three, and that one issue it wants to evaluate is whether it should "reconsider" its State Street Bank ruling. 联邦巡回法院发布了一项不同寻常的命令，声明该案件将由法院的所有12名法官审理，而不是通常的三人小组，并表示法院想要评估的一个议题是是否应该"重新考虑"对道富银行的裁决。（2010年）

alcohol / ˈælkəhɒl / `094`

释 *n.* 酒; 酒精

例 Part of the problem is that many homeless adults are addicted to **alcohol** or drugs. 部分原因是许多无家可归的成年人对酒精或毒品上瘾。（2006年）

派 alcoholic / ˌælkəˈhɒlɪk / *adj.* 酒精的; 含酒精的 *n.* 嗜酒如命者

envelope / ˈenvələup / `095`

释 *n.* 信封

例 Now think of your laptop, thinner than a brown-paper **envelope**, or your cellphone in the palm of your hand. 现在想想你的笔记本电脑, 比牛皮纸信封或者在手中的手机还薄。（2012年）

humiliate / hjuːˈmɪlieɪt / `096`

释 *v.* 羞辱; 使丧失尊严

例 She accused him of trying to **humiliate** her in public. 她指责他企图在公共场合羞辱她。

派 humiliation / hjuːˌmɪliˈeɪʃn / *n.* 耻辱; 丢脸的事或场合

relax / rɪˈlæks / `097`

释 *v.* （使）放松; 休息; （使）冷静; 放宽（限制等）

例 Studies dating back to the 1930s indicate that laughter **relaxes** muscles, decreasing muscle tone for up to 45 minutes after the laugh dies down. 早在20世纪30年代就有研究表明, 笑可以使肌肉放松, 在笑声消失后的45分钟内, 肌肉张力会降低。（2011年）

派 relaxation / ˌriːlækˈseɪʃn / *n.* 放松; 休息; 消遣; 休闲活动

variable / ˈveəriəbl / `098`

释 *n.* 变量; 可变因素 *adj.* 多变的; 易变的; 可变的

例 Temperatures were highly **variable** but more often warm than cold. 气温变化很大, 但往往是温暖多于寒冷。

派 variably / ˈveəriəbli / *adv.* 易变地; 不定地 ‖ variability / ˌveəriəˈbɪləti / *n.* 可变性; 易变性

panorama / ˌpænəˈrɑːmə / `099`

释 *n.* 全景, 远景; 概述, 综述

例 There is a superb **panorama** of the mountains from the hotel. 从旅馆可尽览群山的壮丽全景。

spontaneous / spɒnˈteɪniəs / `100`

释 *adj.* 自然的; 自发的; 非筹划安排的

例 **Spontaneous** smiles were relatively easy to capture by the 1890s, so we must look elsewhere for an explanation of why Victorians still hesitated to smile. 到19世纪90年代, 自然的微笑已经相对比较容易捕捉, 所以我们必须从其他方面寻找维多利亚时代的人为什么对微笑犹豫不决的解释。（2021年）

- ☐ ☐ accord
- ☐ ☐ acquisition
- ☐ ☐ add
- ☐ ☐ addict
- ☐ ☐ adverse
- ☐ ☐ advise
- ☐ ☐ alcohol
- ☐ ☐ alliance
- ☐ ☐ ambiguous
- ☐ ☐ analogy
- ☐ ☐ apologize/-ise
- ☐ ☐ appearance
- ☐ ☐ arrange
- ☐ ☐ assumption
- ☐ ☐ authentic
- ☐ ☐ bid
- ☐ ☐ board
- ☐ ☐ burden
- ☐ ☐ career
- ☐ ☐ casualty
- ☐ ☐ cease
- ☐ ☐ clue
- ☐ ☐ combination
- ☐ ☐ compact
- ☐ ☐ complicated
- ☐ ☐ conception
- ☐ ☐ confine
- ☐ ☐ conscious
- ☐ ☐ consent
- ☐ ☐ conservative
- ☐ ☐ considerable

- ☐ ☐ correspond
- ☐ ☐ crew
- ☐ ☐ declare
- ☐ ☐ dedicate
- ☐ ☐ define
- ☐ ☐ destiny
- ☐ ☐ display
- ☐ ☐ dramatic
- ☐ ☐ envelope
- ☐ ☐ erroneous
- ☐ ☐ ethic
- ☐ ☐ external
- ☐ ☐ fail
- ☐ ☐ fragment
- ☐ ☐ gamble
- ☐ ☐ glare
- ☐ ☐ grieve
- ☐ ☐ humanity
- ☐ ☐ humble
- ☐ ☐ humiliate
- ☐ ☐ illuminate
- ☐ ☐ incorporate
- ☐ ☐ indeed
- ☐ ☐ indispensable
- ☐ ☐ innovation
- ☐ ☐ inspect
- ☐ ☐ intelligence
- ☐ ☐ interact
- ☐ ☐ legacy
- ☐ ☐ legislation
- ☐ ☐ lock

- ☐ ☐ majority
- ☐ ☐ match
- ☐ ☐ minimize/-ise
- ☐ ☐ obscure
- ☐ ☐ observe
- ☐ ☐ obvious
- ☐ ☐ oral
- ☐ ☐ outline
- ☐ ☐ panel
- ☐ ☐ panorama
- ☐ ☐ purse
- ☐ ☐ question
- ☐ ☐ quote
- ☐ ☐ recognition
- ☐ ☐ relax
- ☐ ☐ release
- ☐ ☐ religion
- ☐ ☐ safeguard
- ☐ ☐ satire
- ☐ ☐ scream
- ☐ ☐ seek
- ☐ ☐ seize
- ☐ ☐ shade
- ☐ ☐ shortage
- ☐ ☐ sphere
- ☐ ☐ spontaneous
- ☐ ☐ stern
- ☐ ☐ suggest
- ☐ ☐ supply
- ☐ ☐ surpass
- ☐ ☐ tactic

- ☐ ☐ tissue
- ☐ ☐ trigger
- ☐ ☐ union
- ☐ ☐ upgrade
- ☐ ☐ variable
- ☐ ☐ view
- ☐ ☐ virtue

音频

Previous Check

- □ withstand
- □ precede
- □ manuscript
- □ cement
- □ plague
- □ involve
- □ cast
- □ corporate
- □ deduce
- □ gradual
- □ rate
- □ individual
- □ levy
- □ relief
- □ broad
- □ consequence
- □ intention
- □ sentiment
- □ diminish
- □ enforce
- □ consider
- □ sneak
- □ avoid
- □ diverse
- □ spot
- □ spur
- □ discriminate
- □ distinguish
- □ format
- □ create
- □ transaction

- □ establish
- □ cling
- □ transmit
- □ vocal
- □ gene
- □ resistance
- □ direct
- □ mean
- □ objection
- □ distress
- □ nonsense
- □ whereas
- □ shift
- □ dominant
- □ effort
- □ repel
- □ conscience
- □ controversial
- □ intervene
- □ gigantic
- □ abundant
- □ thrift
- □ notion
- □ breed
- □ reinforce
- □ suppress
- □ exhaust
- □ influence
- □ campaign
- □ prove
- □ undoubtedly

- □ endorse
- □ accurate
- □ boycott
- □ absorb
- □ bleak
- □ outcome
- □ groan
- □ arouse
- □ superiority
- □ mechanism
- □ wild
- □ ordinary
- □ fiscal
- □ internal
- □ theory
- □ smooth
- □ tear
- □ era
- □ civil
- □ fraction
- □ reign
- □ method
- □ treat
- □ edition
- □ painful
- □ model
- □ habit
- □ pregnant
- □ enrol(l)
- □ equal
- □ reply

- □ moment
- □ session
- □ receive
- □ active
- □ defend
- □ voluntary
- □ index

Writing Models ◎

withstand

precede

manuscript

cement

plague

involve

cast

corporate

deduce

gradual

rate

withstand / wɪð'stænd /

释 v. 承受, 抵住, 经受住

例 Moreover, even though humans have been upright for millions of years, our feet and back continue to struggle with bipedal posture and cannot easily **withstand** repeated strain imposed by oversize limbs. 此外, 尽管人类已经直立行走了数百万年, 我们的双脚和背部还在不断地与双足行走的姿态进行抗争, 并且不能轻易承受超重的四肢所造成的持续重压。(2008年)

precede / prɪ'siːd /

释 v. 在……之前发生; 领先, 先于; 走在……前面

例 Although sadness also **precedes** tears, evidence suggests that emotions can flow from muscular responses. 虽然悲伤也会先于流泪, 但有证据表明情绪可以从肌肉反应中流露出来。(2011年)

派 precedent / 'presɪdənt / adj. 在前的; 在先的

manuscript / 'mænjuskrɪpt /

释 n. 手稿; 原稿; 手抄本

搭 in manuscript 未付印的

例 The SBoRE panel will then find external statisticians to review these **manuscripts**. 然后, SBoRE (由审查编辑组成的统计委员会) 小组将寻找外部统计人员来审查这些手稿。(2015年)

cement / sɪ'ment /

释 n. 水泥; 混凝土; 粘合物 v. 使结合; 巩固; 粘牢

例 We need some **cement** to build a house. 我们需要一些水泥来盖房子。

plague / pleɪɡ /

释 n. 瘟疫; 祸患, 灾害

例 There was **plague** everywhere in the history and it brought grave misery. 历史上到处都有瘟疫, 它给人类带来了巨大的苦难。

involve / ɪn'vɒlv /

释 v. 涉及, 使卷入; 需要; 包括

搭 involve sb./sth. in (doing) sth. 使……参与某活动或陷于某种状况

例 The crude technique required educated guesses on exposure times, and **involved** heavy, awkward equipment—several men had to assist in its transportation. 这种粗陋的技术需要有根据地推测曝光时间, 并且需要用沉重不便捷的设备——必须几个人协助运输。(2023年)

派 involved / ɪn'vɒlvd / adj. 有关联的; 复杂的 ‖ involvement / ɪn'vɒlvmənt / n. 关系; 卷入

cast / kɑːst / 007

釋 *v.* 投掷; 投射（光、影子等）; 挑选（演员）; 使……出演（某角色）; 描写, 描绘; 使产生怀疑; 投票 *n.* （一出戏剧或一部电影的）全体演员; 投, 扔; 特征; 外貌

例 Art and mothering, in the romantic imagination, are each **cast** as the kind of labor that consumes wholly, that is worth being consumed by. 在浪漫主义的想象中，艺术和育儿都被描写成一种完全消耗、值得被消耗的劳动。

近 fling / flɪŋ / *v.* 抛, 投 || pitch / pɪtʃ / *v.* 投, 掷

corporate / 'kɔːpərət / 008

釋 *adj.* 公司的; 法人的

搭 corporate social responsibility (CSR) 企业社会责任

例 That is exactly what happened when Norway adopted a nationwide **corporate** gender quota. 这正是挪威在全国范围内实行企业性别配额的结果。（2020年）

派 corporation / ˌkɔːpə'reɪʃn / *n.* （大）公司

deduce / dɪ'djuːs / 009

釋 *v.* 推论; 推断; 演绎

例 This report was originally published in 2023 with the most popular styles of the year, as **deduced** by some stylists' recommendations, and was later updated to reflect the changes that the trends of 2024 brought about. 这篇报道最初发表于2023年，介绍了根据一些造型师的推荐推断出的当年最流行的款式，后来又进行了更新，以反映2024年的流行趋势所带来的变化。

gradual / 'grædʒuəl / 010

釋 *adj.* 逐渐的; 逐步的

例 Intelligence, it turns out, is a high-priced option. It takes more upkeep, burns more fuel and is slow off the starting line because it depends on learning—a **gradual** process—instead of instinct. 事实证明，智能是一种昂贵的选择。它需要更多的维护，消耗更多的燃料，而且起步较慢，因为它依赖于学习——一个循序渐进的过程——而不是本能。（2009年）

rate / reɪt / 011

釋 *n.* 速度; 进度; 比率; 率; 价格; 费用 *v.* 评估; 评价; 估价; 划分等级; 分等; 对（电影或录像片）分级; 值得, 配得上（某种对待）

搭 at any rate 无论如何, 不管怎样; 总而言之, 反正

例 For example, a high growth **rate** placed great strains on the existing structures of governance, of administration, and above all of socialization. 例如，高增长率给现有的治理结构、行政结构，尤其是社会化结构带来了巨大压力。（2021年）

individual

levy

relief

broad

consequence

intention

sentiment

diminish

enforce

consider

sneak

avoid

individual / ˌɪndɪˈvɪdʒuəl /

释 *n.* 个人；个体 *adj.* 个人的；个别的；独特的

搭 individual initiative 个人创业

例 Second, growth obviously affected the absolute size both of systems and **individual** institutions. 其次，（学生人数的）增长对各系统和各院校的绝对规模都有明显影响。（2021年）

近 personal / ˈpɜːsənl / *adj.* 个人的；亲自的 ‖ private / ˈpraɪvət / *adj.* 私人的；私有的

levy / ˈlevi /

释 *n.* 征收额；（尤指）税款 *v.* 征收（税等）

搭 levy on 向某人征收（税款等）

例 The bill requires every rental host to register with the state, mandates they carry insurance, and opens the potential for local taxes on top of a new state **levy**. 该法案要求每个租赁房东都要在州政府登记注册，强制他们购买保险，并有可能在新的州政府征税之外再征收地方税。（2023年）

relief / rɪˈliːf /

释 *n.* （不快过后的）宽慰，轻松；解脱；（痛苦等）减轻，解除；替班者；接替人；救济，救援物品

例 To the anxious travelers the sight of the American shore brought almost inexpressible **relief**. 对于焦虑的旅行者来说，美国海岸的景象几乎给他们带来了难以言喻的宽慰。（2015年）

broad / brɔːd /

释 *adj.* 宽的；宽阔的；广阔的；广泛的；概括的

搭 (in) broad daylight 光天化日（之下）

例 She had been mugged in the street in **broad** daylight. 光天化日之下，她在街上遭到抢劫。

consequence / ˈkɒnsɪkwəns /

释 *n.* 结果；后果；重要性

搭 in consequence (of sth.) 由于；作为……的结果

例 It is too easy, and misleading, to see such court rulings as merely standing up for the rights of land owners when the **consequences** can be so dire for their neighbors. 把这样的法院裁决仅仅看作是维护土地所有者的权利，太容易，也太误导人了，因为其后果对他们的邻居来说可能非常严重。（2024年）

intention / ɪnˈtenʃn /

释 *n.* 打算；计划；意图；目的

搭 have no intention to do sth./of doing sth. 不打算做某事

例 Time, rather than **intention**, has given them legitimacy. 时间，而不是意图，赋予了它们合法性。（2014年）

sentiment / 'sentɪmənt /   018

释 n. 意见，观点；情绪，感情；伤感，哀伤

例 At the next election none of the big parties seem likely to endorse this **sentiment**. 在接下来的一次选举中，似乎没有一个大党会支持这种观点。（2016年）

diminish / dɪ'mɪnɪʃ /   019

释 v.（使）减少；（使）减小；降低

例 His strength has **diminished** because of the illness. 疾病使他的体力衰退。

近 reduce / rɪ'djuːs / v. 减少，缩小 ‖ decrease / dɪ'kriːs / v. 减少，减小

enforce / ɪn'fɔːs /   020

释 v. 强制执行，强行实施（法律或规定）；强迫，迫使

例 In *Arizona v. United States*, the majority overturned three of the four contested provisions of Arizona's controversial plan to have state and local police **enforce** federal immigration law. 在亚利桑那州诉美国一案中，多数法官推翻了亚利桑那州有争议的计划中四项有争议条款中的三项，该计划要求州和地方警察强制执行联邦移民法。（2013年）

consider / kən'sɪdə(r) /   021

释 v. 仔细考虑，细想；认为；以为；体谅；考虑到；顾及；注视

搭 all things considered 从各方面看来；考虑到所有情况；总而言之

例 Nearly 40% of the roughly 350 people who responded to an accompanying poll said they had collaborated with artists; and almost all said they would **consider** doing so in future. 在对一项随附的民意调查做出回应的约350人中，有近40%的人表示，他们曾与艺术家合作过；几乎所有人都表示，他们今后会考虑这样做。（2022年）

sneak / sniːk /   022

释 v. 鬼鬼祟祟做事 n. 鬼鬼祟祟的人

搭 sneak out/away 悄悄地走；溜；潜行

例 I saw you grab your running shoes this morning and **sneak** out. 今天早上我看见你提着跑鞋悄悄溜出去了。

avoid / ə'vɔɪd /   023

释 v. 避免；防止；避开；回避；躲避

例 The researchers first established what kinds of plant the elephants preferred either to eat or **avoid** when foraging freely. 研究人员首先确定了大象在自由觅食时喜欢吃或避免吃的植物种类。（2024年）

diverse / daɪˈvɜːs /

024

释 *adj.* 不同的；各式各样的

例 The smallest nonprofit organizations tend to have more **diverse** leadership than larger organizations. 与规模较大的组织相比，规模最小的非营利组织的领导层往往更加多元化。

spot / spɒt /

025

释 *n.* 斑点；点；场所

例 When we look at a face or a picture, our eyes pause on one **spot** at a time, often on the eyes or mouth. 当我们看一张脸或一张照片时，我们的视线会一次停在一个点上，通常是眼睛或嘴巴。（2020年）

spur / spɜː(r) /

026

释 *v.* 刺激；鞭策 *n.* 刺激因素

例 They have been **spurred** in part by DNA evidence made available in 1998, which almost certainly proved Thomas Jefferson had fathered at least one child with his slave Sally Hemings. 1998年出现的DNA证据在一定程度上刺激了他们，这个证据几乎可以明确证实托马斯·杰斐逊与他的奴隶萨莉·海明斯至少生了一个孩子。（2008年）

近 stimulate / ˈstɪmjuleɪt / *v.* 刺激；激励

discriminate / dɪˈskrɪmɪneɪt /

027

释 *v.* 区别，辨别；有差别地对待，歧视

搭 discriminate against 歧视；排斥

例 You must **discriminate** between facts and opinions. 你必须把事实和看法区别开来。

distinguish / dɪˈstɪŋgwɪʃ /

028

释 *v.* 区分；辨别；分清；认出；使出众

例 Some tasks involve content moderation—helping AI **distinguish** between innocent content and that which contains violence, hate speech, or adult imagery. 有些任务涉及内容审核——帮助人工智能区分无恶意的内容和包含暴力、仇恨言论或成人图像的内容。

format / ˈfɔːmæt /

029

释 *n.* 版式；格式；开本 *v.* 使格式化；设计版式

例 The challenge the computer mounts to television thus bears little similarity to one **format** being replaced by another in the manner of record players being replaced by CD players. 因此，计算机对电视机的挑战与一种格式被另一种格式所取代（如唱片播放机被CD播放机所取代）并无多少相似之处。（2012年）

create / kriˈeɪt /

030

释 *v.* 创造；创作；造成，引起；产生（感觉或印象）

例 The tool, along with other popular image-generation AI models, allows anyone to **create** impressive images based on text prompts. 该工具与其他流行的图像生成人工智能模型一起，让任何人都能根据文本提示创建令人印象深刻的图像。（2024年）

transaction / træn'zækʃn / 031

释 n. (一笔) 交易, 业务, 买卖

例 He prefers to resign rather than take part in such a dishonest **transaction**. 他宁愿辞职也不愿参加这样一桩骗人的交易。

establish / ɪ'stæblɪʃ / 032

释 v. 建立, 确立; 证实

例 That March, President Ulysses S. Grant signed an act into law that **established** Yellowstone as the world's first national park. 同年三月, 尤利西斯·S. 格兰特总统签署了一项法案, 将黄石公园建成世界上第一个国家公园。(2023年)

cling / klɪŋ / 033

释 v. 坚持; 固守; 依附, 依靠

搭 cling to 坚持; 依靠

例 Their recent achievements signal a small breakthrough in an industry that has, for over a century, **clung** to the deeply misguided belief that natives lack the skills to act, write and direct. 一个多世纪以来, 业界一直固守一个深深被误导的信念, 认为土著人缺乏表演、编剧和导演的技能, 而他们最近的成就标志着业界的一个小突破。

近 stick / stɪk / v. 坚持; 黏住 ‖ adhere / əd'hɪə(r) / v. 遵守; 紧贴

transmit / træns'mɪt / 034

释 v. 传送; 传递; 传播 (广播电视节目、计算机信息等); 传播 (疾病); 传达; 传导

例 Men do not make history under circumstances chosen by themselves, but under circumstances directly found, given and **transmitted** from the past. 人类不是在自己选择的环境下创造历史, 而是在直接发现的、给定的或由过去传递下来的环境中创造历史。

派 transmission / træns'mɪʃn / n. 播送; 发射

vocal / 'vəʊkl / 035

释 adj. 嗓音的; 发声的; 直言不讳的, 大声表达的

例 A small but **vocal** group of Hawaiians and environmentalists have long viewed their presence as disrespect for sacred land and a painful reminder of the occupation of what was once a sovereign nation. 一小部分直言不讳的夏威夷人和环保主义者长期以来一直认为, 它们 (望远镜) 的存在是对圣地的不尊重, 是对曾经是主权国家的地方被占领的一个痛苦提醒。(2017年)

gene / dʒiːn / 036

释 n. 基因

搭 a dominant/recessive gene 显性/隐性基因

例 One of the remarkable findings of the study was that the similar **genes** seem to be evolving faster than other **genes**. 这项研究的一个重要发现是, 相似基因的进化速度似乎快于其他基因。(2015年)

Writing Models ◎

resistance

direct

mean

objection

distress

nonsense

whereas

shift

dominant

effort

repel

conscience

037

resistance / rɪ'zɪstəns /

释 *n.* 抵抗, 反抗; 电阻

例 Quebec's **resistance** to a national agency is provincialist ideology. 魁北克对国家机构的抵制是地方意识形态造成的。(2005年)

近 rebellion / rɪ'beljən / *n.* 抵抗, 反抗

038

direct / daɪ'rekt /

释 *v.* 把……对准; 指导; 给……指路; 导演; 指示, 命令; 指挥 *adj.* 直达的; 直接的; 笔直的; 直率的 *adv.* 直达地

例 Although mental health is the cure-all for living our lives, it is perfectly ordinary as you will see that it has been there to **direct** you through all your difficult decisions. 虽然心理健康是我们生活的万灵药, 但它也是再普通不过的, 因为你会发现, 它一直在指导你做出所有艰难的决定。(2016年)

039

mean / miːn /

释 *v.* 意味着; 意思是; 打算 *n.* 平均值; 折中 *adj.* 吝啬的; 不友好的; 熟练的; 平均的

搭 be meant to be sth. 被普遍认为是 ‖ the happy/golden mean 中庸之道

例 Perhaps museums and governments might explore some role for the use of nearly exact reproductions as a **means** of resolving issues relating to returning works of art and antiquities. 也许博物馆和政府可以探索使用几乎完全相同的复制品作为解决艺术品和古董返还问题的一种手段。(2024年)

040

objection / əb'dʒekʃn /

释 *n.* 反对; 异议

例 The 8–0 **objection** to President Obama turns on what Justice Samuel Alito describes in his **objection** as "a shocking assertion of federal executive power". 反对奥巴马总统出现8比0的结果是依靠塞缪尔·阿利托大法官在反对意见中将其描述为"对联邦行政权力令人震惊的维护"。(2013年)

041

distress / dɪ'stres /

释 *n.* 忧虑, 忧伤, 苦恼; 贫困; 危难, 遇险 *v.* 使悲痛; 使苦恼

例 The middle-aged man was in great **distress** over his unemployment. 那位中年男子因为失业而万分苦恼。

042

nonsense / 'nɒnsns /

释 *n.* 胡言乱语; 谬论; 胡扯; 愚蠢的行为

例 There is a great deal of this kind of **nonsense** in the medical journals which, when taken up by broadcasters and the lay press, generates both health scares and short-lived dietary enthusiasms. 医学杂志上有大量这类无稽之谈, 一旦被广播公司和非专业媒体转载, 就会引起健康恐慌和短暂的饮食热情。(2019年)

whereas / ˌweərˈæz / 043

释 *conj.* 然而，但是，尽管

例 In all, the study concludes that **whereas** prosecutors should only evaluate a case based on its merits, they do seem to be influenced by a company's record in CSR. 总之，研究得出结论，尽管检察官只应根据案件的是非曲直进行评估，但他们似乎确实会受到企业社会责任记录的影响。（2016年）

shift / ʃɪft / 044

释 *n.* 稍微改变；轮班 *v.* 变换；转移；换挡；推卸

例 This abrupt **shift** to an "intensive mothering narrative", which suggests that mothers should manage childcare alone, was likely to have been harmful. 这种突然向"密集型育儿理念"，即认为母亲应该独自照顾孩子的转变很可能是有害的。（2024年）

dominant / ˈdɒmɪnənt / 045

释 *adj.* 首要的；占支配地位的；占优势的；显著的；（基因）显性的，优势的

例 According to many books and articles, New England's leaders established the basic themes and preoccupations of an unfolding, **dominant** Puritan tradition in American intellectual life. 许多书籍和文章指出，新英格兰的领袖们确立了在美国知识界逐渐展开的、占主导地位的清教徒传统的基本主题和关注点。（2009年）

effort / ˈefət / 046

释 *n.* 努力；有组织的活动；努力的结果

搭 joint effort 共同的努力

例 One of the turning points in public support for land conservation **efforts**—and recognizing the magnificence of the Yellowstone region in particular—came in the form of vivid photographs. 公众支持土地保护活动的一个转折点，尤其是认识到黄石地区的壮丽景色就是以生动的照片形式出现的。（2023年）

repel / rɪˈpel / 047

释 *v.* 击退；使厌恶；排斥

例 The army has been ready to **repel** an attack. 这支军队已经做好了击退袭击的准备。

conscience / ˈkɒnʃəns / 048

释 *n.* 良心；良知；内疚；愧疚

例 The thief must have had an attack of **conscience**, because he returned the wallet with nothing missing from it. 小偷一定是良心发现了，因为他把钱包还了回来，而且里边的东西一样没少。

controversial

intervene

gigantic

abundant

thrift

notion

breed

reinforce

suppress

exhaust

influence

campaign

prove

controversial / ˌkɒntrəˈvɜːʃ / `049`

释 *adj.* 引起争论的

例 Now the nation's top patent court appears completely ready to scale back on business-method patents, which have been **controversial** ever since they were first authorized 10 years ago. 现在，美国最高专利法院似乎已完全准备好要缩减商业方法专利的范围了，自十年前首次授权以来，这些商业方法专利就一直备受争议。（2010年）

intervene / ˌɪntəˈviːn / `050`

释 *v.* 干涉，干预，介入；发生（以致阻碍某事）

搭 intervene in sth. 干预某事

例 If they do not move fast enough, regulators may have to **intervene** forcefully. 如果他们的行动不够迅速，监管部门可能不得不强行介入其中。

gigantic / dʒaɪˈɡæntɪk / `051`

释 *adj.* 巨大的，庞大的

例 All in all, this clearly seems to be a market in which big retailers could profitably apply their **gigantic** scale, existing infrastructure, and proven skills in the management of product ranges, logistics, and marketing intelligence. 总之，这显然是一个大型零售商可以利用其巨大的规模、现有的基础设施以及在产品系列管理、物流和营销情报方面的成熟技术来获利的市场。（2010年）

abundant / əˈbʌndənt / `052`

释 *adj.* 大量的；丰盛的；充裕的

例 The police have **abundant** evidence to prove his guilt. 警察有大量的证据证明他有罪。

thrift / θrɪft / `053`

释 *n.* 节约，节俭

例 He has the virtues of **thrift** and hard work. 他具备节约和勤奋的美德。

近 frugality / fruˈɡæləti / *n.* 节俭 ‖ economy / ɪˈkɒnəmi / *n.* 节约

notion / ˈnəʊʃn / `054`

释 *n.* 观念，观点；信念；理解

例 "Eye contact and smiles" can signal availability and confidence, a common-sense **notion** supported in studies by psychologist Monica Moore. "目光接触和微笑"可以传递安心和自信的信号，心理学家莫妮卡·摩尔的研究也证实了这一常识性观点。（2020年）

近 concept / ˈkɒnsept / *n.* 概念，观念 ‖ idea / aɪˈdɪə / *n.* 想法，主意

breed / briːd / `055`

释 *v.* 繁殖，生殖；造成，引起；教养，抚养；饲养 *n.* 品种，种类

例 When animals **breed** overly in the wild, they pay a price for this experience. 当动物在自然环境中过度繁衍时，它们就会为这一经历付出代价。

reinforce / ˌriːɪnˈfɔːs / 056

释 v. 加强；巩固；加固；增援

例 Durkheim proposed that religious beliefs functioned to **reinforce** social solidarity. 杜克海姆提出，宗教信仰具有加强社会团结的功能。（2009年）

近 strengthen / ˈstreŋθn / v. 加强；巩固 ‖ intensify / ɪnˈtensɪfaɪ / v. 增强，加强

suppress / səˈpres / 057

释 v. 抑制，阻止；镇压；封锁

例 Despite attempts by the Church to **suppress** this new generation of logicians and rationalists, more explanations for how the universe functioned were being made at a rate that the people could no longer ignore. 尽管教会试图压制这些新一代的逻辑学家和理性主义者，但更多关于宇宙如何运转的解释正以人们再也无法忽视的速度出现。（2020年）

exhaust / ɪgˈzɔːst / 058

释 v. 使筋疲力尽，使疲惫不堪；用完，用光，耗尽

搭 be exhausted from 因……而十分疲乏

例 They worked until **exhausted**, lived with few protections and died young. 他们工作到筋疲力尽，生活没有什么保障，英年早逝。（2006年）

influence / ˈɪnfluəns / 059

释 n. 有影响的人或事物；影响；作用 v. 影响；对……起作用

例 And it's a reminder that the EPA's involvement in the Chesapeake Bay Program has long been crucial as the means to transcend the **influence** of deep-pocketed special interests in neighboring states. 这提醒我们，长期以来，作为超越相邻各州财力雄厚的特殊利益集团影响的手段，环保局参与切萨皮克湾项目一直至关重要。（2024年）

近 affect / əˈfekt / v. 影响 ‖ impress / ɪmˈpres / v. 给……留下深刻印象

campaign / kæmˈpeɪn / 060

释 n. 战役；（有计划的）运动，活动 v. 参加运动，领导运动

搭 election campaign 竞选活动

例 However, its **campaign** risks coming across as being pushy and overprotective. 然而，它的活动有可能给人留下咄咄逼人和过度保护的印象。（2020年）

prove / pruːv / 061

释 v. 证明是；原来是；结果是；证实；显示

例 Employers have long seen the advantages of hiring school leavers who often **prove** themselves to be more committed and loyal employees than graduates. 长期以来，雇主们都看到了雇用离校生的优势，这些离校生常常会证明自己是比毕业生更尽心尽力的忠诚员工。（2022年）

Writing Models ◎

undoubtedly

endorse

accurate

boycott

absorb

bleak

outcome

groan

arouse

superiority

mechanism

wild

ordinary

undoubtedly / ʌnˈdaʊtɪdli /

0 6 2

释 *adv.* 无疑地；千真万确地

例 Progress in education is **undoubtedly** necessary for the social and intellectual development of these nations. 毫无疑问，教育的发展对于这些国家的社会及学术发展而言都是必不可少的。

endorse / ɪnˈdɔːs /

0 6 3

释 *v.* 赞同，认可，支持

例 The Prime Minister is unlikely to **endorse** this view. 首相不太可能支持这一观点。

accurate / ˈækjərət /

0 6 4

释 *adj.* 精确的；准确的

例 This process, along with employees reviewing the contracts, is faster and more **accurate**. 这一过程加上员工对合同的审查，速度会更快，也更准确。（2021年）

boycott / ˈbɔɪkɒt /

0 6 5

释 *v.* 联合抵制；拒绝参加 *n.* 联合抵制

例 If that happens, passionate consumers would try to persuade others to **boycott** products, putting the reputation of the target company at risk. 如果出现这种情况，狂热的消费者就会试图说服其他人联合抵制这些产品，从而危及目标公司的声誉。（2011年）

absorb / əbˈzɔːb /

0 6 6

释 *v.* 吸收（液体、气体、光、热等）；理解；合并；承受；使全神贯注；消减（外力）；花掉（大量金钱）

例 Sharpening judgment by **absorbing** and reflecting on law is a desirable component of a journalist's intellectual preparation for his or her career. 通过理解和思考法律来提高判断力，是记者为其职业生涯做好知识准备的一个理想组成部分。（2007年）

bleak / bliːk /

0 6 7

释 *adj.* 不乐观的；无望的；暗淡的；荒凉的；阴冷的；无遮掩的

例 Last year marked the third year in a row that Indonesia's **bleak** rate of deforestation has slowed in pace. 去年标志着印尼不乐观的森林砍伐速度连续第三年放缓。（2021年）

outcome / ˈaʊtkʌm /

0 6 8

释 *n.* 结果；效果

例 To pressure zoos to spend less on their animals would lead to inhumane **outcomes** for the precious creatures in their care. 如果迫使动物园减少在动物身上的花费，就会给它们照顾的珍贵动物带来非人道的结果。（2022年）

groan / grəʊn /　069

释 *v.* 叹息；呻吟 *n.* 呻吟声；叹息声

例 They're all **groaning** about soaring health budgets, the fastest-growing component of which are pharmaceutical costs. 他们都在抱怨高涨的医疗预算，其中增长最快的部分是药品费用。（2005年）

近 moan / məʊn / *v.* 抱怨；呻吟 ‖ grumble / 'grʌmbl / *v.* 抱怨；发牢骚

arouse / ə'raʊz /　070

释 *v.* 激起，引起；唤起

例 But many middle-class occupations—trucking, financial advice, software engineering—have **aroused** their interest, or soon will. 但许多中产阶级职业——卡车运输、金融咨询、软件工程——已经或即将引起他们的兴趣。（2018年）

superiority / suː,pɪəri'ɒrəti /　071

释 *n.* 优越（性）；优势；优越感

例 His success has given him a false sense of **superiority**. 他的成功给了他一种虚假的优越感。

反 inferiority / ɪn,fɪəri'ɒrəti / *n.* 低等；劣等；劣势

mechanism / 'mekənɪzəm /　072

释 *n.* 方法；机制；机械装置；机件

例 However, the **mechanisms** proposed were unwieldy and the Bill was voted down following the change in government later that year. 然而，所提议的机制难于管理，该法案在当年晚些时候政府换届后被投票否决。（2022年）

wild / waɪld /　073

释 *adj.* 野生的；荒凉的；缺乏管教的

例 Were it not for opportunities to observe these beautiful, **wild** creatures close to home, many more people would be driven by their fascination to travel to **wild** areas to seek out, disturb and even hunt them down. 如果不是有机会在家附近观察这些美丽的野生动物，更多的人会被它们的魅力驱使而前往野外去寻找、打扰，甚至猎杀它们。（2022年）

ordinary / 'ɔːdnri /　074

释 *adj.* 普通的；平常的；平庸的；一般的

例 Consequently—and paradoxically—laws introduced to protect the jobs of **ordinary** workers may be placing those jobs at risk. 因此，矛盾的是，为保护普通工人的工作而出台的法律可能会将这些工作置于危险之中。（2022年）

反 extraordinary / ɪk'strɔːdnri / *adj.* 不平常的；卓越的

fiscal / ˈfɪskl / ⓪⑦⑤

释 *adj.* 财政的；国库的；税收的

搭 fiscal year 财政年度，财年

例 It reported a net loss of $5.6 billion for **fiscal** 2016, the 10th straight year its expenses have exceeded revenue. 该公司报告称，2016财年净亏损56亿美元，这是其连续第10年支出超过收入。（2018年）

internal / ɪnˈtɜːnl / ⓪⑦⑥

释 *adj.* 内部的；里面的；国内的；内政的；本身的；内心的

例 Juvenile birds that hatched in the spring would be taking their first migratory journeys, and their **internal** sense of direction might not be as fine-tuned as for older birds that have flown the route before. 春季孵化的幼鸟将首次踏上迁徙之旅，它们的内在方向感可能不如以前飞过这条路线的大鸟那么敏锐。

反 external / ɪkˈstɜːnl / *adj.* 外部的；与外国有关的；对外的

theory / ˈθɪəri / ⓪⑦⑦

释 *n.* 学说；理论；看法；推测

搭 in theory 理论上；按理说

例 In **theory**, a girl may veto the spouse her parents have chosen. 理论上，女孩可以否决父母为其选择的配偶。（2016年）

smooth / smuːð / ⓪⑦⑧

释 *adj.* 平整的，光滑的；流畅的；顺利的；平稳的 *v.* 使平整；使平坦；使平滑；使光滑；

搭 smooth the path/way 铺平道路 ‖ smooth sth. away/out 消除（问题）

例 In healthy and **smooth** leadership transitions, incoming leaders have strong support from the board, according to Karen. 凯伦表示，在健康、顺利的领导层过渡中，新任领导会得到董事会的大力支持。

反 rough / rʌf / *adj.* 粗糙的；不平滑的

tear ⓪⑦⑨

释 / teə(r) / *v.* 撕碎；撕开 / tɪə(r) / *n.* 眼泪，泪水

搭 burst into tears 放声大哭

例 It was argued at the end of the 19th century that humans do not cry because they are sad but that they become sad when the **tears** begin to flow. 19世纪末有一种观点认为，人类不是因为悲伤而哭泣，而是当眼泪开始流淌时人们才变得悲伤。（2011年）

era / ˈɪərə / ⓪⑧⓪

释 *n.* 时代；年代；纪元

例 As many took on the duty of trying to integrate reasoning and scientific philosophies into the world, the Renaissance was over and it was time for a new **era**—the Age of Reason. 当很多人承担起将理性和科学哲学融入这个世界的责任时，文艺复兴时代就谢幕了，一个新的时代——理性时代开启了。（2020年）

civil / 'sɪvl / 081

释 *adj.* 国民的; 平民的; 国家的; 民事的

例 Some relatively poor European countries have seen huge improvements across measures including **civil** society, income equality and the environment. 一些相对贫穷的欧洲国家通过各种措施, 在包括公民社会、收入平等和环境方面取得了巨大的进步。(2017年)

fraction / 'frækʃn / 082

释 *n.* 小部分; 少量; 一点儿

搭 a fraction of 少量

例 This year's rise, an average of 2.7 percent, may be a **fraction** lower than last year's, but it is still well above the official Consumer Price Index (CPI) measure of inflation. 今年的平均涨幅为2.7%, 可能比去年略低, 但仍远高于官方衡量通货膨胀的消费者价格指数(CPI)。

reign / reɪn / 083

释 *n.* 任期; 当政期; 君主统治时期 *v.* 统治; 当政; 盛行; 成为最佳

例 Generally, Victorian style refers to the **reign** of the British Queen Victoria from 1837 to 1901. 一般来说, 维多利亚风格是指1837年至1901年英国维多利亚女王当政期的风格。

method / 'meθəd / 084

释 *n.* 方法; 办法; 措施

例 The cameras have been the city's main **method** of traffic enforcement and can issue fines up to $500. 这些摄像头一直是该市交通执法的主要措施, 可以开出高达500美元的罚款。

treat / triːt / 085

释 *v.* 对待; 处理; 治疗; 款待 *n.* 款待

例 "I think the question is, shouldn't a developer who's really building a hotel, but disguising it as not a hotel, be **treated** and taxed and regulated like a hotel?" Horn said. "我认为问题在于, 一个实际上建的是酒店, 但把它伪装成不是酒店的开发商, 难道不应该像酒店一样被对待、征税和监管吗?" 霍恩说。(2023年)

派 treatment / 'triːtmənt / *n.* 治疗; 对待; 处理

edition / ɪ'dɪʃn / 086

释 *n.* 版本; 版次

例 Overhead may be high and circulation lower, but rushing to eliminate its print **edition** would be a mistake, says BuzzFeed CEO Jonah Peretti. BuzzFeed的首席执行官乔纳·佩雷蒂表示, 可能运营成本很高, 而发行量较少, 但急于取消其印刷版将是一个错误。(2016年)

painful / 'peɪnfl / 087

释 *adj.* 令人痛苦(或难过、难堪)的; 不愉快的

例 It is **painful** to read these roundabout accounts today. 今天读到这些迂回曲折的叙述, 令人痛心疾首。(2010年)

model / 'mɒdl / 088

释 *n.* 模型；模特儿；样式；样本；模范

例 In contrast to France's actions, Denmark's fashion industry agreed last month on rules and sanctions regarding the age, health, and other characteristics of **models**. 与法国的做法形成鲜明对比的是，丹麦时装业上个月对于模特的年龄、健康状况和其他特征的规定和制裁达成了一致。（2016年）

habit / 'hæbɪt / 089

释 *n.* 习惯；惯常行为；习性；（吸毒、喝酒、抽烟的）瘾

搭 make a habit of 使成为习惯

例 An emerging body of research shows that positive health **habits**—as well as negative ones—spread through networks of friends via social communication. 一项新的研究表明，积极的健康习惯——以及消极的习惯——都会通过社交传播到朋友圈。（2012年）

派 habitual / hə'bɪtʃuəl / *adj.* 习惯性的

pregnant / 'pregnənt / 090

释 *adj.* 怀孕的；饱含，充溢着

例 There are also stories about newly adoptive—and newly single-mom Sandra Bullock, as well as the usual "Jennifer Aniston is **pregnant**" news. 也有关于新的领养妈妈和单亲妈妈桑德拉·布洛克的故事，以及常见的"詹妮弗·安妮斯顿怀孕了"的新闻。（2011年）

派 pregnancy / 'pregnənsi / *n.* 怀孕；孕期

enrol(l) / ɪn'rəʊl / 091

释 *v.* 吸收（成员），（使）加入；注册；登记；编入

例 The TSA wants to **enroll** 25 million people in PreCheck. （美国）运输安全管理局希望将2 500万人纳入预检。（2017年）

派 enrollment / ɪn'rəʊlmənt / *n.* 入学（会、伍）；注册；登记；参加

equal / 'iːkwəl / 092

释 *adj.* （大小、数量、价值等）相同的；相等的；平等的；能胜任的
v. 与……相等，等于；比得上；导致，结果为 *n.* 同等的人；相等物

搭 be without equal/have no equal 无与伦比

例 Because the California law applies to all boards, even where there is no history of prior discrimination, courts are likely to rule that the law violates the constitutional guarantee of "**equal** protection." 由于加州法律适用于所有董事会，即使没有歧视前科，法院也很可能会裁定该法违反了宪法对"平等保护"的保障。（2020年）

派 equality / i'kwɒləti / *n.* 平等；均等；相等

reply / rɪ'plaɪ / 093

释 *v./n.* 回答；答复；回应

例 Raise objections and listen carefully to their **replies**. 提出反对意见并仔细倾听他们的回答。（2019年）

moment / ˈməʊmənt / [094]

释 *n.* 片刻; 瞬间; 时机; 机遇

搭 for the moment 目前; 暂时 ‖ the last moment 最后一刻, 紧要关头

例 The cast gave speeches about their memorable **moments** on the show. 全体演员就自己在剧中的难忘时刻发表了演讲。

session / ˈseʃn / [095]

释 *n.* 一场 (活动); 一段时间; (议会等的) 会议; (法庭的) 开庭; 学年

例 You are going to host a club reading **session**. 你将主持一场俱乐部读书会。(2015年)

receive / rɪˈsiːv / [096]

释 *v.* 接到; 收到; 受到; 接待; 回应

例 However, there is a strong case that those who have been worst affected by industrial action should **receive** compensation for the disruption they have suffered. 不过, 有充分的理由认为, 那些受工业行动影响最严重的人应该得到补偿, 以弥补他们所遭受的干扰。(2021年)

active / ˈæktɪv / [097]

释 *adj.* 积极的; 好动的; 忙碌的, 活跃的; 起作用的

例 But they show comprehension to consist not just of passive assimilation but of **active** engagement in inference and problem-solving. 但它们 (这些阅读方式) 表明, 理解不仅包括被动地吸收, 还包括积极地参与推理和解决问题。(2015年)

defend / dɪˈfend / [098]

释 *v.* 保护; 为……争辩

例 It is what any county would do to **defend** its territory and its people. 这是任何一个国家为了保卫自己的领土和人民都会做的事情。

voluntary / ˈvɒləntri / [099]

释 *adj.* 自愿的; 主动的; 自发的; 无偿的; 义务性的

例 In Denmark, the United States, and a few other countries, it is trying to set **voluntary** standards for models and fashion images that rely more on peer pressure for enforcement. 在丹麦、美国和其他一些国家, 它 (时尚业) 正试图为模特和时尚形象制定自愿遵照的标准, 这些标准的实施更多地依靠同行压力。(2016年)

反 compulsory / kəmˈpʌlsəri / *adj.* 强制的

index / ˈɪndeks / [100]

释 *n.* 索引; 指数; 标志; 指标 *v.* 为……编索引; 将……编入索引

例 This is the famed citation **index**, that is to say the number of times a paper has been quoted elsewhere in the scientific literature, the assumption being that an important paper will be cited more often than one of small account. 这是著名的引用指数, 也就是说一篇论文在科学文献中被引用的次数, 其假设是一篇重要的论文比一篇不重要的文章被引用的次数更多。(2019年)

Day 04

- ☐ ☐ absorb
- ☐ ☐ abundant
- ☐ ☐ accurate
- ☐ ☐ active
- ☐ ☐ arouse
- ☐ ☐ avoid
- ☐ ☐ bleak
- ☐ ☐ boycott
- ☐ ☐ breed
- ☐ ☐ broad
- ☐ ☐ campaign
- ☐ ☐ cast
- ☐ ☐ cement
- ☐ ☐ civil
- ☐ ☐ cling
- ☐ ☐ conscience
- ☐ ☐ consequence
- ☐ ☐ consider
- ☐ ☐ controversial
- ☐ ☐ corporate
- ☐ ☐ create
- ☐ ☐ deduce
- ☐ ☐ defend
- ☐ ☐ diminish
- ☐ ☐ direct
- ☐ ☐ discriminate
- ☐ ☐ distinguish
- ☐ ☐ distress
- ☐ ☐ diverse
- ☐ ☐ dominant
- ☐ ☐ edition

- ☐ ☐ effort
- ☐ ☐ endorse
- ☐ ☐ enforce
- ☐ ☐ enrol(l)
- ☐ ☐ equal
- ☐ ☐ era
- ☐ ☐ establish
- ☐ ☐ exhaust
- ☐ ☐ fiscal
- ☐ ☐ format
- ☐ ☐ fraction
- ☐ ☐ gene
- ☐ ☐ gigantic
- ☐ ☐ gradual
- ☐ ☐ groan
- ☐ ☐ habit
- ☐ ☐ index
- ☐ ☐ individual
- ☐ ☐ influence
- ☐ ☐ intention
- ☐ ☐ internal
- ☐ ☐ intervene
- ☐ ☐ involve
- ☐ ☐ levy
- ☐ ☐ manuscript
- ☐ ☐ mean
- ☐ ☐ mechanism
- ☐ ☐ method
- ☐ ☐ model
- ☐ ☐ moment
- ☐ ☐ nonsense

- ☐ ☐ notion
- ☐ ☐ objection
- ☐ ☐ ordinary
- ☐ ☐ outcome
- ☐ ☐ painful
- ☐ ☐ plague
- ☐ ☐ precede
- ☐ ☐ pregnant
- ☐ ☐ prove
- ☐ ☐ rate
- ☐ ☐ receive
- ☐ ☐ reign
- ☐ ☐ reinforce
- ☐ ☐ relief
- ☐ ☐ repel
- ☐ ☐ reply
- ☐ ☐ resistance
- ☐ ☐ sentiment
- ☐ ☐ session
- ☐ ☐ shift
- ☐ ☐ smooth
- ☐ ☐ sneak
- ☐ ☐ spot
- ☐ ☐ spur
- ☐ ☐ superiority
- ☐ ☐ suppress
- ☐ ☐ tear
- ☐ ☐ theory
- ☐ ☐ thrift
- ☐ ☐ transaction
- ☐ ☐ transmit

- ☐ ☐ treat
- ☐ ☐ undoubtedly
- ☐ ☐ vocal
- ☐ ☐ voluntary
- ☐ ☐ whereas
- ☐ ☐ wild
- ☐ ☐ withstand

音频

- ☐ resent
- ☐ major
- ☐ limit
- ☐ work
- ☐ assist
- ☐ league
- ☐ attract
- ☐ rely
- ☐ conviction
- ☐ settle
- ☐ charter
- ☐ moan
- ☐ formidable
- ☐ examine
- ☐ notice
- ☐ press
- ☐ locate
- ☐ nonetheless
- ☐ intrude
- ☐ pray
- ☐ guarantee
- ☐ curb
- ☐ insult
- ☐ steer
- ☐ signify
- ☐ definition
- ☐ speculate
- ☐ diplomatic
- ☐ dictate
- ☐ absolute
- ☐ frequency

- ☐ regulation
- ☐ upright
- ☐ institute
- ☐ affair
- ☐ route
- ☐ toss
- ☐ flee
- ☐ dealer
- ☐ minimum
- ☐ recession
- ☐ enlarge
- ☐ commodity
- ☐ peer
- ☐ snack
- ☐ fatigue
- ☐ temperament
- ☐ decent
- ☐ sue
- ☐ legal
- ☐ output
- ☐ afford
- ☐ incidence
- ☐ appoint
- ☐ transfer
- ☐ ensure
- ☐ gaze
- ☐ restrain
- ☐ govern
- ☐ trust
- ☐ physical
- ☐ performance

- ☐ reference
- ☐ judge
- ☐ correlate
- ☐ brief
- ☐ unique
- ☐ regard
- ☐ mental
- ☐ collaborate
- ☐ novel
- ☐ bet
- ☐ apology
- ☐ central
- ☐ reception
- ☐ instruction
- ☐ liberty
- ☐ embrace
- ☐ skill
- ☐ link
- ☐ launch
- ☐ power
- ☐ comfort
- ☐ super
- ☐ drag
- ☐ opinion
- ☐ multiply
- ☐ medium
- ☐ site
- ☐ tap
- ☐ soak
- ☐ crash
- ☐ quit

- ☐ brand
- ☐ attention
- ☐ mix
- ☐ alien
- ☐ tendency
- ☐ victim
- ☐ mutual

Writing Models ◎

resent

major

limit

work

assist

league

attract

rely

conviction

settle

charter

---

resent / rɪ'zent / ⓪⓪1

釋 *v.* 怨恨; 憎恶; 愤恨

搭 resent sb. doing sth. 讨厌某人做某事

例 At the end of 2023, however, TikTok's dominance in the music industry has been repeatedly and widely established—to the point where the platform is sometimes **resented**. 然而，在2023年末，TikTok在音乐行业的主导地位已一再得到广泛认可——以至于该平台有时会被怨恨。

近 hate / heɪt / *v.* 憎恨; 讨厌

---

major / 'meɪdʒə(r) / ⓪⓪2

釋 *adj.* 主要的; 重要的 *n.* 主修课程; 专业课; 少校 *v.* 主修; 专攻

搭 major in 主修 ‖ major on 专门研究（课题、问题等）

例 What played the **major** role in lowering the price of nails after the late 1700s? 18世纪晚期之后，是什么在降低钉子价格方面发挥了重要作用？（2024年）

派 majority / mə'dʒɒrəti / *n.* 大多数; 多数票

近 chief / tʃiːf / *adj.* 主要的; 首席的 ‖ main / meɪn / *adj.* 主要的

反 minor / 'maɪnə(r) / *adj.* 较小的; 次要的

---

limit / 'lɪmɪt / ⓪⓪3

釋 *v.* 限制; 限定 *n.* 限度; 限制; 极限; 界限, 范围

例 A pressure-sensitive mat would be more appropriate to **limit** the surveyed area. 使用压敏垫来限制勘测区域更为合适。（2024年）

派 limitation / ˌlɪmɪ'teɪʃn / *n.* 限制; 局限性

近 restrict / rɪ'strɪkt / *v.* 限制; 约束; 阻碍

---

work / wɜːk / ⓪⓪4

釋 *v.* 工作; 产生……作用; 争取; （使）运转 *n.* 工作; 工作成果; 作品

例 Yet the new system has not **worked** out any cheaper for the universities. 然而，新制度并没有为大学节省多少费用。（2020年）

派 coworker / 'kəʊwɜːkə(r) / *n.* 同事 ‖ workforce / 'wɜːkfɔːs / *n.* 劳动力; 全体员工

近 labo(u)r / 'leɪbə(r) / *n.* 劳动;（统称）劳工 *v.* 努力做（困难的事）

---

assist / ə'sɪst / ⓪⓪5

釋 *n.* 帮助; 助攻 *v.* 帮助; 协助

搭 assists in 帮助, 协助

例 Fewer artists than scientists responded to the *Nature* poll; however, several respondents noted that artists do not simply **assist** scientists with their communication requirements. 对《自然》民意调查给出答复的艺术家要少于科学家；然而，一些答复者指出，艺术家并不只是协助科学家满足他们的交流要求。（2022年）

辨 help和assist都有"帮助"的意思。help为最普通用词，含义广泛，侧重积极地帮助他人; assist强调所给的帮助起从属的作用。

league / li:g /

⊕ *n.* 联盟; 同盟;（体育运动队的）联合会, 联赛; 级别, 档次; 里格（长度单位）

⊕ Said one recorder of events, "The air at twelve **leagues**' distance smelt as sweet as a new-blown garden." 一位事件记录者说:"在12里格的距离上, 空气闻起来就像新开花的花园一样甜美。"（2015年）

attract / ə'trækt /

⊕ *v.* 吸引, 引诱; 引起……的兴趣; 吸引（支持或资金等）

⊕ A town of culture award could, it is argued, become an annual event, **attracting** funding and creating jobs. 可以说, 文化之城奖可以成为一项年度活动, 吸引资金并创造就业机会。（2020年）

rely / rɪ'laɪ /

⊕ *v.* 依赖, 依靠; 信任, 信赖

⊕ rely on/upon 依赖, 依靠

⊕ To find their sites, archaeologists today **rely** heavily on systematic survey methods and a variety of high-technology tools and techniques. 如今, 考古学家要找到他们的遗址, 在很大程度上要依赖于系统的调查方法和各种高科技工具和技术。（2014年）

conviction / kən'vɪkʃn /

⊕ *n.* 坚定的信仰; 确信; 判罪

⊕ religious conviction 宗教信仰

⊕ The criminal has five previous **convictions**. 这名罪犯有五次犯罪前科。

settle / 'setl /

⊕ *v.* 解决、结束（争端、分歧等）; 决定, 确定; 安排好; 定居; 把……放好; 付清（欠款）; 结算; 结账

⊕ settle down 在某地定居下来, 过安定的生活; 坐下或躺下;（使某人）安静下来

⊕ They were determined to **settle** the dispute before going home for the day. 他们决心在当天回家之前解决那个争端。

charter / 'tʃɑːtə(r) /

⊕ *n.* 特许状, 许可证, 凭照; 宪章;（法律或政策的）缺陷、疏漏 *v.* 包租（飞机、船等）; 特许设立, 给……发许可证或凭照

⊕ Reform has been vigorously opposed, perhaps most notoriously in education, where **charter** schools, academies and merit pay all faced drawn-out battles. 改革一直遭到强烈反对, 最明显的可能是在教育领域: 特许学校、学院和绩效工资都面临着旷日持久的斗争。（2012年）

moan

formidable

examine

notice

press

locate

nonetheless

intrude

pray

guarantee

curb

moan / məʊn /

㊉ *v.* 抱怨；呻吟 *n.* 呻吟声；抱怨；（尤指风的）呼啸声

㊋ Their rules, **moan** the banks, have forced them to report enormous losses, and it's just not fair. 银行抱怨说，他们的规则迫使银行报告巨额亏损，而这是不公平的。（2010年）

㊍ moanful / 'məʊnful / *adj.* 悲叹的；呻吟的

㊎ groan / grəʊn / *v.* 呻吟；抱怨 ‖ sigh / saɪ / *v.* 叹气；叹息

formidable / fə'mɪdəbl /

㊉ *adj.* 可怕的，令人敬畏的；难对付的

㊋ Even Tommasini, who had advocated Gilbert's appointment in the *Times*, calls him "an unpretentious musician with no air of the **formidable** conductor about him." 就连曾在《纽约时报》上主张任命吉尔伯特的托马西尼也称他为"一位朴实无华的音乐家，身上丝毫没有那种令人生畏的指挥家气质"。（2011年）

㊎ dreadful / 'dredfl / *adj.* 可怕的；令人敬畏的

examine / ɪɡ'zæmɪn /

㊉ *v.* 审查；调查；考查；检查；检验；考，测验（某人）；审问

㊋ And only over the past 30 years have scholars **examined** history from the bottom up. 而只有在过去的30年里，学者们才自上而下地考查历史。（2008年）

㊎ inspect / ɪn'spekt / *v.* 检查

notice / 'nəʊtɪs /

㊉ *n.* 通知；注意 *v.* 注意到；通知；留心

㊋ Long gone are the days when a boss could simply give an employee contractual **notice**. 老板可以简单地以合同形式通知员工的时代已经一去不复返了。（2022年）

press / pres /

㊉ *n.* 报刊；印刷机；媒体评论；新闻界；出版社；按压 *v.* 按压；敦促；逼迫；推进

㊋ The really successful holders of such titles are those that do a great deal more than fill hotel bedrooms and bring in high-profile arts events and good **press** for a year. 真正成功的此类头衔拥有者，是那些除了让酒店房间爆满、带来高知名度的艺术活动和一年的良好媒体报道之外，还能做更多事情的人。（2020年）

㊎ squeeze / skwiːz / *v.* 挤压；挤出；压榨

locate / 'ləʊkeɪt /

㊉ *v.* 找到准确位置或地点；把……建在；定居

㊋ Free-ranging elephants presumably also use this information to **locate** their preferred food. 自由觅食的大象大概也会利用这些信息来寻找自己喜欢的食物。（2024年）

㊍ location / ləʊ'keɪʃn / *n.* 地方，位置

㊎ place / pleɪs / *v.* 将某物放置于…… ‖ settle / 'setl / *v.* 定居

nonetheless / ˌnʌnðə'les / ⁰¹⁸

释 *adv.* 尽管如此；然而

例 Even if families don't sit down to eat together as frequently as before, millions of Britons will **nonetheless** have got a share this weekend of one of the nation's great traditions: the Sunday roast. 尽管一家人不再像以前那样经常坐在一起吃饭，但数百万英国人还是会在本周末品尝到英国最伟大的传统之一：周日烤肉。（2020年）

近 nevertheless / ˌnevəðə'les / *adv.* 尽管如此；然而

intrude / ɪn'truːd / ⁰¹⁹

释 *v.* 侵扰；打扰；干扰；扰乱；侵入；闯入；把（思想等）强加于

搭 intrude upon 打扰

例 On the overturned provisions the majority held that Congress had deliberately "occupied the field", and Arizona had thus **intruded** on the federal's privileged powers. 关于被推翻的条款，多数人认为国会故意"占领了这一领域"，亚利桑那州因此扰乱了联邦的特权。（2013年）

pray / preɪ / ⁰²⁰

释 *v.* 祈祷；祷告；祈求

例 I had decided I must go on as usual, follow my normal routine, and hope and **pray**. 我打定主意必须像平时一样生活，遵循自己通常的作息规律，同时怀抱希望、虔诚祈祷。

guarantee / ˌgærən'tiː / ⁰²¹

释 *v.* 保证；担保；保障；使必然发生，确保；为……作保 *n.* 保证；保修单；保证金；抵押品

搭 be guaranteed to do sth. 肯定会做某事；必定会做某事

例 Yet as we report now, the food police are determined that this enjoyment should be rendered yet another guilty pleasure **guaranteed** to damage our health. 然而，正如我们现在所报道的那样，食品警察坚决认为，这种享受应该是另一种罪恶的快乐，必然会损害我们的健康。（2020年）

近 pledge / pledʒ / *v.* 承诺 *n.* 保证

curb / kɜːb / ⁰²²

释 *v.* 控制；抑制，遏制；限定；约束 *n.* 起控制（或限制）作用的事物

例 The use of privacy law to **curb** the tech giants in this instance feels slightly maladapted. 在这种情况下，利用隐私法来遏制科技巨头的做法让人感觉有些不妥。（2018年）

近 control / kən'trəʊl / *v.* 控制；掌控

辨 curb和control都有"控制"的意思。curb指果断地制止，也可指用严格的方法加以控制；control是含义广泛的常用词，指对人或物进行约束或控制。

insult
023

释 / ɪnˈsʌlt / v. 侮辱; 辱骂; 冒犯; ˈɪnsʌlt / n. 侮辱; 辱骂

例 Emma Marris's article is an **insult** and a disservice to the thousands of passionate, dedicated people who work tirelessly to improve the lives of animals and protect our planet. 艾玛·马里斯的文章是对成千上万为改善动物生活和保护我们的星球而不懈努力的热心人的侮辱和伤害。(2022年)

steer / stɪə(r) /
024

释 v. 引导, 引领; 驾驶

搭 steer clear of 有意避开……

例 Far less certain, however, is how successfully experts and bureaucrats can select our peer groups and **steer** their activities in virtuous directions. 然而, 专家和官僚如何成功地选择我们的同龄群体, 并引导他们的行动朝着良性的方向发展, 这一点就不那么确定了。(2023年)

signify / ˈsɪɡnɪfaɪ /
025

释 v. 表示; 意味着; 象征; (用符号或手势)表达

例 They also focused on important rituals that appeared to preserve a people's social structure, such as initiation ceremonies that formally **signify** children's entrance into adulthood. 他们也关注那些看上去能够保存一个民族的社会结构的重要仪式, 诸如象征着孩子们正式进入成年时期的开启典礼等。(2009年)

派 signification / ˌsɪɡnɪfɪˈkeɪʃn / n. (尤指词或短语的)意思, 意义

definition / ˌdefɪˈnɪʃn /
026

释 n. 定义, 释义; 清晰(度), 鲜明(度)

搭 by definition 根据定义; 就定义来看

例 This **definition** excludes many individuals usually referred to as intellectuals—the average scientist, for one. 这个定义排除了许多通常被称为知识分子的人, 普通的科学家算是一个。(2006年)

speculate / ˈspekjuleɪt /
027

释 v. 预测, 推断; 猜测

例 It is **speculated** that gardens arise from a basic human need in the individuals who made them: the need for creative expression. 据推断, 花园源于建造者的一种基本人类需求: 创造性表达的需求。(2013年)

diplomatic / ˌdɪpləˈmætɪk /
028

释 adj. 外交的, 从事外交的; 有策略的, 有手腕的

例 The country is pursuing **diplomatic** channels to solve the problem. 该国正在寻求外交途径来解决这个问题。

dictate

[029]

释 / dɪkˈteɪt / *v.* 听写; 口述; 支配; 摆布; 决定 / ˈdɪkteɪt / *n.* 命令; 规定

搭 dictate sth. to sb. 向某人口述某事 ‖ dictate to sb. 向某人发号施令

例 I had not realized how profoundly marketing trends **dictated** our perception of what is natural to kids, including our core beliefs about their psychological development. 我没有意识到，营销趋势在多大程度上决定着我们对孩子天性的认识，包括我们对孩子心理发展的核心理念。

派 dictation / dɪkˈteɪʃn / *n.* 口授笔录; 听写 ‖ dictator / dɪkˈteɪtə(r) / *n.* 独裁者，专制者

absolute / ˈæbsəluːt /

[030]

释 *adj.* 绝对的; 完全的; 专制的; 肯定的; 无疑的; 不受约束的

例 France, which prides itself as the global innovator of fashion, has decided its fashion industry has lost an **absolute** right to define physical beauty for women. 以全球时尚创新者自居的法国决定，其时尚产业已经丧失了定义女性形体美的绝对权利。（2016年）

frequency / ˈfriːkwənsi /

[031]

释 *n.* 频率

例 The ear is fatigued with a certain **frequency**. 耳朵听某种特定的频率会感到疲劳。

regulation / ˌreɡjuˈleɪʃn /

[032]

释 *n.* 章程; 规章制度; 规则; 法规; 管理，控制

例 The group is in its early days of mobilization, which could involve pushing for new policies or **regulation**. 该小组正处于早期动员阶段，可能涉及推动新的政策或法规。（2024年）

upright / ˈʌpraɪt /

[033]

释 *adj.* 直立的，挺直的; 正直的 *n.*（支撑用的）直柱，立柱 *adv.* 直立地

例 Humans are often thought to be insensitive smellers compared with animals, but this is largely because, unlike animals, we stand **upright**. 与动物相比，人类通常被认为嗅觉不灵敏，但这主要是因为人类与动物不同，我们是直立站立的。（2005年）

institute / ˈɪnstɪtjuːt /

[034]

释 *n.* 研究所; 协会 *v.* 制定（体系、政策等）

例 A group of labour MPs, among them Yvette Cooper, are bringing in the new year with a call to **institute** a UK "town of culture" award. 包含伊薇特·库珀在内的一批工党议员在新年伊始就呼吁设立英国"文化之城"奖。（2020年）

近 establish / ɪˈstæblɪʃ / *v.* 建立（尤指正式关系）; 确立（地位）

affair / əˈfeə(r) / 035

释 *n.* [pl.]公共事务，政治事务；事件；事情；[pl.]私通，风流韵事；私人业务

例 The report also advocates greater study of foreign languages, international **affairs** and the expansion of study abroad programs. 报告还提倡加强外语和国际事务学习，扩大出国留学计划。（2014年）

route / ruːt / 036

释 *n.* 路线；途径 *v.* 按某路线发送

例 The researchers are convinced that the elephants always know precisely where they are in relation to all the resources they need, and can therefore take shortcuts, as well as following familiar **routes**. 研究人员确信，大象总是能精确地感知它们相对于所有所需资源的位置，因此它们不但可以沿着熟悉的路线前进，还可以抄近路。（2024年）

toss / tɒs / 037

释 *v.* 扔；抛；掷；（使）摇摆，颠簸；甩（表愤怒等）*n.* 抛硬币的方法

搭 toss and turn 辗转反侧

例 And if one received a grape without having to provide her token in exchange at all, the other either **tossed** her own token at the researcher or out of the chamber, or refused to accept the slice of cucumber. 如果一只猴子根本不需要提供她的代币就得到了一颗葡萄，那么另一只猴子要么把她的代币扔给研究者或扔出密室，要么拒绝接受黄瓜片。（2005年）

flee / fliː / 038

释 *v.* 逃走；逃避

搭 flee from 逃离；避开

例 The animals **fled** in all direction at the sight of the hunters. 动物们一看到猎人就四下里逃散了。

dealer / ˈdiːlə(r) / 039

释 *n.* 贸易商

例 In the late 1800s British archaeologist Sir Arthur Evans combed antique **dealers'** stores in Athens, Greece. 19世纪晚期，英国考古学家阿瑟·埃文斯爵士在希腊雅典的古董商店里搜寻古董（2014年）

minimum / ˈmɪnɪməm / 040

释 *adj.* 最低的；最小的；最低限度的 *n.* 最小值；最少量；最低限度

例 Imagine that you favor increasing the **minimum** wage in our state, and I do not. 试想一下，你赞成提高本州的最低工资标准，而我不赞成。（2019年）

recession / rɪˈseʃn /

041

- 释 *n.* 经济衰退, 不景气; 退后; 撤回
- 搭 economic recession 经济衰退; 经济萧条
- 例 Not long ago, with the country entering a **recession** and Japan at its pre-bubble peak, the U.S. workforce was derided as poorly educated and one of the primary causes of the poor U.S. economic performance. 不久前, 随着美国经济进入衰退期, 日本也处于泡沫经济前的高峰期, 美国劳动力被嘲笑为教育水平低下, 是美国经济表现不佳的主要原因之一。(2009年)

enlarge / ɪnˈlɑːdʒ /

042

- 释 *v.* 扩大; 增大; 扩充; 扩展; 放大 (照片或文件)
- 搭 enlarge on/upon 详述; 细说
- 例 Its volunteers work with someone in need to enhance their personal skills, **enlarge** their business opportunities and improve their day-to-day lives. 它的志愿者与有需要的人合作, 提高他们的个人技能, 扩大他们的商业机会, 改善他们的日常生活。

commodity / kəˈmɒdəti /

043

- 释 *n.* 商品, 货物
- 例 It was a year before she became head of a tiny Internet-based **commodities** exchange. 一年后, 她成为一家小型互联网商品交易所的负责人。(2011年)

peer / pɪə(r) /

044

- 释 *n.* 同龄人; 同等地位的人; 同伴 *v.* 仔细看, 费力地看; 凝视
- 搭 peer pressure 同辈压力 ‖ peer into 检查; 仔细看
- 例 This is a subtle form of **peer** pressure: we unconsciously imitate the behavior we see every day. 这是一种微妙的同辈压力: 我们会不自觉地模仿自己每天看到的行为。(2012年)
- 派 peerless / ˈpɪələs / *adj.* 无与伦比的, 出类拔萃的
- 近 counterpart / ˈkaʊntəpɑːt / *n.* 职位 (或作用) 相当的人

snack / snæk /

045

- 释 *n.* 零食, 小吃; 快餐, 便餐 *v.* 吃快餐, 吃点心
- 例 Such food service operators range from **snack** machines to large institutional catering ventures, but most of these businesses are known in the trade as "horeca": hotels, restaurants, and cafés. 这些餐饮业者的经营范围从小吃店到大型机构餐饮企业不等, 但这些企业大多数在业内被称为 "horeca", 即酒店、餐馆和咖啡馆。(2010年)

fatigue / fəˈtiːg /

046

- 释 *n.* 疲劳
- 例 Instead, use it as an opportunity to reduce decision **fatigue**. 相反, 应将其作为减少决策疲劳的机会。(2016年)

Writing Models

temperament

decent

sue

legal

output

afford

incidence

appoint

transfer

ensure

gaze

---

temperament / ˈtemprəmənt /   047

释 *n.* 性情, 性格; 气质

例 In this new book he hits off the Chinese **temperament** with amazing insight. 在这本新书里, 他对中国人性格的描写表现出惊人的洞察力。

近 disposition / ˌdɪspəˈzɪʃn / *n.* 脾气; 性格 ‖ character / ˈkærəktə(r) / *n.* 性格; 特征

---

decent / ˈdiːsnt /   048

释 *adj.* 像样的; 体面的; 得体的, 合宜的; 正直的, 正派的

例 Millennials were told that if you did well in school, got a **decent** degree, you would be set up for life. 千禧一代被告知, 如果你在学校表现出色, 拿到一个像样的学位, 你的人生就有了保障。(2022年)

---

sue / suː /   049

释 *v.* 控告, 提起诉讼; 提出请求

搭 sue for peace 谈和, 求和

例 The company could be **sued** for damages. 该公司可能会因为造成损失被起诉。

---

legal / ˈliːgl /   050

释 *adj.* 合法的; 法律的; 法律要求的; 法律允许的; 与法律有关的

例 The endless **legal** battles and back-and-forth at the FCC cry out for Congress to act. 针对联邦通信委员会的无休止的法律诉讼和反复折腾都要求国会采取行动。(2021年)

---

output / ˈaʊtpʊt /   051

释 *n.* 产量; 产生; 输出

搭 carbon-dioxide output 二氧化碳排放量

例 Boiling down an individual's **output** to simple metrics, such as number of publications or journal impacts, entails considerable savings in time, energy and ambiguity. 将一个人的产出归结为简单的指标, 如发表论文的数量或期刊影响, 可以大大节省时间、精力, 减少模棱两可。(2019年)

---

afford / əˈfɔːd /   052

释 *v.* 支付得起; 承担得起; 提供; 给予

例 They **afford** an opportunity for people from all backgrounds to encounter a range of animals, from drone bees to springbok or salmon, to better understand the natural world we live in. 它们(动物园)为各种背景的人们提供了接触各种动物的机会, 从雄蜂到跳羚或鲑鱼, 让人们更好地了解我们生活的自然世界。(2022年)

········· ◎ Study Notes

incidence / 'ɪnsɪdəns / 〔053〕

释 *n.* 发生范围; 发生率; 影响程度; 入射（角）

例 Bone loss is progressive in both men and women, with the **incidence** rising as people age. 男性和女性的骨质流失都是渐进性的，随着年龄的增长，发病率也会上升。

appoint / ə'pɔɪnt / 〔054〕

释 *v.* 任命; 指派; 下令; 布置

例 Working with the American Statistical Association, the journal has **appointed** seven experts to a statistics board of reviewing editors (SBoRE). 该期刊与美国统计协会合作，任命了七位专家加入由审查编辑组成的统计委员会（SBoRE）。（2015年）

派 appointee / ə,pɔɪn'ti: / *n.* 被任命者

近 designate / 'dezɪgneɪt / *v.* 命名; 任命, 选定; 指派 ‖ assign / ə'saɪn / *v.* 指派; 选派

辨 designate、appoint和assign都有"任命; 指派"的意思。designate 为书面用语，侧重当权者或机构的选拔或任命，有时含强行指定的意味；appoint通常指不经过选择的官方委任；assign主要指将某项任务指派给某人去完成。

transfer 〔055〕

释 / 'trænsfɜ:(r) / *n.* 转移; 调动; 换乘 / træns'fɜ:(r) / *v.* （使）转移; 调动; 移交

例 I would ask that the foreign nations and the original country discuss the terms of **transfer**. 我要求外国和原属国讨论移交条件。（2024年）

ensure / ɪn'ʃʊə(r) / 〔056〕

释 *v.* 确保, 保证; 担保

例 A pair of bills sponsored by Massachusetts state Senator Jason Lewis and House Speaker Pro Tempore Patricia Haddad, to **ensure** "gender parity" on boards and commissions, provide a case in point. 由马萨诸塞州参议员杰森·刘易斯和众议院临时议长帕特里夏·哈达德发起的旨在确保董事会和委员会中"性别均等"的两项法案就是一个很好的例子。（2020年）

近 guarantee / ,gærən'ti: / *v.* 确保, 保证

gaze / geɪz / 〔057〕

释 *v.* 凝视, 注视 *n.* 凝视

搭 gaze at 凝视, 看着

例 We know that a typical infant will instinctively **gaze** into its mother's eyes, and she will look back. 我们知道，一个典型的婴儿会本能地注视母亲的眼睛，而母亲也会回望。（2020年）

辨 stare、gaze和glimpse都有"看"的意思。stare强调由于好奇、害怕或无意地睁大眼睛盯着看；gaze强调由于惊奇、兴趣而目不转睛地注视；glimpse指有意地匆匆地看一眼。

restrain / rɪ'streɪn /

058

释 *v.* 抑制; 制止; 限制

搭 restrain sb. from (doing) sth. 制止某人做某事

例 In musical expression, he did not feel **restrained** by the weight of convention. 在音乐表现方面, 他并不觉得受到惯例的限制。（2014年）

govern / 'ɡʌvn /

059

释 *v.* 统治; 控制; 管理; 治理; 支配

例 Sensible ideas have been around for a long time, but the state-level bodies that **govern** the profession have been too conservative to implement them. 合理的想法由来已久, 但管理该行业的州级机构却过于保守, 不敢付诸实施。（2014年）

trust / trʌst /

060

释 *n.* 相信; 信托; 受托基金机构; 委托 *v.* 相信; 托付

搭 mutual trust 相互信任

例 While eye contact may be a sign of connection or **trust** in friendly situations, it's more likely to be associated with dominance or intimidation in adversarial situations. 在友好的情况下, 目光接触可能是联系或信任的标志, 但在敌对的情况下, 它更可能与支配或恐吓联系在一起。（2020年）

physical / 'fɪzɪkl /

061

释 *adj.* 实物的; 外在的; 物理的; 身体的

搭 physical fitness 身体健康

例 Like **physical** fights, verbal fights can leave both sides bloodied. 与肢体冲突一样, 言语冲突也会让双方伤痕累累。（2019年）

performance / pə'fɔːməns /

062

释 *n.* 表演; 演出; 表现; 业绩; 性能; 运行情况; 执行; 履行

例 The **performance** was a creative call to action ahead of November's United Nations Climate Change Conference in Glasgow, UK. 在11月于英国格拉斯哥举行的联合国气候变化大会之前, 这场表演是一次富有创意的行动号召。（2022年）

reference / 'refrəns /

063

释 *n.* 说到（或写到）的事; 提到; 谈及; 涉及; 参考; 查询; 查阅; 参考书目; 标记; 编号; 推荐人或信; 介绍人或信 *v.* 查阅; 参考; 给（书等）附参考资料

搭 in/with reference to (所述内容) 关于

例 In effect, you try to reconstruct the likely meanings or effects that any given sentence, image or **reference** might have had: These might be the ones the author intended. 实际上, 你是在试图重建任何特定句子、图像或参考书目可能具有的含义或效果: 这些可能就是作者想要表达的意思。（2015年）

judge / dʒʌdʒ /

释 v. 判断; 评判; 估计 n. 法官; 裁判员

例 It is hard, the state argues, for **judges** to assess the implications of new and rapidly changing technologies. 该州认为, 法官很难评估日新月异的新技术的影响。(2015年)

064

correlate / 'kɒrəleɪt /

释 v. 和……相关; 使……相互关联

搭 correlate with (使) 相互关联; 极为相似

例 That's because economic growth can be **correlated** with environmental degradation, while protecting the environment is sometimes **correlated** with greater poverty. 这是因为经济增长可能与环境退化相关, 而保护环境有时又与更加贫困相关。(2021年)

065

brief / briːf /

释 adj. 简短的; 短暂的; 草率的 n. 摘要, 简报 v. 摘要; 做……的提要

例 Neuroscientist Bonnie Auyeung found that the hormone oxytocin increased the amount of eye contact from men toward the interviewer during a **brief** interview when the direction of their gaze was recorded. 神经科学家邦妮·奥阳发现, 在一次简短的采访中, 当记录男性的注视方向时, 荷尔蒙催产素会增加男性对访谈者的目光接触次数。(2020年)

066

unique / juːˈniːk /

释 adj. 独特的; 唯一的; 独一无二的; 独具的, 特有的; 罕见的

例 AI can also be used to identify the lifestyle choices of customers regarding their hobbies, favourite celebrities, and fashions to provide **unique** content in marketing messages put out through social media. 人工智能还可用于识别客户的生活方式选择, 包括他们的爱好、喜欢的名人和时尚, 从而在通过社交媒体发布的营销信息中提供独特的内容。(2023年)

067

regard / rɪˈɡɑːd /

释 v. 将……认为; 把……视为 n. 注意; 关注; 尊重; 敬佩

搭 in/with regard to sb./sth. 关于; 至于

例 When GDP is no longer **regarded** as the sole measure of a country's success, the world looks very different. 当国内生产总值不再被视为衡量一个国家成功与否的唯一标准时, 世界的面貌就大不一样了。(2017年)

068

mental / 'mentl /

释 adj. 智力的; 精神健康的

搭 mental health 心理健康

例 As you will come to see, knowing that **mental** health is always available and knowing to trust it allow us to slow down to the moment and live life happily. 正如你将看到的那样, 知道心理健康总是可以获得的, 并懂得信任它, 就能让我们放慢脚步, 快乐地生活。(2016年)

069

Writing Models ◎

collaborate

novel

bet

apology

central

reception

instruction

liberty

embrace

skill

link

collaborate / kəˈlæbəreɪt /

070

释 v.（尤指著书或进行研究时的）合作

搭 collaborate with 与……协作、合作

例 Annie **collaborated** on a book with her friends. 安妮和她的朋友们合著了一本书。

辨 cooperate和collaborate都有"合作"的意思。cooperate指为相互支持而进行的合作或协作，强调通力合作；collaborate多指文化领域中的合作。

novel / ˈnɒvl /

071

释 adj. 新的；新奇的；新颖的；与众不同的；珍奇的 n.（长篇）小说

例 Two centuries ago, the idea of preserving nature, rather than exploiting it, was a **novel** one to many U.S. settlers. 两个世纪前，对许多美国移民来说，保护自然而不是开发自然，是一个新奇的理念。（2023年）

派 novelty / ˈnɒvlti / n. 新奇；新颖；新奇的事物（或人、环境）

bet / bet /

072

释 n. 打赌；赌注 v. 下赌注（于）；用……打赌；敢说

例 The **bet** seems to have paid off: The streamer says the audience for the show on the platform grew 20 percent over its 2023 number. 这个赌注似乎得到了回报：该主播表示，这个节目在该平台上的观众数量比2023年增长了20%。

近 gamble / ˈɡæmbl / v./n. 赌博，打赌

apology / əˈpɒlədʒi /

073

释 n. 道歉

搭 make an apology 道歉

例 The **apology**, however, did little to calm the fury over the artist's original comments, with few, if any, other artists or friends speaking out publicly to support him. 然而，这一道歉并没有平息人们对这位艺术家最初言论的愤怒，几乎没有其他艺术家或朋友公开站出来支持他。

派 apologize / əˈpɒlədʒaɪz / v. 道歉；谢罪

central / ˈsentrəl /

074

释 adj. 中心的；中央的；主要的；最重要的；起支配作用的

例 Other scientists perform the specialised work of peer review also for free, because it is a **central** element in the acquisition of status and the production of scientific knowledge. 其他科学家也免费从事同行评议的专业工作，因为这是获得地位和产生科学知识的主要因素。（2020年）

派 centralise / ˈsentrəlaɪz / v. 集权控制；实行集中

reception / rɪˈsepʃn / 075

释 *n.* （宾馆的）前台；（办公室或医院的）接待处，服务台；欢迎会，招待会；接待；迎接

例 Neil was seen in the video holding hands with Naomi as the two danced in front of guests at the **reception**. 视频中可以看到尼尔和娜奥米手牵着手，在欢迎会上当着宾客的面跳舞。

instruction / ɪnˈstrʌkʃn / 076

释 *n.* 用法说明；操作指南；指示；命令；教导

例 Ms Brooks may or may not have had suspicions about how her journalists got their stories, but she asked no questions, gave no **instructions**—nor received traceable, recorded answers. 布鲁克斯女士可能怀疑过，也可能没有怀疑过她的记者是如何获取新闻报道的，但她没有提出任何问题，也没有给出任何指示，也没有收到可追溯的、有记录的答复。（2015年）

liberty / ˈlɪbəti / 077

释 *n.* 自由

搭 at liberty 不再受监禁；自由 ‖ at liberty to do sth. 有权做某事；有做某事的自由

例 Scientific method, reductionism and the questioning of Church ideals was to be encouraged, as were ideas of **liberty**, tolerance and progress. 科学方法、还原论和质疑教会的思想，以及自由、宽容和进步的思想都受到鼓励。（2020年）

embrace / ɪmˈbreɪs / 078

释 *v.* 拥抱；乐意采纳，欣然接受；包括；接纳 *n.* 拥抱

例 Marketers have **embraced** the two-step flow because it suggests that if they can just find and influence the influentials, those select people will do most of the work for them. 营销人员之所以欣然接受二级传播理论，是因为它表明，只要他们能找到并影响有影响力的人，这些被选中的人就会为他们完成大部分工作。（2010年）

skill / skɪl / 079

释 *n.* 技巧；技艺；技术；技能

例 Yet as distrust has risen toward all media, people may be starting to beef up their media literacy **skills**. 然而，随着对所有媒体的不信任度上升，人们可能会开始加强他们的媒体识读技能。（2018年）

派 skillful / ˈskɪlfl / *adj.* 熟练的 ‖ skilled / skɪld / *adj.* 有技术的；熟练的

link / lɪŋk / 080

释 *n.* 联系，连接；关系，纽带；链接 *v.* 使联系起来；连接；接合

例 On the assumption that they will become relevant later, you make a mental note of discourse entities as well as possible **links** between them. 假设它们稍后会变得有关联，你就会在脑海中记下话语里的字词以及它们之间可能存在的联系。（2015年）

launch

power

comfort

super

drag

opinion

multiply

medium

site

tap

soak

crash

launch / lɔːntʃ /　⓿⓼⓵

释 *v.* 发射（火箭、导弹或卫星）；推出，发布（新产品）；开展（重大活动）；发起；发动（军事袭击等）；使（船）下水 *n.* 发射；（船的）下水；上市；（事件的）发起

搭 launch out 开始从事，投身于

例 A century ago Octavia Hill **launched** the National Trust not to rescue stylish houses but to save "the beauty of natural places for everyone forever." 一个世纪前，奥克塔维亚·希尔发起成立了国民信托基金，目的不是拯救别具风格的房子，而是"为每个人永久保存自然之美"。（2016年）

power / 'paʊə(r) /　⓿⓼⓶

释 *n.* 权力；能力；强国

搭 in power 当权

例 "This is all part of a wider change towards concentration of **power**," says literary agent Andrew Lownie. 文学经纪人安德鲁·洛尼表示："这是权力集中的更广泛变化的一部分。"（2023年）

派 powerful / 'paʊfl / *adj.* 有影响力的；强壮的

comfort / 'kʌmfət /　⓿⓼⓷

释 *n.* 舒适，舒服；安慰 *v.* 安慰

例 In fact, the more new things we try—the more we step outside our **comfort** zone—the more inherently creative we become, both in the workplace and in our personal lives. 事实上，我们尝试的新事物越多，走出舒适区的次数越多，我们就越有内在的创造力，无论是在工作场所还是在个人生活中。（2009年）

派 comfortable / 'kʌmfətəbl / *adj.* 使人舒服的；舒适的

super / 'suːpə(r) /　⓿⓼⓸

释 *adj.* 顶好的；超级的 *adv.* 特别；超级地

例 This **super** soft blanket is the perfect travel companion and is made of the highest quality Scottish Cashmere. 这条超级柔软的毯子是完美的旅行伴侣，由最高品质的苏格兰开士米制成。

drag / dræg /　⓿⓼⓹

释 *v.* （费力地）拖，拉，拽；缓慢而费力地移动（或行进）

例 And it should: Wasted time is a **drag** on Americans' economic and private lives, not to mention infuriating. 应该这么说：浪费的时间拖累了美国人的经济和私人生活，更不用说激怒他们了。（2017年）

opinion / ə'pɪnjən /　⓿⓼⓺

释 *n.* 意见；想法；看法；（对某人的）评价，印象；舆论；（群体的）信仰，观点

例 This board discussion, in my **opinion**, was the highlight of the conference. 在我看来，这次董事会的讨论是本次会议的亮点。

近 view / vjuː / *n.* 观点；看法；方式；视野；风景

multiply / ˈmʌltɪplaɪ / 087

释 v. 乘; 乘以; (使) 大大增加

例 Beyond this date, the safety of consuming these items becomes increasingly uncertain, as bacteria could have **multiplied** to levels that could pose health risks. 超过这个日期, 食用这些食品的安全性变得越来越不确定, 因为细菌可能会增加到可能构成健康风险的程度。

反 divide / dɪˈvaɪd / v. 除; 分割; 分离; 分配

medium / ˈmiːdiəm / 088

释 adj. 中等的; 中等程度的 n. 媒介物

例 But in the **medium** term, middle-class workers may need a lot of help adjusting. 但从中期来看, 中产阶级工人可能需要很多帮助来调整。(2018年)

site / saɪt / 089

释 n. 场地; 场所; 现场; 发生地; 网站 v. 使坐落在; 为……选址

搭 on site 在工地上; 在现场

例 Communities throughout New England have been attempting to regulate short-term rentals since **sites** like Airbnb took off in the 2010s. 在二十一世纪的第二个十年, Airbnb等网站兴起以来, 新英格兰各地的社区一直在试图规范短期租赁。(2023年)

tap / tæp / 090

释 n. 水龙头; 阀门; 轻击; 轻拍 v. 轻敲; 利用, 开发, 发掘

例 Television is a one-way **tap** flowing into our homes. 电视是流入我们家庭的一个单向水龙头。(2012年)

soak / səʊk / 091

释 v. 浸泡; 浸湿; 湿透; 向(某人)敲竹杠; 宰(某人); 向(某人)征收重税 n. 浸泡; 浸渍; 湿透

搭 soak up 吸收, 吸掉

例 Be sure to **soak** and rinse the rice before adding it to the pot, which ensures that the grains cook up light and separate. 把米放入锅里之前, 一定要浸泡并淘洗干净, 这样可以确保米粒煮得清淡且颗颗分离。

crash / kræʃ / 092

释 n. 撞车; 碰撞; 暴跌; 倒闭, 破产; (计算机或计算机程序)崩溃, 瘫痪 v. (使)碰撞; 撞击; 倒闭, 破产

例 Yes, there has been a budding economic recovery since the 2008 global **crash**, but in key indicators in areas such as health and education, major economies have continued to decline. 是的, 自2008年全球金融危机以来, 经济出现了复苏的苗头, 但在卫生和教育等领域的关键指标上, 主要经济体仍在继续下滑。(2017年)

quit

brand

attention

mix

alien

tendency

victim

mutual

quit / kwɪt /　093

释 v. 放弃, 辞去（工作）; 停止; 退出; 放弃; 离开（某地）

例 Ellen Marram **quit** as chief of Tropicana a decade ago, saying she wanted to be a CEO. 埃伦·马拉姆十年前辞去纯果乐的主管职务时表示, 她想成为一名首席执行官。（2011年）

brand / brænd /　094

释 n. 品牌

例 By offering on-trend items at dirt-cheap prices, Cline argues, these **brands** have hijacked fashion cycles, shaking an industry long accustomed to a seasonal pace. 克莱恩认为, 这些品牌以极低的价格提供紧跟潮流的商品, 劫持了时尚流行周期, 撼动了这个长期以来习惯于季节性节奏的行业。（2013年）

attention / əˈtenʃn /　095

释 n. 注意; 专心; 留心; 注意力

搭 pay attention to 注意

例 In a social situation, eye contact with another person can show that you are paying **attention** in a friendly way. 在社交场合, 与他人的目光接触可以表示你在友好地关注对方。（2020年）

mix / mɪks /　096

释 v. （使）混合, 掺和; 融合; 调配, 配制; 混录, 混音

搭 mix in 掺入 ‖ mix up 弄错; 弄乱

例 Her work **mixes** the hallmarks of traditional English country homes, including fine arts, antiques and fabrics, with American ease and livability. 她的作品融合了传统英国乡村住宅的特点, 包括美术、古董和织物, 以及美国的舒适和宜居性。

派 mixture / ˈmɪkstʃə(r) / n. 混合; 混合物 ‖ mixed / mɪkst / adj. 混合的; 混杂的

alien / ˈeɪliən /　097

释 n. 外星人; 外星生物 adj. 陌生的; 不熟悉的; 外国的; 不相容的

例 The actor transformed into an **alien** with reflective makeup and a pink bob. 这位演员摇身一变成了一个化着反光妆, 留着粉色波波头的外星人。

tendency / ˈtendənsi /　098

释 n. 倾向; 偏好; 趋势

例 The findings do not simply explain people's **tendency** to befriend those of similar ethnic backgrounds, say the researchers. 研究人员说, 这些发现并不能简单地解释人们喜欢与种族背景相似的人交朋友的偏好。（2015年）

近 trend / trend / n. 趋势; 时尚

victim / 'vɪktɪm /   099

释 *n.* 受害者；牺牲品

搭 fall victim (to sth.) 受伤；受损；被害

例 The **victims** of this revolution, of course, are not limited to designers. 当然，这场革命的受害者并不局限于设计师。（2013年）

mutual / 'mjuːtʃuəl /   100

释 *adj.* 相互的；彼此的；共有的，共同的

例 If we readjust our view of arguments—from a verbal fight or tennis game to a reasoned exchange through which we all gain **mutual** respect and understanding—then we change the very nature of what it means to "win" an argument. 如果我们重新调整我们对争论的看法——从一场口水战或你来我往的争论转变为一种理性的交流，通过这种交流，我们都能获得相互尊重和理解——那么我们就改变了"赢得"争论的本质。（2019年）

☐ ☐ absolute	☐ ☐ fatigue	☐ ☐ opinion	☐ ☐ toss
☐ ☐ affair	☐ ☐ flee	☐ ☐ output	☐ ☐ transfer
☐ ☐ afford	☐ ☐ formidable	☐ ☐ peer	☐ ☐ trust
☐ ☐ alien	☐ ☐ frequency	☐ ☐ performance	☐ ☐ unique
☐ ☐ apology	☐ ☐ gaze	☐ ☐ physical	☐ ☐ upright
☐ ☐ appoint	☐ ☐ govern	☐ ☐ power	☐ ☐ victim
☐ ☐ assist	☐ ☐ guarantee	☐ ☐ pray	☐ ☐ work
☐ ☐ attention	☐ ☐ incidence	☐ ☐ press	
☐ ☐ attract	☐ ☐ institute	☐ ☐ quit	
☐ ☐ bet	☐ ☐ instruction	☐ ☐ reception	
☐ ☐ brand	☐ ☐ insult	☐ ☐ recession	
☐ ☐ brief	☐ ☐ intrude	☐ ☐ reference	
☐ ☐ central	☐ ☐ judge	☐ ☐ regard	
☐ ☐ charter	☐ ☐ launch	☐ ☐ regulation	
☐ ☐ collaborate	☐ ☐ league	☐ ☐ rely	
☐ ☐ comfort	☐ ☐ legal	☐ ☐ resent	
☐ ☐ commodity	☐ ☐ liberty	☐ ☐ restrain	
☐ ☐ conviction	☐ ☐ limit	☐ ☐ route	
☐ ☐ correlate	☐ ☐ link	☐ ☐ settle	
☐ ☐ crash	☐ ☐ locate	☐ ☐ signify	
☐ ☐ curb	☐ ☐ major	☐ ☐ site	
☐ ☐ dealer	☐ ☐ medium	☐ ☐ skill	
☐ ☐ decent	☐ ☐ mental	☐ ☐ snack	
☐ ☐ definition	☐ ☐ minimum	☐ ☐ soak	
☐ ☐ dictate	☐ ☐ mix	☐ ☐ speculate	
☐ ☐ diplomatic	☐ ☐ moan	☐ ☐ steer	
☐ ☐ drag	☐ ☐ multiply	☐ ☐ sue	
☐ ☐ embrace	☐ ☐ mutual	☐ ☐ super	
☐ ☐ enlarge	☐ ☐ nonetheless	☐ ☐ tap	
☐ ☐ ensure	☐ ☐ notice	☐ ☐ temperament	
☐ ☐ examine	☐ ☐ novel	☐ ☐ tendency	

音频

Previous Check

- [ ] promise
- [ ] discipline
- [ ] resemble
- [ ] aware
- [ ] candidate
- [ ] worth
- [ ] justice
- [ ] feat
- [ ] contemplate
- [ ] pit
- [ ] impair
- [ ] underlying
- [ ] grant
- [ ] weave
- [ ] strip
- [ ] intense
- [ ] boast
- [ ] deal
- [ ] assume
- [ ] ease
- [ ] incredible
- [ ] propaganda
- [ ] series
- [ ] criterion
- [ ] terror
- [ ] set
- [ ] deny
- [ ] investigate
- [ ] form
- [ ] equality
- [ ] privacy

- [ ] invent
- [ ] recite
- [ ] responsibility
- [ ] federal
- [ ] observation
- [ ] uncover
- [ ] comment
- [ ] ability
- [ ] vanity
- [ ] soar
- [ ] mood
- [ ] publication
- [ ] nutrition
- [ ] force
- [ ] mark
- [ ] manipulate
- [ ] pursue
- [ ] suicide
- [ ] consistent
- [ ] tolerant
- [ ] acquire
- [ ] skim
- [ ] competition
- [ ] stimulate
- [ ] convey
- [ ] estate
- [ ] consumption
- [ ] boost
- [ ] professional
- [ ] renaissance
- [ ] alleviate

- [ ] devote
- [ ] persist
- [ ] tend
- [ ] routine
- [ ] stretch
- [ ] weigh
- [ ] energy
- [ ] contempt
- [ ] result
- [ ] win
- [ ] residence
- [ ] solid
- [ ] raw
- [ ] stability
- [ ] integrate
- [ ] pure
- [ ] mention
- [ ] excellent
- [ ] durable
- [ ] bring
- [ ] urban
- [ ] record
- [ ] exaggerate
- [ ] welfare
- [ ] eclipse
- [ ] skeptical
- [ ] boil
- [ ] hit
- [ ] landscape
- [ ] lure
- [ ] preference

- [ ] cruel
- [ ] disturb
- [ ] transparent
- [ ] surgery
- [ ] block
- [ ] global
- [ ] widespread

promise / 'prɒmɪs / 001

释 *v.* 许诺；承诺；答应；保证；使很可能，预示 *n.* 诺言；许诺；承诺；吉兆

搭 break the promise 违背承诺

例 If software **promises** to save lives on the scale that drugs now can, big data may be expected to behave as a big pharma has done. 如果软件有望像现在的药物一样拯救生命，那么大数据也有望像大型制药公司那样发挥作用。（2018年）

近 guarantee / ˌɡærən'tiː / *v.* 保证 *n.* 保证

discipline / 'dɪsəplɪn / 002

释 *n.* 纪律；自律；训练；行为准则；自制力；（尤指大学的）专业，科目 *v.* 训练；管教；惩罚

例 Law is a **discipline** which encourages responsible judgment. 法律是一门鼓励负责任判断的科目。（2007年）

近 training / 'treɪnɪŋ / *n.* 训练；培养

resemble / rɪ'zembl / 003

释 *v.* 像；类似于；看起来像；显得像

例 In some ways the scientific publishing model **resembles** the economy of the social Internet: labour is provided free in exchange for the hope of status, while huge profits are made by a few big firms who run the market places. 在某些方面，科学出版模式类似于社交互联网经济：免费提供劳动力以换取（更高）地位的希望，而巨额利润则由少数几家主导市场的大公司赚取。（2020年）

aware / ə'weə(r) / 004

释 *adj.* 意识到⋯⋯的；觉察到⋯⋯的

例 We are not **aware** of the usual smell of our own house, but we notice new smells when we visit someone else's. 我们不会觉察到自己家里常有的气味，但当我们去别人家做客时，我们会觉察到新的气味。（2005年）

candidate / 'kændɪdət / 005

释 *n.* 候选人；申请人；被认定适合者

例 AI looks at résumés in greater numbers than humans would be able to, and selects the more promising **candidates**. 人工智能查看简历的数量远多于人类，并能筛选出更有潜力的候选人。（2021年）

worth / wɜːθ / 006

释 *adj.* 有⋯⋯价值；值⋯⋯钱；（指行动）值得；值得（费周折）*n.* 价值；意义；作用

例 Good governance rests on an understanding of the inherent **worth** of each individual. 善政建立在对每个人内在价值的理解之上。（2017年）

justice / ˈdʒʌstɪs /

释 *n.* 公正; 公平; 正义; 合理; 司法制度; 审判

搭 bring sb. to justice (将某人)绳之以法 ‖ do justice to sb./sth. 公平对待某人(某事)

例 Words degraded to the margin have been **justice**, fairness, tolerance, proportionality and accountability. 正义、公平、宽容、相称性和问责制等词已沦为边缘。(2015年)

feat / fiːt /

释 *n.* 功绩, 壮举

搭 accomplish a feat 建功立业

例 Man's landing on the moon was an extraordinary **feat**. 人类登月是一次非凡的壮举。

contemplate / ˈkɒntəmpleɪt /

释 *v.* 考虑; 沉思; 凝视

例 At the same time, the European Union, Spain, Britain and several other countries have all seriously **contemplated** digital services taxes. 与此同时, 欧盟、西班牙、英国和其他一些国家都在认真考虑征收数字服务税。(2020年)

pit / pɪt /

释 *n.* 坑; 陷阱; 矿; 矿井

例 The children tumbled about in the sand **pit**. 小孩在沙坑里翻滚着玩。

impair / ɪmˈpeə(r) /

释 *v.* 损害, 削弱

例 The patient's intelligence has been **impaired** by a brain injury. 这个病人因脑部受伤而智力受损。

近 harm / hɑːm / *v.* 伤害, 损害 ‖ damage / ˈdæmɪdʒ / *v.* 损害, 毁坏

辨 impair、damage和harm作动词时, 都有"损害, 损伤"的意思。impair通常用于物, 指对某物造成损坏或损伤; damage用于物时, 通常指有形的破坏或损失, 用于人时, 通常指无形的伤害, 如对人的精神、感情或名誉的伤害等; harm既可用于人, 也可用于物, 多用于那些带来痛苦、悲伤、损失或损害的抽象事物。

underlying / ˌʌndəˈlaɪɪŋ /

释 *adj.* 潜在的; 根本的; 下层的, 表面下的

例 In contrast to previous drugs, which can temporarily improve symptoms of the disease, such as memory loss and agitation, this new treatment addresses the **underlying** cause of the disease. 不同于以往的药物只能暂时改善该病的症状, 如记忆力减退和烦躁不安, 而这种新疗法能从根本上解决该病的病因。

grant / grɑːnt /

释 *v.* 同意，准予，允许；承认 *n.* 拨款（政府、机构的）
搭 take sb./sth. for granted 认为……理所当然；对……不予重视
例 The interdependence of the forest and its constituent tree species, ground flora, and fauna is taken for **granted**. 森林及其组成树种、地面植物群和动物群之间的相互依存关系被认为是理所当然的。（2010年） 013

weave / wiːv /

释 *v.* 编，编织
例 The spider **wove** a web in a corner of the storage unit. 蜘蛛在仓库的一个角落里织了张网。 014

strip / strɪp /

释 *n.* 条，带；狭长区域；带状 *v.* 除去；剥去；拆卸，拆开；脱衣服
例 Roman lamps and Roman chariots are very different from LED **strips** and sports cars, but Roman nails are still clearly nails. 罗马灯和罗马战车与LED灯带和跑车截然不同，但罗马钉显然还是钉子。（2024年） 015

intense / ɪn'tens /

释 *adj.* 剧烈的；极度的；集中的；紧张的；热切的
例 Although good TV shows can help stir children's interest in conservation, they cannot replace the excitement of a zoo visit as an **intense**, immersive and interactive experience. 虽然优秀的电视节目有助于激发儿童对动物保护的兴趣，但它们无法取代参观动物园这种紧张刺激、身临其境的互动体验。（2022年）
派 intensity / ɪn'tensəti / *n.* 强烈；紧张；强度 ‖ intensive / ɪn'tensɪv / *adj.* 集中的；密集的 016

boast / bəʊst /

释 *n.* 自吹自擂；足以自豪的事物 *v.* 自夸；吹嘘
搭 boast about/of 吹牛，自夸
例 That is nothing to **boast** of. 那没有什么值得夸耀的。 017

deal / diːl /

释 *v.* 经营；买卖；贩卖（毒品）；发（牌）*n.* 协议；（尤指）交易；大量；很多
搭 deal with 解决；处理；对待（某人）；涉及
例 Elected leaders must be allowed to help supporters **deal** with bureaucratic problems without fear of prosecution for bribery. 必须允许民选领导人帮助支持者解决官僚问题，而不必担心因贿赂而被起诉。（2017年） 018

assume / ə'sjuːm /

🔵 *v.* 假定，设想

🟠 Should advertisers **assume** that people are happy to be tracked and sent behavioral ads? Or should they have explicit permission? 广告商是否应该假设人们乐意被跟踪并发送行为广告，还是他们应该得到人们的明确许可？（2013年）

🔵 suppose / sə'pəʊz / *v.* 推想，假设

🟣 assume和suppose都有"假设"的意思。assume强调未经证实把有分歧的事作为假设，suppose常指根据一些证据进行推断。

ease / iːz /

🔵 *v.* 缓解；减轻；缓和；降低；（使）宽慰 *n.* 容易；安逸

🟠 As so often is the case, stating that principle doesn't **ease** the challenge of line-drawing. 通常情况下，说明这一原则并不能减轻划定界限的挑战。（2015年）

🔵 relieve / rɪ'liːv / *v.* 缓解；解除 ‖ alleviate / ə'liːvieɪt / *v.* 减轻

incredible / ɪn'kredəbl /

🔵 *adj.* 令人难以置信的；了不起的

🟠 When I was 12, I ran my first full marathon and it was an **incredible** feeling for me. 我12岁时第一次跑了全程马拉松，这对我来说是一种难以置信的感觉。

🔵 unbelievable / ˌʌnbɪ'liːvəbl / *adj.* 令人难以置信的

propaganda / ˌprɒpə'gændə /

🔵 *n.* 宣传；鼓吹

🟠 Sadly, the spirit of inquiry once at home on campus has been replaced by the use of the humanities and social sciences as vehicles for publicizing "progressive," or left-liberal **propaganda**. 可悲的是，在（美国）国内校园中曾存在的探究精神已经被用作宣传"进步派"或左翼自由主义工具的人文和社会科学所取代。（2014年）

series / 'sɪəriːz /

🔵 *n.* 一系列，连续；系列节目；串联

🟢 a series of 一系列的

🟠 These journals can act as milk cows where every single article in an issue may cite a specific paper or a **series** of papers. 这些期刊可以充当奶牛的角色，一期中的每一篇文章都可以引用一篇特定的论文或一系列论文。（2023年）

criterion / kraɪ'tɪəriən /

🔵 *n.* （评判的）标准，准则

🟠 In fact, a listing in Scopus seems to be a **criterion** to be targeted in this type of citation manipulation. 事实上，被Scopus收录似乎是这种引用操作的目标标准。（2023年）

terror / 'terə(r) / 025

释 *n.* 恐怖；恐惧；恐怖行动；可怕的人；恐怖的事；可怕的情况

例 Its Campaign to Protect Rural England struck **terror** into many local Conservative parties. 它发起的"保护英格兰农村运动"让许多地方保守政党感到恐惧。（2016年）

set / set / 026

释 *n.* 一组，一套（配套使用的东西）；电视机 *v.* 确定；使处于某种状况；创立；放；把故事情节安排在；摆放餐具 *adj.* 套（餐）的；安排好的

例 Karla Ortiz, an illustrator based in San Francisco who found her work in Stable Diffusion's data **set**, has been raising awareness about the issues around AI art and copyright. 旧金山的一位插画家卡拉·奥尔蒂斯在SD绘画软件的数据组中找到了自己的作品，她一直在提高人们对人工智能艺术和版权问题的认识。（2024年）

deny / dɪ'naɪ / 027

释 *v.* 否认；拒绝接受

例 The charter's main tool of enforcement is to **deny** access for designers and modeling agencies to Copenhagen Fashion Week (CFW), which is run by the Danish Fashion Institute. 该宪章的主要执行手段是拒绝设计师和模特经纪公司参加丹麦时装学院举办的哥本哈根时装周（CFW）。（2016年）

派 denial / dɪ'naɪəl / *n.* 否认，拒绝

反 acknowledge / ək'nɒlɪdʒ / *v.* 承认 ‖ admit / əd'mɪt / *v.* 承认

investigate / ɪn'vestɪgeɪt / 028

释 *v.* 调查；审查；研究

例 After a spouse has been selected, each family **investigates** the other to make sure its child is marrying into a good family. 选定配偶后，每个家庭都会对对方进行调查，以确保自己的孩子与好人家联姻。（2016年）

近 inspect / ɪn'spekt / *v.* 检查；视察 ‖ survey / sə'veɪ / *v.* 查看；审查

form / fɔːm / 029

释 *n.* 类型，种类；形式；外表；表格；形状；体形；惯常做法 *v.* 使形成；（使）出现，产生；（使）形成；组织；建立

例 Light was a something that both artists and scientists had an interest in, and therefore could **form** the basis of collaboration. 光是艺术家和科学家都感兴趣的东西，因此可以形成合作的基础。（2022年）

equality / i'kwɒləti / 030

释 *n.* 平等；均等；相等

例 Progressives often support diversity mandates as a path to **equality** and a way to level the playing field. 进步派经常支持多元化授权，将其作为实现平等的途径和创造公平竞争环境的方法。（2020年）

privacy / ˈprɪvəsi / 031

释 *n.* 隐私；秘密

例 But it's also a lot more personal, Ortiz says, arguing that because art is so closely linked to a person, it could raise data protection and **privacy** problems. 但奥尔蒂斯说，这也更加个人化，他认为，由于艺术与人的关系如此密切，它可能会引发数据保护和隐私问题。（2024年）

近 secrecy / ˈsiːkrəsi / *n.* 秘密，保密

invent / ɪnˈvent / 032

释 *v.* 发明；创造；编造；虚构；捏造

例 When one of these noneconomic categories is threatened and, if we happen to love it, we **invent** excuses to give it economic importance. 当这些非经济类别中的一个（物种）有灭绝危险时，如果我们碰巧喜欢它，我们就会编造借口赋予它经济上的重要性。（2010年）

recite / rɪˈsaɪt / 033

释 *v.* 背诵；吟诵，朗诵

例 Buddhist priests offer a short sermon and **recite** prayers of blessing. 佛教祭司进行简短的布道，并诵读祝福祷文。（2016年）

responsibility / rɪˌspɒnsəˈbɪləti / 034

释 *n.* 责任

搭 social responsibility 社会责任 ‖ sense of responsibility 责任感

例 We are aware of and take **responsibility** for the impact the fashion industry has on body ideals, especially on young people. 我们意识到时尚产业对理想身材的影响，尤其是对年轻人的影响，并为此承担责任。（2016年）

federal / ˈfedərəl / 035

释 *adj.* 联邦制的；联邦（政府）的

例 There are many reasons this formerly stable **federal** institution finds itself on the verge of bankruptcy. 这个昔日稳定的联邦机构发现自己濒临破产的原因有很多。（2018年）

observation / ˌɒbzəˈveɪʃn / 036

释 *n.* 观察；评论

例 While hunter-gatherer children learnt from **observation** and imitation in mixed-age playgroups, researchers said that western "instructive teaching", where pupils are asked to sit still, may contribute to conditions such as attention deficit hyperactivity disorder. 研究人员说，狩猎采集儿童在混合年龄游戏小组中通过观察和模仿来学习，而西方的"指令性教学"，要求学生坐着不动，可能会导致诸如注意缺陷多动障碍等疾病。（2024年）

uncover / ʌnˈkʌvə(r) / 037

释 *v.* 揭开，揭露
例 The police **uncovered** the cause of Tom's death. 警方揭开了汤姆死亡的原因。

comment / ˈkɒment / 038

释 *v.* 表达意见 *n.* 议论；评论；解释；批评；指责
例 To those of you in the **comments** section who are having strong feelings about artifacts being removed from cities in the U.S. and Britain and returned to their countries of origin, I would ask you to consider why do you think Americans have more of a right to easily access the Benin Bronzes than the people of Nigeria? 对于评论区中那些将文物从美国和英国的城市被移走并送回其原属国有强烈感受的人，我想请你们思考一下，为什么你们认为美国人比尼日利亚人民更有权利更容易看到贝宁青铜器？（2024年）

ability / əˈbɪləti / 039

释 *n.* 能力；才能；技能
搭 intellectual ability 智力
例 Waterstones are currently operating with reduced credit terms from PRH, the only publisher in the UK to place any limitations on our **ability** to trade. 目前，水石书店是在企鹅兰登降低了信贷条件下运营的，企鹅兰登是英国唯一一家对我们的贸易能力施加任何限制的出版商。（2023年）

vanity / ˈvænəti / 040

释 *n.* 虚荣（心）；自负
例 **Vanity** is a constant; people will only start shopping more sustainably when they can't afford not to. 虚荣心是永恒不变的；当人们无法承受不这样做时，他们只会开始更可持续地购物。（2013年）

soar / sɔː(r) / 041

释 *v.* 急升；猛涨
例 Prices are **soaring**, causing high inflation rate. 物价正在飞涨，造成了高通货膨胀率。

mood / muːd / 042

释 *n.* 心情，情绪；语气；气氛，氛围
例 But some of it remains in the brain, where it influences **mood**, behavior and physiology. 但其中一些仍留在大脑中，对情绪、行为和生理产生影响。（2017年）

publication / ˌpʌblɪˈkeɪʃn / 043

释 *n.* 出版；出版物；发表，公布
例 What is important is not truth, but **publication**, which has become almost an end in itself. 重要的不是真相，而是发表，发表本身几乎已成为目的了。（2019年）

nutrition / njuˈtrɪʃn /

释 *n.* 营养；滋养；营养的补给

例 It is like the immune system of the body, which under stress or through lack of **nutrition** or exercise can be weakened, but which never leaves us. 它就像人体的免疫系统，处于压力下或缺乏营养或运动时，免疫系统会被削弱，但它永远不会消失。（2016年）

force / fɔːs /

释 *n.* 武力；暴力；力量；影响大的人（或事物）；权力；兵力，武装力量 *v.* 促使；强迫；用力，强行

搭 come/enter into force（使法律、规则等）开始生效，开始实施

例 Then I counter with another reasonable argument: that a higher minimum wage will **force** businesses to employ fewer people for less time. 然后，我用另一个合理的论点来反驳：提高最低工资会迫使企业在更短的时间内雇用更少的人。（2019年）

派 enforce / ɪnˈfɔːs / *v.* 执行

近 compel / kəmˈpel / *v.* 迫使 ‖ oblige / əˈblaɪdʒ / *v.* 迫使

mark / mɑːk /

释 *n.* 污点；污渍；符号；记号；标志；迹象；表示 *v.* 做记号；做标记；留下痕迹；弄脏；标明方位；标示；成为……的征兆；打分，评分

搭 mark down 减价；打折；记下

例 Finally, assuming you're lost in an area humans tend to frequent, look for the **marks** we leave on the landscape. 最后，假设你在人类经常出现的地方迷路了，请寻找我们在景观上留下的记号。（2019年）

manipulate / məˈnɪpjuleɪt /

释 *v.*（暗中）操控，操纵；使用；影响

搭 manipulate sb. into (doing) sth. 操控某人做某事

例 Intelligence seeks to grasp, **manipulate**, re-order, and adjust, while intellect examines, ponders, wonders, theorizes, criticizes and imagines. 智力寻求的是领会、使用、重置和调节，而智慧寻求的是审视、思考、求真、推理、批判和想象。

pursue / pəˈsjuː /

释 *v.* 追求；努力实现；追赶；执行

搭 pursue a goal 追求目标

例 Rather than cloaking his exit in the usual vague excuses, he came right out and said he was leaving "to **pursue** my goal of running a company." 他没有像通常那样用含糊不清的借口来掩饰自己的离职，而是直截了当地说，他离职是"为了追求自己经营一家公司的目标"。（2011年）

Writing Models ◎

suicide

consistent

tolerant

acquire

skim

competition

stimulate

convey

estate

consumption

boost

professional

suicide / 'suːɪsaɪd /

049

释 *n.* 自杀; 自杀行为; 自杀者

搭 commit suicide 自杀

例 Seymour made the change, went into his backyard, and expressed his displeasure by committing **suicide**. 西摩做出了改变, 走进自家后院, 用自杀表达了他的不满。(2017年)

consistent / kən'sɪstənt /

050

释 *adj.* 始终如一的; 相符的; 一致的

例 While all of these countries face their own challenges, there are a number of **consistent** themes. 虽然所有这些国家都面临着各自的挑战, 但有一些主题是一致的。(2017年)

tolerant / 'tɒlərənt /

051

释 *adj.* 容忍的, 宽容的; 能耐……的

例 In many respects, the U.S. was more socially **tolerant** entering this widespread recession than at any time in its history, and a variety of national polls on social conflict since then have shown mixed results. 在这次广泛的经济衰退中, 美国在社会的很多方面都表现出前所未有的宽容, 从那时起, 关于社会矛盾的各种各样的全国性民意调查都显示出复杂多样的结果。

派 tolerance / 'tɒlərəns / *n.* 容忍, 宽容

acquire / ə'kwaɪə(r) /

052

释 *v.* 获得; 学到

例 Professionals trying to **acquire** new skills will be able to do so without going into debt. 努力学习新技能的专业人员将能够在不负债的情况下完成学业。(2018年)

近 obtain / əb'teɪn / *v.* 获得, 得到 ‖ gain / geɪn / *v.* 获得, 赢得

辨 acquire、obtain和gain都有"获得"的意思。acquire多指经过努力逐步获得才能、知识、习惯等; obtain为较正式用词, 指通过努力、要求而得到所需或盼望已久的东西; gain指取得某种利益或好处。

skim / skɪm /

053

释 *v.* 浏览, 略读

例 If you have nothing to do, you can **skim** the news of the day. 要是没事干, 你可以浏览一下今天的新闻。

competition / ˌkɒmpə'tɪʃn /

054

释 *n.* 比赛; 竞争; 竞争产品; 竞争对手

例 Your prospects would be almost as dismal if arguments were even just **competitions**—like, say, tennis games. 如果争论仅仅是比赛, 比如像是网球比赛, 你的前景几乎同样渺茫。(2019年)

stimulate / ˈstɪmjuleɪt / 05 5

释 v. 刺激, 激励

例 Likewise, automation should eventually boost productivity, **stimulate** demand by driving down prices, and free workers from hard, boring work. 同样, 自动化最终也会提高生产率, 通过降低价格来刺激需求, 并将工人从艰苦、枯燥的工作中解放出来。（2018年）

convey / kənˈveɪ / 05 6

释 v. 表达, 传递; 传达; 传送; 运送; 输送

例 In some settings, red sneakers or dress T-shirts can **convey** status; in others not so much. 在某些场合, 红色运动鞋或正装T恤可以传达身份地位, 但在其他场合则不尽然。（2016年）

estate / ɪˈsteɪt / 05 7

释 n. 庄园; 住宅区; 遗产; 个人财产

搭 real estate 房地产

例 The typical Chinese household only has access to a very limited range of savings and investments: essentially bank accounts, domestic stocks and real **estate**. 典型的中国家庭只能接触到非常有限的储蓄和投资: 基本上是银行储蓄、国内股市和房地产。

近 property / ˈprɒpəti / n. 财产 ‖ possession / pəˈzeʃn / n. 占有; 所有物

consumption / kənˈsʌmpʃn / 05 8

释 n. 消费; 消耗; 肺病

例 First, most people do not realise that there are strong commercial agendas at work to keep them in passive **consumption** mode. 首先, 大多数人并没有意识到, 有强烈的商业目的在起作用, 使他们处于被动消费状态。（2012年）

boost / buːst / 05 9

释 v. 使增长, 使兴旺; 提高, 提升 n. 推动力; 刺激; 增长

搭 boost up 提高, 增强

例 This would **boost** incomes, encourage work, reward companies for job creation, and reduce inequality. 这将提高收入, 鼓励工作, 奖励创造就业机会的公司, 并减少不平等现象。（2018年）

近 advance / ədˈvɑːns / v. 促进; 使加速 ‖ promote / prəˈməʊt / v. 提升; 促销

professional / prəˈfeʃənl / 06 0

释 adj. 专业的, 职业的 n. 专业人员

例 Enlist the support of **professionals** and share with them your goals and context. 争取专业人士的支持, 与他们分享你的目标和背景。（2016年）

反 amateur / ˈæmətə(r) / adj. 业余的; 外行的

Writing Models ◎

renaissance

alleviate

devote

persist

tend

routine

stretch

weigh

energy

contempt

result

renaissance / rɪˈneɪsns /   0 6 1

释 n.（欧洲14~17世纪的）文艺复兴，文艺复兴时期；新生

例 Hawaiian culture is not a relic of the past; it is a living culture undergoing a **renaissance** today. 夏威夷文化不是过去的遗迹，而是今天正在复兴的鲜活文化。（2017年）

近 revival / rɪˈvaɪvl / n. 苏醒；复兴 ‖ renewal / rɪˈnjuːəl / n. 复兴；恢复

alleviate / əˈliːvieɪt /   0 6 2

释 v. 减轻，缓和

例 The doctor gave her an injection to **alleviate** cold symptoms. 医生给她打了一针以缓解感冒症状。

派 alleviation / əˌliːviˈeɪʃn / n. 减轻；镇痛物

近 relieve / rɪˈliːv / v. 缓解，使轻松 ‖ ease / iːz / v. 减轻，减缓

devote / dɪˈvəʊt /   0 6 3

释 v. 献（身）；奉献，投入（时间、精力等）

搭 devote oneself to 献身；致力；专心

例 Human beings **devote** enormous time, energy and resources to taking care of our children and parents, our partners and friends, the sick and the needy, without expecting a return. 人类投入了大量的时间、精力和资源来照顾我们的子女和父母、伴侣和朋友、病人和有需要的人，却不求回报。

persist / pəˈsɪst /   0 6 4

释 v.（尤指不合意的事物）继续存在；坚持

搭 persist in 坚持……

例 The belief that the earth was flat **persisted** for many centuries. "地球是平的"这种看法持续了许多个世纪。

派 persistence / pəˈsɪstəns / n. 坚持；持续 ‖ persistent / pəˈsɪstənt / adj. 执着的；持续的

近 continue / kənˈtɪnju / v. 持续；不断发生 ‖ last / lɑːst / v. 持续

tend / tend /   0 6 5

释 v. 往往会，常常会；趋向；倾向；照料；照管；护理

例 Beethoven's music **tends** to move from chaos to order as if order were an imperative of human existence. 贝多芬的音乐倾向于从混乱走向秩序，仿佛秩序是人类生存的必然要求。（2014年）

routine / ruːˈtiːn /   0 6 6

释 n. 惯例；常规；例行公事 adj. 例行的；常规的；惯常的

例 Habits are a funny thing. We reach for them mindlessly, setting our brains on auto-pilot and relaxing into the unconscious comfort of familiar **routine**. 习惯是个有趣的东西。我们会不自觉地养成习惯，让大脑处于自动驾驶状态，在熟悉的例行公事中不知不觉地放松下来。（2009年）

.... ◎ Study Notes

`0 6 7`

stretch / stretʃ /

释 *n.* 伸展; 舒展; 一段时间; 一片, 一段; 弹性 *v.* 伸展; 舒展; 拉长; 伸出; 延伸; 绵延; 拉紧; 拉直; 包括, 涉及

搭 stretch out 躺下 (通常为休息或睡觉)‖ at full stretch 竭尽全力

例 At the same time, listening through earphones to the same monotonous beats for long **stretches** encourages kids to stay inside their bubble instead of pursuing other endeavors. 同时, 长时间通过耳机听着同样单调的节拍, 也会鼓励孩子们沉浸在自己的幻想中, 而不是去追求其他的东西。(2007年)

`0 6 8`

weigh / weɪ /

释 *v.* 有……重; 称重量; 认真考虑; 权衡; 有影响; 有分量

搭 weigh in 参加, 参与 (讨论等), 对……发表意见; 称重‖ weigh out 称出……的重量

例 A federal appeals court **weighed** in again Tuesday, but instead of providing a badly needed resolution, it only prolonged the fight. 联邦上诉法院周二再次介入, 但它非但没有提供一个急需的解决方案, 反而延长了这场斗争。(2021年)

`0 6 9`

energy / 'enədʒi /

释 *n.* 能源; 精力; 能量

搭 efficient energy 高效能源

例 Pat Hardy, who sympathises with the views of the **energy** sector, is resisting proposed changes to science standards for pre-teen pupils. 帕特·哈迪对能源部门的观点深表同情, 他正在抵制针对十岁刚出头的学生的科学标准修改建议。(2023年)

派 energetic / ˌenə'dʒetɪk / *adj.* 精力充沛的

`0 7 0`

contempt / kən'tempt /

释 *n.* 蔑视; 藐视, 不顾

例 He feels that wealthy people view him with **contempt** because he is poor. 他觉得有钱人看不起他, 因为他穷。

派 contemptible / kən'temptəbl / *adj.* 可鄙的

`0 7 1`

result / rɪ'zʌlt /

释 *n.* 结果; 后果; 成果; 成绩

搭 as a result 因此‖ as a result of 由于; 因为‖ result in 致使‖ result from 起因于

例 One possibility was that they merely used their eyes and tried out the plants they found, but that would probably **result** in a lot of wasted time and energy, not least because their eyesight is actually not very good. 一种可能是, 它们 (大象) 只是用眼睛看, 并尝试它们找到的植物, 但这可能会导致大量的时间和精力浪费, 尤其是因为它们的视力实际上并不是很好。(2024年)

win

residence

solid

raw

stability

integrate

pure

mention

excellent

durable

bring

urban

win / wɪn / 072

释 *v.* 获胜；赢得；取得

例 There is a better way to **win** arguments. 有一种更好的方法来赢得争论。（2019年）

派 winner / 'wɪnə(r) / *n.* 获胜的人

residence / 'rezɪdəns / 073

释 *n.* 住所；住房；居住；定居

例 The 1990 Census revealed that "a majority of immigrants from each of the fifteen most common countries of origin spoke English 'well' or 'very well' after ten years of **residence**." 1990年的人口普查显示，"来自15个最常见的原籍国的大多数移民在居住十年后英语都能说得'好'或'非常好'"。（2006年）

solid / 'sɒlɪd / 074

释 *adj.* 固体的；结实的；坚固的；可靠的；可信赖的；实心的；立体的；立方的 *n.* 固体；形状；立体图形

例 There is **solid** evidence that security cameras help solve crimes. 有可靠的证据表明，监控摄像头有助于破案。

派 solidity / sə'lɪdəti / *n.* 固态；坚固性；可靠性

raw / rɔː / 075

释 *adj.* 原始的；未经加工的；（食物）生的；粗犷的；没有经验的

例 The country has to import most of its **raw** materials. 那个国家不得不进口其大多数原料。

stability / stə'bɪləti / 076

释 *n.* 稳定（性）；稳固（性）

例 To be sure, the ability to consistently pay a dividend over a long time-span is often a mark of a company's **stability**. 可以肯定的是，在很长一段时间内持续支付股息的能力通常是公司稳定性的标志。

派 instability / ˌɪnstə'bɪləti / *n.* 不稳定；不稳固

integrate / 'ɪntɪɡreɪt / 077

释 *v.* （使）合并，成为一体；（使）加入

搭 integrate into（使）加入

例 And in Europe, some are up in arms over a proposal to drop a specific funding category for social-science research and to **integrate** it within cross-cutting topics of sustainable development. 在欧洲，一些人对取消社会科学研究专项经费类别，并将其纳入可持续发展横向专题的建议大为不满。（2013年）

派 integration / ˌɪntɪ'ɡreɪʃn / *n.* 结合，融合

pure / pjʊə(r) / `078`

释 *adj.* 纯粹的；洁净的

例 While some influencer restaurants might be vanity projects or **pure** money-making ventures, Jibawi says sharing his family's recipes—and staying true to them—is his ultimate motivation. 虽然一些网红餐厅可能是虚荣项目或纯粹的赚钱项目，但吉巴维说，分享他的家庭食谱——并忠于它们——是他的最终动机。

mention / ˈmenʃn / `079`

释 *v.* 提到；提及

例 He also found that, while the number of job postings that **mention** pensions remains low, that figure has shot up roughly 130 percent over the past three years. 他还发现，虽然提到养老金的招聘信息数量仍然很少，但这一数字在过去三年里飙升了大约130%。

excellent / ˈeksələnt / `080`

释 *adj.* 极好的；优秀的；好极了

例 Major retailers like Amazon and Macy's have truly **excellent** Black Friday sales including clothing deals on puffer jackets, trench coats, parkas, etc. 像亚马逊和梅西百货这样的大型零售商的"黑色星期五"都有非常棒的促销活动，包括超轻款羽绒服、风衣、派克大衣等服装优惠。

派 excellence / ˈeksələns / *n.* 优秀；杰出；卓越

durable / ˈdjʊərəbl / `081`

释 *adj.* 耐用的；持久的

例 He wanted viewers to walk around on the carpets—which meant they had to be **durable**. 他想让观众在地毯上走来走去，这意味着地毯必须耐用。（2022年）

派 durability / ˌdjʊərəˈbɪləti / *n.* 持久性，耐用性

bring / brɪŋ / `082`

释 *v.* 带来；取来；提供；供给

搭 bring about 引起，导致 ‖ bring up 提出；养育

例 Besides helping you feel close and connected to people you care about, it turns out that hugs can **bring** a host of health benefits to your body and mind. 事实证明，拥抱除了能让你感到与你关心的人亲密无间之外，还能为你的身心带来诸多健康益处。（2017年）

urban / ˈɜːbən / `083`

释 *adj.* 城市的；都市的

例 We do not ruin **urban** conservation areas. Why ruin rural ones? 我们不破坏城市保护区。那为什么要破坏农村地区呢？（2016年）

反 rural / ˈrʊərəl / *adj.* 乡村的；农村的

Writing Models ◎ ⋯⋯⋯⋯

record
⁰⁸⁴

释 / 'rekɔːd / n. 记录; 纪录 / rɪ'kɔːd / v. 记录; 记载

例 Now, with **record**-high home prices and historically low inventory, there's an increased urgency in such regulation, particularly among those who worry that developers will come in and buy up swaths of housing to flip for a fortune on the short-term rental market. 如今, 在房价创历史新高、库存处于历史低位的情况下, 这样的监管措施变得越来越紧迫, 尤其是那些担心开发商会进来买下大片房屋, 然后在短期租赁市场上大赚一笔的人。(2023年)

exaggerate / ɪg'zædʒəreɪt /
⁰⁸⁵

释 v. 夸张; 夸大; 突出

例 She **exaggerates** the existing panic. 她夸大了现有的恐慌。(2023年)

派 exaggerated / ɪg'zædʒəreɪtɪd / adj. 夸大的; 故作姿态的 ‖ exaggeration / ɪgˌzædʒə'reɪʃn / n. 夸大; 夸张

welfare / 'welfeə(r) /
⁰⁸⁶

释 n. 幸福; 福利

例 The principle of British **welfare** is no longer that you can insure yourself against the risk of unemployment and receive unconditional payments if the disaster happens. 英国的福利原则不再是你可以为自己投保以抵御失业风险, 以及如果灾难发生, 你可以无条件地领取失业救济金。(2014年)

近 well-being / 'wel biːɪŋ / n. 健康; 安乐; 康乐

eclipse / ɪ'klɪps /
⁰⁸⁷

释 v. 使相形见绌; 使失色; 遮住……的光; 使丧失重要性 n. (重要性、权势等的)丧失, 黯然失色, 暗淡; 日食; 月食

例 With the Church's teachings and ways of thinking being **eclipsed** by the Renaissance, the gap between the Medieval and modern periods had been bridged, leading to new and unexplored intellectual territories. 随着文艺复兴使教会的教义及其思维方式黯然失色, 中世纪和现代之间的鸿沟才得以弥合, 从而带来了新的、无人涉足的知识领域。(2020年)

skeptical / 'skeptɪkl /
⁰⁸⁸

释 adj. 表示怀疑的

搭 be skeptical about/of 对……持怀疑态度

例 But banks' shares trade below their book value, suggesting that investors are **skeptical**. 但银行股的交易价格低于其账面价值, 这表明投资者持怀疑态度。(2010年)

boil / bɔɪl /
⁰⁸⁹

释 v. (使)沸腾; 烧开

例 Doubtless a piece of **boiled** beef can always be served up on Sunday alongside some steamed vegetables, without the Yorkshire pudding and no wine. 毫无疑问, 在周日, 一块煮牛肉总是可以和一些蒸蔬菜一起端上来, 不需要约克郡布丁, 也不需要葡萄酒。(2020年)

hit / hɪt /

090

🔘 *v.* 击，打；碰撞；打击；危害 *n.* 打；击；击中；风行一时的流行歌曲（或唱片）

📖 "The visualization, particularly those photographs, really **hit** home that this is something that has to be protected," says Alicia Murphy, Yellowstone's park historian. 黄石公园的历史学家艾丽西亚·墨菲说："可视化，尤其是那些照片，真的让人深刻意识到这是必须受到保护的东西。"（2023年）

landscape / ˈlændskeɪp /

091

🔘 *n.* 风景，景色；乡村风景画

📖 Last year marked the 150th anniversary of a series of Yellowstone photographs by the renowned **landscape** photographer William Henry Jackson. 去年是著名风景摄影师威廉·亨利·杰克逊拍摄黄石公园系列照片150周年。（2023年）

近 scenery / ˈsiːnəri / *n.* 风景；景色；风光

lure / lʊə(r) /

092

🔘 *v.* 劝诱；引诱；诱惑 *n.* 诱惑力；魅力；鱼饵；诱饵

📖 And since these messages have an agenda—to **lure** us to open our wallets—they make the very idea of happiness seem unreliable. 由于这些信息有一个目的——引诱我们打开钱包——它们使幸福的概念看起来不可靠。（2006年）

近 entice / ɪnˈtaɪs / *v.* 诱使；引诱

preference / ˈprefrəns /

093

🔘 *n.* 偏爱；爱好；偏爱的事物

搭 in preference to 相较于；而不是；优先于

📖 For example, AI can be used to analyse what type of advertising content or copy would be appropriate to "speak" to a specific target customer group by revealing information about trends and **preferences** through the analysis of big data. 例如，人工智能可以通过分析大数据来揭示趋势和偏好信息，从而被用来分析哪种类型的广告内容或文案适合与特定的目标客户群体"对话"。（2023年）

cruel / ˈkruːəl /

094

🔘 *adj.* 残酷的；冷酷的；残忍的；残暴的；引起痛苦的

📖 As a zoology professor, I agree with Emma Marris that zoo displays can be sad and **cruel**. 作为一名动物学教授，我同意艾玛·马里斯的观点，动物园的表演可能是悲伤、残酷的。（2022年）

派 cruelty / ˈkruːəlti / *n.* 残酷，残忍，残暴；残暴的行为

disturb / dɪˈstɜːb /

095

🔘 *v.* 打扰；干扰；妨碍；搅乱；弄乱

📖 She doesn't want to be **disturbed** while she's working. 她工作时不想被打扰。

Writing Models ◎

transparent

surgery

block

global

widespread

096

transparent / træns'pærənt /

释 *adj.* 透明的；清澈的

例 So does the idea that decisions made by AI systems should be explainable, **transparent**, and fair. 人工智能系统做出的决定应该是可解释的、透明的和公平的。（2019年）

派 transparency / træns'pærənsi / *n.* 透明；透明性

097

surgery / 'sɜːdʒəri /

释 *n.* 外科手术；诊室；门诊处；应诊时间

例 Or, put another way, expert performers—whether in memory or **surgery**, ballet or computer programming—are nearly always made, not born. 或者，换句话说，专业的高手——无论是在记忆方面还是外科手术方面，在芭蕾方面还是计算机编程方面——几乎都是后天培养出来的，而不是天生的。（2007年）

098

block / blɒk /

释 *n.* 大楼，大厦；（长方形）块，大块；街区 *v.* 堵塞；阻塞；堵住；阻止；妨碍

搭 block in 阻挡，挡住 ‖ block out 挡住，遮住

例 In the meantime, the court threw out the FCC's attempt to **block** all state rules on net neutrality, while preserving the commission's power to preempt individual state laws that undermine its order. 与此同时，最高法院驳回了联邦通信委员会试图阻止所有州关于网络中立性的规定的企图，同时保留了委员会先发制人的权力，以防止个别州的法律破坏它的秩序。（2021年）

099

global / 'gləʊbl /

释 *adj.* 全球的；全世界的

例 According to a study by Catalyst, between 2010 and 2015 the share of women on the boards of **global** corporations increased by 54 percent. 根据Catalyst的一项研究，2010年至2015年间，全球企业董事会中，女性的比例增加了54%。（2020年）

派 globalization / ˌgləʊbələr'zeɪʃn / *n.* 全球化；传播，流传

100

widespread / 'waɪdspred /

释 *adj.* 广泛的；普遍的；分布广的

例 Court, school, organizations of amateurs, and the traveling actors were all rivals in supplying a **widespread** desire for dramatic entertainment; and no boy who went to a grammar school could be ignorant that the drama was a form of literature which gave glory to Greece and Rome and might yet bring honor to England. 宫廷、学校、业余爱好者组织和巡回演出者在满足人们对戏剧娱乐的广泛渴望方面都是竞争对手；而且上过文法学校的男孩都不会不知道，戏剧是一种文学形式，它给希腊和罗马带来了荣耀，也可能给英国带来荣耀。（2018年）

Review

- ☐ ☐ ability
- ☐ ☐ acquire
- ☐ ☐ alleviate
- ☐ ☐ assume
- ☐ ☐ aware
- ☐ ☐ block
- ☐ ☐ boast
- ☐ ☐ boil
- ☐ ☐ boost
- ☐ ☐ bring
- ☐ ☐ candidate
- ☐ ☐ comment
- ☐ ☐ competition
- ☐ ☐ consistent
- ☐ ☐ consumption
- ☐ ☐ contemplate
- ☐ ☐ contempt
- ☐ ☐ convey
- ☐ ☐ criterion
- ☐ ☐ cruel
- ☐ ☐ deal
- ☐ ☐ deny
- ☐ ☐ devote
- ☐ ☐ discipline
- ☐ ☐ disturb
- ☐ ☐ durable
- ☐ ☐ ease
- ☐ ☐ eclipse
- ☐ ☐ energy
- ☐ ☐ equality
- ☐ ☐ estate

- ☐ ☐ exaggerate
- ☐ ☐ excellent
- ☐ ☐ feat
- ☐ ☐ federal
- ☐ ☐ force
- ☐ ☐ form
- ☐ ☐ global
- ☐ ☐ grant
- ☐ ☐ hit
- ☐ ☐ impair
- ☐ ☐ incredible
- ☐ ☐ integrate
- ☐ ☐ intense
- ☐ ☐ invent
- ☐ ☐ investigate
- ☐ ☐ justice
- ☐ ☐ landscape
- ☐ ☐ lure
- ☐ ☐ manipulate
- ☐ ☐ mark
- ☐ ☐ mention
- ☐ ☐ mood
- ☐ ☐ nutrition
- ☐ ☐ observation
- ☐ ☐ persist
- ☐ ☐ pit
- ☐ ☐ preference
- ☐ ☐ privacy
- ☐ ☐ professional
- ☐ ☐ promise
- ☐ ☐ propaganda

- ☐ ☐ publication
- ☐ ☐ pure
- ☐ ☐ pursue
- ☐ ☐ raw
- ☐ ☐ recite
- ☐ ☐ record
- ☐ ☐ renaissance
- ☐ ☐ resemble
- ☐ ☐ residence
- ☐ ☐ responsibility
- ☐ ☐ result
- ☐ ☐ routine
- ☐ ☐ series
- ☐ ☐ set
- ☐ ☐ skeptical
- ☐ ☐ skim
- ☐ ☐ soar
- ☐ ☐ solid
- ☐ ☐ stability
- ☐ ☐ stimulate
- ☐ ☐ stretch
- ☐ ☐ strip
- ☐ ☐ suicide
- ☐ ☐ surgery
- ☐ ☐ tend
- ☐ ☐ terror
- ☐ ☐ tolerant
- ☐ ☐ transparent
- ☐ ☐ uncover
- ☐ ☐ underlying
- ☐ ☐ urban

- ☐ ☐ vanity
- ☐ ☐ weave
- ☐ ☐ weigh
- ☐ ☐ welfare
- ☐ ☐ widespread
- ☐ ☐ win
- ☐ ☐ worth

音频

☐ relieve	☐ recur	☐ extra	☐ target
☐ comparable	☐ natural	☐ debate	☐ beat
☐ phenomenon	☐ heighten	☐ affect	☐ antique
☐ overlook	☐ summon	☐ scale	☐ variety
☐ assess	☐ abstract	☐ justify	☐ addition
☐ asset	☐ remind	☐ displace	☐ cooperate
☐ democratic	☐ quota	☐ genius	☐ bare
☐ attendant	☐ require	☐ figure	
☐ legitimate	☐ sole	☐ adopt	
☐ enthusiasm	☐ accumulate	☐ pace	
☐ convention	☐ loyalty	☐ fill	
☐ crucial	☐ concentrate	☐ recover	
☐ immediate	☐ illustrate	☐ tense	
☐ community	☐ verge	☐ program	
☐ erect	☐ conceive	☐ possess	
☐ artistic	☐ rural	☐ treasure	
☐ vital	☐ imagine	☐ symptom	
☐ typical	☐ occupy	☐ pioneer	
☐ conspiracy	☐ urge	☐ root	
☐ detect	☐ provoke	☐ eminent	
☐ appear	☐ account	☐ except	
☐ weird	☐ resolution	☐ cure	
☐ guilty	☐ faculty	☐ angle	
☐ lean	☐ confusion	☐ monitor	
☐ pursuit	☐ reflect	☐ clinic	
☐ classify	☐ information	☐ height	
☐ evidence	☐ destruction	☐ decorate	
☐ scrap	☐ revise	☐ myth	
☐ spy	☐ promote	☐ pollution	
☐ ally	☐ regulate	☐ ritual	
☐ extravagant	☐ disclose	☐ twist	

relieve / rɪˈliːv / 　　　　　　　　　　001

释 v. 缓解, 减轻; 使解脱; 使解除(职务)

例 She became immensely **relieved** when she knew the result. 知道结果后, 她大大松了一口气。

comparable / ˈkɒmpərəbl / 　　　　　　002

释 adj. (数量、重要性等)相当的; 可比较的

例 The author believes that exploring one's phone contents is **comparable** to getting into one's residence. 作者认为, 探查一个人的手机内容就相当于进入一个人的住所。(2015年)

phenomenon / fəˈnɒmɪnən / 　　　　　　003

释 n. [pl. phenomena] 现象

搭 the social phenomenon 社会现象

例 If you then examined the European national youth teams that feed the World Cup and professional ranks, you would find this strange **phenomenon** to be even more pronounced. 如果你再考察一下为世界杯和职业球队输送人才的欧洲国家青年队, 你会发现这种奇怪的现象甚至更加明显。(2007年)

overlook / ˌəʊvəˈlʊk / 　　　　　　　　004

释 v. 忽略; 不予理会; 俯视; 眺望

例 Its negative effects on businesses are often **overlooked**. 它对企业的负面影响往往被忽视。(2016年)

assess / əˈses / 　　　　　　　　　　　005

释 v. 评估; 计算, 估算

例 Insurance companies, meanwhile, can base their premiums on AI models that more accurately **assess** risk. 与此同时, 保险公司可以根据能更准确评估风险的人工智能模型来确定保费。(2021年)

派 assessable / əˈsesəbl / adj. 可估价的 ‖ assessment / əˈsesmənt / n. 估价

近 evaluate / ɪˈvæljueɪt / v. 评价; 估价 ‖ estimate / ˈestɪmeɪt / v. 估计, 估量; 估价

辨 assess指为确定某物的价值而进行的权威估价; evaluate强调在确定价值时经过了深思熟虑; estimate强调评价的主观性和不精确性。

asset / ˈæset / 　　　　　　　　　　　006

释 n. 资产, 财产; 有价值的人(或物)

搭 liquid assets 流动资产 ‖ net assets 净资产

例 America's new plan to buy up toxic **assets** will not work unless banks mark **assets** to levels which buyers find attractive. 除非银行将资产标记到买家认为有吸引力的水平, 否则美国收购有毒资产的新计划将不会奏效。(2010年)

近 property / ˈprɒpəti / n. 财产; 所有物

democratic / ˌdeməˈkrætɪk /

007

释 *adj.* 民主的；民主管理的；[D-]（美国）民主党的

搭 democratic society 民主社会

例 If connections can be bought, a basic premise of **democratic** society—that all are equal in treatment by government—is undermined. 如果人脉可以被收买，民主社会的一个基本前提——政府对所有人一视同仁——就会遭到破坏。（2017年）

attendant / əˈtendənt /

008

释 *adj.* 伴随的，随之而来的 *n.* 服务员；随从，侍从

例 Even demographics are working against the middle class family, as the odds of having a weak elderly parent—and all the **attendant** need for physical and financial assistance—have jumped eightfold in just one generation. 甚至连人口统计数据也对中产阶级家庭不利，因为父母年迈体弱的几率——以及随之而来的对身体和经济援助的需求——在短短一代人的时间里猛增了八倍。（2007年）

近 subsequent / ˈsʌbsɪkwənt / *adj.* 后来的；随后的

legitimate / lɪˈdʒɪtɪmət /

009

释 *adj.* 合法的；正当合理的

例 As *Nature* has pointed out before, there are some **legitimate** concerns about how science prizes—both new and old—are distributed. 正如《自然》杂志之前指出的那样，人们对新老科学奖项的颁发方式有一些合理的担忧。（2014年）

enthusiasm / ɪnˈθjuːziæzəm /

010

释 *n.* 热情，热心

例 No disciplines have seized on professionalism with as much **enthusiasm** as the humanities. 没有哪个学科像人文学科那样对专业性如此热情。（2011年）

convention / kənˈvenʃn /

011

释 *n.* 常规，惯例；习俗；（国家或首脑间的）公约，协定；大会，集会

搭 social convention 社会惯例

例 He freed music from hitherto prevailing **conventions** of harmony and structure. 他将音乐从迄今为止流行的和声与结构的惯例中解放出来。（2014年）

近 custom / ˈkʌstəm / *n.* 惯例；习俗 ‖ tradition / trəˈdɪʃn / *n.* 传统，惯例

crucial / ˈkruːʃl /

012

释 *adj.* 至关重要的；决定性的

搭 play a crucial role/part in sth. 在……中扮演至关重要的角色

例 If we are ever going to protect the atmosphere, it is **crucial** that those new plants be environmentally sound. 如果我们要保护大气环境，那么让这些新建的工厂对环境无害是至关重要的。（2005年）

immediate

community

erect

artistic

vital

typical

conspiracy

detect

appear

weird

guilty

lean

immediate / ɪˈmiːdiət / 013

释 *adj.* 立即的，立刻的；目前的；迫切的；直接的；直系的
搭 immediate feedback 即时反馈 ‖ immediate family 直系亲属
例 Perhaps willfully, it may be easier to think about such lengthy timescales than about the more **immediate** future. 也许是有意为之，考虑如此漫长的时间尺度可能比考虑更直接的未来更容易。（2013年）
近 instant / ˈɪnstənt / *adj.* 立即的，即刻的 ‖ prompt / prɒmpt / *adj.* 立刻的；迅速的

community / kəˈmjuːnəti / 014

释 *n.* 界；社区；社会；团体
例 Another measure could be encouraging friendships between children in different school years to mirror the unsupervised mixed-age playgroups in hunter-gatherer **communities**. 另一项措施可以是鼓励不同学年的孩子之间建立友谊，模仿狩猎采集者社区中无人监管的混龄游戏小组。（2024年）

erect / ɪˈrekt / 015

释 *adj.* 直立的；垂直的 *v.* 树立，建立
例 This monument was **erected** in honor of the martyrs during the internal war. 这座纪念碑是为了纪念在内战中牺牲的烈士们而建立的。

artistic / ɑːˈtɪstɪk / 016

释 *adj.* 艺术（家）的，美术（家）的
搭 artistic abilities 艺术才能
例 These recordings are cheap, available everywhere, and very often much higher in **artistic** quality than today's live performances; moreover, they can be "consumed" at a time and place of the listener's choosing. 这些录音价格低廉，随处可得，艺术质量往往比今天的现场表演高出许多；此外，听众还可以在自己选择的时间和地点对其"消费"。（2011年）

vital / ˈvaɪtl / 017

释 *adj.* 必不可少的；对……极重要的；充满生机的；热情洋溢的
例 Pricing is **vital** to environment-friendly purchasing. 定价对环保采购至关重要。（2013年）

typical / ˈtɪpɪkl / 018

释 *adj.* 典型的；特有的；一贯的
例 The discovery of the Higgs boson is a **typical** case which involves the joint effort of modern researchers. 希格斯玻色子的发现是现代研究人员共同努力的一个典型事例。（2014年）

conspiracy / kən'spɪrəsi /

079

释 *n.* 共谋; 阴谋

例 We successfully thwarted the enemy's **conspiracy**. 我们成功地挫败了敌人的阴谋。

detect / dɪ'tekt /

020

释 *v.* 探测; 察觉; 发现, 查明

例 Scopus itself has all the data necessary to **detect** this malpractice. Scopus本身拥有发现这种不当行为所需的所有数据。（2023年）

派 detection / dɪ'tekʃn / *n.* 察觉; 侦查 ‖ detective / dɪ'tektɪv / *n.* 侦探; 警探

appear / ə'pɪə(r) /

021

释 *v.* 看起来; 出现; 产生; 出场; 出版

例 Since students and parents expect a college degree to lead to a job, it is in the best interest of a school to turn out graduates who are as qualified as possible—or at least **appear** to be. 由于学生和家长都期望大学学位能带来一份工作，因此对学校最有利的就是培养出尽可能合格的毕业生——至少看起来是合格的。（2019年）

派 appearance / ə'pɪərəns / *n.* 外貌, 外观

weird / wɪəd /

022

释 *adj.* 不自然的; 怪异的, 古怪的; 不寻常的

例 I found some of her novels a bit **weird**. 我觉得她的一些小说有点儿怪。

近 odd / ɒd / *adj.* 古怪的

guilty / 'ɡɪlti /

023

释 *adj.* 内疚的; 犯罪的; 罪恶的; 有过失的

搭 be guilty of (a crime) 犯有……罪

例 It can be inferred from Paragraph 3 that more journalists may be found **guilty** of phone hacking. 从第三段可以推断，可能会有更多的记者被判犯有电话窃听罪。（2015年）

lean / liːn /

024

释 *v.* 身体倾斜; 靠 (在……上); 倾斜 *adj.* 脂肪少的; 贫乏的; 清瘦而健康的

搭 lean on 依靠, 依赖

例 The man was staggering and had to **lean** on the table. 那个男人走路摇摇晃晃，不得不靠在桌子上。

近 depend / dɪ'pend / *v.* 依靠, 依赖

辨 lean和depend都有"依靠"的意思。lean指为获取帮助或支持而依靠; depend更加侧重抽象意义上的依靠, 如精神依靠。

Writing Models ◎

pursuit

classify

evidence

scrap

spy

ally

extravagant

recur

natural

heighten

summon

abstract

remind

pursuit / pə'sjuːt / 025

释 *n.* 追赶，追求；消遣活动

例 The New England colonies were the scenes of important episodes in the **pursuit** of widely understood ideals of civility and virtuosity. 在人们追求普遍理解的文明和高尚理想上，新英格兰殖民地是重要事件的发生地。（2009年）

classify / 'klæsɪfaɪ / 026

释 *v.* 将……分类；将……归类；划分，界定

例 In Spain, there have been rules for **classifying** wine since 1982, with the lower run of the designation labeled cosechas, which are inexpensive wines aged fewer than three months. 在西班牙，葡萄酒的分类规则从1982年开始就有了，其中较低一级的名称标签为cosechas，即陈酿时间少于三个月的廉价葡萄酒。

evidence / 'evɪdəns / 027

释 *n.* 根据；证明；证据；证词；人证；物证 *v.* 证明；表明；作为……的证据

搭 (be) in evidence 显眼；显而易见

例 Perhaps most importantly, these images provided documentary **evidence** that later made its way to government officials. 也许最重要的是，这些图像提供了书面证据，后来传到了政府官员手里。（2023年）

scrap / skræp / 028

释 *v.* 废除；抛弃；报废；取消；打架 *n.* 小块；碎片；废品；打架

例 The committee has **scrapped** the current way of choosing host cities. 委员会废除了现行的选择主办城市的方法。

spy / spaɪ / 029

释 *n.* 间谍；密探 *v.* 从事间谍活动；搜集情报

例 There may have been many **spies** and intelligence officers during the Napoleonic Wars, but it is usually extremely difficult to find the material they actually provided or worked on. 拿破仑战争期间可能有许多间谍和情报人员，但通常很难找到他们实际提供或研究的材料。（2022年）

ally / 'ælaɪ / 030

释 *v.* （使）结盟 *n.* 同盟国；伙伴

搭 ally with 与……结盟

例 During World War II, Great Britain **allied** with the United States. 二战期间，英美两国结了盟。

extravagant / ɪk'strævəgənt / 031

释 *adj.* 奢侈的，浪费的；消费过多的

例 Martin was so **extravagant** that he was always in debt. 马丁消费太多，以至于他总是负债累累。

recur / rɪˈkɜː(r) / [0]3[2]

释 v. 重现; 复发

例 Cartwright believes one can exercise conscious control over **recurring** bad dreams. 卡特赖特认为，人们可以练习有意识地控制反复出现的噩梦。（2005年）

派 recurrence / rɪˈkʌrəns / n. 重现; 再发生

natural / ˈnætʃrəl / [0]3[3]

释 adj. 自然的; 正常的; 天赋的; 本能的

搭 natural resources 自然资源 ‖ natural selection 自然选择

例 Zoos are at the forefront of conservation and constantly evolving to improve how they care for animals and protect each species in its **natural** habitat. 动物园是保护动物的前沿阵地，它们在不断改进照料动物的方式，以及保护自然栖息地里的每个物种。（2022年）

heighten / ˈhaɪtn / [0]3[4]

释 v. 加强, 提高; 增加

例 Talent is one of the largest expenses on a company's balance sheet, but employers are not ignorant of the consequences of widespread layoffs, such as knowledge loss, **heightened** anxiety for remaining employees, and even the immediate financial cost of letting people go. 人才是公司资产负债表上最大的支出之一，但雇主们并非不知道大范围裁员的后果，如知识流失、留守员工焦虑加剧，甚至提高了辞退员工的直接经济成本。

summon / ˈsʌmən / [0]3[5]

释 v. 召集; 召唤

例 The pupils were **summoned** in the school hall. 学生们被召集到了学校的礼堂。

abstract [0]3[6]

释 / ˈæbstrækt / adj. 抽象的; 深奥的 n. 摘要; 抽象; 抽象派作品 / æbˈstrækt / v. 提取, 分离; 写出摘要

例 He asserted, also, that his power to follow a long and purely **abstract** train of thought was very limited, for which reason he felt certain that he never could have succeeded with mathematics. 他还断言，他的能力非常有限，无法按照纯粹抽象的思路进行长时间的思考，因此他认为自己在数学方面注定无法取得成功。（2008年）

remind / rɪˈmaɪnd / [0]3[7]

释 v. 提醒; 使想起

搭 remind sb. of sb./sth. 使某人想起

例 **Remind** the person that this is your point of view, and then invite critique. Be open to hearing other opinions. 提醒对方这是你的观点，然后请他批评。要虚心听取其他意见。

quota / ˈkwəʊtə /

038

释 *n.* 定额，限额，配额

搭 output quotas *产品定额*

例 In order to ensure that elite women have more such opportunities, they have proposed imposing government **quotas**. 为了确保精英女性有更多这样的机会，她们建议实行政府配额制。（2020年）

require / rɪˈkwaɪə(r) /

039

释 *v.* 需要；要求

例 The bills are similar to a measure recently adopted in California, which last year became the first state to **require** gender quotas for private companies. 这些法案与加利福尼亚州最近通过的一项措施类似，该州去年成为第一个要求私营公司实行性别配额的州。（2020年）

sole / səʊl /

040

释 *adj.* 唯一的，仅有的；专有的 *n.* 脚底；鞋底（不包括后跟）*v.* 给（鞋）换底

例 In some families of that country, the man is the **sole** wage earner. 在那个国家的某些家庭中，男人是唯一赚薪水的人。

accumulate / əˈkjuːmjəleɪt /

041

释 *v.* 积累；积聚；（数量）逐渐增加；（数额）逐渐增长

例 The scientific community measures the quality of those papers in a number of ways, including the perceived quality of the journal (as reflected by the title's impact factor) and the number of citations a specific paper **accumulates**. 科学界通过多种方式来衡量这些论文的质量，包括对期刊品质的认知（期刊名称的影响因子反映了这一点）以及特定论文累积的引用次数。（2023年）

loyalty / ˈlɔɪəlti /

042

释 *n.* 忠诚；忠实；忠心耿耿

例 Transient investors, who demand high quarterly profits from companies, can hinder a firm's efforts to invest in long-term research or to build up customer **loyalty**. 短期的投资者要求公司每季度获得高额利润，这会阻碍公司投资于长期研究或建立客户忠诚度的努力。（2019年）

concentrate / ˈkɒnsntreɪt /

043

释 *v.* 集中（心思）；专心；使清楚地思考

搭 concentrate on *专心于*

例 Ms. Denham chose to **concentrate** the blame on the NHS trust, since under existing law it "controlled" the data and DeepMind merely "processed" it. 德纳姆女士选择将责任集中在NHS信托公司身上，因为根据现行法律，它"控制"了数据，而DeepMind只是"处理"了数据。（2018年）

illustrate / ˈɪləstreɪt /

044

释 v.（用示例、图画）说明，解释；加插图于；显示……存在

例 The U.S. and France examples are used to **illustrate** the approaches to promoting "long-termism". 美国和法国的例子是用来说明促进 "长期主义" 的方法。（2019年）

派 illustration / ˌɪlə'streɪʃn / n. 实例；插图

verge / vɜːdʒ /

045

释 n. 边，边缘 v. 濒临，接近

搭 on the verge of 接近于，濒于

例 John's eyes are half closed and it looks like he's on the **verge** of falling asleep. 约翰双眼半睁，看上去好像快睡着了。

conceive / kənˈsiːv /

046

释 v. 想象；相信；认为；设想；怀孕

搭 conceive of (doing) sth. 设想（做）某事

例 **Conceived** in this way, comprehension will not follow exactly the same track for each reader. 在这样的构思下，每个读者的理解不会完全遵循相同的轨迹。（2015年）

派 conception / kənˈsepʃn / n. 构想；怀孕

近 imagine / ɪ'mædʒɪn / v. 想象，设想

rural / ˈrʊrəl /

047

释 adj. 农村的，乡村的

例 That's likely because the **rural** poor are using the money as makeshift insurance policies against inclement weather, Ferraro says. 费拉罗说，这很可能是因为农村贫困人口把这些钱当作应对恶劣天气的临时保险单。（2021年）

imagine / ɪ'mædʒɪn /

048

释 v. 想象，设想；认为，猜测；误以为；胡乱猜想

例 It is difficult to the point of impossibility for the average reader under the age of forty to **imagine** a time when high-quality arts criticism could be found in most big-city newspapers. 对于40岁以下的普通读者来说，想象一个在大多数大城市的报纸上还能看到高水平的艺术评论的时代，几乎不可能。（2010年）

occupy / ˈɒkjupaɪ /

049

释 v. 使用，占用；侵占；占领；任职；忙着（做某事）

例 The theatre has broken attendance records for three years in a row. Last year its 1,431 seats were 94 percent **occupied** all year long and this year they'll do better. 剧院已连续三年打破上座率记录。去年，1 431个座位的全年使用率达到了94%，今年的情况会更好。（2006年）

Writing Models ◎

urge

provoke

account

resolution

faculty

confusion

reflect

information

destruction

revise

promote

regulate

urge / ɜːdʒ /

释 v. 敦促; 催促; 力劝; 竭力主张; 驱赶 n. 强烈的欲望; 冲动

例 There is no doubt that gardens evidence an irrepressible **urge** to create, express, fashion, and beautify and that self-expression is a basic human **urge**. 毫无疑问, 花园表明一种不可抑制的创造、表达、塑造和美化的欲望, 而且自我表达是人类的一种基本的欲望。(2013年)

provoke / prəˈvəʊk /

释 v. 激起, 引起; 刺激; 挑衅, 激怒

搭 provoke sb. into (doing) sth. 刺激某人去做某事

例 Second, novelty itself frequently **provokes** disbelief. 其次, 新奇事物本身经常会引起人们的怀疑。(2012年)

近 irritate / ˈɪrɪteɪt / v. 刺激; 激怒

account / əˈkaʊnt /

释 v. (在数量、比例方面)占; 说明, 解释 n. 账目; 账户

搭 account for (在数量、比例方面)占; 说明 (原因等) ‖ take... into account 考虑

例 There's no change to collective bargaining at the USPS, a major omission considering that personnel **accounts** for 80 percent of the agency's costs. 美国邮政的集体谈判没有变化, 考虑到人事费用占该机构支出的80%, 这是一个重大疏漏。(2018年)

resolution / ˌrezəˈluːʃn /

释 n. 决心; 正式决议

例 Always bear in mind that your own **resolution** to succeed is more important than anything else. 要永远记住: 自己想要成功的决心比其他任何事情都重要。

faculty / ˈfæklti /

释 n. 机能; 天赋; 全体教员; (高等院校的)系, 院

例 In the 1960s and 1970s, European universities saw marked changes in their governance arrangements, with the empowerment of junior **faculty** and to some degree of students as well. 20世纪60年代和70年代, 欧洲大学的管理安排发生了显著变化, 青年教师获得了权力, 学生也在一定程度上获得了权力。(2021年)

confusion / kənˈfjuːʒn /

释 n. 困惑; 不确定; 混淆; 混乱局面; 困窘; 局促不安

搭 confusion over/about 关于……的困惑

例 She looked at me in **confusion** and did not know what to do next. 她困惑地看着我, 不知道接下来该做什么。

reflect / rɪ'flekt / 056

释 *v.* 反映; 表现; 显示; 反射; 想到（某事）

搭 reflect on 深思

例 And third, growth was **reflected** in changes in the proportion of the relevant age group enrolled in institutions of higher education. 第三，增长反映在相关年龄组在高等教育机构就读比例的变化上。（2021年）

information / ˌɪnfə'meɪʃn / 057

释 *n.* 信息;（计算机程序储存和使用的）数据; 情报; 资料

例 If customers are not willing to share data, AI will be starved of essential **information** and will not be able to function effectively or employ machine learning to improve its marketing content and communication. 如果客户不愿意分享数据，人工智能就会缺乏必要的信息，从而无法有效发挥作用，或者无法利用机器学习来改进营销内容和沟通。（2023年）

destruction / dɪ'strʌkʃn / 058

释 *n.* 破坏; 摧毁; 毁坏; 毁灭

例 To paraphrase the great social scientist Joseph Schumpeter: there is no radical innovation without creative **destruction**. 套用伟大的社会学家约瑟夫·熊彼特的一句话：没有创造性的破坏，就没有彻底的创新。（2013年）

revise / rɪ'vaɪz / 059

释 *v.* 修改，修订; 修正（对某事的想法）; 复习

例 We reason together, challenge, **revise**, and complete each other's reasoning and each other's conceptions of reason. 我们共同推理、质疑、修改并且完善彼此的推理以及推理概念。（2012年）

派 revision / rɪ'vɪʒn / *n.* 修订; 修改

近 review / rɪ'vjuː / *v.* 复习 ‖ amend / ə'mend / *v.* 改善; 修改

promote / prə'məʊt / 060

释 *v.* 促进; 推动; 促销; 推销; 提升; 晋升; 晋级

例 We have to suspect that continuing economic growth **promotes** the development of education even when governments don't force it. 我们不得不怀疑，即使政府不推进，持续的经济增长也会促进教育的发展。（2009年）

regulate / 'reɡjuleɪt / 061

释 *v.* 调节，控制（速度、压力、温度等）;（用规则、条例）约束，控制，管理

例 For AI to be successful, data needs to be accessible, but the use of personal data is becoming more **regulated** and the automated sharing of data is becoming more difficult. 人工智能要想取得成功，就必须能够获取数据，但个人数据的使用正受到更多的监管，数据的自动共享也变得更困难。（2023年）

近 adjust / ə'dʒʌst / *v.* 调节 ‖ manage / 'mænɪdʒ / *v.* 管理

disclose / dɪsˈkləʊz / 062

释 v.（尤指在被隐瞒后）透露；揭露；泄露；公开（某事）

例 Meanwhile, the theft of information about some 40 million credit-card accounts in America, **disclosed** on June 17th, overshadowed a decision a day earlier by America's Federal Trade Commission (FTC) that puts corporate America on notice that regulators will act if firms fail to provide adequate data security. 与此同时，6月17日披露的美国约4 000万个信用卡账户信息被盗事件，为一天前美国联邦贸易委员会（FTC）做出的一项决定蒙上了阴影，该决定提醒美国企业，如果公司未能提供足够的数据安全，监管机构将采取行动。（2007年）

派 disclosure / dɪsˈkləʊʒə(r) / n. 揭发；披露

近 reveal / rɪˈviːl / v. 显示，揭露

反 conceal / kənˈsiːl / v. 隐藏，隐瞒 ‖ hide / haɪd / v. 隐藏，隐瞒

extra / ˈekstrə / 063

释 adj. 额外的

例 It could make **extra** training and instruction affordable. 它可以使额外的培训和指导变得能负担得起。（2018年）

debate / dɪˈbeɪt / 064

释 n. 争论，辩论，讨论 v. 辩论；考虑

例 Today, the social sciences are largely focused on disciplinary problems and internal scholarly **debates**, rather than on topics with external impact. 如今，社会科学主要侧重于学科问题和内部学术争论，而不是具有外部影响的课题。（2013年）

affect / əˈfekt / 065

释 v. 影响；使感染；感动；假装

例 Stringent job dismissal regulations adversely **affect** productivity growth and hamper both prosperity and overall well-being. 严苛的解雇规定对生产力的增长产生了不利影响，阻碍了繁荣和整体福祉。（2022年）

scale / skeɪl / 066

释 n. 规模；范围；等级；音阶；秤；鳞

搭 on a large scale 大规模地

例 We're also giving our customers better channels versus picking up the phone to accomplish something beyond human **scale**. 我们还为客户提供了更好的渠道，而不是拿起电话就能完成超越人力规模的任务。（2021年）

近 scope / skəʊp / n. 范围；机会

justify / ˈdʒʌstɪfaɪ / 067

释 v. 证明（其正当性），证实；是……的正当理由；调整

例 How can Britain's train operators possibly **justify** yet another increase to rail passenger fares? 英国的火车运营商怎么可能有理由再次提高铁路乘客票价？（2021年）

派 justification / ˌdʒʌstɪfɪˈkeɪʃn / n. 辩护

displace / dɪsˈpleɪs / 068

释 *v.* 取代, 代替

例 The Industrial Revolution didn't go so well for Luddites whose jobs were **displaced** by mechanized looms, but it eventually raised living standards and created more jobs than it destroyed. 对于那些被机械化织布机取代了工作的卢德分子来说, 工业革命并不顺利, 但它最终提高了生活水平, 创造的就业机会多于破坏的就业机会。（2018年）

genius / ˈdʒiːniəs / 069

释 *n.* 天才, 天赋; 才能; 天才人物

例 In the course of my long life, I've known two real **geniuses**. 在我漫长的一生中, 我结识过两位真正的天才。

近 talent / ˈtælənt / *n.* 天赋; 才能 ‖ gift / ɡɪft / *n.* 天赋; 礼物

辨 genius、talent和gift都有"天赋"的意思。genius语气最强, 指极高的天赋与智力; talent指人在某方面具有突出的才能, 但语气比genius弱; gift指个人的天赋才能或在某方面的显著本领, 常暗含不能用一般规律做解释的意味。

figure / ˈfɪɡə(r) / 070

释 *n.* 数字; 身影; 人像; 重要人物; 图表; 数字符号; 位数 *v.* 认为; 猜想; 估计; 出现; 显出……的样子

搭 figure out 弄清楚; 弄明白; 计算

例 "There is a coalition growing within artist industries to **figure** out how to tackle or mitigate this," says Ortiz. 奥尔蒂斯说: "艺术家行业内部正在形成一个联盟, 共同研究如何解决或缓解这一问题。"（2024年）

adopt / əˈdɒpt / 071

释 *v.* 采用; 采取; 收养

例 Among the most popular: paternity and kinship testing, which **adopted** children can use to find their biological relatives and families can use to track down kids put up for adoption. 其中最受欢迎的是亲子鉴定和亲属鉴定, 被收养的孩子可以用这种方法找到他们的生物学上的亲属, 而家庭可以用这种方法找到被收养的孩子。（2009年）

派 adoption / əˈdɒpʃn / *n.* 采用; 收养; 领养 ‖ adoptive / əˈdɒptɪv / *adj.* 收养的; 有收养关系的

pace / peɪs / 072

释 *n.* 速度; 步速; 节奏; 迅速出现（或变化等）

搭 keep pace (with)（与……）并驾齐驱;（与……）步调一致

例 Overall, Europe's wholesale market for food and drink is growing at the same sluggish **pace** as the retail market, but the figures, when added together, mask two opposing trends. 总体而言, 欧洲食品和饮料批发市场的增长速度与零售市场的增长速度一样缓慢, 但这些数据加在一起时, 会掩盖这两种相反的趋势。（2020年）

fill

recover

tense

program

possess

treasure

symptom

pioneer

root

eminent

except

cure

073

fill / fɪl /

释 *v.* （使）充满，装满，注满，填满

搭 fill in 填写；填满；打发（时间）‖ fill up（使）填满；充满

例 *Join the Club* is **filled** with too much irrelevant detail and not enough exploration of the social and biological factors that make peer pressure so powerful. 《加入俱乐部》充满了太多无关紧要的细节信息，而针对社会和使同辈压力如此强大的生物因素的探究却不够深入。（2012年）

074

recover / rɪˈkʌvə(r) /

释 *v.* 恢复健康；复原；好转，扭转；恢复；重新找到，重新拿回

例 The chip industry, which was in a prolonged slump, has largely **recovered** due to factors like demand for AI. 受人工智能需求等因素的影响，曾长期低迷的芯片行业已基本复苏。

派 recovery / rɪˈkʌvəri / *n.* 恢复；痊愈；好转；复苏

075

tense / tens /

释 *adj.* 紧张的；焦虑的；无法放松的；（肌肉）紧绷的 *n.* 时态

例 Older generations often talk about their degree in the present and personal **tense**: "I am a geographer" or "I am a classist". 老一辈的人经常用现在时态和个人角度来谈论他们的学位："我是地理学家"或"我是一个阶级主义者"。（2022年）

076

program / ˈprəʊɡræm /

释 *n.* 程序；计划；方案；节目 *v.* 编写程序

例 The zoology **program** at my university attracts students for whom zoo visits were the crucial formative experience that led them to major in biological sciences. 我所在大学的动物学项目吸引了很多学生，对他们来说，参观动物园是促使他们主修生物科学的重要成长经历。（2022年）

077

possess / pəˈzes /

释 *v.* 拥有；具有（特质）

例 Beginning in 2006, some scientists have argued that plants **possess** neuron-like cells that interact with hormones and neurotransmitters, forming "a plant nervous system, analogous to that in animals," said lead study author Lincoln Taiz. 从2006年开始，一些科学家认为植物拥有与激素和神经递质相互作用的神经元样细胞，形成了"植物神经系统，类似动物的神经系统"，该研究的主要作者林肯·塔伊兹说。（2022年）

派 possession / pəˈzeʃn / *n.* 具有；拥有

078

treasure / ˈtreʒə(r) /

释 *n.* 极贵重的物品；珍宝；财富 *v.* 珍视；珍爱

例 The virgin forest with its richness and variety of trees was a real **treasure**-house which extended from Maine all the way down to Georgia. 枝繁叶茂、树木种类繁多的原始森林是一座从缅因州一直绵延到佐治亚州的真正的天然宝库。（2015年）

symptom / 'sɪmptəm / 079

释 n. 症状；征兆

例 This was also found in high-functioning men with some autistic spectrum **symptoms**, who may tend to avoid eye contact. 在有一些自闭症谱系症状的高功能男性中也发现了这种情况，他们可能倾向于回避目光接触。（2020年）

pioneer / ˌpaɪə'nɪə(r) / 080

释 n. 先驱；先锋；开发者；拓荒者 v. 当开拓者；做先锋

例 Certain artifacts are especially vulnerable because some **pioneers** in plastic art didn't always know how to mix ingredients properly, says Thea van Oosten, a polymer chemist who, until retiring a few years ago, worked for decades at the Cultural Heritage Agency of the Netherlands. 聚合物化学家西娅·范·奥斯滕在荷兰文化遗产局工作了几十年，直到几年前才退休，她说，某些文物特别脆弱，因为一些造型艺术的先驱并不总是知道如何正确地混合成分。（2022年）

root / ruːt / 081

释 n. 根；根源；起因 v.（使）生根

搭 take root 生根 ‖ root up 连根拔起

例 The idea that plants have some degree of consciousness first took **root** in the early 2000s. 植物有某种程度的意识这一观点最早是在21世纪初生根发芽的。（2022年）

eminent / 'emɪnənt / 082

释 adj. 卓越的；有名望的；著名的；杰出的

例 This description even fits the majority of **eminent** scholars. 这一描述甚至适用于大多数著名学者。（2006年）

except / ɪk'sept / 083

释 prep. 除……之外 conj. 除了

例 Robert F. Kennedy once said that a country's GDP measures "everything **except** that which makes life worthwhile." 罗伯特·F. 肯尼迪曾经说过，一个国家的GDP衡量的是"除了让生活有价值的东西之外的一切"。（2017年）

派 exception / ɪk'sepʃn / n. 例外 ‖ exceptional / ɪk'sepʃənl / adj. 特别的；杰出的

cure / kjʊə(r) / 084

释 v. 治愈，治好 n. 药；药物；治疗；措施，对策

例 But on the general effectiveness of the social **cure**, Rosenberg is less persuasive. 但就社会治疗的总体效果而言，罗森博格的说法不那么有说服力。（2012年）

angle / 'æŋgl / [0][8][5]

释 *n.* 角；角度；观点；立场；侧重点；倾向性 *v.*（使）朝向；（使）转向

例 But privacy is not the only **angle** in this case and not even the most important. 但隐私并不是本案的唯一侧重点，甚至也不是最重要的观点。（2018年）

monitor / 'mɒnɪtə(r) / [0][8][6]

释 *n.* 显示屏；监视器；班长；监督员 *v.* 监视；监听

例 Board members like her "casually dismiss the career work of scholars and scientists as just another misguided opinion," says Dan Quinn, senior communications strategist at the Texas Freedom Network, a non-profit group that **monitors** public education. 得克萨斯自由网络是一个监督公共教育的非营利组织，该组织的高级传播策略师丹·奎恩表示，像她这样的董事会成员都"随意地将学者和科学家的职业工作视为另一种误导的观点"。（2023年）

clinic / 'klɪnɪk / [0][8][7]

释 *n.* 诊所；（医院的）门诊部

例 The link between dreams and emotions shows up among the patients in Cartwright's **clinic**. 梦和情绪之间的联系在卡特赖特诊所的病人身上得到了体现。（2005年）

height / haɪt / [0][8][8]

释 *n.* 高度；身高；高；高处

例 And if you need to predict human **height** in the near future to design a piece of equipment, Gordon says that by and large, "you could use today's data and feel fairly confident." 戈登说，如果你需要预测人类在不久的将来的身高，以便设计一种设备，总的来说，"你可以使用当今的数据，且可以感到相当自信"。（2008年）

派 heighten / 'haɪtn / *v.*（使）加强，提高，增加

decorate / 'dekəreɪt / [0][8][9]

释 *v.* 装饰；装潢；点缀；装点

例 Those pieces included small beds of roses and other items as well as a few dozen "nature carpets"—large rectangles **decorated** with foam pumpkins, cabbages, and watermelons. 这些作品包括小型玫瑰花床和其他物品，以及几十个"自然地毯"——用泡沫南瓜、卷心菜和西瓜装饰的大长方形地毯。（2022年）

派 decoration / ˌdekə'reɪʃn / *n.* 装饰；装潢；装饰品；装饰风格

myth / mɪθ / [0][9][0]

释 *n.* 神话；神话故事；谬见

例 They perpetuate the **myth** of the lone genius. 它们（奖项）延续了孤独天才的神话。（2014年）

pollution / pəˈluːʃn /   0 9 1

释 *n.* 污染; 污染物

例 This can provide for reduced road congestion, less parking space requirement, and lower air **pollution**. 这可以减少道路拥堵，减少停车位需求，并降低空气污染水平。

ritual / ˈrɪtʃuəl /   0 9 2

释 *n.* 宗教仪式; 典礼; 习俗 *adj.* 仪式性的; 传统的; 习惯性的

例 Parts of the ceremony involve **ritual** hair cutting, tying cotton threads soaked in holy water around the bride's and groom's wrists, and passing a candle around a circle of happily married and respected couples to bless the union. 婚礼的部分仪式包括传统的剪头发，将浸过圣水的棉线绑在新娘和新郎的手腕上，并在一圈幸福的已婚夫妇和受人尊敬的夫妇周围传递蜡烛，以祝福他们的结合。(2016年)

twist / twɪst /   0 9 3

释 *v.* 扭曲; 拧; 扭伤; 转动 *n.* 扭动; 转折，转变; 曲折处

例 Like Dakhil, Sarandon's words were quickly **twisted** and weaponized against her. 和达希尔一样，萨兰登的话很快就被曲解，变成了针对她的武器。

target / ˈtɑːɡɪt /   0 9 4

释 *n.* 目标; 指标; 靶子 *v.* 面向，把……对准

搭 target at 以……为目标

例 Digital services include everything from providing a platform for selling goods and services online to **targeting** advertising based on user data, and the tax applies to gross revenue from such services. 数字服务包括所有服务，从提供线上销售商品和服务的平台，到基于用户数据的定向广告，而该税适用于此类服务的总收入。(2020年)

beat / biːt /   0 9 5

释 *v.* 赢，打败; 难倒 *n.* (鼓的)一击; (心脏等的)跳动; 节拍

例 These tools can help you win every argument—not in the unhelpful sense of **beating** your opponents but in the better sense of learning about the issues that divide people, learning why they disagree with us and learning to talk and work together with them. 这些工具可以帮助你赢得每一场争论——不是毫无用处地打败对手，而是更好地了解导致人们产生分歧的问题，了解他们为什么不同意我们的观点，并学会与他们交谈和合作。(2019年)

antique / ænˈtiːk /   0 9 6

释 *n.* 古董

例 There is so much comedic talent among these four actors crammed into that little, cluttered **antique** shop. 挤在那间杂乱无章的小古董店里的这四位演员的喜剧天赋实在是太高了。

Writing Models ◎ ┄┄┄┄┄

variety

addition

cooperate

bare

variety / vəˈraɪəti /

097

釋 *n.* 不同种类, 多种式样; 多样化; 品种; 变体

搭 a variety of 各种各样的

例 The **variety** of plastic objects at risk is dizzying: early radios, avant-garde sculptures, celluloid animation stills from Disney films, the first artificial heart. 面临风险的塑料制品种类之多令人眼花缭乱: 早期的收音机、前卫的雕塑、迪士尼电影中的胶片动画剧照、第一颗人造心脏。(2022年)

addition / əˈdɪʃn /

098

釋 *n.* 加; 加法; 增加; 增加物

搭 in addition (to) 除……以外 (还)

例 In **addition** to the entourage of scientists, the team also included artists: Painter Thomas Moran and photographer Jackson were charged with capturing this astounding natural beauty and sharing it with the world. 除了科学家的随行人员外, 该团队还包括艺术家: 画家托马斯·莫兰和摄影师杰克逊负责抓拍并与全世界分享这一惊人的自然美景。(2023年)

cooperate / kəʊˈɒpəreɪt /

099

釋 *v.* 合作; 协作; 协助; 配合

例 That's because Congress has always envisioned joint federal-state immigration enforcement and explicitly encourages state officers to share information and **cooperate** with federal colleagues. 这是因为国会一直都希望联邦政府和州政府能够联合执行移民法, 并明确鼓励州政府官员与联邦政府的官员分享信息和合作。(2013年)

派 cooperation / kəʊˌɒpəˈreɪʃn / *n.* 合作; 协作

bare / beə(r) /

100

釋 *adj.* 荒芜的; 裸露的; 空的; 仅够的

例 If it clears the House, this measure would still have to get through the Senate—where someone is bound to point out that it amounts to the **bare**, **bare** minimum necessary to keep the Postal Service afloat, not comprehensive reform. 如果这项措施在众议院获得通过, 那么它还需要在参议院获得通过——在参议院, 肯定会有人指出, 这只是维持邮政服务运转所需的最基本、最起码的措施, 而不是全面的改革。(2018年)

Review

- ☐ ☐ abstract
- ☐ ☐ account
- ☐ ☐ accumulate
- ☐ ☐ addition
- ☐ ☐ adopt
- ☐ ☐ affect
- ☐ ☐ ally
- ☐ ☐ angle
- ☐ ☐ antique
- ☐ ☐ appear
- ☐ ☐ artistic
- ☐ ☐ assess
- ☐ ☐ asset
- ☐ ☐ attendant
- ☐ ☐ bare
- ☐ ☐ beat
- ☐ ☐ classify
- ☐ ☐ clinic
- ☐ ☐ community
- ☐ ☐ comparable
- ☐ ☐ conceive
- ☐ ☐ concentrate
- ☐ ☐ confusion
- ☐ ☐ conspiracy
- ☐ ☐ convention
- ☐ ☐ cooperate
- ☐ ☐ crucial
- ☐ ☐ cure
- ☐ ☐ debate
- ☐ ☐ decorate
- ☐ ☐ democratic

- ☐ ☐ destruction
- ☐ ☐ detect
- ☐ ☐ disclose
- ☐ ☐ displace
- ☐ ☐ eminent
- ☐ ☐ enthusiasm
- ☐ ☐ erect
- ☐ ☐ evidence
- ☐ ☐ except
- ☐ ☐ extra
- ☐ ☐ extravagant
- ☐ ☐ faculty
- ☐ ☐ figure
- ☐ ☐ fill
- ☐ ☐ genius
- ☐ ☐ guilty
- ☐ ☐ height
- ☐ ☐ heighten
- ☐ ☐ illustrate
- ☐ ☐ imagine
- ☐ ☐ immediate
- ☐ ☐ information
- ☐ ☐ justify
- ☐ ☐ lean
- ☐ ☐ legitimate
- ☐ ☐ loyalty
- ☐ ☐ monitor
- ☐ ☐ myth
- ☐ ☐ natural
- ☐ ☐ occupy
- ☐ ☐ overlook

- ☐ ☐ pace
- ☐ ☐ phenomenon
- ☐ ☐ pioneer
- ☐ ☐ pollution
- ☐ ☐ possess
- ☐ ☐ program
- ☐ ☐ promote
- ☐ ☐ provoke
- ☐ ☐ pursuit
- ☐ ☐ quota
- ☐ ☐ recover
- ☐ ☐ recur
- ☐ ☐ reflect
- ☐ ☐ regulate
- ☐ ☐ relieve
- ☐ ☐ remind
- ☐ ☐ require
- ☐ ☐ resolution
- ☐ ☐ revise
- ☐ ☐ ritual
- ☐ ☐ root
- ☐ ☐ rural
- ☐ ☐ scale
- ☐ ☐ scrap
- ☐ ☐ sole
- ☐ ☐ spy
- ☐ ☐ summon
- ☐ ☐ symptom
- ☐ ☐ target
- ☐ ☐ tense
- ☐ ☐ treasure

- ☐ ☐ twist
- ☐ ☐ typical
- ☐ ☐ urge
- ☐ ☐ variety
- ☐ ☐ verge
- ☐ ☐ vital
- ☐ ☐ weird

Previous Check

- [ ] hostage
- [ ] preach
- [ ] improve
- [ ] impression
- [ ] pressure
- [ ] employ
- [ ] render
- [ ] largely
- [ ] conclude
- [ ] compare
- [ ] category
- [ ] accomplish
- [ ] restore
- [ ] attend
- [ ] ideology
- [ ] senior
- [ ] provide
- [ ] warrant
- [ ] seal
- [ ] owe
- [ ] plead
- [ ] essential
- [ ] companion
- [ ] historic
- [ ] advocate
- [ ] image
- [ ] decline
- [ ] bleed
- [ ] stock
- [ ] influential
- [ ] eliminate

- [ ] security
- [ ] presence
- [ ] senator
- [ ] discover
- [ ] sufficient
- [ ] carry
- [ ] decisive
- [ ] character
- [ ] impact
- [ ] workout
- [ ] resort
- [ ] competitive
- [ ] element
- [ ] construct
- [ ] obstacle
- [ ] remain
- [ ] purpose
- [ ] specify
- [ ] specific
- [ ] monopoly
- [ ] feature
- [ ] commerce
- [ ] ruin
- [ ] evolution
- [ ] species
- [ ] habitat
- [ ] massacre
- [ ] forgive
- [ ] differ
- [ ] investment
- [ ] crisis

- [ ] regime
- [ ] synthetic
- [ ] scatter
- [ ] mission
- [ ] adhere
- [ ] passion
- [ ] struggle
- [ ] contract
- [ ] rule
- [ ] network
- [ ] receipt
- [ ] carrier
- [ ] amount
- [ ] navy
- [ ] innocent
- [ ] argu(e)ment
- [ ] shed
- [ ] size
- [ ] melt
- [ ] flow
- [ ] shadow
- [ ] agency
- [ ] motive
- [ ] score
- [ ] heroic
- [ ] equipment
- [ ] fragile
- [ ] apt
- [ ] enlighten
- [ ] mixture
- [ ] rank

- [ ] praise
- [ ] joint
- [ ] desperate
- [ ] trick
- [ ] ambition
- [ ] fluid
- [ ] underline

hostage / 'hɒstɪdʒ / 〔001〕

释 *n.* 人质

搭 hold/take sb. hostage 把某人持为人质

例 The gunman told the police to back off or he would shoot a **hostage**. 持枪歹徒要求警方退后，否则他就要枪杀一名人质。

preach / priːtʃ / 〔002〕

释 *v.* 讲道，布道；宣扬，宣讲

例 He was always **preaching** the advantages of capitalism. 他总是鼓吹资本主义的长处。

派 preachy / 'priːtʃi / *adj.* 说教的；劝诫的

近 sermonize / 'sɜːmənaɪz / *v.* 说教；布道

improve / ɪm'pruːv / 〔003〕

释 *v.* 改进；提高；康复

例 Technology will **improve** society in ways big and small over the next few years, yet this will be little comfort to those who find their lives and careers upended by automation. 在未来几年里，技术将以大大小小的方式改善社会，但这对那些发现自己的生活和事业被自动化颠覆的人来说，并不是什么安慰。（2018年）

impression / ɪm'preʃn / 〔004〕

释 *n.* 印象；影响；效果；压痕；（虚假的）外观；感想；印象画；重印本

例 Concluding paragraphs demand equal attention because they leave the reader with a final **impression**. 结尾段落同样需要关注，因为它们会给读者留下最后的印象。（2008年）

pressure / 'preʃə(r) / 〔005〕

释 *n.* 压力 *v.* 对……施加压力

例 He gave in to the social **pressures** to act and dress like everybody else. 他屈服于社会压力，在行为和穿着上与其他人无异。

employ / ɪm'plɔɪ / 〔006〕

释 *v.* 采用；雇用；使忙于 *n.* 使用；雇用

例 During peak avalanche season, the center **employs** three full-time avalanche forecasters to monitor weather, snowpack and other conditions to issue the daily forecast. 在雪崩高峰期，该中心聘用了三名全职雪崩预报员，负责监测天气、积雪和其他情况，以发布每日预报。

派 employee / ɪm'plɔɪiː / *n.* 雇员 ‖ employer / ɪm'plɔɪə(r) / *n.* 雇主

render / 'rendə(r) / 〔007〕

释 *v.* 使成为，使变得；给予，提供；递交；表达

例 The news **rendered** her speechless. 这个消息使她一时说不出话来。

largely / 'lɑːdʒli /

释 *adv.* 大部分，主要地，基本上，在很大程度上；大规模地，大量地

例 He has failed to understand that monarchies have **largely** survived because they provide a service—as non-controversial and non-political heads of state. 他不明白，君主制之所以得以延续，在很大程度上是因为它们提供了一种服务——作为不具争议性和非政治性的国家元首。（2015年）

conclude / kən'kluːd /

释 *v.* 得出结论，推断出；（使）结束；订立，缔结（协定）

例 "Many young people assume a great deal of personal responsibility for educating themselves and actively seeking out opposing viewpoints," the survey **concluded**. 调查得出结论："许多年轻人在自我教育和积极寻求反对观点方面要承担很大的个人责任。"（2018年）

派 conclusion / kən'kluːʒn / *n.* 结论；推论

近 infer / ɪn'fɜː(r) / *v.* 推断；推论 ‖ deduce / dɪ'djuːs / *v.* 推断；演绎出

compare / kəm'peə(r) /

释 *v.* 比较；对比；与……类似（或相似）；将……比作 *n.* 比较

搭 beyond/without compare 无与伦比；举世无双

例 They cannot be **compared** to works of art produced for sale which can be passed from hand to hand and place to place by purchase. 它们不能与为销售而制作的艺术品相提并论，因为后者可以通过购买从一个人手中传到另一个人手中，从一个地方传到另一个地方。（2024年）

category / 'kætəgəri /

释 *n.* 种类，类别；范畴

例 This **category** is the one most likely to involve different hair types (fine, medium, or thick) and also combine wavy and coily strands. 这一类最有可能涉及不同的发质（细、中或粗），同时也结合了波浪状和卷曲状发丝。

accomplish / ə'kʌmplɪʃ /

释 *v.* 完成；实现；达到

例 In fact, instead of straining muscles to build them, as exercise does, laughter apparently **accomplishes** the opposite. 事实上，笑声并不像运动那样使肌肉紧张，看来它起到相反的作用。（2011年）

restore / rɪ'stɔː(r) /

释 *v.* 恢复；修复

例 If you've explored the area before, keep an eye out for familiar sights—you may be surprised how quickly identifying a distinctive rock or tree can **restore** your bearings. 如果你以前探索过该地区，请留意熟悉的景象——你可能会惊讶地发现，认出一块独特的岩石或一棵树能让你如此迅速地恢复你的方位。（2019年）

近 recover / rɪ'kʌvə(r) / *v.* 恢复 ‖ repair / rɪ'peə(r) / *v.* 修理；恢复

Writing Models ◎

attend

ideology

senior

provide

warrant

seal

owe

plead

essential

companion

historic

advocate

attend / əˈtend / 　014

释 *v.* 出席；参加；上（学）；去（教堂）；照顾；陪伴

搭 attend to sb./sth. 处理；对付；照料；关怀

例 3,000 people from around the world were invited to **attend** the conference. 来自世界各地的3 000人应邀出席了会议。

派 attendance / əˈtendəns / *n.* 出席；上学

ideology / ˌaɪdiˈɒlədʒi / 　015

释 *n.* 思想体系，思想意识；意识形态

例 The rise of anti-happy art almost exactly tracks the emergence of mass media, and with it, a commercial culture in which happiness is not just an ideal but an **ideology**. 反快乐艺术的兴起几乎与大众传媒的兴起如出一辙，随之而来的是一种商业文化，在这种文化中，快乐不仅是一种理想，更是一种意识形态。（2006年）

senior / ˈsiːniə(r) / 　016

释 *adj.* 级别高的，资深的；（比赛）成人的；较年长的；高水平的 *n.* 高年级学生；资深运动员

例 The decision to quit a **senior** position to look for a better one is unconventional. 辞去高级职位去寻找一个更好的职位是个不因循守旧的决定。（2011年）

provide / prəˈvaɪd / 　017

释 *v.* 提供；规定；供应；给予

例 The industry also claims that people who lay fake grass spend an average of £500 on trees or shrubs for their garden, which **provides** habitat for insects. 该行业还声称，铺设假草的人平均花费500英镑为他们的花园购买树木或灌木，这为昆虫提供了栖息地。

warrant / ˈwɒrənt / 　018

释 *n.* 正当理由；搜查令；拘捕令 *v.* 保证，担保；批准

搭 warrant for sth./doing sth. 做某事的正当理由

例 The Supreme Court will now consider whether police can search the contents of a mobile phone without a **warrant** if the phone is on or around a person during an arrest. 最高法院现在将审议，在逮捕过程中，如果手机在某人身上或周围，警方是否可以在没有搜查令的情况下搜查手机内容。（2015年）

seal / siːl / 　019

释 *v.* 封住；封闭；封锁；粘住（信封）*n.* 印章；印记；封条；火漆；密封处；海豹

搭 under seal （文件）密封；加盖印信

例 The crew released carbon dioxide into the hold and **sealed** it over concerns of an explosion. 由于担心发生爆炸，全体船员向船舱释放了二氧化碳，并将其封闭。

owe / əʊ /
020

釋 *v.* 欠; 感激; 应给予; 得益于; 应该把……归功于

搭 owing to 由于; 因为

例 Customers were generally responsible for paying the sales tax to the state themselves if they weren't charged it, but most didn't realize they **owed** it and few paid. 如果州政府没有向顾客收取销售税，顾客一般有责任自己向州政府缴纳，但大多数顾客并没有意识到自己应缴纳销售税，也很少有人缴纳。（2019年）

plead / pliːd /
021

釋 *v.* 恳求, 乞求; 为……辩护; 以……为借口

搭 plead for/against 为……辩护 ‖ plead with sb. 恳求某人

例 The lady **pleaded** with her son to come back home. 这位女士恳求她的儿子回家。

近 appeal / ə'piːl / *v.* 恳求; 上诉

essential / ɪ'senʃl /
022

釋 *adj.* 必要的, 必不可少的; 本质的, 基本的 *n.* 必需品; 必不可少的东西

搭 be essential to 对……是必不可少的

例 By all accounts he was a freethinking person, and a courageous one, and I find courage an **essential** quality for the understanding, let alone the performance, of his works. 无论从哪个角度看，他都是一个思想自由、勇敢的人，而且我发现勇气是理解他的作品的基本品质，更不用说表演他的作品了。（2014年）

companion / kəm'pænjən /
023

釋 *n.* 伙伴, 同伴; 伴侣; 陪伴; 陪护; （用于书名）指南, 手册

例 We became **companions** in misfortune. 我们成了患难之交。

historic / hɪ'stɒrɪk /
024

釋 *adj.* 有历史意义的; 历史的

搭 historic site 古迹

例 It is a **historic** meeting between the two leaders. 这是两位领导人之间一次具有历史意义的会晤。

advocate
025

釋 / 'ædvəkət / *n.* 倡导者; 辩护律师; 为（某团体）谋利益者
/ 'ædvəkeɪt / *v.* 拥护; 鼓吹, 提倡

例 In New Hampshire, where the rental vacancy rate has dropped below 1 percent, housing **advocates** fear unchecked short-term rentals will put further pressure on an already strained market. 在新罕布什尔州，房屋出租空置率已降至1%以下，住房倡导者担心，不加控制的短期租赁将给本已紧张的市场带来更大压力。（2023年）

image / 'ɪmɪdʒ / 026

释 *n.* 形象; 印象; 声誉; 图像; 画像; 雕像

搭 be the image of sb./sth. 极像某人/某物; 和……几乎完全一样

例 Artists say they risk losing income as people start using AI-generated **images** based on copyrighted material for commercial purposes. 艺术家们说, 由于人们开始将基于版权材料的人工智能生成图像用于商业目的, 他们面临着失去收入的风险。(2024年)

近 impression / ɪm'preʃn / *n.* 印象

decline / dɪ'klaɪn / 027

释 *v.* 下降; 减少; 衰退; 衰落; 婉拒; 谢绝 *n.* 下降; 减少; 衰落

搭 in decline/on the decline 正在衰退

例 Some of the **decline** was expected, and revenue projections were lowered in those categories in the city's new budget. 其中一些下降是预料之中的, 并且在该城市新的预算中, 这些类别的收入预测被下调了。

bleed / bliːd / 028

释 *v.* 流血; 使出血; 榨取 (某人的钱); 渗开

例 He is **bleeding** me for every penny I have. 他在榨取我的每一分钱。

stock / stɒk / 029

释 *n.* 股份, 股票; 贮存量

例 The average time for holding a **stock** in both the United States and Britain, he notes, has dropped from seven years to seven months in recent decades. 他指出, 近几十年来, 在美国和英国, 人们持有一只股票的平均时间都从七年降到了七个月。(2019年)

influential / ˌɪnfluˈenʃl / 030

释 *n.* 有影响力的人或物 *adj.* 有影响的, 有影响力的; 有权势的

搭 be influential in 对……有影响

例 The committee was **influential** in formulating government policy on employment. 该委员会在制定政府就业政策方面具有影响力。

eliminate / ɪ'lɪmɪneɪt / 031

释 *v.* 消除; 根除; 消灭; (比赛中) 淘汰

例 It's past time for transparency with these institutions, and it's past time to **eliminate** zoos from our culture. 是时候让这些机构透明化了, 也是时候从我们的文化中消除动物园了。(2022年)

security / sɪ'kjʊərəti / 032

释 *n.* 安全; 安全措施; 有价证券

例 Yes, there is the risk that the original country will not have as good **security** as do the foreign countries. 是的, 存在这样一种风险, 即原属国的安全状况不如外国好。(2024年)

◎ Study Notes

033
presence / 'prezns /

释 *n.* 出席，到场；存在；出现；仪态；风度；气质

搭 in the presence of sth. 存在……的情况下；有……的存在

例 The ruling is a victory for big chains with a **presence** in many states, since they usually collect sales tax on online purchases already. 这一裁决对于在许多州都有业务的大型连锁店来说是一场胜利，因为它们通常已经对网上购物征收销售税。（2019年）

反 absence / 'æbsəns / *n.* 缺席；缺乏

034
senator / 'senətə(r) /

释 *n.* 参议员

例 **Senator** Smith spoke at length about the proposed legislation. 史密斯参议员就所提立法议案做了详细的发言。

035
discover / dɪ'skʌvə(r) /

释 *v.* （第一个）发现；（出乎意料地）发现，找到；了解到；认识到；查明

例 I first **discovered** the Napoleonic code-breaking battle a few years ago when I was reading Sir Charles Oman's epic *History of the Peninsular War.* 几年前，我在阅读查尔斯·阿曼爵士史诗般的《半岛战争史》时，第一次发现了拿破仑时期的密码破译战。（2022年）

036
sufficient / sə'fɪʃnt /

释 *adj.* 充足的；足够的

例 This increasingly high level of education is probably a necessary, but not a **sufficient**, condition for the complex political systems required by advanced economic performance. 这种日益提高的教育水平可能是先进的经济表现所要求的复杂政治制度的必要条件，但不是充分条件。（2009年）

近 adequate / 'ædɪkwət / *adj.* 充足的；适当的

辨 sufficient和adequate都有"充足的"意思。sufficient是正式用词，侧重数目、数量或程度满足某一特定要求或需要；adequate指数量上足够，质量上适当。

037
carry / 'kæri /

释 *v.* 拿，带；带来（某种结果或后果）；销售；刊登；承担（责任、负担等）；传播（疾病）

例 And, unless banks **carry** toxic assets at prices that attract buyers, reviving the banking system will be difficult. 而且，除非银行以吸引买家的价格出售有毒资产，否则很难重振银行系统。（2010年）

038
decisive / dɪ'saɪsɪv /

释 *adj.* 决定性的；果断的

例 Their key player is a **decisive** factor in the game. 他们的核心队员是这场比赛胜负的决定性因素。

Writing Models

character

impact

workout

resort

competitive

element

construct

obstacle

remain

purpose

specify

specific

---

character / ˈkærəktə(r) /

释 *n.* 性格; 品质; 人物; 角色

例 A moralist, satirist, and social reformer, Dickens crafted complex plots and striking **characters** that capture the panorama of English society. 狄更斯是道德家、讽刺作家和社会改革家，他的作品情节复杂、人物鲜明，展现了英国社会的全景。（2017年）

近 quality / ˈkwɒləti / *n.* 品质，特质 ‖ characteristic / ˌkærəktəˈrɪstɪk / *n.* 特征

---

impact 040

释 / ɪmˈpækt / *v.* 有影响，有作用 / ˈɪmpækt / *n.* 影响，作用; 冲撞冲击力

例 Some believe that AI is negatively **impacting** on the marketer's role by reducing creativity and removing jobs, but they are aware that it is a way of reducing costs and creating new information. 有些人认为，人工智能降低了创造力，减少了工作岗位，对营销人员的角色产生了负面影响，但他们也意识到，人工智能是降低成本和创造新信息的一种方式。（2023年）

近 influence / ˈɪnfluəns / *n./v.* 影响

---

workout / ˈwɜːkaʊt / 041

释 *n.* 锻炼; 体育训练

例 It turns out that the brain needs exercise in much the same way our muscles do, and the right mental **workouts** can significantly improve our basic cognitive functions. 事实证明，大脑和我们的肌肉一样需要锻炼，正确的脑力锻炼可以显著提高我们的基本认知功能。（2014年）

---

resort / rɪˈzɔːt / 042

释 *v.* 采取（某手段或方法）; 求助，诉诸 *n.* 凭借，手段; 度假胜地

搭 resort to 求助于……

例 We mustn't **resort** to violence no matter what difficulties we meet. 无论遇到什么困难，我们都不要诉诸暴力。

近 appeal / əˈpiːl / *v.* 求助，诉诸

---

competitive / kəmˈpetətɪv / 043

释 *adj.* 有竞争力的

例 When the **competitive** environment pushed our ancestors to achieve that potential, they could in turn afford more education. 当竞争环境促使我们的祖先获得这种潜能时，他们反过来也能接受更多的教育。（2009年）

---

element / ˈelɪmənt / 044

释 *n.* 组成部分; 元素; 成分

例 Some software programs can also check spelling and certain grammatical **elements** in your writing. 有些软件程序还可以检查你作文中的拼写和某些语法成分。（2008年）

045
construct

释 / 'kɒnstrʌkt / n. （根据不总是真实的各种证据得出的）构想；概念；建造物；构筑物 / kən'strʌkt / v. 建造；组成；创建；绘制

例 In plays, novels and narrative poems, characters speak as **constructs** created by the author, not necessarily as mouthpieces for the author's own thoughts. 在戏剧、小说和叙事诗中，人物都是按照作者的构想来表达，而不一定是作者本人思想的传声筒。（2015年）

046
obstacle / 'ɒbstəkl /

释 n. 障碍；妨碍

例 Particularly useful in busy locations or during times of emergency, the doors act as crowd management by reducing the **obstacles** put in people's way. 在繁忙地点或紧急情况下，这种门尤其有用，它们可以减少人们前进道路上的障碍，起到人群管理的作用。（2024年）

近 barrier / 'bæriə(r) / n. 障碍 ‖ obstruction / əb'strʌkʃn / n. 障碍

反 assistance / ə'sɪstəns / n. 帮助，援助

047
remain / rɪ'meɪn /

释 v. 保持，仍然是；剩余

例 When we don't understand the value of mental health and we don't know how to gain access to it, mental health will **remain** hidden from us. 当我们不了解心理健康的价值，不知道如何获取心理健康时，心理健康仍将被我们所忽视。（2016年）

048
purpose / 'pɜːpəs /

释 n. 目的；目标；用途；意志

搭 on purpose 故意地

例 In many respects, the dearth of moral **purpose** frames not only the fact of such widespread phone hacking but the terms on which the trial took place. 在许多方面，道德目的的缺失不仅造成了如此广泛的电话黑客行为，也造成了审判条件的缺失。（2015年）

049
specify / 'spesɪfaɪ /

释 v. 具体制定，详细说明

例 The justices had to **specify** novel rules for the new personal domain of the passenger car then; they must sort out how the Fourth Amendment applies to digital information now. 当时，大法官们必须为客车这一新的个人领域制定新规则；现在，他们必须理清第四修正案如何适用于数字信息。（2015年）

050
specific / spə'sɪfɪk /

释 adj. 特有的；特定的；具体的，确切的；针对……的

例 There are many different types of automatic door, with each relying on **specific** signals to tell them when to open. 自动门有许多不同的类型，每种类型都依靠特定的信号来告诉它们何时打开。（2024年）

monopoly / məˈnɒpəli /
0 5 1

释 *n.* 垄断；专卖权

搭 monopoly in/of/on sth. 独占或垄断某物

例 Liberty and **monopoly** cannot live together. 自由与垄断不能共存。

feature / ˈfiːtʃə(r) /
0 5 2

释 *n.* 特点；（报纸、电视等的）特写 *v.* 以……为特色；起重要作用

例 Aerial surveys locate general areas of interest or larger buried **features**, such as ancient buildings or fields. 航空勘测可确定感兴趣的大致目标区域或较大的被埋藏遗址的特征，如古建筑或田野。（2014年）

commerce / ˈkɒmɜːs /
0 5 3

释 *n.* 商业，商务，贸易

例 We define such sold media as owned media whose traffic is so strong that other organizations place their content or e-**commerce** engines within that environment. 我们将这种"售出媒介"定义为自有媒体，其流量巨大，以至于其他机构将它们的内容或电子商务引擎置于其环境中。（2011年）

ruin / ˈruːɪn /
0 5 4

释 *v.* 毁坏；破坏；糟蹋；使破产 *n.* 破产；祸根；一无所有

搭 in ruins 毁坏；严重受损；破败不堪

例 It was to **ruin** lives in the quest for circulation and impact. 这是为了追求发行量和影响力而毁掉生活。（2015年）

evolution / ˌevəˈluːʃn /
0 5 5

释 *n.* 进化；演化；发展

例 Studying this could help understand why human **evolution** picked pace in the last 30,000 years, with social environment being a major contributory factor. 研究这一点有助于理解为什么人类的进化在过去三万年里加快了步伐，而社会环境是一个重要的促成因素。（2015年）

species / ˈspiːʃiːz /
0 5 6

释 *n.* （物）种，种类

例 The shallows provide homes for hundreds of **species** while storing floodwaters, filtering pollutants from water, and protecting nearby communities from potentially destructive storm surges. 浅滩为数以百计的物种提供家园，同时储存洪水，过滤水中的污染物，保护附近社区免受潜在的破坏性风暴潮的影响。（2024年）

habitat / ˈhæbɪtæt /
0 5 7

释 *n.* （动物或植物的）栖息地，生活环境；住处

例 They move between a variety of **habitats**, including forests, grasslands, woodlands, wetlands and agricultural land. 它们（大象）在森林、草原、林地、湿地和农田等各种栖息地之间穿梭。（2024年）

058
massacre / ˈmæsəkə(r) /

释 *n.* 大屠杀

例 It was a **massacre** of thousands of people for their religious beliefs. 这是一场因宗教信仰而对成千上万人进行的大屠杀。

近 slaughter / ˈslɔːtə(r) / *n.* 宰杀

059
forgive / fəˈɡɪv /

释 *v.* 原谅，饶恕

搭 forgive and forget 不念旧恶，不记仇

例 Provided you have the courage to admit your mistakes, I will **forgive** you. 要是你有勇气承认自己的错误，我就会原谅你。

060
differ / ˈdɪfə(r) /

释 *v.* 不同于；有区别；相异；不同意，持不同看法，意见相左

例 Plant biology is complex and fascinating, but it **differs** so greatly from that of animals that so-called evidence of plants' intelligence is inconclusive, the authors wrote. 作者们写道，植物生物学复杂而迷人，但它与动物的生物学差异很大，因此所谓的植物智慧证据并不确凿。（2022年）

061
investment / ɪnˈvestmənt /

释 *n.* 投资；投资金额；（时间、精力的）投入；值得买的东西；有用的投资物

例 In France, shareholders who hold onto a company **investment** for at least two years can sometimes earn more voting rights in a company. 在法国，持有公司投资至少两年的股东有时可以获得更多的公司投票权。（2019年）

062
crisis / ˈkraɪsɪs /

释 *n.* 危机；危难时刻，病危期

搭 financial crisis 金融危机

例 The idea that "housing **crisis**" equals "concreted meadows" is pure lobby talk. "住房危机"等同于"水泥草地"的说法纯属游说之词。（2016年）

063
regime / reɪˈʒiːm /

释 *n.* 政权，政体；管理，方法

例 If he were to meet all of the protesters' demands, his **regime** might be fatally weakened. 如果他满足抗议者的所有要求，他的政权可能会受到严重削弱。

064
synthetic / sɪnˈθetɪk /

释 *adj.* 合成的 *n.* 合成物

例 I think the boots made from **synthetic** materials can be washed in a machine. 我认为这双用合成材料做成的靴子可以机洗。

scatter / ˈskætə(r) / 　　　065

释 v. 撒; 撒播; 散开; 使分散 n. 分散; 散播

例 The goals of the prize-givers seem as **scattered** as the criticism. Some want to shock, others to draw people into science, or to better reward those who have made their careers in research. 颁奖人的目标似乎和批评一样分散。一些人希望震撼人心，另一些人则希望吸引人们投身科学，或者更好地奖励那些以研究为职业的人。（2014年）

mission / ˈmɪʃn / 　　　066

释 n. 任务; 使命, 天职; 驻外使团; 传教活动

搭 military mission 军事任务

例 She uses outdated research and decades-old examples to undermine the noble **mission** of organizations committed to connecting children to a world beyond their own. 她用过时的研究和几十年前的例子去破坏那些致力于将儿童与他们自己以外的世界联系起来的组织的崇高任务。（2022年）

近 task / tɑːsk / n. 工作，任务

adhere / ədˈhɪə(r) / 　　　067

释 v. 遵守; 坚持; 紧贴; 黏附

例 For years executives and headhunters have **adhered** to the rule that the most attractive CEO candidates are the ones who must be poached. 多年以来，经理们和猎头们都坚持这样一个原则：最具吸引力的首席执行官候选人一定是被挖来的。（2011年）

passion / ˈpæʃn / 　　　068

释 n. 激情, 热情; 酷爱

例 Big-name PRH authors may suffer a bit, but it's those mid-list authors, who normally rely on Waterstones staff's **passion** for promoting books by lesser-known writers, who will be praying for an end to the dispute. 大名鼎鼎的企鹅兰登的作家可能会受到一些影响，但那些通常依靠水石书店店员的热情来推广知名度较低作家的作品的中等知名度作家，他们将会祈求结束这场纠纷。（2023年）

近 zeal / ziːl / n. 热情; 热诚

struggle / ˈstrʌɡl / 　　　069

释 v. 奋斗; 争取; 斗争; 搏斗; 扭打; 争论; 艰难地行进 n. 斗争; 奋斗; 难事; 搏斗; 扭打

例 The court's ruling is a step forward in the **struggle** against both corruption and official favoritism. 法院的裁决是在打击腐败和官官相护的斗争中向前迈出的一步。（2017年）

contract

`070`

释 / 'kɒntrækt / *n.* 合同; 合约; 契约 / kən'trækt / *v.* （使）收缩, 缩小; 与……订立合同（婚约、契约或同盟）; 订立……的合同（或契约）

搭 contract in (to sth.) 订约参与 ‖ contract out (of sth.) 退出（或不参加）……合约

例 But under anti-bribery laws, proof must be made of concrete benefits, such as approval of a **contract** or regulation. 但根据反贿赂法, 必须证明具体的利益, 如批准合同或法规。（2017年）

rule / ruːl /

`071`

释 *n.* 规则; 原则; 惯例; 统治 *v.* 统治; 支配

例 That's why there has been such a strong demand for **rules** that would prevent broadband providers from picking winners and losers online, preserving the freedom and innovation that have been the lifeblood of the Internet. 这就是为什么人们强烈要求制定规则, 防止宽带提供商在网上挑选赢家和输家, 以保护互联网的命脉——自由和创新。（2021年）

network / 'netwɜːk /

`072`

释 *n.* 网络; 关系网; 人际网; 网状物; 网状系统 *v.* 联播; 建立工作关系; 将……连接成网络

例 The term caravan was used to describe groups of people who travelled together across the ancient **network** for safety reasons, such as merchants, travellers or pilgrims. "商队"一词被用来描述出于安全原因一起穿行古老的交通网络的人群, 比如商人、旅行者或朝圣者。（2023年）

receipt / rɪ'siːt /

`073`

释 *n.* 收据; 收条; 接收; 收到

例 Shoppers can submit **receipts** of $50 or more spent at Ocean Beach businesses for a chance to win gift cards. 购物者可以提交在Ocean Beach商店消费的50美元或以上金额的收据, 以获得赢得礼品卡的机会。

carrier / 'kæriə(r) /

`074`

释 *n.* 载体;（尤指经营空运的）运输公司; 军用运输车; 运输舰; 航空母舰; 病原携带者

例 But in keeping with our examination of southern intellectual life, we may consider the original Puritans as **carriers** of European culture, adjusting to New World circumstances. 但根据我们对南方知识分子生活的考察, 我们可以把最初的清教徒看作是欧洲文化的承载者, 他们在适应新世界的环境。（2009年）

Writing Models ◎

amount

navy

innocent

argu(e)ment

shed

size

melt

flow

shadow

agency

motive

score

heroic

---

amount / ə'maʊnt /

075

释 *n.* 金额；数量；数额

搭 a large amount of 大量 ‖ amount to 总计，共计

例 "It's like baking a cake: If you don't have exact **amounts**, it goes wrong," she says. 她说："这就像烤蛋糕一样：如果你用量不准，就会出问题。"（2022年）

navy / 'neɪvi /

076

释 *n.* 海军；海军部队

例 Although the Dutch invented it, peacoats made their way into the British **navy** and eventually across the pond to America. 虽然是荷兰人发明的，但厚呢短大衣却进入了英国海军，并最终漂洋过海来到了美国。

innocent / 'ɪnəsnt /

077

释 *adj.* 无辜的；清白的；无恶意的；纯真的

例 While seemingly **innocent**, this loss of mental focus can potentially have a damaging impact on our professional, social, and personal wellbeing. 这种精神上的注意力缺失看似无伤大雅，但却可能会对我们的职业、社会和个人健康产生破坏性的影响。（2014年）

argu(e)ment / 'ɑːgjumənt /

078

释 *n.* 论据；讨论；辩论；争吵

例 Why, the **argument** goes, should a car-driving pensioner from Lincolnshire have to subsidise the daily commute of a stockbroker from Surrey? 争论的问题是：为什么林肯郡的一位自己开车的、领取养老金的人必须补贴萨里郡的一位股票经纪人的日常通勤？（2021年）

shed / ʃed /

079

释 *v.* 去除；摆脱；落（泪）*n.* 棚屋；棚式建筑

例 Now, a new research **sheds** light on just how Americans feel about this proposal. 现在，一项新的研究揭示了美国人对这项提议的看法。

size / saɪz /

080

释 *n.* 大小；尺寸；规模

例 Throughout the trip, Jackson juggled multiple cameras and plate **sizes** using the collodion process that involved coating the plates with a chemical mixture, exposing them and developing the resulting images with a portable darkroom. 在整个旅途中，杰克逊使用多台相机和不同尺寸的底片，使用火棉胶法包括在底片上涂抹化学混合物、使用便携式暗房曝光以及冲洗出最终的照片。（2023年）

melt / melt / 0 8 1

释 v. (使)融化;(使)熔化;(情绪等)消失、平息;逐渐融入(黑暗、人群等)

搭 melt away (使)慢慢消失 ‖ melt into 逐渐融入

例 In Pakistan during 2022, for instance, warming caused glaciers to **melt** and rivers to surge in the north of the country. 例如, 在巴基斯坦, 2022年期间, 气候变暖导致该国北部的冰川融化和河流水位上涨。

flow / fləʊ / 0 8 2

释 n. 流动;流通 v. 流动

搭 go with the flow 随大溜

例 We think of it simply as a healthy and helpful **flow** of intelligent thought. 我们认为它只是一种健康有益的智慧思想流。(2016年)

shadow / 'ʃædəʊ / 0 8 3

释 n. 阴影;影子;眼影;坏影响;虚幻的事物 v. 跟踪;在……上投下阴影

搭 cast a shadow on 给……投下阴影

例 Her hair is shaped into an old-fashioned bob and her eyes are painted with harsh red **shadow**. 她的头发梳成了老式的波波头, 眼睛涂上了刺眼的红色眼影。

agency / 'eɪdʒənsi / 0 8 4

释 n. 机构;(政府的)专门机构;代理机构;服务机构

例 They wouldn't like a national **agency**, but self-interest would lead them to deal with it. 他们不喜欢一个国家的专门机构, 但自身利益会促使他们与之打交道。(2005年)

motive / 'məʊtɪv / 0 8 5

释 n. 动机;原因;目的

例 Such measures have a couple of uplifting **motives**. 这些措施有几个令人振奋的动机。(2016年)

score / skɔː(r) / 0 8 6

释 v. 得分;分值是 n. 得分, 比分;成绩

例 They found that middle-aged people with higher measures of abdominal fat **scored** worse on measures of fluid intelligence as the years went by. 他们发现, 随着时间的推移, 腹部脂肪含量较高的中年人在流体智力测试中得分更低。(2021年)

heroic / hə'rəʊɪk / 0 8 7

释 adj. 英勇的;英雄的;有必胜决心的;不畏艰难的;非常大的;巨大的

例 His **heroic** deeds were celebrated in every corner of the country. 他的英雄事迹在全国各地都受到颂扬。

派 heroically / hə'rəʊɪkli / adv. 英勇地

Writing Models ◎

equipment

fragile

apt

enlighten

mixture

rank

praise

joint

desperate

trick

ambition

fluid

underline

equipment / ɪˈkwɪpmənt / `088`

释 *n.* 设备；器材；配备；装备

例 Airborne technologies, such as different types of radar and photographic **equipment** carried by airplanes or spacecraft, allow archaeologists to learn about what lies beneath the ground without digging. 机载技术，如飞机或宇宙飞船携带的不同类型的雷达和摄影设备，使考古学家无须挖掘就能了解地表下面有什么。（2014年）

fragile / ˈfrædʒaɪl / `089`

释 *adj.* 易碎的；脆弱的；虚弱的

例 They did not always prioritize the protection of Mauna Kea's **fragile** ecosystems or its holiness to the islands' inhabitants. 他们并不总是将保护莫纳克亚山脆弱的生态系统或它对岛上居民的神圣意义放在首位。（2017年）

派 fragility / frəˈdʒɪləti / *n.* 易碎；脆弱；虚弱

apt / æpt / `090`

释 *adj.* 恰当的；易于……；有……倾向

例 Researchers examined the question of why teens were more **apt** to take risks in the company of other teenagers. 研究人员研究了为什么青少年在其他青少年的陪伴下更敢于冒险这一问题。

enlighten / ɪnˈlaɪtn / `091`

释 *v.* 启发；开导；阐明

例 There is nothing quite like a good documentary, one with the power to both entertain and **enlighten**. 没有什么能像一部优秀的纪录片那样，既有娱乐的功能，还有启发的作用。

派 enlightenment / ɪnˈlaɪtnmənt / *n.* 启迪

mixture / ˈmɪkstʃə(r) / `092`

释 *n.* 混合；混合物

例 History and news become confused, and one's impressions tend to be a **mixture** of skepticism and optimism. 历史和新闻变得混淆，人们的印象往往是怀疑和乐观兼而有之。（2005年）

rank / ræŋk / `093`

释 *n.* 地位；级别；队列 *v.* 属于某等级；排列

例 The prices of his works **rank** high among contemporary photographers. 他的作品价格在当代摄影师中名列前茅。

praise / preɪz / `094`

释 *n.* 赞扬；称赞；赞美 *v.* 表扬；赞扬；称赞

例 Retail trade groups **praised** the ruling, saying it levels the playing field for local and online businesses. 零售贸易组织称赞了这一裁决，称它为本地企业和线上企业创造了公平的竞争环境。（2019年）

joint / dʒɔɪnt /

释 *adj.* 联合的；共同的 *n.* 关节；接头

搭 joint effort 共同努力

例 Football Australia and the PFA held a **joint** press conference. 澳大利亚足球协会和英格兰职业足球运动员协会举行了一场联合新闻发布会。

派 jointly / 'dʒɔɪntli / *adv.* 共同地

095

desperate / 'despərət /

释 *adj.* 绝望的；不顾一切的；极度渴望的

例 Instead, the company has done precisely what it had long promised it would not: challenge the constitutionality of Vermont's rules in the federal court, as part of a **desperate** effort to keep its Vermont Yankee nuclear power plant running. 相反，该公司恰恰做了它长期以来承诺不会做的事情：在联邦法庭质疑佛蒙特州法规是否符合宪法，这也是该公司为维持其佛蒙特扬基核电站运转而做出的不顾一切的努力的一部分。（2012年）

派 desperation / ˌdespə'reɪʃn / *n.* 绝望

096

trick / trɪk /

释 *n.* 诡计；花招；把戏；技巧 *v.* 欺骗；欺诈

搭 trick sb. into (doing) sth. 诱使某人做某事

例 If you get lost without a phone or a compass, and you gradually can't find north, a few **tricks** may help you navigate back to civilization, one of which is to follow the land. 如果你在没有手机或指南针的情况下迷路了，并且你逐渐找不着北，有几个小技巧或许能帮你回到文明世界，其中之一就是沿着陆地前进。（2019年）

097

ambition / æm'bɪʃn /

释 *n.* 雄心；野心；志向；抱负

例 Robert Willumstad left Citigroup in 2005 with **ambitions** to be a CEO. 罗伯特·威伦斯塔德在2005年离开了花旗集团，雄心勃勃地想成为一名首席执行官。（2011年）

派 ambitious / æm'bɪʃəs / *adj.* 有野心的；有雄心的

098

fluid / 'fluːɪd /

释 *n.* 液体；流体 *adj.* 流动的；流体的；不稳定的

例 One study found that muscle loss and the accumulation of body fat around the abdomen are associated with a decline in **fluid** intelligence. 一项研究发现，肌肉减少和腹部周围脂肪的堆积与流体智力下降有关。（2021年）

099

underline / ˌʌndə'laɪn /

释 *v.* （在词语等下）画线；强调；凸显

例 This alone demonstrates that the television business is not an easy world to survive in, a fact **underlined** by statistics that show that out of eighty European television networks, no less than 50% took a loss in 1989. 这一点就足以表明，要在电视行业里生存下来并非易事，统计数字凸显了这一事实：在80家欧洲电视网中，在1989年亏损的不少于50%。（2005年）

100

☐ ☐ accomplish
☐ ☐ adhere
☐ ☐ advocate
☐ ☐ agency
☐ ☐ ambition
☐ ☐ amount
☐ ☐ apt
☐ ☐ argu(e)ment
☐ ☐ attend
☐ ☐ bleed
☐ ☐ carrier
☐ ☐ carry
☐ ☐ category
☐ ☐ character
☐ ☐ commerce
☐ ☐ companion
☐ ☐ compare
☐ ☐ competitive
☐ ☐ conclude
☐ ☐ construct
☐ ☐ contract
☐ ☐ crisis
☐ ☐ decisive
☐ ☐ decline
☐ ☐ desperate
☐ ☐ differ
☐ ☐ discover
☐ ☐ element
☐ ☐ eliminate
☐ ☐ employ
☐ ☐ enlighten

☐ ☐ equipment
☐ ☐ essential
☐ ☐ evolution
☐ ☐ feature
☐ ☐ flow
☐ ☐ fluid
☐ ☐ forgive
☐ ☐ fragile
☐ ☐ habitat
☐ ☐ heroic
☐ ☐ historic
☐ ☐ hostage
☐ ☐ ideology
☐ ☐ image
☐ ☐ impact
☐ ☐ impression
☐ ☐ improve
☐ ☐ influential
☐ ☐ innocent
☐ ☐ investment
☐ ☐ joint
☐ ☐ largely
☐ ☐ massacre
☐ ☐ melt
☐ ☐ mission
☐ ☐ mixture
☐ ☐ monopoly
☐ ☐ motive
☐ ☐ navy
☐ ☐ network
☐ ☐ obstacle

☐ ☐ owe
☐ ☐ passion
☐ ☐ plead
☐ ☐ praise
☐ ☐ preach
☐ ☐ presence
☐ ☐ pressure
☐ ☐ provide
☐ ☐ purpose
☐ ☐ rank
☐ ☐ receipt
☐ ☐ regime
☐ ☐ remain
☐ ☐ render
☐ ☐ resort
☐ ☐ restore
☐ ☐ ruin
☐ ☐ rule
☐ ☐ scatter
☐ ☐ score
☐ ☐ seal
☐ ☐ security
☐ ☐ senator
☐ ☐ senior
☐ ☐ shadow
☐ ☐ shed
☐ ☐ size
☐ ☐ species
☐ ☐ specific
☐ ☐ specify
☐ ☐ stock

☐ ☐ struggle
☐ ☐ sufficient
☐ ☐ synthetic
☐ ☐ trick
☐ ☐ underline
☐ ☐ warrant
☐ ☐ workout

音频

- [ ] complex
- [ ] cater
- [ ] inherent
- [ ] margin
- [ ] announce
- [ ] flaw
- [ ] spectacle
- [ ] republic
- [ ] facilitate
- [ ] credit
- [ ] temporary
- [ ] venture
- [ ] aspire
- [ ] simplify
- [ ] oppose
- [ ] flexible
- [ ] manual
- [ ] deadline
- [ ] divide
- [ ] maintenance
- [ ] principle
- [ ] database
- [ ] analyze/-yse
- [ ] acknowledge
- [ ] contain
- [ ] select
- [ ] perspective
- [ ] succeed
- [ ] revelation
- [ ] modify
- [ ] chancellor

- [ ] maintain
- [ ] essence
- [ ] sponsor
- [ ] interior
- [ ] prosper
- [ ] random
- [ ] absence
- [ ] descend
- [ ] unexpected
- [ ] supplement
- [ ] probe
- [ ] snap
- [ ] ban
- [ ] compel
- [ ] spread
- [ ] underestimate
- [ ] scope
- [ ] fearful
- [ ] undermine
- [ ] hostile
- [ ] coherent
- [ ] delivery
- [ ] input
- [ ] firm
- [ ] portray
- [ ] undergo
- [ ] sarcastic
- [ ] statistics
- [ ] genetic
- [ ] assemble
- [ ] enormous

- [ ] concession
- [ ] extract
- [ ] term
- [ ] check
- [ ] mode
- [ ] behave
- [ ] assurance
- [ ] adapt
- [ ] celebrate
- [ ] cost
- [ ] dean
- [ ] official
- [ ] pull
- [ ] scan
- [ ] transition
- [ ] sum
- [ ] admire
- [ ] fear
- [ ] fair
- [ ] quarrel
- [ ] dissolve
- [ ] click
- [ ] posture
- [ ] speed
- [ ] radical
- [ ] fuel
- [ ] host
- [ ] pour
- [ ] pass
- [ ] heel
- [ ] classic

- [ ] characterize/-ise
- [ ] error
- [ ] roll
- [ ] mend
- [ ] overhead
- [ ] stem
- [ ] coach

001

complex / ˈkɒmpleks /

釋 *adj.* 复杂的；难懂的；费解的；[语法]复合的 *n.*（类型相似的）建筑群；情结

例 Their reactions may be a **complex** combination of instant reflexes, input from past driving experiences, and what their eyes and ears tell them in that moment. 他们的反应可能是瞬间反射、过去驾驶经验的输入以及他们的眼睛和耳朵在那一刻告诉他们的信息的复杂组合。（2019年）

002

cater / ˈkeɪtə(r) /

釋 *v.* 满足……的需要，为……提供服务；接待；（为社交活动）提供饮食；考虑到

搭 cater for 满足需要；适合 ‖ cater to 迎合

例 The plans need to be flexible enough to **cater** for the needs of everyone. 这些计划需要能够变通，以满足每个人的需要。

003

inherent / ɪnˈhɪrənt /

釋 *adj.* 内在的，固有的

例 The fashion industry knows it has an **inherent** problem in focusing on material adornment and idealized body types. 时尚界知道，注重物质装饰和理想化体型是其固有的问题。（2016年）

004

margin / ˈmɑːdʒɪn /

釋 *n.* 页边空白，白边；差数，差额；备用的时间；界限，边缘

搭 profit margin 利润率

例 Scientific publishers routinely report profit **margins** approaching 40% on their operations, at a time when the rest of the publishing industry is in an existential crisis. 科学出版商经常报告其业务利润率接近40%，而此时出版业的其他部门正面临生存危机。（2020年）

005

announce / əˈnaʊns /

釋 *v.* 宣布，宣告（决定、计划等）；通知；声称

例 The journal *Science* is adding an extra round of statistical checks to its peer-review process, editor-in-chief Marcia McNutt **announced** today.《科学》杂志主编玛西娅·麦克纳特今天宣布，该杂志将在同行评审过程中增加一轮额外的统计检查。（2015年）

派 announcement / əˈnaʊnsmənt / *n.* 宣告

006

flaw / flɔː /

釋 *n.* 缺点，错误；裂缝；（性格上的）弱点，缺点

例 The most glaring **flaw** of the social cure as it's presented here is that it doesn't work very well for very long. 这里所介绍的社会疗法最明显的缺陷是，它不能很好地长期发挥作用。（2012年）

派 flawed / flɔːd / *adj.* 有缺点的；有瑕疵的 ‖ flawless / ˈflɔːləs / *adj.* 完美的；无瑕的

近 fault / fɔːlt / *n.* 缺点；过错 ‖ defect / ˈdiːfekt / *n.* 缺点；不足之处

spectacle / 'spektəkl /

释 *n.* 景象；奇观

搭 make a spectacle of oneself 使自己出丑；出洋相

例 The sunrise from the sea is indeed a **spectacle**. 海上日出真是一个奇观。

007

republic / rɪ'pʌblɪk /

释 *n.* 共和国

例 The declaration proclaimed the full sovereignty of the **republic**. 这份宣言宣告这个共和国完全独立自主。

008

facilitate / fə'sɪlɪteɪt /

释 *v.* 促进；使便利；促使

例 The moderator's role is to **facilitate** the discussion by asking appropriate questions. 主持人的作用是通过提出适当的问题来促进讨论。

009

credit / 'kredɪt /

释 *n.* 名誉，名望；信用，信任；学分；赞扬；认可 *v.* 相信，信任

例 According to Sichel, although the falling price of nails was driven partly by cheaper iron and cheaper energy, most of the **credit** goes to nail manufacturers who simply found more efficient ways to turn steel into nails. 西谢尔认为，虽然钉子价格下降的部分原因是铁更便宜、能源更便宜，但大部分功劳要归功于钉子制造商，因为他们找到了更有效地将钢铁变成钉子的方法。（2024年）

010

temporary / 'temprəri /

释 *adj.* 暂时的；临时的；短暂的

例 Today they argue that market prices overstate losses, because they largely reflect the **temporary** illiquidity of markets, not the likely extent of bad debts. 如今，他们认为市场价格高估了损失，因为市场价格在很大程度上反映的是市场的流动性暂时不足，而不是坏账的可能程度。（2010年）

011

venture / 'ventʃə(r) /

释 *n.* 风险项目；冒险活动 *v.* 冒险做；冒险去某处

例 He is about to embark on a new business **venture**. 他正准备开始新的商业冒险活动。

012

aspire / ə'spaɪə(r) /

释 *v.* 渴望（成就），有志（成为）

搭 aspire to 渴望，立志

例 For us, winning the championship is the thing that we may **aspire** to but can never attain. 对我们来说，赢得冠军是我们可望而不可即的事情。

派 aspiration / ˌæspə'reɪʃn / *n.* 渴望；抱负

013

Writing Models ◎

simplify

oppose

flexible

manual

deadline

divide

maintenance

principle

database

analyze/-yse

acknowledge

contain

simplify / ˈsɪmplɪfaɪ / `0 1 4`

释 *v.* 使简化；使简易

例 This perspective makes sense if you **simplify** the workings of a complex brain, reducing it to an array of electrical pulses; cells in plants also communicate through electrical signals. 如果你将复杂的大脑工作简化为一系列电脉冲，这种观点就有意义了；植物细胞也通过电信号进行交流。（2022年）

oppose / əˈpəʊz / `0 1 5`

释 *v.* 反对；抵制；阻挠；（在竞赛中）与……对垒，与……角逐

例 While some locals **opposed** the designation, the decision was largely accepted—and Jackson's photos played a key role in the fight to protect the area. 虽然一些当地人反对这一指定，但这一决定在很大程度上被接受了——杰克逊的照片在保护该地区的斗争中发挥了关键作用。（2023年）

flexible / ˈfleksəbl / `0 1 6`

释 *adj.* 能适应新情况的；灵活的；可变动的；可弯曲的；有弹性的

例 The functioning of the market is based on **flexible** trends dominated by potential buyers. 市场运作以潜在买家主导的灵活趋势为基础。（2010年）

manual / ˈmænjuəl / `0 1 7`

释 *n.* 使用手册，指南 *adj.* 手工的；体力的；手动的

例 The fourth edition of the *Diagnostic and Statistical **Manual** of Mental Disorders* says "pathological gambling" involves persistent, recurring and uncontrollable pursuit less of money than of the thrill of taking risks in quest of a windfall.《精神疾病诊断与统计手册》第四版指出，"病态赌博"是指持续、反复和无法控制地追求，与其说是对金钱的追求，不如说是为了追求意外之财而冒险的刺激。（2006年）

近 guidebook / ˈɡaɪdbʊk / *n.* 指南 ‖ handbook / ˈhændbʊk / *n.* 手册

deadline / ˈdedlaɪn / `0 1 8`

释 *n.* 截止日期

例 Assign responsibilities around the house and make sure homework **deadlines** are met.（给孩子）布置一些家务活并督促他们按时完成家庭作业。（2007年）

divide / dɪˈvaɪd / `0 1 9`

释 *v.* （使）分开，分散，分割；[数]除，除以；分配；分担；使产生分歧；把（时间、精力等）分别用于 *n.* 不同；分歧；差异；分水岭

例 None of these tricks will help you understand them, their positions or the issues that **divide** you, but they can help you win—in one way. 这些技巧都无法帮助你理解他们、他们的立场或造成你们分歧的问题，但它可以帮助你获胜——在某种程度上。（2019年）

maintenance / ˈmeɪntənəns /
020

㉿ *n.* 维护；检修；维持

㋡ Yes, more investment is needed, but passengers will not be willing to pay more indefinitely if they must also endure cramped, unreliable services, interrupted by regular chaos when timetables are changed, or planned **maintenance** is managed incompetently. 是的，（铁路）还需要更多的投资，但如果乘客必须忍受出行拥挤，忍受不可靠的服务，忍受常因时刻表更改或常规性维护管理不当而带来的混乱，那么他们就不会愿意无限期地支付更多了。（2021年）

principle / ˈprɪnsəpl /
021

㉿ *n.* 法则；原则；原理；道德原则；行为准则；观念；定律

㋡ in principle 原则上；理论上；基础上

㋡ On the basis of the precautionary **principle**, it could be argued that it is advisable to follow the FSA advice. 根据预防原则，可以说遵循金融服务管理局的建议是可取的。（2020年）

database / ˈdeɪtəbeɪs /
022

㉿ *n.* 数据库

㋡ The problem is rampant in Scopus, a citation **database**, which includes a high number of the new "international" journals. 这个问题在Scopus数据库中非常普遍，Scopus中包括大量新的"国际"期刊。（2023年）

analyze/-yse / ˈænəlaɪz /
023

㉿ *v.* 对……进行分析；分解

㋡ Some AI software can **analyze** and optimize marketing email subject lines to increase open rates. 一些人工智能软件可以分析和优化营销电子邮件主题文字，以提高打开率。（2021年）

acknowledge / əkˈnɒlɪdʒ /
024

㉿ *v.* 认可；承认；确认收到；向……致意

㋡ be acknowledged as 被公认为

㋡ This is hacking on an industrial scale, as was **acknowledged** by Glenn Mulcaire, the man hired by the *News of the World* in 2001 to be the point person for phone hacking. 正如《世界新闻报》2001年聘请的电话黑客负责人格伦·穆尔凯尔所承认的那样，这是工业规模的黑客行为。（2015年）

㋡ admit / ədˈmɪt / *v.* 承认

contain / kənˈteɪn /
025

㉿ *v.* 包含，含有；容纳；控制，克制，抑制（感情）

㋡ Mental health is the seed that **contains** self-esteem—confidence in ourselves and an ability to trust in our common sense. 心理健康是蕴含自尊的种子——对自己有信心，能够相信自己的常识。（2016年）

select / sɪˈlekt / 026

释 v. 挑选；选择；选拔 adj. 精选的；第一流的

例 Elephants are very choosy eaters, but until recently little was known about how they **selected** their food. 大象是非常挑剔的食客，但直到最近，人们对它们如何选择食物还知之甚少。（2024年）

perspective / pəˈspektɪv / 027

释 n. 观点，看法；远景

搭 in perspective 正确地

例 They cross-check sources and prefer news from different **perspectives**—especially those that are open about any bias. 他们会交叉检查消息来源，喜欢不同视角的新闻，尤其是那些对任何偏见持开放态度的新闻。（2018年）

近 view / vjuː / n. 意见 ‖ opinion / əˈpɪnjən / n. 意见；主张

succeed / səkˈsiːd / 028

释 v. 成功；有成就；实现目标；做到；接替；继任；随后出现

搭 succeed in (doing) sth. 做成某事

例 These benefactors have **succeeded** in their chosen fields, they say, and they want to use their wealth to draw attention to those who have **succeeded** in science. 他们说，这些资助者在自己选择的领域取得了成功，他们希望用自己的财富来吸引那些在科学领域取得成功的人。（2014年）

revelation / ˌrevəˈleɪʃn / 029

释 n. 揭示；启示，默示；被揭示的真相

例 It was with these great **revelations** that a new kind of philosophy founded in reason was born. 正是在这些伟大的启示下，一种建立在理性基础上的新哲学诞生了。（2020年）

modify / ˈmɒdɪfaɪ / 030

释 v. 调整，改变，稍做修改；缓和；修饰

例 The United States is the product of two principal forces—the immigration of European peoples with their varied ideas, customs, and national characteristics and the impact of a new country which **modified** these traits. 美国是两股主要力量的产物——带有不同思想、习俗和民族特色的欧洲移民，以及改变了这些特征的新国家的影响。（2015年）

派 modification / ˌmɒdɪfɪˈkeɪʃn / n. 修改，修正

近 alter / ˈɔːltə(r) / v. 改变，更改 ‖ change / tʃeɪndʒ / v. 改变；更换

辨 modify、alter和change都有"改变"的意思。modify强调限定作用的变化或变更，常含"缓和"的意味；alter常指轻微的改变，强调在基本上保持原状的情况下所进行的部分改变；change指任何变化，强调与原先的情况有明显的不同。

chancellor / ˈtʃɑːnsələ(r) / 031

释 *n.* （美国）大学校长；（德国或奥地利）总理；（英国）财政大臣

例 British people are waiting for the **chancellor**'s announcement. 英国人正等待财政大臣发布公告。

maintain / meɪnˈteɪn / 032

释 *v.* 保持，维持；维修；抚养

例 Meanwhile, there are steps you can take to help reduce abdominal fat and **maintain** lean muscle mass as you age in order to protect both your physical and mental wellbeing. 同时，随着年龄的增长，你可以采取一些措施来帮助减少腹部脂肪，保持瘦肌肉质量，以保护你的身心健康。（2021年）

essence / ˈesns / 033

释 *n.* 本质，实质；精髓；精油

搭 in essence 本质上，实质上 ‖ be of the essence 至关重要的

例 The Administration was in **essence** asserting that because it didn't want to carry out Congress's immigration wishes, no state should be allowed to do so either. 政府实质上是在坚称因为它不想执行国会的移民意愿，所以任何州都不应该允许这样做。（2013年）

派 essential / ɪˈsenʃl / *adj.* 必要的；本质的

sponsor / ˈspɒnsə(r) / 034

释 *n.* 赞助人；赞助机构；倡议人 *v.* 资助；赞助；组织，主办；倡议，发起

例 They include materials **sponsored** by energy industry associations. 它们中包括能源行业协会赞助的材料。（2023年）

interior / ɪnˈtɪəriə(r) / 035

释 *adj.* 内部的；里面的；内政的 *n.* 内部；内陆；内政

例 The **interior** walls of the house are all painted white. 这个房子内部的墙都被刷成了白色。

反 exterior / ɪkˈstɪəriə(r) / *adj.* 外部的 *n.* 外部

prosper / ˈprɒspə(r) / 036

释 *v.* 繁荣，昌盛；成功

例 But the professional companies **prospered** in their permanent theaters, and university men with literary ambitions were quick to turn to these theaters as offering a means of livelihood. 但是，专业剧团在他们的固定剧场中发展壮大，有文学抱负的大学生们很快转向这些剧场，因为它们提供了谋生的手段。（2018年）

random / ˈrændəm / 037

释 *adj.* 随机的，随意的 *n.* 随意，随机

搭 at random 随意，随机

例 Men are exposed to more acts of **random** physical violence. 男性遭受的随机身体暴力行为更多。（2008年）

038

absence / 'æbsəns /

释 *n.* 缺乏, 不存在; 缺席

搭 in the absence of 缺乏……

例 It's increasingly apparent that the **absence** of purpose, of a moral language within government, media or business could become one of the most dangerous goals for capitalism and freedom. 越来越明显的是，在政府、媒体或企业内部缺乏目标、缺乏道德语言，可能会成为资本主义和自由最危险的目标之一。（2015年）

近 lack / læk / *n.* 缺乏; 不足 ‖ shortage / 'ʃɔːtɪdʒ / *n.* 缺少, 不足

039

descend / dɪ'send /

释 *v.* 下来; 下降; 降临;（大批人）突然到来, 突然造访; 降低身份; 沦落

例 In less than a year, millions of spectators will **descend** on the French capital for what is poised to be the event of the decade: the Summer Olympics and Paralympics. 在不到一年的时间里，数百万观众将涌向法国首都，参加即将成为十年盛事的夏季奥运会和残奥会。

040

unexpected / ˌʌnɪk'spektɪd /

释 *adj.* 意想不到的, 意外的

例 The theory also seems to explain the sudden and **unexpected** popularity of certain looks, brands, or neighborhoods. 这一理论似乎可以解释为什么某些装扮、品牌或街区会突然得到意外的追捧。（2010年）

041

supplement

释 / 'sʌplɪmənt / *n.* 补充; 增刊; 补编, 附录 / 'sʌplɪment / *v.* 补充

例 Typically, if rains are delayed, people may clear land to plant more rice to **supplement** their harvests. 通常情况下，如果降雨延迟，人们可能会开荒种植更多水稻，以补充收成。（2021年）

近 complement / 'kɒmplɪmənt / *n.* 补充物;[语法]补语

042

probe / prəʊb /

释 *v.* 调查; 探查, 检查, 探测; 搜寻; 侦察, 侦探 *n.* 航天探测器; 太空探测器; 探针

例 From psychological thrillers to absurdist comedies, his movies all tend to land as social commentary, steeped in **probing** curiosity about the world. 从心理惊悚片到荒诞喜剧，他的电影都倾向于以社会评论的形式呈现，蕴含着对世界的好奇探究。

043

snap / snæp /

释 *v.* 咔嚓折断; 猛咬; 猛然断裂; 突然发怒; 打响指; 拍照 *n.* 照片; 打响指

搭 snap one's fingers 打响指

例 When the thief was climbing up, the rope **snapped**. 小偷向上爬的时候，绳子突然断了。

ban / bæn /

044

释 *v.* 明令禁止; 取缔; 禁止 (做某事) *n.* 禁令

例 The **bans**, if fully enforced, would suggest to women (and many men) that they should not let others be arbiters of their beauty. 这些禁令如果得到充分执行, 将向女性 (以及许多男性) 建议, 她们不应该让他人成为她们美貌的仲裁者。(2016年)

compel / kəm'pel /

045

释 *v.* 驱使; 强迫

例 Most living creatures are capable of adaptation when **compelled** to do so. 大多数生物都能在迫于压力的情况下适应新环境。

spread / spred /

046

释 *v.* 展开; 打开; (使) 传播; (使) 扩散; 延伸; 扩张 *n.* 传播; 蔓延; 涉及区域; 活动范围; 宽度; 面积

搭 spread out 伸展身体; 散开

例 Pennsylvania farmers, to use one telling example, aren't thinking about next year's blue crab harvest in Maryland when they decide whether to **spread** animal waste on their fields, yet the runoff into nearby creeks can have enormous impact downstream. 举一个很好的例子, 宾夕法尼亚州的农民在决定是否在自家田地里撒动物粪便时, 并没有考虑到马里兰州来年的蓝蟹收成, 但这些粪便流入附近的小溪会对下游产生巨大影响。(2024年)

underestimate

047

释 / ˌʌndər'estɪmət / *n.* 低估; 估计不足 / ˌʌndər'estɪmeɪt / *v.* 低估; 对……估计不足

例 Some individuals would therefore not have been caught, since no baited hooks would have been available to trap them, leading to an **underestimate** of fish stocks in the past. 因此, 有些鱼不会被捕获, 因为没有诱饵钩可以捕获它们, 从而导致人们过去低估了鱼类种群数量。(2006年)

反 overestimate / ˌəʊvər'estɪmeɪt / *v.* 对……评价过高 || overrate / ˌəʊvə'reɪt / *v.* 高估

scope / skəʊp /

048

释 *n.* 范围; 机会

例 This narrowing of the regulatory **scope** was a victory for builders, mining operators and other commercial interests often at odds with environmental rules. 监管范围的缩小是建筑商、矿业经营者和其他商业利益的胜利, 这些利益往往与环境规则相冲突。(2024年)

近 scale / skeɪl / *n.* 范围 || dimension / daɪ'menʃn / *n.* 程度

辨 scope多指某项活动、主题或工作所涵盖的范围; scale多用于不可计算的数量或不可丈量的事物, 强调其规模或范围大小; dimension多指情况或难题的范围、程度。

fearful / ˈfɪəfl /　049

释 *adj.* 可怕的；担心的；极严重的

例 The fisherman gaped in **fearful** disbelief at this display of power by the monster. 渔夫吓得目瞪口呆，不敢相信怪物展示的力量。

undermine / ˌʌndəˈmaɪn /　050

释 *v.* 逐渐削弱；逐渐动摇；破坏，损害

例 But demanding too much of air travelers or providing too little security in return **undermines** public support for the process. 但是，对航空旅客的要求过高或提供的安全保障过低，反过来都会削弱公众对这一进程的支持。（2017年）

近 weaken / ˈwiːkən / *v.* 削弱；使变弱

反 strengthen / ˈstreŋθn / *v.* 加强；巩固 ‖ intensify / ɪnˈtensɪfaɪ / *v.* 增强；加强

hostile / ˈhɒstaɪl /　051

释 *adj.* 敌意的，敌对的；反对的；怀有敌意的

例 Stratford-on-Avon, as we all know, has only one industry—William Shakespeare—but there are two distinctly separate and increasingly **hostile** branches. 众所周知，埃文河畔斯特拉特福只有一个产业——威廉·莎士比亚，但却有两个截然不同且日益敌对的分支。（2006年）

coherent / kəʊˈhɪərənt /　052

释 *adj.* 连贯的；合乎逻辑的；条理清楚的

例 His composition is **coherent** and easy to be understood. 他的作品条理清楚，容易理解。

delivery / dɪˈlɪvəri /　053

释 *n.* 传送；递送；交付；分娩；演讲方式；表演风格；投球

例 Can anyone really think it's a good idea to allow Amazon **deliveries** to your tent in Yosemite or food trucks to line up under the redwood trees at Sequoia National Park? 难道真的有人会认为，让亚马逊送货到你在约塞米蒂国家公园的帐篷里，或者让餐车在红杉国家公园的红杉树下排队是个好主意吗？

input / ˈɪnpʊt /　054

释 *n.* 投入；投资；输入 *v.* 输入

例 The data should be **input** to our computer system as soon as possible. 该数据应当尽快输入我们的电脑系统。

firm / fɜːm /　055

释 *n.* 公司 *adj.* 坚固的；坚定的 *v.* 使坚固

例 One accounting **firm**, EY, uses an AI system that helps review contracts during an audit. 安永会计师事务所在审计过程中使用人工智能系统帮助其审查合同。（2021年）

portray / pɔː'treɪ /

`056`

释 v. 扮演, 饰演; 描写, 描绘

例 Some of the soldiers Pyle interviewed **portrayed** themselves in the film. 佩里采访的一些士兵在电影中饰演他们自己。

派 portrayal / pɔː'treɪəl / n. 描绘; 画像

undergo / ˌʌndə'ɡəʊ /

`057`

释 v. 遭受; 承受; 经历

例 You may have to **undergo** countless hardships and tremendous sacrifice to achieve a success. 想获得成功, 你可能都要经历无数的磨难, 做出巨大的牺牲。

sarcastic / saː'kæstɪk /

`058`

释 adj. 讽刺的, 挖苦的, 嘲笑的

例 John's **sarcastic** comments insulted David. 约翰带有讽刺意味的评论侮辱了大卫。

statistics / stə'tɪstɪks /

`059`

释 n. 统计数字; 统计资料; 统计学

例 "Machine learning often provides a more reliable form of **statistics**, which makes data more valuable," says Winston. 温斯顿说: "机器学习通常能提供更可靠的统计数字形式, 从而使数据更有价值。"（2021年）

genetic / dʒə'netɪk /

`060`

释 adj. 遗传的; 基因的

搭 genetic variation 遗传变异

例 Critics also argue that commercial **genetic** testing is only as good as the reference collections to which a sample is compared. 批评者还认为, 商业基因检测的好坏取决于与之进行比较的样本参照库。（2009年）

近 inborn / ˌɪn'bɔːn / adj. 天生的; 生来的 ‖ innate / ɪ'neɪt / adj. 天生的; 固有的

assemble / ə'sembl /

`061`

释 v. 收集; 集合; 整理; 装配, 组装

例 How the whole image is then **assembled** and perceived is still a mystery although it is the subject of current research. 整个图像之后是如何收集并被感知的, 这仍然是一个谜, 尽管它是当前研究的主题。（2020年）

近 gather / 'ɡæðə(r) / v. 聚集, 集合

enormous / ɪ'nɔːməs /

`062`

释 adj. 巨大的; 庞大的; 极大的

例 There's no doubt that our peer groups exert **enormous** influence on our behavior. 毫无疑问, 我们的同伴群体对我们的行为施加了巨大的影响。（2012年）

concession / kən'seʃn / ⓪⑥③

釋 *n.* 让步，妥协；承认，许可

例 But by giving in to critics now they are inviting pressure to make more **concessions**. 但是，他们现在向批评者让步，就会招致压力，迫使他们做出更多妥协。（2010年）

extract ⓪⑥④

釋 / ɪk'strækt / *v.* （用力）拔出；提取 / 'ekstrækt / *n.* 摘录；提取物

例 Our studies focused on the impact of zoo experiences on how people think about themselves and nature, and the data points **extracted** from our studies do not, in any way, discount what is learned in a zoo visit. 我们的研究侧重于动物园体验对人们如何看待自己和自然的影响，从我们的研究中提取的数据点丝毫没有低估在动物园参观中所学到的东西。（2022年）

term / tɜːm / ⓪⑥⑤

釋 *n.* 期限；[pl.]条款；（工作或居住）期间；词语；术语

例 The **term** "plant neurobiology" was coined around the notion that some aspects of plant behavior could be compared to intelligence in animals. "植物神经生物学"是围绕植物行为的某些方面可以与动物的智力相比较这一概念而产生的术语。（2022年）

check / tʃek / ⓪⑥⑥

釋 *n.* 核查，核实；支票（=cheque）*v.* 核查，核实；查看；打钩

例 Most Americans rely on social media to **check** daily headlines. 大多数美国人依靠社交媒体查看每日头条新闻。（2018年）

mode / məʊd / ⓪⑥⑦

釋 *n.* 方式；风格；样式；（设备的）模式

例 For all the possibilities of our new culture machines, most people are still stuck in download **mode**. 尽管我们的新型文化机器具有各种可能性，但大多数人仍然停留在下载模式。（2012年）

behave / bɪ'heɪv / ⓪⑥⑧

釋 *v.* 表现；（机器等）运转；规则地行事

搭 behave oneself 使举止规矩

例 The court cannot maintain its legitimacy as guardian of the rule of law when justices **behave** like politicians. 如果法官的行为像政客，法院就无法维持其作为法治守护者的合法性。（2012年）

assurance / ə'ʃʊərəns / ⓪⑥⑨

釋 *n.* 保证；担保；自信；人寿保险

例 This **assurance** allows producers to focus on the creation of content without getting distracted by sourcing capital. 这种保证使制作人能够专注于内容创作，而不必为寻找资金而分心。

adapt / əˈdæpt / 070

释 v. （使）适应；使适合；改编，改写

例 Destroying the machines that are coming for our jobs would be nuts. But policies to help workers **adapt** will be indispensable. 摧毁那些来抢我们饭碗的机器将是痴人说梦，但帮助工人适应的政策将是不可或缺的。（2018年）

celebrate / ˈselɪbreɪt / 071

释 v. 庆祝，庆贺；赞美；颂扬

例 A "town of culture" could be not just about the arts but about honouring a town's peculiarities—helping sustain its high street, supporting local facilities and above all **celebrating** its people. 一座"文化之城"不应该仅仅有关艺术，还可以是对一个城市独特性的尊重——帮助维持它的商业街，支持当地的设施，最重要的是赞美它的人民。（2020年）

派 celebrated / ˈselɪbreɪtɪd / adj. 著名的 ‖ celebration / ˌselɪˈbreɪʃn / n. 庆祝活动

cost / kɒst / 072

释 n. 费用；成本；代价 v. 需付费；价钱为；使损失；使付出努力

搭 at a cost of 以……为代价 ‖ at all cost 不惜任何代价 ‖ at any cost 无论如何

例 Even if the maintenance work were completed, the value of the vessel would be less than the **cost** of fixing it up. 即使完成了维修工作，这艘船的价值也会低于维修费用。

dean / diːn / 073

释 n. （大学的）学院院长，系主任

例 Robert Storr, who directed the Venice Biennale and is a former **dean** of the Yale School of Art, said the rising costs of shipping and other logistics make the system unsustainable. 威尼斯双年展的导演罗伯特·斯托尔是耶鲁大学艺术学院的前院长，他说，航运和其他物流成本的上升使这个体系难以为继。

official / əˈfɪʃl / 074

释 adj. 官方的；正式的；官僚的 n. 官员

例 Branch points out that, even if a growing number of **official** guidelines and textbooks reflect scientific consensus on climate change, unofficial educational materials that convey more biased perspectives are being distributed to teachers. 布兰奇指出，尽管越来越多的官方指南和教科书反映了对气候变化的科学共识，但向教师分发的非官方教材传达了更多偏颇的观点。（2023年）

Writing Models ◎

pull

scan

transition

sum

admire

fear

fair

quarrel

dissolve

click

posture

speed

---

pull / pʊl / ⓪⑦⑤

释 *v.* 拉；拽；拔出；吸引

例 Nearly 2,000 years ago, as the Romans began to **pull** out of Scotland, they left behind a curious treasure: 10 tons of nails, nearly a million of the things. 将近2 000年前，当罗马人开始撤离苏格兰时，他们留下了一个奇特的宝藏：10吨钉子，将近100万枚。（2024年）

---

scan / skæn / ⓪⑦⑥

释 *v.* 浏览；仔细察看；扫描 *n.* （身体）扫描检查

例 The new technique uses a much faster laser system for **scanning**—the device can now print 660 times as fast as before. 这项新技术使用了更快的激光扫描系统——该设备现在的打印速度是以前的660倍。

---

transition / trænˈzɪʃn / ⓪⑦⑦

释 *n.* 过渡；转变；转型

例 When this practice first started decades ago, it was usually limited to freshmen, to give them a second chance to take a class in their first year if they struggled in their **transition** to college-level courses. 几十年前，这种做法刚开始的时候，通常仅限于大一新生，如果他们在过渡到大学水平课程的过程中遇到困难，可以在第一年给他们第二次选课的机会。（2019年）

派 transitional / trænˈzɪʃənl / *adj.* 暂时的；转型的；过渡的

---

sum / sʌm / ⓪⑦⑧

释 *n.* 金额；款项；总和；总数 *v.* 总结；概括

搭 sum up 总而言之

例 The candidates had two minutes to make opening remarks, take questions, then **sum** it up. 候选人有两分钟的时间致开场白，回答问题，之后进行总结。

---

admire / ədˈmaɪə(r) / ⓪⑦⑨

释 *v.* 钦佩；仰慕；赞赏；欣赏

例 The path lets walkers traverse Switzer and Juniper canyons, located within South Park, as well as explore the neighborhood and **admire** its historical homes. 步行者可以通过这条小路穿过位于南方公园内的瑞士峡谷和杜松峡谷，也可以探索附近的社区，欣赏那里历史悠久的住宅。

派 admiration / ˌædməˈreɪʃn / *n.* 钦佩；赞赏；羡慕

---

fear / fɪə(r) / ⓪⑧⓪

释 *n./v.* 害怕；惧怕；担忧

搭 for fear of (doing) / for fear (that)... 唯恐，以免（发生危险）

例 Many work for the mine, though some residents organize protests, **fearing** environmental damage. 尽管一些居民因担心环境遭到破坏而组织了抗议活动，但许多人还是为这个矿山工作。

fair / feə(r) / 081

释 *adj.* 合理的; 恰当的; 公正的; 相当大或好的 *adv.* 公正地; 公平合理地 *n.* 集市; 展销会

例 To be **fair**, the FSA says it is not telling people to cut out roast foods entirely, but to reduce their lifetime intake. 公平地说, 英国食品标准局表示, 它并不是要人们完全不吃烧烤食品, 而是要减少他们一生的摄入量。(2020年)

quarrel / ˈkwɒrəl / 082

释 *n.* 口角; 争吵 *v.* 争吵; 吵嘴; 吵架

例 The discussion escalated to a loud **quarrel** involving several cast mates over who was in the right, before Brandi stepped in to defend Cardona. 在布兰迪出面为卡多纳辩护之前, 讨论升级为几位演员为谁是对的而大声争吵。

dissolve / dɪˈzɒlv / 083

释 *v.* (使)溶解; 解散; (使)消失

例 Hopes for peace **dissolved** in renewed violence. 和平的希望在新的暴力中破灭了。

click / klɪk / 084

释 *v.* 使发出咔嗒声; 点击, 单击(鼠标) *n.* 咔嗒声; 点按, 单击(鼠标)

搭 click through 点击, 点进

例 By watching what people search for, **click** on and say online, companies can aim "behavioral" ads at those most likely to buy. 通过观察人们在网上搜索、点击和说的内容, 公司可以针对那些最有可能购买的人投放"行为"广告。(2013年)

posture / ˈpɒstʃə(r) / 085

释 *n.* 姿势; 态度; 看法; 立场 *v.* 故作姿态; 装样子

例 They believe that these individuals pose a grave threat to America's national security **posture**. 他们认为这些人对美国的国家安全立场构成了严重威胁。

speed / spiːd / 086

释 *n.* 速度 *v.* 加速; 促进

搭 speed up 加速

例 The robots can increase the **speed** and accuracy of processing orders, keep better track of inventory and save space by fetching products that are stacked higher in the building, he said. 他说, 机器人可以提高处理订单的速度和准确性, 更好地跟踪库存, 并通过抓取在建筑物中被堆放得较高的产品来节省空间。

radical / ˈrædɪkl /　〔087〕

释 *adj.* 根本的；彻底的；激进的 *n.* 激进分子

例 The 17th and 18th centuries were times of **radical** change and curiosity. 17世纪和18世纪是充满巨变和好奇心的时代。（2020年）

fuel / ˈfjuːəl /　〔088〕

释 *n.* 燃料 *v.* 加剧；给（交通工具）加油

例 Here was abundant **fuel** and lumber. 这里有丰富的燃料和木材。（2015年）

host / həʊst /　〔089〕

释 *n.* 主人；节目主持人 *v.* 主办

搭 a host of (=hosts of) 大量

例 To realize how great was the dramatic activity, we must remember further that **hosts** of plays have been lost, and that probably there is no author of note whose entire work has survived. 要认识到当时的戏剧活动有多么辉煌，我们还必须记住，大量剧作都已丢失，可能没有全部作品都幸存的知名作者。（2018年）

派 hostess / ˈhəʊstəs; həʊˈstes / *n.* 女主人；女主持人

pour / pɔː(r) /　〔090〕

释 *v.* 倾倒；倒出；（雨）倾盆而下

搭 pour into 大量投资于 ‖ pour out 畅所欲言；（感情或说话）奔涌，迸发

例 She **poured** salt into the palm of her hand and then sprinkled it over the stew. 她把盐倒在自己的手掌里，然后撒在炖菜上。

pass / pɑːs /　〔091〕

释 *v.* 走过；经过；传递；通过（考试）；（时间）消逝 *n.* 通行证；车票；关口

例 Last Thursday, the French Senate **passed** a digital services tax, which would impose an entirely new tax on large multinationals that provide digital services to consumers or users in France. 上周四，法国参议院通过了一项数字服务税，该税将对向法国的消费者或用户提供数字服务的大型跨国公司征收一种全新的税。（2020年）

heel / hiːl /　〔092〕

释 *n.* 脚后跟；鞋后跟；女高跟鞋

例 Shelves of **heels** and boots could be seen in the background of the photo. 在照片的背景中可以看到高跟鞋和靴子的货架。

classic / ˈklæsɪk /　〔093〕

释 *adj.* 典型的；经典的；第一流的 *n.* 经典作品，名著，杰作

例 This **classic** cookware is built to last, and extremely inexpensive. 这款经典的炊具经久耐用，而且价格低廉。

characterize/-ise / ˈkærəktəraɪz / |094|

释 *v.* 以……为特征; 描述为

例 Which of the following **characterises** the scientific publishing model? 以下哪项是科学出版模式的特征?(2020年)

error / ˈerə(r) / |095|

释 *n.* 错误

搭 in error 错误地

例 Good writing most often occurs when you are in hot pursuit of an idea rather than in a nervous search for **errors**. 好的写作往往发生在你热衷于追求一个想法,而不是紧张地寻找错误的时候。(2008年)

roll / rəʊl / |096|

释 *v.*(使)翻滚,滚动; 把(衣服的边)卷起来 *n.* 卷; 卷轴

例 We watched the waves **rolling** onto the beach. 我们注视着波浪涌向海滩。

mend / mend / |097|

释 *v.* 修理; 修补; 弥合(分歧)

例 We don't have to learn how to be mentally healthy; it is built into us in the same way that our bodies know how to heal a cut or **mend** a broken bone. 我们不需要去学习如何保持心理健康,它是我们生来就有的,正如我们的身体知道如何治愈伤口或者修复断裂的骨头一样。(2016年)

overhead / ˌəʊvəˈhed / |098|

释 *adv.* 在头上方; 在空中 *adj.* 头上方的 *n.* 营运费用; 经常性开支

例 With seaside surroundings and strings of fairy lights **overhead**, a meal on Ibn's terrace has a distinct holiday dining feel. 有海边的环境和头顶上的仙女灯串相伴,在伊本的露台上吃饭有一种独特的假日用餐的感觉。

stem / stem / |099|

释 *n.*(植物的)秆,茎,梗; [语法]词干 *v.* 起源于,来自; 阻止; 封堵; 遏止

搭 stem from 是……的结果; 起源于; 根源是

例 The experts will allow for a plant with multiple **stems** that grows taller than 13 feet to be considered a tree. 专家们将允许把长有多根茎、高度超过13英尺的植物视为树木。

coach / kəʊtʃ / |100|

释 *n.* 教练; 私人教师 *v.* 训练,培养; 辅导

例 The only American public-sector workers who earn well above $250,000 a year are university sports **coaches** and the president of the United States. 年收入远高于25万美元的美国公共部门工作人员只有大学体育教练和美国总统。(2012年)

☐ ☐ absence
☐ ☐ acknowledge
☐ ☐ adapt
☐ ☐ admire
☐ ☐ analyze/-yse
☐ ☐ announce
☐ ☐ aspire
☐ ☐ assemble
☐ ☐ assurance
☐ ☐ ban
☐ ☐ behave
☐ ☐ cater
☐ ☐ celebrate
☐ ☐ chancellor
☐ ☐ characterize/-ise
☐ ☐ check
☐ ☐ classic
☐ ☐ click
☐ ☐ coach
☐ ☐ coherent
☐ ☐ compel
☐ ☐ complex
☐ ☐ concession
☐ ☐ contain
☐ ☐ cost
☐ ☐ credit
☐ ☐ database
☐ ☐ deadline
☐ ☐ dean
☐ ☐ delivery
☐ ☐ descend

☐ ☐ dissolve
☐ ☐ divide
☐ ☐ enormous
☐ ☐ error
☐ ☐ essence
☐ ☐ extract
☐ ☐ facilitate
☐ ☐ fair
☐ ☐ fear
☐ ☐ fearful
☐ ☐ firm
☐ ☐ flaw
☐ ☐ flexible
☐ ☐ fuel
☐ ☐ genetic
☐ ☐ heel
☐ ☐ host
☐ ☐ hostile
☐ ☐ inherent
☐ ☐ input
☐ ☐ interior
☐ ☐ maintain
☐ ☐ maintenance
☐ ☐ manual
☐ ☐ margin
☐ ☐ mend
☐ ☐ mode
☐ ☐ modify
☐ ☐ official
☐ ☐ oppose
☐ ☐ overhead

☐ ☐ pass
☐ ☐ perspective
☐ ☐ portray
☐ ☐ posture
☐ ☐ pour
☐ ☐ principle
☐ ☐ probe
☐ ☐ prosper
☐ ☐ pull
☐ ☐ quarrel
☐ ☐ radical
☐ ☐ random
☐ ☐ republic
☐ ☐ revelation
☐ ☐ roll
☐ ☐ sarcastic
☐ ☐ scan
☐ ☐ scope
☐ ☐ select
☐ ☐ simplify
☐ ☐ snap
☐ ☐ spectacle
☐ ☐ speed
☐ ☐ sponsor
☐ ☐ spread
☐ ☐ statistics
☐ ☐ stem
☐ ☐ succeed
☐ ☐ sum
☐ ☐ supplement
☐ ☐ temporary

☐ ☐ term
☐ ☐ transition
☐ ☐ underestimate
☐ ☐ undergo
☐ ☐ undermine
☐ ☐ unexpected
☐ ☐ venture

音频

Day 10

- [ ] episode
- [ ] negotiate
- [ ] detector
- [ ] productive
- [ ] decrease
- [ ] refusal
- [ ] superb
- [ ] superfluous
- [ ] impressive
- [ ] circumstance
- [ ] mostly
- [ ] compose
- [ ] aim
- [ ] preferable
- [ ] explain
- [ ] nuisance
- [ ] tradition
- [ ] peak
- [ ] partial
- [ ] resolve
- [ ] standard
- [ ] sign
- [ ] comparative
- [ ] detach
- [ ] constant
- [ ] segment
- [ ] vivid
- [ ] equivalent
- [ ] executive
- [ ] mass
- [ ] restrict

- [ ] possibility
- [ ] vulnerable
- [ ] hono(u)r
- [ ] visual
- [ ] occur
- [ ] purchase
- [ ] defeat
- [ ] behalf
- [ ] coincide
- [ ] exposure
- [ ] conflict
- [ ] poisonous
- [ ] generate
- [ ] break
- [ ] reputation
- [ ] conjunction
- [ ] advance
- [ ] entail
- [ ] pay
- [ ] course
- [ ] eager
- [ ] responsible
- [ ] potential
- [ ] fatal
- [ ] comparison
- [ ] yield
- [ ] succession
- [ ] ignore
- [ ] virtual
- [ ] scandal
- [ ] alter

- [ ] complaint
- [ ] foremost
- [ ] superstition
- [ ] bias
- [ ] gap
- [ ] trace
- [ ] remarkable
- [ ] survey
- [ ] tremendous
- [ ] bold
- [ ] mankind
- [ ] slack
- [ ] patent
- [ ] slave
- [ ] underground
- [ ] warn
- [ ] curiosity
- [ ] shock
- [ ] starve
- [ ] spend
- [ ] puzzle
- [ ] push
- [ ] common
- [ ] noble
- [ ] gain
- [ ] discount
- [ ] banner
- [ ] situation
- [ ] translate
- [ ] branch
- [ ] repeat

- [ ] chaos
- [ ] sober
- [ ] upward
- [ ] gift
- [ ] forget
- [ ] impulse
- [ ] request

episode / ˈepɪsəʊd /

001

释 *n.* 片段; 逸事; (连续剧的) 一集; 情节

例 One of the funniest **episodes** in the book occurs in Chapter 6. 书中最有趣的片段之一出现在第六章。

negotiate / nɪˈgəʊʃɪeɪt /

002

释 *v.* 谈判; 协商; 达成 (协议)

例 Either way, one benefit of a "national" organization would be to **negotiate** better prices, if possible, with drug manufacturers. 无论如何, "全国性"组织的一个好处是, 如果可能的话, 可以与药品生产商谈判更优惠的价格。(2005年)

detector / dɪˈtektə(r) /

003

释 *n.* 探测器; 检测器

例 In keeping with security regulations, everyone must pass through the metal **detector**. 根据安全规定, 每个人都必须通过金属探测器检测。

productive / prəˈdʌktɪv /

004

释 *adj.* 生产的; 生产力高的; 富有成效的

例 Only when humanity began to get its food in a more **productive** way was there time for other things. 只有当人类开始以更具生产力的方式获取食物时, 才有时间做其他事情。(2009年)

decrease / dɪˈkriːs /

005

释 *v./n.* 减少; 降低; 减小

例 This might sound small, but to undo the effects of such a **decrease** a candidate would need 30 more GMAT points than would otherwise have been necessary. 这听起来似乎很小, 但要消除这种下降的影响, 申请者的GMAT成绩要比原本需要的多30分。(2013年)

refusal / rɪˈfjuːzl /

006

释 *n.* 拒绝

例 In the final paragraph about the significance of the setting in "A & P," the student brings together the reasons Sammy quit his job by referring to his **refusal** to accept Lengel's store policies. 在最后一段关于 "A & P" 中背景的意义, 学生提到萨米拒绝接受伦格尔的商店政策, 从而将其辞职的原因归纳到一起。(2008年)

superb / suːˈpɜːb /

007

释 *adj.* 质量极高的; 极佳的; 卓越的

例 There is the Royal Shakespeare Company (RSC), which presents **superb** productions of the plays at the Shakespeare Memorial Theatre on the Avon. (两者中的) 一个是皇家莎士比亚剧团 (RSC), 它在雅芳河畔的莎士比亚纪念剧院上演极佳的戏剧演出。(2006年)

superfluous / suːˈpɜːfluəs /

释 *adj.* 多余的；过剩的；不必要的

例 Humans are unique in their capacity to not only make tools but then turn around and use them to create **superfluous** material goods—paintings, sculpture and architecture—and **superfluous** experiences—music, literature, religion and philosophy. 人类的独特之处在于，他们不仅能制造工具，反过来还能利用工具创造不必要的物质产品——绘画、雕塑和建筑，以及不必要的体验——音乐、文学、宗教和哲学。（2012年）

近 unnecessary / ʌnˈnesəsəri / *adj.* 不必要的，多余的 ‖ surplus / ˈsɜːpləs / *adj.* 过剩的，多余的

impressive / ɪmˈpresɪv /

释 *adj.* 给人印象深刻的；令人赞叹的；令人敬佩的

例 The early settlers of Massachusetts Bay included men of **impressive** achievements and influence in England. 马萨诸塞湾的早期移民中包括在英格兰拥有令人钦佩的成就并具有影响力的人物。（2009年）

circumstance / ˈsɜːkəmstəns /

释 *n.* 条件；状况；环境

例 In fact, **circumstances** seem to be designed to bring out the best in us, and if we feel that we have been "wronged" then we are unlikely to begin a conscious effort to escape from our situation. 事实上，环境似乎就是为了激发我们最好的一面，如果我们觉得自己"受了委屈"，那么我们就不太可能开始有意识地努力摆脱困境。（2011年）

mostly / ˈməʊstli /

释 *adv.* 主要地；大部分；通常

例 These are **mostly** students who had no opportunity as children to travel to wilderness areas, wildlife refuges or national parks. 这些学生大多在孩提时代没有机会前往荒野地区、野生动物保护区或国家公园。（2022年）

compose / kəmˈpəʊz /

释 *v.* 创作；组成，构成

搭 be composed of 由……组成

例 Do not attempt to **compose** a perfectly correct draft the first time around. 不要试图第一次就创作出十分准确的草稿。（2008年）

派 composed / kəmˈpəʊzd / *adj.* 沉着的 ‖ composer / kəmˈpəʊzə(r) / *n.* 作曲家；创作者

近 constitute / ˈkɒnstɪtjuːt / *v.* 组成；构成

辨 compose和constitute都有"组成；构成"的意思。compose多用于被动语态，指将两个或两个以上的人或物放到一起形成一个整体；constitute指由某些部分组成一个整体或构成某物的基本成分。

Writing Models ⦿

aim

preferable

explain

nuisance

tradition

peak

partial

resolve

standard

sign

comparative

detach

---

aim / eɪm /

🔘 **释** *n.* 目的 *v.* 以……为目标; 打算; 针对

🔘 **例** That's why Hayden's expedition **aimed** to produce a fuller understanding of the Yellowstone River region, from its hot springs and waterfalls to its variety of flora and fauna. 这就是为什么海登的探险旨在更全面地了解黄石河地区, 从它的温泉、瀑布到各种动植物。(2023年)

🔘 **近** purpose / 'pɜːpəs / *n.* 目的; 目标

013

preferable / 'prefrəbl /

🔘 **释** *adj.* 更可取的, 较适合的

🔘 **例** While comment and reaction from lawyers may enhance stories, it is **preferable** for journalists to rely on their own notions of significance and make their own judgments. 尽管律师的评论和反应可能会提升新闻报道的价值, 但是新闻工作者们最好还是依靠自己对事件重要性的认识来做出自己的判断。(2007年)

014

explain / ɪk'spleɪn /

🔘 **释** *v.* 解释; 说明 (……的) 原因

🔘 **例** It is hoped that future studies could **explain** these differences and perhaps lead to different treatments for men and women. 希望未来的研究能解释这些差异, 或许它能为男性和女性提供不同的治疗方法。(2021年)

🔘 **派** explanation / ˌeksplə'neɪʃn / *n.* 解释; 原因

015

nuisance / 'nuːsns /

🔘 **释** *n.* 讨厌的人 (或东西); 麻烦事

🔘 **例** Many of them instead become the kind of **nuisance**-lawsuit filer that makes the tort system a costly nightmare. 他们中的许多人反而成了那种滋扰性诉讼的提起者, 使侵权制度成为一场代价高昂的噩梦。(2014年)

016

tradition / trə'dɪʃn /

🔘 **释** *n.* 传统; 传说

🔘 **例** A native literary drama had been created, its alliance with the public playhouses established, and at least some of its great **traditions** had been begun. 本土文学戏剧已经诞生, 它与公共剧场的联盟已经建立, 至少它的一些伟大传统已经开始。(2018年)

017

peak / piːk /

🔘 **释** *v.* 达到顶点; 达到顶峰; 达到最高值 *n.* 顶点; 顶峰; 山峰; 山顶

🔘 **搭** at the peak of 在……高峰期

🔘 **例** It **peaks** in young adulthood, levels out for a period of time, and then generally starts to slowly decline as we age. 它 (流体智力) 在青壮年时期达到顶峰, 在一段时间内趋于平稳, 然后随着年龄的增长开始缓慢下降。(2021年)

🔘 **近** summit / 'sʌmɪt / *n.* 顶点; 最高级会议 ‖ climax / 'klaɪmæks / *n.* 顶点; 高潮

018

partial / ˈpɑːʃl /

0|1|9

釋 *adj.* 部分的；偏袒的，偏爱的

例 This performance is only a **partial** success. 这次表演仅获得了部分成功。

resolve / rɪˈzɒlv /

0|2|0

釋 *v.* 解决；表决；下决心 *n.* 决心，坚定的信念

例 They should also learn how to solve problems and **resolve** conflicts, ways to brainstorm and think critically. 他们应该学会如何解决问题和矛盾，学会集思广益和批判性地思考。（2007年）

派 resolved / rɪˈzɒlvd / *adj.* 下定决心的

近 solve / sɒlv / *v.* 解决；解答

standard / ˈstændəd /

0|2|1

釋 *n.* 标准 *adj.* 标准的

搭 living standards 生活水平

例 Even if a state is considered a high performer in its science **standards**, "that does not mean it will be taught", he says. 他说，即使一个州被认为在科学标准方面表现出色，"也并不意味着会教授它（气候变化）"。（2023年）

近 criterion / kraɪˈtɪəriən / *n.*（判定的）标准 ‖ norm / nɔːm / *n.* 正常行为；规范

sign / saɪn /

0|2|2

釋 *v.* 签字（或署名）于；签署（信、文件等）*n.* 迹象，征兆，预兆；标牌，标志

例 Therefore, unless customers are prepared to **sign** release agreements, the use of AI may become somewhat restricted in the future. 因此，除非客户准备签署免责协议，否则人工智能的使用今后可能会受到一定限制。（2023年）

comparative / kəmˈpærətɪv /

0|2|3

釋 *adj.* 比较的，相比的；相对的 *n.*（形容词或副词的）比较级形式

例 That, at least, is the hope. But a **comparative** study of linguistic traits published online today supplies a reality check. 这至少是一种希望。但是，今天在网络发表的一项语言特征比较研究提供了一个现实的检验。（2012年）

detach / dɪˈtætʃ /

0|2|4

釋 *v.* 拆卸；（使）分开，脱离；挣脱；摆脱；离开；派遣

例 Otherwise, academics will continue to think dangerously alike, increasingly **detached** from the societies which they study, investigate and criticise. 否则，学者们的思维将继续危险地趋同，越来越脱离他们所研究、调查和批评的社会。（2011年）

constant / ˈkɒnstənt /　　025

释 *adj.* 连续发生的; 不断的; 重复的; 不变的; 固定的; 恒定的 *n.* 常数; 常量

例 **Constant** health scares just end up with no one listening. 一味地担心健康问题, 最终只会无人倾听。(2020年)

segment　　026

释 / ˈsegmənt / *n.* 部分; 份; 段 / segˈment / *v.* 分割; 划分

例 In so doing they give composure to a **segment** of the inarticulate environment in which they take their stand. 通过这种方式, 他们就将宁静赋予了自己所处的那一小块难以名状的环境中。(2013年)

vivid / ˈvɪvɪd /　　027

释 *adj.* (记忆、描述等) 清晰的; 生动的; 鲜明的

例 While veterans of previous expeditions had written at length about stunning sights, these **vivid** photographs were another thing entirely. 虽然前几次探险的老兵们曾用大量篇幅描写过令人惊叹的景色, 但这些生动的照片完全是另一回事。(2023年)

equivalent / ɪˈkwɪvələnt /　　028

释 *adj.* 相等的, 相当的; 等价的, 等值的 *n.* 对等物

搭 (be) equivalent to 相当于

例 In a society that so persistently celebrates procreation, is it any wonder that admitting you regret having children is **equivalent** to admitting you support kitten-killing? 在一个一味崇尚生育的社会里, 承认自己后悔生孩子就等同于承认自己支持杀害小猫, 这有什么好奇怪的呢? (2011年)

executive / ɪɡˈzekjətɪv /　　029

释 *adj.* 有执行权的, 实施的; 行政的 *n.* 经理; 主管; 领导层

例 In its latest survey of CEO pay, *The Wall Street Journal* finds that "a substantial part" of **executive** pay is now tied to performance. 《华尔街日报》在针对首席执行官薪酬的最新调查中发现, 现在高管薪酬的 "很大一部分" 与业绩挂钩。(2019年)

近 director / dəˈrektə(r) / *n.* 主管; 董事 ‖ president / ˈprezɪdənt / *n.* 总统; 董事长; 主席

mass / mæs /　　030

释 *n.* 块; 团; 堆; [pl.]普通百姓; 质量 *adj.* 人数众多的 *v.* 聚集

搭 a mass of 一堆; 大量 ‖ mass media 大众传媒

例 Under the law, using a fashion model that does not meet a government-defined index of body **mass** could result in a $85,000 fine and six months in prison. 根据这项法律, 使用不符合政府规定的身体质量指数的时装模特可能会被处以85 000美元的罚款和六个月的监禁。(2016年)

restrict / rɪ'strɪkt / 031

释 *v.* 限制

搭 restrict... to... 把……限制于……

例 The sale of alcoholic beverages is **restricted** to those over 21 in that country. 在那个国家，酒精类饮料的出售只限于21岁以上的人。

近 limit / 'lɪmɪt / *v.* 限制

possibility / ˌpɒsə'bɪləti / 032

释 *n.* 可能，可能性；机会

例 Travellers on the Silk Road faced the **possibility** of being attacked by thieves or being subjected to extreme weather conditions. 丝绸之路上的旅行者可能会遭到盗贼的袭击，或遭受极端天气条件的影响。（2023年）

近 probability / ˌprɒbə'bɪləti / *n.* 概率；可能性

vulnerable / 'vʌlnərəbl / 033

释 *adj.* 易受伤害的；容易患……病的

搭 be vulnerable to 易受……的伤害

例 It's especially **vulnerable** to light damage, and by the mid-1990s, Gilardi's pumpkins, roses, and other figures were splitting and crumbling. 它特别容易受到光线的损害，到了20世纪90年代中期，吉拉尔迪的南瓜、玫瑰和其他雕像都出现了裂缝和破损。（2022年）

hono(u)r / 'ɒnə(r) / 034

释 *v.* 给予表扬（或奖励、头衔、称号）；尊重，尊敬 *n.* 尊敬，尊重；名誉

搭 in honor of 为纪念……，向……表示敬意

例 He was knighted in 1967, the first music critic to be so **honored**. 1967年，他被授予爵士称号，是首位获此殊荣的音乐评论家。（2010年）

近 respect / rɪ'spekt / *v.* 尊敬，尊重 ‖ esteem / ɪ'stiːm / *v.* 尊敬；认为

反 dishonor / dɪs'ɒnə(r) / *v.* 侮辱；使……蒙羞 ‖ disgrace / dɪs'ɡreɪs / *v.* 使丢脸；使蒙受耻辱

visual / 'vɪʒuəl / 035

释 *adj.* 视力的；视觉的 *n.* 视觉资料

例 An effective Washington operator, Hayden sensed that he could capitalize on the expedition's stunning **visuals**. 海登是华盛顿的一名能干的操作员，他认为自己可以利用探险队令人惊叹的视觉资料。（2023年）

occur / ə'kɜː(r) / 036

释 *v.* 发生；出现；存在于；出现在

搭 occur to sb. （观念或想法）出现在某人的头脑中

例 In fact, all of these cultural developments **occurred** separately at different times in many parts of the world. 事实上，这些文化发展都是在世界许多地方的不同时期分别出现的。（2009年）

purchase / ˈpɜːtʃəs / 037

释 *n.* 购买; 购买的东西 *v.* 购买

例 Having said that, I do feel that whatever artifacts find their way to public museums should, in fact, be sanctioned as having been obtained on loan, legally **purchased**, or obtained by treaty. 尽管如此，我还是认为，无论什么文物进入公共博物馆，事实上都应该被认定为是借用、合法购买或通过条约获得的。（2024年）

defeat / dɪˈfiːt / 038

释 *v.* 击败; 使失败; 战胜; 挫败; 使困惑; 难住 *n.* 击败; 失败; 战胜; 战败; 挫败

例 But on the more important matter of the Constitution, the decision was an 8-0 **defeat** for the Administration's effort to upset the balance of power between the federal government and the states. 但在更重要的宪法问题上，该裁决以8比0的比分击败了政府打破联邦政府与各州之间权力平衡的努力。（2013年）

behalf / bɪˈhɑːf / 039

释 *n.* 代表

搭 on behalf of sb. 代表某人

例 The ability to guard customer data is the key to market value, which the board is responsible for on **behalf** of shareholders. 保护客户数据的能力是市场价值的关键，而董事会则代表股东对此负责。（2007年）

coincide / ˌkəʊɪnˈsaɪd / 040

释 *v.* 同时发生; 一致, 符合

搭 coincide with 与……同时发生

例 **Coinciding** with the groundbreaking theory of biological evolution proposed by British naturalist Charles Darwin in the 1860s, British social philosopher Herbert Spencer put forward his own theory of biological and cultural evolution. 19世纪60年代，英国博物学家查尔斯·达尔文提出了具有开创意义的生物进化论，与此同时，英国社会哲学家赫伯特·斯宾塞也提出了自己的生物和文化进化论。

exposure / ɪkˈspəʊʒə(r) / 041

释 *n.* [摄]曝光; 遭受; 接触

例 But **exposure** times were much quicker by the 1880s, and the introduction of the Box Brownie and other portable cameras meant that, though slow by today's digital standards, the **exposure** was almost instantaneous. 但到了19世纪80年代，曝光时间已经大大缩短，而盒式布朗尼相机和其他便携式相机的问世意味着，尽管以今天的数码标准来看曝光速度较慢，但曝光几乎是瞬间完成的。（2021年）

conflict 042

释 / kənˈflɪkt / v. （两种思想、信仰、说法等）冲突，抵触
/ ˈkɒnflɪkt / n. 争执；分歧；冲突；矛盾，不一致；（军事）冲突

例 The White House argued that Arizona's laws **conflicted** with its enforcement priorities, even if state laws complied with federal statutes to the letter. 白宫认为，亚利桑那州的法律与其执法重点相冲突，即使该州的法律完全符合联邦法规。（2013年）

poisonous / ˈpɔɪzənəs / 043

释 adj. 有毒的；引起中毒的；分泌毒素的；恶毒的；极端讨厌（或不友善）的

例 Immigrants are quickly fitting into this common culture, which may not be altogether elevating but is hardly **poisonous**. 移民很快就融入了这种共同的文化，这种文化也许并不完全令人振奋，但也几乎没有毒害。（2006年）

generate / ˈdʒenəreɪt / 044

释 v. 产生；生成；引起

搭 generate electricity/heat/power 发电/发热/产生动力

例 At the same time AI can also be used to **generate** content for social media posts and chat sites. 同时，人工智能还可用于为社交媒体发布和聊天网站生成内容。（2023年）

break / breɪk / 045

释 v. 打碎；打破（沉默、传统、纪录）；违反；戒除（习惯）；破解（密码）n. 中止；休息时间；短假；骨折；间隔；缝隙；机遇；机会

搭 break through 冲破障碍；获得成功 ‖ break down（机器、车辆等）出故障；系统瘫痪；破除（障碍、偏见等）‖ break up（婚姻、恋爱关系）破裂，分手；解散 ‖ break out（战争、斗殴、疾病等）爆发 ‖ break in 破门而入；打断 ‖ break off 终止，突然停止 ‖ take a break 休息一下

例 The self-help expert's guide aims to build good habits and **break** bad ones via tiny changes in behavior. 自助专家的指南旨在通过微小的行为改变，养成好习惯，改掉坏习惯。

reputation / ˌrepjuˈteɪʃn / 046

释 n. 名望；声誉

例 It is only the Queen who has preserved the monarchy's **reputation** with her rather ordinary (if well-heeled) granny style. 只有女王以她那相当普通（虽然富裕）的老太太风格维护了君主制的声誉。（2015年）

conjunction / kənˈdʒʌŋkʃn / 047

释 n. 结合，连接；联合；[语法]连（接）词

搭 in conjunction with sb./sth. 与某人/某事相关联

例 Seat belts are more effective when used in **conjunction** with air bags. 安全带和安全气囊一起使用时效果更佳。

Writing Models ◎

advance

entail

pay

course

eager

responsible

potential

fatal

comparison

yield

succession

ignore

---

advance / əd'vɑːns / [048]

释 *n./v.* 进步，进展；前进，行进 *adj.* 预先的，事先的

搭 in advance (of sth.)（在某事前）预先，事先

例 In the last decade or so, **advances** in technology have allowed mass-market labels such as Zara, H&M, and Uniqlo to react to trends more quickly and anticipate demand more precisely. 在过去十年左右的时间里，技术的进步让Zara、H&M和优衣库等大众品牌能够更快地对潮流做出反应，更准确地预测需求。（2013年）

---

entail / ɪn'teɪl / [049]

释 *v.* 牵涉；需要；使必要；势必造成

例 It is becoming less clear, however, that such a theory would be a simplification, given the dimensions and universes that it might **entail**. 然而，考虑到这种理论可能牵涉的维度和宇宙，它是否是一种简化变得不那么清楚了。（2012年）

近 encompass / ɪn'kʌmpəs / *v.* 包含；涉及 ‖ demand / dɪ'mɑːnd / *v.* 需要，要求

---

pay / peɪ / [050]

释 *v.* 付款；付出；受益 *n.* 工资，薪金

例 In this age of generalists, it **pays** to have specific knowledge or skills. 在这个通才辈出的时代，拥有特定的知识或技能是有益的。（2022年）

派 payment / 'peɪmənt / *n.* 支付；支付的款项

---

course / kɔːs / [051]

释 *n.* 课程；一道菜；航线；进程；行动方式

例 Before the Depression ends, it will likely change the life **course** and character of a generation of young adults. 在经济大萧条结束之前，它很可能会影响人们的人生历程，改变年轻一代的性格。

---

eager / 'iːɡə(r) / [052]

释 *adj.* 热切的；渴望的

例 There have been signs that voters are unhappy with the ruling party and **eager** to express their discontent, especially over stagnating economic growth. 有迹象表明，选民对执政党不满，渴望表达他们的不满，尤其是对经济增长停滞不前的不满。

派 eagerness / 'iːɡənəs / *n.* 渴望；热心

---

responsible / rɪ'spɒnsəbl / [053]

释 *adj.* 负责的；有责任心的

搭 be responsible for 对……负责

例 Teachers are **responsible** for teaching kids how to learn; parents should be **responsible** for teaching them how to work. 老师有责任教孩子们如何学习，家长则应负责教他们如何工作。（2007年）

---

potential / pə'tenʃl / 054

🔷 n. 可能性; 潜在性; 潜力; 潜质 adj. 潜在的; 可能的

🔷 Surely there must be some middle ground that balances zoos' treatment of animals with their educational **potential**. 当然, 一定存在某种中间地带能够平衡动物园对待动物的方式与动物园的教育潜力。(2022年)

fatal / 'feɪtl / 055

🔷 adj. 致命的; 毁灭性的; 灾难性的; 导致失败的

🔷 Since the beginning, this price tag has been PreCheck's **fatal** flaw. 从一开始, 这个价格标签就是PreCheck的致命缺陷。(2017年)

comparison / kəm'pærɪsn / 056

🔷 n. 比较, 对比

🔷 in comparison with 与……相比

🔷 However, a **comparison** with data for weeks when there was no experimentation showed that output always went up on Mondays. 然而, 与没有进行实验的几周的数据进行比较后发现, 周一的产出总是上升的。(2010年)

🔷 analogy / ə'nælədʒi / n. 类推, 类比 ‖ distinction / dɪ'stɪŋkʃn / n. 区别

yield / jiːld / 057

🔷 v. 出产 (作物); 产生 (收益、效益等); 提供; 屈服, 让步; 变形, 弯曲 n. 产量, 产出; 利润

🔷 yield to sb./sth. 屈服于某人或某物

🔷 Typically, they survey and sample (make test excavations on) large areas of terrain to determine where excavation will **yield** useful information. 通常情况下, 他们会对大面积地形进行勘测和取样 (进行试掘), 以确定在哪些地方进行挖掘可以产出有用的信息。(2014年)

succession / sək'seʃn / 058

🔷 n. 继承; 继任; (尤指王位的) 继承权; 一系列, 连续; 交替; 更迭

🔷 As boards scrutinize **succession** plans in response to shareholder pressure, executives who don't get the nod also may wish to move on. 在股东的压力下, 董事会对继任计划进行了严格审查, 未获提名的高管也可能希望继续留任。(2011年)

🔷 successor / sək'sesə(r) / n. 继承人 ‖ successive / sək'sesɪv / adj. 接连的, 连续的

ignore / ɪg'nɔː(r) / 059

🔷 v. 忽视; 对……不予理会; 佯装未见

🔷 It tends to **ignore**, and thus eventually to eliminate, many elements in the land community that lack commercial value, but that are essential to its healthy functioning. 它 (这种保护体系) 往往会忽视陆地群落里那些缺乏商业价值的 (物种), 但这些 (物种) 是对其健康运作至关重要的要素。(2010年)

virtual / 'vɜːtʃuəl /　060

释 *adj.* 实际上的，事实上的；虚拟的

例 The best uses of 3D printers and **virtual** reality haven't been invented yet. 3D打印机和虚拟现实技术的最佳用途尚未被发明出来。（2018年）

scandal / 'skændl /　061

释 *n.* 丑闻；流言蜚语

例 The **scandal** has made them the laughing stock of the country. 那条丑闻使他们成为举国上下的笑柄。

alter / 'ɔːltə(r) /　062

释 *v.* 改变，更改

例 An awareness that they were being experimented upon seemed to be enough to **alter** workers' behavior by itself. 意识到自己正在被试验，似乎本身就足以改变工人的行为。（2010年）

派 alternate / 'ɔːltəneɪt / *v.* 交替，轮换 ‖ alteration / ˌɔːltə'reɪʃn / *n.* 改变，变更

近 shift / ʃɪft / *v.* 转变 ‖ transform / træns'fɔːm / *v.* 变形

complaint / kəm'pleɪnt /　063

释 *n.* 抱怨；诉苦

例 The long-standing **complaint** by the USPS and its unions can be addressed by removing its burden of retiree health care. 美国邮政及其工会长期以来的抱怨可以通过消除退休人员医疗负担来解决。（2018年）

foremost / 'fɔːməʊst /　064

释 *adj.* 最重要的；最著名的

例 During his lifetime, though, he was also one of England's **foremost** classical-music critics, and a stylist so widely admired that his *Autobiography* (1947) became a best-seller. 不过，他生前也是英国最重要的古典音乐评论家之一，还是一位广受推崇的造型设计师，也因此他的《自传》（1947年）成了畅销书。（2010年）

superstition / ˌsuːpə'stɪʃn /　065

释 *n.* 迷信，迷信观念（或思想）

例 Ignorance and **superstition** prevent them from benefiting from modern medicine. 无知和迷信使他们无法享受现代医学所带来的好处。

bias / 'baɪəs /　066

释 *n.* 偏见；偏爱 *v.* 使有偏见；影响……以致产生偏差

例 It uses analytics to help identify where there may be **bias** in the hiring process. 它利用数据分析帮助识别招聘过程中可能存在的偏见。（2021年）

近 prejudice / 'predʒudɪs / *n.* 成见，偏见 *v.* 使存有偏见

◎ Study Notes

gap / gæp /

067

释 *n.* 分歧, 差距; 缺口

搭 gap year 空缺年 (源自英国, 通常指中学毕业后进入大学前的1年假期, 常用于实习或旅游。)

例 Finally, because automation threatens to widen the **gap** between capital income and labor income, taxes and the safety net will have to be rethought. 最后, 由于自动化有可能扩大资本收入与劳动收入之间的差距, 因此必须重新考虑税收和安全网。(2018年)

trace / treɪs /

068

释 *v.* 追溯; 发现, 找到; 追踪; 描绘 (事物的过程或发展); 记述; 勾画出 *n.* 痕迹, 踪迹

搭 disappear without a trace 消失得无影无踪

例 In *Oliver Twist*, he **traces** an orphan's progress from the workhouse to the criminal slums of London. 在《雾都孤儿》中, 他描绘了一个孤儿从救济院到伦敦犯罪贫民窟的经历。(2017年)

remarkable / rɪˈmɑːkəbl /

069

释 *adj.* 卓越的, 非凡的; 值得注意的

例 Even before the invention of the electric light bulb, the author produced a **remarkable** work of speculative fiction that would foreshadow many ethical questions to be raised by technologies yet to come. 甚至在电灯泡发明之前, 作者就已经创作了一部出色的推理小说, 这部小说预示着未来技术将引发的许多伦理问题。(2019年)

survey

070

释 / ˈsɜːveɪ / *n.* 调查; 全面检查; 概述 / səˈveɪ / *v.* 调查; 审视; 全面评述; 勘测

例 The **survey** stated that, within the next decade, AI programs will have a 50% or greater chance of completing the vast majority of various tasks, including writing songs or installing wiring into a new home. 这项调查指出, 在未来十年内, 人工智能程序将有50%或更大的概率完成各种各样的绝大多数任务, 包括编写歌曲或为新家安装供电线路。

近 research / rɪˈsɜːtʃ / *n.* 研究, 调查

tremendous / trəˈmendəs /

071

释 *adj.* 巨大的; 极大的; 极好的

例 And for those able to navigate today's startup journey, the rewards can be **tremendous**—for investors, founders, and the Innovation Economy at large. 对于那些能够驾驭当今创业之旅的人来说, 回报可能是巨大的——对投资者、创始人和整个创新经济来说都是如此。

派 tremendously / trəˈmendəsli / *adv.* 非常地; 极大地

Writing Models ◎

bold

mankind

slack

patent

slave

underground

warn

curiosity

shock

starve

spend

puzzle

bold / bəuld /   072

释 *adj.* 大胆的；勇敢的；（色彩或图案）醒目的；放肆的，莽撞的
n. [印刷字体]粗体字，黑体字

例 They transform the aspirations of the people who live there; they nudge the self-image of the city into a **bolder** and more optimistic light. 它们改变了居住在那里的人们的愿望；它们将城市的自我形象推向更大胆、更乐观的一面。（2020年）

mankind / mæn'kaɪnd /   073

释 *n.* 人类

例 As the debate about how AI will shape **mankind**'s future rages on, some tech experts have insisted the technology will coexist with workers rather than replace them, and even fuel a strong labor market by creating new jobs. 随着人工智能将如何塑造人类未来的争论愈演愈烈，一些技术专家坚持认为，这项技术将与工人共存，而不是取代他们，甚至通过创造新的就业机会来促进劳动力市场的繁荣。

slack / slæk /   074

释 *adj.* 松弛的；萧条的；懈怠的 *v.* 懈怠；怠惰；偷懒 *n.* （绳索的）松弛部分；煤屑

搭 slack off 松懈，放松；懈怠

例 Although the causes of the recent bank meltdowns aren't yet fully known, some industry observers have pointed to **slack** risk management. 虽然近期银行倒闭的原因尚不完全清楚，但一些行业观察人士指出，原因在于风险管理不力。

patent / 'pætnt /   075

释 *n.* 专利权；专利证书 *adj.* 受专利保护的；明显的

例 The Federal Circuit's action comes in the wake of a series of recent decisions by the Supreme Court that has narrowed the scope of protections for **patent** holders. 在联邦巡回法院采取这一行动之前，最高法院最近做出了一系列裁决，缩小了对专利持有人的保护范围。（2010年）

slave / sleɪv /   076

释 *n.* 奴隶 *v.* 苦干；辛勤地工作

例 **Slaves** in the old days did not have the right to vote. 过去，奴隶没有选举权。（2008年）

派 slavery / 'sleɪvəri / *n.* 奴隶制

underground   077

释 / ˌʌndə'graʊnd / *adj.* 地下的；暗中的 *adv.* 在地下；隐蔽地 / 'ʌndəgraʊnd / *n.* 地铁

例 These pockets of hot water deep **underground** do not exist everywhere. 这些深藏在地下的热水注并非到处都有。

warn / wɔːn / 〔078〕

释 v. 警告; 提醒; 告诫

例 This year, Williams **warns** that businesses are about to experience the opposite phenomenon: There's plenty of supply but shopper's savings have dried up. 威廉姆斯警告说, 今年商家将经历相反的现象: 供应充足, 但消费者的储蓄已经枯竭。

派 warning / 'wɔːnɪŋ / n. 警告, 警示

curiosity / ˌkjʊəri'ɒsəti / 〔079〕

释 n. 好奇心; 求知欲

例 The same **curiosity** to find what lies beyond the horizon that first brought early Polynesians to Hawaii's shores inspires astronomers today to explore the heavens. 寻找地平线以外的世界的好奇心, 最初将波利尼西亚人带到了夏威夷海岸, 这种同样的好奇心激励着当今的天文学家们探索天空。(2017年)

shock / ʃɒk / 〔080〕

释 v. 使震惊 n. 震惊; 令人震惊的事; 休克

例 The move **shocked** not only industry insiders and investors, but executive-level employees at the company, as well. 这一举动不仅震惊了业内人士和投资者, 也震惊了公司高层员工。

派 shocking / 'ʃɒkɪŋ / adj. 令人震惊的

starve / staːv / 〔081〕

释 v. (使)挨饿, 饿死; 缺乏……的; 急需……的

搭 starve of 缺乏

例 Going into a meal **starving** often leads to more impulsive choices, eating too quickly, and overeating. 饥肠辘辘地进餐往往会导致更多冲动的选择、吃得太快和暴饮暴食。

spend / spend / 〔082〕

释 v. 花 (钱、时间、精力); 度过

搭 spend sth. on (doing) sth. 花某事物做某事

例 Researchers admit that their study does not answer the question of how much businesses ought to **spend** on CSR. 研究人员承认, 他们的研究并没有回答企业应该在企业社会责任上花多少钱的问题。(2016年)

puzzle / 'pʌzl / 〔083〕

释 n. 谜 v. 使……迷惑不解

例 Scientists are still **puzzled** by the factors that lead to rapid climate intensification. 科学家们仍然对导致气候迅速加剧的因素感到困惑。

push / pʊʃ /　　　　　　　　　　　　　0 8 4

释 *v.* 推；推动；促使；说服；劝解；施压 *n.* 推；鼓励；进攻；坚定的努力

搭 push sth. back 推迟；延迟 ‖ push forward 继续前进

例 In the U.S., the Sarbanes-Oxley Act of 2002 has **pushed** most public companies to defer performance bonuses for senior executives by about a year, slightly helping reduce "short-termism". 在美国，2002年的萨班斯-奥克斯利法案迫使大多数上市公司将高管的绩效奖金推迟一年左右发放，这略微有助于减少"短期行为"。（2019年）

common / 'kɒmən /　　　　　　　　　　0 8 5

释 *adj.* 常见的；共同的；普通的；普遍的

例 Worse, biodegradable plastics, designed to disintegrate, are increasingly **common**. 更糟糕的是，被设计成可分解的可生物降解塑料越来越普遍。（2022年）

反 uncommon / ʌn'kɒmən / *adj.* 不常有的；罕见的

noble / 'nəʊbl /　　　　　　　　　　　0 8 6

释 *adj.* 高尚的；高贵的 *n.* 出身高贵的人；贵族成员

例 At the height of the Italian Renaissance, the House of Borromeo, a **noble** family descended from a long line of merchants and bankers, played an important role in shaping Milanese society. 在意大利文艺复兴的鼎盛时期，博罗梅奥家族——一个由商人和银行家组成的贵族家族——在塑造米兰社会方面发挥了重要作用。

派 nobility / nəʊ'bɪləti / *n.* 贵族；高贵的品质

反 ignoble / ɪɡ'nəʊbl / *adj.* 卑劣的；不诚实的；不光彩的

gain / ɡeɪn /　　　　　　　　　　　　0 8 7

释 *v.* 获得；赢得；（从……中）受益，获益；增加 *n.* 增值，增加；好处；利益；利润

例 Alongside that, many countries are introducing English into the primary-school curriculum but British schoolchildren and students do not appear to be **gaining** greater encouragement to achieve fluency in other languages. 与此同时，许多国家正在将英语引入小学课程，但英国的中小学生似乎并没有得到更多的鼓励去学会流利地使用其他语言。（2017年）

近 obtain / əb'teɪn / *v.* 获得，赢得

discount / 'dɪskaʊnt /　　　　　　　　0 8 8

释 *n.* 折扣 *v.* 打折；低估

搭 at a discount 打折

例 Outdoor security cameras are also on sale, coming in at just $34 after a 74-percent **discount**. 户外监控摄像头也在打折销售中，打七四折后，售价仅为34美元。

banner / 'bænə(r) / ⓪⑧⑨

释 *n.* 横幅

例 His image was featured in schools and on **banners** hung along the main street leading into the city. 他的画像出现在多所学校和通往城市的主要街道两边悬挂的横幅上。

situation / ˌsɪtʃu'eɪʃn / ⓪⑨⓪

释 *n.* 情况；形势

例 And to anticipate every imaginable driving **situation** is a difficult programming problem. 预测所有可能的驾驶情况是一个难度很大的编程问题。（2019年）

translate / trænz'leɪt / ⓪⑨①

释 *v.* （被）翻译；（使）转变，变为；（以某种方式）理解；给予（某种含义）

例 Across the 163 countries measured, the UK is one of the poorest performers in ensuring that economic growth is **translated** into meaningful improvements for its citizens. 在所检测的163个国家中，在确保经济增长转化为对公民有意义的改善方面，英国是表现最差的国家之一。（2017年）

派 translation / trænz'leɪʃn / *n.* 翻译；译文 ‖ translator / trænz'leɪtə(r) / *n.* 译者

branch / brɑːntʃ / ⓪⑨②

释 *n.* 树枝；（企业或机构的）分支 *v.* 分开；分岔

例 Waterstones **branches** suffer a severe reduction in revenue. 水石分公司的收入严重减少。（2023年）

repeat / rɪ'piːt / ⓪⑨③

释 *v.* 重复；重说；重做；复述；再次发生

例 Deliberate practice entails more than simply **repeating** a task. 刻意练习不仅仅是简单地重复做一项任务。（2007年）

派 repetition / ˌrepə'tɪʃn / *n.* 重复；重做；重说

chaos / 'keɪɒs / ⓪⑨④

释 *n.* 混乱；杂乱；紊乱

搭 in chaos 处于混乱状态

例 Despite all their disagreements, everyone agreed the **chaos** should not spill into next week, one insider said. 一位知情人士说，尽管各方意见不一，但所有人都认为混乱局面不应延续到下周。

派 chaotic / keɪ'ɒtɪk / *adj.* 混乱的

sober / 'səʊbə(r) / ⓪⑨⑤

释 *adj.* 未醉的；头脑清醒的；严肃的；审慎的；（颜色、衣服）素淡的

例 When **sober**, he can come across as an extremely pleasant and charming young man. 在他清醒的时候，他可能给人一种极其友善、富有魅力的年轻人的印象。

upward

gift

forget

impulse

request

---

upward / ˈʌpwəd / [096]

释 *adj.* 向上的; 朝上的; 向高处的; (价格等) 上升的 *adv.* (=upwards) 向上; 向高处

例 Economists revised the growth forecast **upward** for the third quarter, showing that the U.S. economy grew by more than five percent. 经济学家上调了第三季度的增长预测, 预测显示美国经济增长超过5%。

---

gift / ɡɪft / [097]

释 *n.* 礼物; 天赋

例 Officials must not be allowed to play favorites in providing information or in arranging meetings simply because an individual or group provides a campaign donation or a personal **gift**. 决不允许官员在提供信息或安排会议时, 仅仅因为某个人或团体提供了竞选捐款或私人礼物而有所偏袒。(2017年)

近 present / ˈpreznt / *n.* 礼物; 现在 *adj.* 当前的

---

forget / fəˈget / [098]

释 *v.* 忘记, 遗忘; 忘记 (做); 落下; 不再想; 不再把……放在心上

例 The long-term result is that the customer won't **forget** it, and the business benefits from a grassroots supporter. 长期效果是客户不会忘记, 企业也能从基层支持者那里获益。

派 forgetful / fəˈgetfl / *adj.* 健忘的 ‖ forgettable / fəˈgetəbl / *adj.* 易被忘记的

---

impulse / ˈɪmpʌls / [099]

释 *n.* 冲动; 心血来潮; 一时的念头; 推动力; 刺激; 脉冲

搭 on impulse 凭一时冲动

例 In physics, one approach takes this **impulse** for unification to its extreme, and seeks a theory of everything—a single generative equation for all we see. 在物理学领域, 有一种方法将这种追求统一的冲动发挥到了极致, 它寻求一种万有理论, 即一种单一的能够解释我们所能看到的一切的通用公式。(2012年)

派 impulsive / ɪmˈpʌlsɪv / *adj.* 易冲动的

---

request / rɪˈkwest / [100]

释 *n./v.* 要求, 请求

例 They can now **request** a hearing, after which the Commission will decide whether the acquisition breaks the antitrust law. 他们现在可以要求举行听证会, 之后委员会将决定此次收购是否违反了反垄断法。

☐ ☐ advance
☐ ☐ aim
☐ ☐ alter
☐ ☐ banner
☐ ☐ behalf
☐ ☐ bias
☐ ☐ bold
☐ ☐ branch
☐ ☐ break
☐ ☐ chaos
☐ ☐ circumstance
☐ ☐ coincide
☐ ☐ common
☐ ☐ comparative
☐ ☐ comparison
☐ ☐ complaint
☐ ☐ compose
☐ ☐ conflict
☐ ☐ conjunction
☐ ☐ constant
☐ ☐ course
☐ ☐ curiosity
☐ ☐ decrease
☐ ☐ defeat
☐ ☐ detach
☐ ☐ detector
☐ ☐ discount
☐ ☐ eager
☐ ☐ entail
☐ ☐ episode
☐ ☐ equivalent

☐ ☐ executive
☐ ☐ explain
☐ ☐ exposure
☐ ☐ fatal
☐ ☐ foremost
☐ ☐ forget
☐ ☐ gain
☐ ☐ gap
☐ ☐ generate
☐ ☐ gift
☐ ☐ hono(u)r
☐ ☐ ignore
☐ ☐ impressive
☐ ☐ impulse
☐ ☐ mankind
☐ ☐ mass
☐ ☐ mostly
☐ ☐ negotiate
☐ ☐ noble
☐ ☐ nuisance
☐ ☐ occur
☐ ☐ partial
☐ ☐ patent
☐ ☐ pay
☐ ☐ peak
☐ ☐ poisonous
☐ ☐ possibility
☐ ☐ potential
☐ ☐ preferable
☐ ☐ productive
☐ ☐ purchase

☐ ☐ push
☐ ☐ puzzle
☐ ☐ refusal
☐ ☐ remarkable
☐ ☐ repeat
☐ ☐ reputation
☐ ☐ request
☐ ☐ resolve
☐ ☐ responsible
☐ ☐ restrict
☐ ☐ scandal
☐ ☐ segment
☐ ☐ shock
☐ ☐ sign
☐ ☐ situation
☐ ☐ slack
☐ ☐ slave
☐ ☐ sober
☐ ☐ spend
☐ ☐ standard
☐ ☐ starve
☐ ☐ succession
☐ ☐ superb
☐ ☐ superfluous
☐ ☐ superstition
☐ ☐ survey
☐ ☐ trace
☐ ☐ tradition
☐ ☐ translate
☐ ☐ tremendous
☐ ☐ underground

☐ ☐ upward
☐ ☐ virtual
☐ ☐ visual
☐ ☐ vivid
☐ ☐ vulnerable
☐ ☐ warn
☐ ☐ yield

音频

Previous Check

- ☐ profit
- ☐ implement
- ☐ ideal
- ☐ susceptible
- ☐ entitle
- ☐ foresee
- ☐ capable
- ☐ progressive
- ☐ hesitate
- ☐ glimpse
- ☐ arrest
- ☐ fake
- ☐ counterpart
- ☐ discourage
- ☐ exclusive
- ☐ remark
- ☐ perform
- ☐ intelligent
- ☐ cue
- ☐ cover
- ☐ invisible
- ☐ affirm
- ☐ lack
- ☐ charge
- ☐ sustain
- ☐ territory
- ☐ secure
- ☐ quality
- ☐ interview
- ☐ identical
- ☐ embody

- ☐ efficient
- ☐ military
- ☐ relate
- ☐ prestige
- ☐ perceive
- ☐ depart
- ☐ urgent
- ☐ hygiene
- ☐ offer
- ☐ throughout
- ☐ communicate
- ☐ primitive
- ☐ rival
- ☐ describe
- ☐ glory
- ☐ reject
- ☐ trade
- ☐ betray
- ☐ solution
- ☐ odd
- ☐ elect
- ☐ handle
- ☐ minor
- ☐ productivity
- ☐ suppose
- ☐ prepare
- ☐ illusion
- ☐ veto
- ☐ extent
- ☐ arise
- ☐ violate

- ☐ universe
- ☐ precedent
- ☐ attempt
- ☐ effect
- ☐ limitation
- ☐ fall
- ☐ accompany
- ☐ claim
- ☐ quest
- ☐ edit
- ☐ flourish
- ☐ complete
- ☐ package
- ☐ sentence
- ☐ rescue
- ☐ feed
- ☐ agenda
- ☐ instant
- ☐ optimistic
- ☐ glance
- ☐ call
- ☐ cycle
- ☐ creativity
- ☐ dumb
- ☐ native
- ☐ slow
- ☐ boom
- ☐ factor
- ☐ suitable
- ☐ mirror
- ☐ fierce

- ☐ organ
- ☐ prey
- ☐ wing
- ☐ lottery
- ☐ postpone
- ☐ frank
- ☐ exit

profit / ˈprɒfɪt / `001`

释 *n.* 利润; 收益; 赢利; 好处 *v.* 获益; 得到好处

例 "Short-termism," or the desire for quick **profits**, has worsened in publicly traded companies, says the Bank of England's top economist, Andrew Haldane. 英格兰银行的首席经济学家安德鲁·霍尔丹表示, "短期主义"或急功近利的心态在上市公司中愈演愈烈。(2019年)

implement `002`

释 / ˈɪmplɪment / *v.* 使生效; 实施; 执行, 贯彻 / ˈɪmplɪmənt / *n.* 工具, 器具

例 Bill **implemented** his investment plan and quickly doubled his money. 比尔实施了他的投资计划, 很快使资金翻了一番。

ideal / aɪˈdiːəl / `003`

释 *adj.* 理想的; 完美的 *n.* 理想; 完美的人(或事物)

例 Mauna Kea is deemed as an **ideal** astronomical site due to its geographical features. 由于其地理特征, 莫纳克被视为理想的天文观测站。(2017年)

susceptible / səˈseptəbl / `004`

释 *adj.* 易受影响的; 易动感情的; 易患(病)的; 易受伤的

例 Women are particularly **susceptible** to developing depression and anxiety disorders in response to stress compared to men. 和男性相比, 女性在面对压力时极其容易患上抑郁症和焦虑症。

近 vulnerable / ˈvʌlnərəbl / *adj.* 易受伤害的; 脆弱的

entitle / ɪnˈtaɪtl / `005`

释 *v.* 给……权利(或资格); 给……题名

搭 be entitled to... 有权……, 有资格……

例 Why are people who live within a day's drive of London **entitled** to go and see the Elgin Marbles whenever they want, but the people of Athens aren't? 为什么住在伦敦一天车程范围内的人可以随时去看埃尔金大理石雕塑, 而雅典人却不行? (2024年)

派 entitlement / ɪnˈtaɪtlmənt / *n.* 权利

foresee / fɔːˈsiː / `006`

释 *v.* 预料, 预见; 预知

例 Either Entergy never really intended to live by those commitments, or it simply didn't **foresee** what would happen next. 要么安特吉公司从来就没有打算信守那些承诺, 要么它只是没有预料到接下来会发生什么。(2012年)

capable / ˈkeɪpəbl / 007

- 释 *adj.* 有能力的，有才能的；足以胜任的
- 搭 be capable of sth./doing sth. 有能力做某事
- 例 Our mental health doesn't really go anywhere; like the sun behind a cloud, it can be temporarily hidden from view, but it is fully **capable** of being restored in an instant. 我们的心理健康不会真正消失；就像云层背后的太阳，它可以暂时被遮蔽，但完全有能力在瞬间恢复。（2016年）
- 派 capability / ˌkeɪpəˈbɪləti / *n.* 能力；性能
- 近 competent / ˈkɒmpɪtənt / *adj.* 能力强的；可以胜任的

progressive / prəˈɡresɪv / 008

- 释 *adj.* 进步的；先进的；（变化等）逐步发生的
- 例 One prominent symptom of the disease is **progressive** loss of memory. 这种疾病的一个显著症状就是记忆逐渐丧失。

hesitate / ˈhezɪteɪt / 009

- 释 *v.* 犹豫；（对某事）迟疑不决；疑虑；顾虑
- 例 Waterstones staff **hesitate** to promote big-name authors' books. 水石书店的员工在宣传大牌作家的书籍时犹豫不决。（2023年）

glimpse / ɡlɪmps / 010

- 释 *n.* 一瞥，一看 *v.* 瞥见；开始认识到
- 搭 catch/get a glimpse of 瞥见
- 例 The colonists' first **glimpse** of the new land was a sight of dense woods. 殖民者们第一眼看到的新土地是一片茂密的树林。（2015年）

arrest / əˈrest / 011

- 释 *v.* 逮捕，拘留；阻止；中止；心跳停止 *n.* 逮捕，拘捕；停止，中止
- 例 He was **arrested** on charges of domestic abuse. 他因实施家暴而被捕。

fake / feɪk / 012

- 释 *adj.* 假的；冒充的
- 例 About a third say the problem of **fake** news lies in "misinterpretation or exaggeration of actual news" via social media. 约三分之一的人表示，假新闻的问题在于通过社交媒体"曲解或夸大新闻事实"。（2018年）

counterpart / ˈkaʊntəpɑːt / 013

- 释 *n.* 对应的人或物
- 例 And though print ad sales still dwarf their online and mobile **counterparts**, revenue from print is still declining. 尽管纸质广告的销售额仍使网络和移动广告相形见绌，但纸质广告的收入仍在下降。（2016年）

discourage / dɪsˈkʌrɪdʒ /   0 1 4

释 v. 阻拦，阻止；使灰心，使泄气

例 When asked what they want to do, they should be **discouraged** from saying "I have no idea." 在问他们想做什么时，不要让他们说"我不知道"。(2007年)

exclusive / ɪkˈskluːsɪv /   0 1 5

释 adj. 专有的，独占的；排他的 n. 独家新闻，独家报道

搭 mutually exclusive 相互排斥

例 That ruling produced an explosion in business-method patent filings, initially by emerging Internet companies trying to stake out **exclusive** rights to specific types of online transactions. 这一裁决引发了商业方法专利申请的激增，始于新兴互联网公司试图在特定类型的在线交易中获得独家权。(2010年)

反 inclusive / ɪnˈkluːsɪv / adj. 包括的，包含的

remark / rɪˈmɑːk /   0 1 6

释 n. 言论；评论；意见 v. 评论；说起

例 "It's a really hard thing to do and it's a tremendous luxury that BuzzFeed doesn't have a legacy business," Peretti **remarked**. 佩雷蒂评论道："这真的是一件很难的事情，而且BuzzFeed没有传统业务是一件非常奢侈的事情。"(2016年)

perform / pəˈfɔːm /   0 1 7

释 v. 执行；工作，运转（好/不好）；履行；表演，演出

例 As countless boards and business owners will attest, constraining firms from firing poorly **performing**, high-earning managers is a handbrake on boosting productivity and overall performance. 无数董事会和企业主都会证明，限制企业解雇表现不佳的高薪经理人，是在对提高生产率和整体业绩拉手刹。(2022年)

intelligent / ɪnˈtelɪdʒənt /   0 1 8

释 adj. 聪明的；有智力的；智能的

搭 intelligent beings 智慧生物，外星人

例 How can we make sure that the thinking of **intelligent** machines reflects humanity's highest values? 我们如何确保智能机器的思维体现人类的最高价值？(2019年)

cue / kjuː /   0 1 9

释 n. 提示；暗示；线索；信号 v. 提示

例 Although the **cues** used by African elephants for long-distance navigation are not yet understood, smell may well play a part. 虽然非洲象用于远距离导航的线索尚不清楚，但嗅觉很可能在其中发挥了作用。(2024年)

近 clue / kluː / n. 线索；提示 ‖ suggestion / səˈdʒestʃən / n. 暗示

cover / ˈkʌvə(r) /   020

释 *v.* 包括; 足以支付; 遮盖; 报道 *n.* 封面

例 Surveys can **cover** a single large settlement or entire landscapes. 调查范围可以是一个大型定居点, 也可以是整个地区。(2014年)

invisible / ɪnˈvɪzəbl /   021

释 *adj.* 看不见的; 隐形的; 被忽视的

例 The English language teaching sector directly earns nearly £1.3 billion for the UK in **invisible** exports and our other education related exports earn up to £10 billion a year more. 英语教学部门直接为英国创造了近13亿英镑的隐形出口收入, 而我们与教育相关的其他出口收入每年高达100亿英镑。(2017年)

affirm / əˈfɜːm /   022

释 *v.* 肯定; 断言

例 We neither **affirm** nor deny it; we simply can't comment on it as scientists. 我们不会肯定它, 也不会否定它; 作为科学家, 我们对此没有发言权。

派 affirmation / ˌæfəˈmeɪʃn / *n.* 证实

近 claim / kleɪm / *v.* 要求; 声称; 断言

lack / læk /   023

释 *n./v.* 缺乏; 匮乏; 短缺

例 Teens who don't get enough sleep may suffer from weak academic performance, a **lack** of organizational skills and decision-making. 睡眠不足的青少年可能会学习成绩差, 缺乏组织和决策能力。

charge / tʃɑːdʒ /   024

释 *n.* 指控; 主管; 要价 *v.* (向……)收费; 控告; 指责; 使……承担责任

例 The government agency in **charge** of protecting consumers' finances introduced a new rule to rein in overdraft fees **charged** by banks. 负责保护消费者金融权益的政府机构出台了一项新规定, 以控制银行收取的透支费。

sustain / səˈsteɪn /   025

释 *v.* 维持; 支撑; 遭受

例 The most loyal customers would still get the product they favor, the idea goes, and they'd feel like they were helping **sustain** the quality of something they believe in. 这样一来, 最忠实的顾客仍然可以得到他们喜欢的产品, 而且他们会觉得自己在帮助维持他们所信赖的东西的质量。(2016年)

派 sustainable / səˈsteɪnəbl / *adj.* 可持续的; 能承受的

近 maintain / meɪnˈteɪn / *v.* 保持, 维持

026

territory / ˈterətri /

释 n. 领土；地域

例 The first shiploads of immigrants bound for the **territory** which is now the United States crossed the Atlantic more than a hundred years after the 15th-and-16th-century explorations of North America. 在15世纪和16世纪对北美的探索结束一百多年后，第一批满载移民的船只才横渡大西洋，驶向如今是美国的那片土地。（2015年）

近 realm / relm / n. 领域；王国 ‖ domain / dəˈmeɪn / n.（知识、活动的）领域；领土

027

secure / sɪˈkjʊə(r) /

释 v.（使）获得；保护，（使）安全 adj. 可靠的；安心的

例 Education was no longer a **secure** route of social mobility. 教育不再是社会流动的可靠途径。（2022年）

028

quality / ˈkwɒləti /

释 n. 质量；品质；特性

例 It does not include important factors such as environmental **quality** or education outcomes—all things that contribute to a person's sense of well-being. 它不包括环境质量或教育成果等重要因素——所有有助于提高一个人的幸福感的东西。（2017年）

029

interview / ˈɪntəvjuː /

释 v./n. 采访；面试

例 Almost everyone who was **interviewed** for this special report said that the biggest problem at the moment is not a lack of demand but a lack of good work to sell. 几乎每个接受这个特别报道采访的人都说，现在这个时期最大的问题不在于没有需求，而是没有可以拍卖的好作品。

030

identical / aɪˈdentɪkl /

释 adj. 同一的，完全相同的

搭 identical to/with 与……完全相同或相似

例 The two conclusions are in effect **identical**. 这两种结论实际上是相同的。

031

embody / ɪmˈbɒdi /

释 v. 体现，使具体化；包含，收录

例 The Spanish case provides arguments both for and against monarchy. When public opinion is particularly polarised, as it was following the end of the Franco regime, monarchs can rise above "mere" politics and "**embody**" a spirit of national unity. 西班牙的情况为支持和反对君主制提供了论据。当公众舆论特别两极分化时，就像佛朗哥政权倒台后那样，君主可以超越"单纯的"政治，"体现"国家团结的精神。（2015年）

efficient / ɪ'fɪʃnt / 032

释 adj. 效率高的；效能高的

例 The long-term effects of the changes will be more comfortable and energy-**efficient** homes. 这些变化的长期效果将会是更舒适和更节能的住宅。

military / 'mɪlətri / 033

释 adj. 军事的，军队的；武装的 n. 军人；军队；军方

例 She says that, unlike those for basketball, the length of **military** uniforms has not changed for some time. 她说，与篮球服不同，军装的长度已经有一段时间没有变化了。（2008年）

近 troop / truːp / n. 军队，部队

relate / rɪ'leɪt / 034

释 v. 把……联系起来；讲述；与……有关

例 Though not biologically **related**, friends are as "**related**" as fourth cousins, sharing about 1% of genes. 虽然没有血缘关系，但朋友之间的"关系"不亚于四从兄弟姐妹，共享约1%的基因。（2015年）

派 relation / rɪ'leɪʃn / n. 关系；亲属

prestige / pre'stiːʒ / 035

释 n. 威信，威望，名声

例 You cannot buy class, as the old saying goes, and these upstart entrepreneurs cannot buy their prizes the **prestige** of the Nobels. 俗话说"阶级是买不来的"，这些新贵企业家也无法为自己（资助）的奖项买来像诺贝尔奖那样的声誉。（2014年）

近 reputation / ˌrepju'teɪʃn / n. 名声，名誉

perceive / pə'siːv / 036

释 v. 察觉，感知；理解，领悟；认为

例 For another, it may be to be **perceived** as more approachable, or more modern and stylish. 对另一个人来说，目标则可能是让自己看起来更平易近人，或者更现代、更时尚。（2016年）

depart / dɪ'pɑːt / 037

释 v. 离开；离去；起程；出发；离职

例 When Liam McGee **departed** as president of Bank of America in August, his explanation was surprisingly straight up. 今年8月，利亚姆·麦基卸任美国银行行长一职时，他的解释出人意料地直截了当。（2011年）

urgent / 'ɜːdʒənt / 038

释 adj. 紧急的；紧迫的；迫切的；催促的

例 The need of training is too evident and the pressure to accomplish a change in their attitude and habits is too **urgent** to leave these consequences wholly out of account. 培训的必要性太明显，改变他们的态度和习惯的压力太紧迫，因此不能完全不考虑这些后果。（2009年）

Writing Models ◎

hygiene

offer

throughout

communicate

primitive

rival

describe

glory

reject

trade

betray

solution

odd

039

hygiene / 'haɪdʒiːn /

释 *n.* 卫生

搭 food hygiene 食品卫生 ‖ personal hygiene 个人卫生

例 A flashing set of healthy and clean, regular "pearly whites" was a rare sight in Victorian society, the preserve of the super-rich (and even then, dental **hygiene** was not guaranteed). 在维多利亚时代的社会中，一口闪亮健康、干净整洁的"珍珠白"牙齿是非常罕见的，那是大富豪的专利（并且即便如此，他们也很难保证口腔卫生）。（2021年）

040

offer / 'ɒfə(r) /

释 *v.* 提供（某物给某人）；给予；表示；出价 *n.* 提议；提供物；特价；赠品；出价

搭 on offer 可使用；提供的；可买到

例 Each set of circumstances, however bad, **offers** a unique opportunity for growth. 每一种情况，无论多么糟糕，都提供了一个独特的成长机会。（2011年）

041

throughout / θruː'aʊt /

释 *prep.* 遍及；自始至终 *adv.* 自始至终；各处

例 This is a skill that will help them all **throughout** life. 这是一个会使他们终生受用的技能。

042

communicate / kə'mjuːnɪkeɪt /

释 *v.* 传达，传递（想法、感情、思想等）；沟通

搭 communicate with sb. 与某人交流

例 Scientists must **communicate** their messages to the public in a compassionate, understandable way—in human terms, not in the language of molecular biology. 科学家必须用富有同情心和易于理解的方式——用一般人能够明白的语言，而不是用分子生物学术语——向公众传达他们的信息。

近 convey / kən'veɪ / *v.* 传达；运送

043

primitive / 'prɪmətɪv /

释 *adj.* 原始的；未开化的；（动植物）低等的，进化初期的；古老的；简陋的

例 **Primitive** humans needed to be able to react like this to escape from dangerous animals. 原始人必须要能做出这样的反应以逃避危险的动物。

044

rival / 'raɪvl /

释 *n.* 对手，竞争者 *v.* 与……相匹敌，比得上

例 Now, **rivals** will be charging sales tax where they hadn't before. 现在，竞争对手将在以前不征收销售税的地方征税。（2019年）

近 opponent / ə'pəʊnənt / *n.* 对手；反对者

---

describe / dɪˈskraɪb /

0 4 5

释 *v.* 描述；形容；把……称为；做……运动；画出……图形；形成……形状

例 Emma Marris selectively **describes** and misrepresents the findings of our research. 艾玛·马里斯有选择性地描述和歪曲了我们的研究结果。（2022年）

glory / ˈɡlɔːri /

0 4 6

释 *n.* 荣誉；光荣；桂冠；壮丽；辉煌；灿烂；（对上帝的）赞颂，赞美，崇拜 *v.* 因……而欣喜；为……而喜悦

例 The garden was almost destroyed by a fire in the 1700s and was left abandoned until it was lovingly restored to its former **glory**. 在18世纪的一场大火中，这个花园几乎毁于一旦，后来被荒废，直到经过精心修复才重现昔日的辉煌。

reject

0 4 7

释 / rɪˈdʒekt / *v.* 拒绝接受；不予考虑；拒收；不录用；不出版；排斥，排异（移植的器官）；不够关心 / ˈriːdʒekt / *n.* 废品；次品；不合格者；被剔除者；被拒收者

例 This means that people should avoid crisping their roast potatoes, **reject** thin-crust pizzas and only partially toast their bread. 这就意味着，人们应该避免把烤土豆烤脆，拒绝薄皮比萨，以及只烤部分面包。（2020年）

trade / treɪd /

0 4 8

释 *n.* 贸易；生意

例 Caravanserais were also an important marketplace for commodities and aided in the **trade** of goods along the Silk Road. 商队客店也是重要的商品市场，有助于丝绸之路沿线的商品贸易。（2023年）

betray / bɪˈtreɪ /

0 4 9

释 *v.* 背叛；出卖；泄露（秘密）；露出……迹象

例 She **betrayed** his trust over and over again. 她一次又一次地辜负了他的信任。

solution / səˈluːʃn /

0 5 0

释 *n.* 解决办法；谜底；答案；溶液

例 The **solution** to the ethical issues brought by autonomous vehicles is still beyond our capacity. 解决自动驾驶汽车带来的伦理问题尚不在我们的能力范围。（2019年）

odd / ɒd /

0 5 1

释 *adj.* 奇怪的，举止怪异的；奇数的，单的

搭 odd number 奇数

例 He gets **odder** as he grows older. 随着年岁的增长，他变得越来越古怪。

Writing Models

elect

handle

minor

productivity

suppose

prepare

illusion

veto

extent

arise

violate

universe

precedent

---

elect / ɪˈlekt / `052`

释 *v.* 选举；推选；选择，决定（做某事）*adj.* 当选而尚未就职的，候任的

例 I shall define him as an individual who has **elected** as his primary duty and pleasure in life the activity of thinking in a Socratic way about moral problems. 我将把他定义为这样一个人：他选择把以苏格拉底的方式思考道德问题作为自己的首要职责和人生乐趣。（2006年）

handle / ˈhændl / `053`

释 *v.* 处理，应付；控制，操纵 *n.* 把手；拉手

搭 get/have a handle on sb./sth. 理解；弄明白

例 There was widespread criticism of the way that the government **handled** the disaster. 政府对灾难的处理方式遭到了普遍的批评。

minor / ˈmaɪnə(r) / `054`

释 *adj.* 较小的；次要的；轻微的 *n.* 未成年人；辅修科目

例 The young actor was given a **minor** part in the new play. 那位年轻的男演员在这出新戏里被分派了一个小角色。

productivity / ˌprɒdʌkˈtɪvəti / `055`

释 *n.* 生产率；生产效率

例 It hoped they would learn how shop-floor lighting affected workers' **productivity**. 它（美国国家研究委员会）希望他们能了解车间照明对工人生产率的影响。（2010年）

suppose / səˈpəʊz / `056`

释 *v.* 认为，推断，料想；假定；假设；设想；（婉转表达）我看，要不

例 In contrast, **suppose** you give a reasonable argument: that full-time workers should not have to live in poverty. 相反，假设你提出一个合理的理由：全职工人不应该生活在贫困之中。（2009年）

prepare / prɪˈpeə(r) / `057`

释 *v.* 准备；预备（饭菜）

例 Studies from the United States and Australia show that students who take a gap year are generally better **prepared** for and perform better in college than those who do not. 美国和澳大利亚的研究表明，和那些直接上大学的人相比，休间隔年的学生通常做了更好的准备，在进入大学之后表现也更好。

illusion / ɪˈluːʒn / `058`

释 *n.* 幻想的事物；幻觉；假象

例 Sometimes he couldn't distinguish between **illusion** and reality. 有时他分不清幻觉和现实。

近 fantasy / ˈfæntəsi / *n.* 幻想；空想的产物 ‖ delusion / dɪˈluːʒn / *n.* 错觉；妄想

veto / ˈviːtəʊ /
〔059〕

释 v. 否决 n. 否决；否决权

例 The chairman has the right to **veto** any of the board's proposals. 董事长有权否决董事会的任何提议。

extent / ɪkˈstent /
〔060〕

释 n. 程度，限度；长度；广度；范围

搭 to some extent 在某种程度上

例 How we read a given text also depends to some **extent** on our particular interest in reading it. 我们如何阅读某一特定文本，在一定程度上也取决于我们对阅读该文本所持有的兴趣。（2015年）

近 degree / dɪˈɡriː / n. 程度

arise / əˈraɪz /
〔061〕

释 v. 出现，发生；起床；起立

搭 arise from... 由……引起

例 Another urge or need that these gardens appear to respond to, or to **arise** from, is so intrinsic that we are barely ever conscious of its abiding claims on us. 这些花园似乎是在回应或源于另一种冲动或需求，这种冲动或需求是如此内在，以至于我们几乎从未意识到它对我们的持久要求。（2013年）

近 rise / raɪz / v. 上升 ‖ raise / reɪz / v. 升起；提高

violate / ˈvaɪəleɪt /
〔062〕

释 v. 违反，违背（法律、协议等）；侵犯（隐私等）；搅扰；亵渎，污损（神圣之地）

例 The court has ruled that police don't **violate** the Fourth Amendment when they go through the wallet or pocketbook of an arrestee without a warrant. 法院裁定，警方在没有搜查证的情况下翻看被捕者的钱包或皮夹并不违反第四条修正案。（2015年）

universe / ˈjuːnɪvɜːs /
〔063〕

释 n. 宇宙；天地万物；万象；经验领域

例 Take a broader look at our species' place in the **universe**, and it becomes clear that we have an excellent chance of surviving for tens, if not hundreds, of thousands of years. 从更广阔的角度审视我们这个物种在宇宙中的地位，很明显，我们有极大的机会存活几十年，如果不是几百年，甚至几千年。（2013年）

precedent / ˈpresɪdənt /
〔064〕

释 n. 先例，惯例；实例；范例 adj. 在前的；在先的

例 He says that the government will set a dangerous **precedent** if it refuses to allow the protesters to hold a rally. 他说，如果政府拒绝允许抗议者举行集会，则将开创一个危险的先例。

近 prior / ˈpraɪə(r) / adj. 优先的；在先的

attempt / ə'tempt / 065

释 *n.* 企图, 努力 *v.* 尝试, 试图

例 Issues arise, however, when developers **attempt** to create large-scale short-term rental facilities—de facto hotels—to bypass taxes and regulations. 然而，当开发商试图建立大规模短期租赁设施——事实上的酒店——以绕过税收和法规时，问题就出现了。（2023年）

近 endeavor / ɪn'devə(r) / *v.* 竭力, 试图 ‖ strive / straɪv / *v.* 努力

effect / ɪ'fekt / 066

释 *n.* 效应；影响；结果；外观，印象；效果 *v.* 使发生；实现；引起

搭 in effect 实际上；在实施中 ‖ come into effect 生效；开始实施

例 Nor does it reveal how much companies are banking on the halo **effect**, rather than the other possible benefits, when they decide their do-gooding policies. 它也没有揭示公司在决定其公益政策时，在多大程度上依赖于光环效应，而不是其他可能的好处。（2016年）

limitation / ˌlɪmɪ'teɪʃn / 067

释 *n.* 限制，控制；局限；限度

搭 limitation of actions 诉讼时效

例 The upside is the possibilities contained in knowing that everything is up to us; where before we were experts in the array of **limitations**, now we become authorities of what is possible. 好的一面是，我们知道一切都取决于我们自己，从而蕴含着无限可能；以前，我们是"限制"的专家，而现在，我们成了"可能"的权威。（2011年）

近 restriction / rɪ'strɪkʃn / *n.* 限制，约束

辨 limitation指事先确定的空间、时间或数量的极限，一旦超越限度，就会造成不良结果，也可指自然的或固有的界限；restriction指把某人或某物限制在一定的范围之内。

fall / fɔːl / 068

释 *v.* 落下；跌倒；下降；倒下 *n.* 落下；下降

例 Sales of books by mid-list PRH writers **fall** off considerably. 企鹅兰登的中等知名度作家作品的销量大幅下滑。（2023年）

accompany / ə'kʌmpəni / 069

释 *v.* 陪伴，伴随；伴奏，伴唱；与……同时发生

例 The major has gone to **accompany** a delegation on a visit abroad. 那位市长随同代表团出国访问去了。

claim / kleɪm / 070

释 *v.* 声称；断言；要求，请求 *n.* 宣称；断言；要求；索赔

例 They even **claimed** that plants have "brain-like command centers" at their root tips. 他们甚至声称，植物的根尖有"类似大脑的指挥中心"。（2022年）

近 announce / ə'naʊns / *v.* 宣布，宣告 ‖ assert / ə's3ːt / *v.* 断言；声称

quest / kwest /　　071

释 *n.* 追求；寻找 *v.* 追求；寻找；探索

搭 in quest of 探寻，寻求；为了追求……

例 In some ways, this **quest** for commonalities defines science. 在某些方面，这种对共性的追求决定了科学的定义。（2012年）

近 search / sɜːtʃ / *n./v.* 搜寻 ‖ pursuit / pəˈsjuːt / *n.* 追逐，追寻

edit / ˈedɪt /　　072

释 *v.* 编辑；编选；主编；剪辑

例 Moral awareness matters in **editing** a newspaper. 在编辑报纸时，道德意识很重要。（2015年）

派 editor / ˈedɪtə(r) / *n.* 编辑；主编；剪辑师 ‖ editorial / ˌedɪˈtɔːriəl / *n.* 社论

flourish / ˈflʌrɪʃ /　　073

释 *v.* 繁荣；兴旺；旺盛；茁壮成长

例 Renaissance ideas had spread throughout Europe well into the 17th century, with the arts and sciences **flourishing** extraordinarily among those with a more logical disposition. 文艺复兴的思想在17世纪已经传遍了整个欧洲，艺术和科学在逻辑性较强的人群中异常繁荣。（2020年）

近 thrive / θraɪv / *v.* 繁荣；蓬勃发展；茁壮成长

complete / kəmˈpliːt /　　074

释 *adj.* 完全的，彻底的；全部的；整个的 *v.* 完成；结束

例 The six-member band is also busy **completing** a run of dates across theaters in the United States. 这支由六名成员组成的乐队也正忙着完成在美国各剧院一系列的演出。

反 incomplete / ˌɪnkəmˈpliːt / *adj.* 不完整的；不完全的

package / ˈpækɪdʒ /　　075

释 *n.* 包裹；包；袋；一揽子建议 *v.* 将……包装好

例 This should form part of a wider **package** of measures to address the long-running problems on Britain's railways. 这应该成为解决英国铁路长期存在的问题的系列措施之一。（2021年）

近 parcel / ˈpɑːsl / *n.* 包裹

sentence / ˈsentəns /　　076

释 *n.* 句子；判刑 *v.* 判决；判刑

例 For example, he theorised that a judge fearful of appearing too soft on crime might be more likely to send someone to prison if he had already **sentenced** five or six other defendants only to forced community service on that day. 例如，他推论说，如果一位法官当天已经对五六名被告只判处了强制性社区服务，但他担心自己对犯罪行为表现得太过仁慈，那么他更有可能会将接下来要审判的某人送进监狱。（2013年）

Writing Models ⊙

rescue

feed

agenda

instant

optimistic

glance

call

cycle

creativity

dumb

native

rescue / 'reskjuː / ⓿❼❼

释 *v./n.* 营救；援救；抢救

例 Scientists jumped to the **rescue** with some distinctly shaky evidence to the effect that insects would eat us up if birds failed to control them. 科学家们带着一些明显不可靠的证据跳出来救场，大意是说，如果鸟类不能控制昆虫的数量，昆虫就会吞噬我们人类。（2010年）

feed / fiːd / ⓿❼❽

释 *v.* 喂养；饲养；进食；养，养活

搭 feed on 以……为食

例 Worse, the crucial income to **feed** yourself and your family and pay the bills has disappeared. 更糟糕的是，养活自己和家人以及支付账单的关键收入已经消失了。（2014年）

agenda / ə'dʒendə / ⓿❼❾

释 *n.* 议程；议事日程；（会议的）议程表

搭 on the agenda 在议程上 ‖ hidden agenda（言语或行为背后的）隐秘意图，秘密目的

例 I think we've just about covered everything on the **agenda**. 我想我们几乎已把议程上所有的事项都讨论过了。

instant / 'ɪnstənt / ⓿❽⓿

释 *adj.* 立即的；即食的；速溶的；方便的 *n.* 瞬间；片刻

例 The company, like other dealers, also has an online tool that provides customers with **instant** offers on their vehicles. 与其他经销商一样，该公司也有一个在线工具，可以为客户提供汽车的即时报价。

近 immediate / ɪ'miːdiət / *adj.* 立刻的；即时的

optimistic / ˌɒptɪ'mɪstɪk / ⓿❽❶

释 *adj.* 乐观的；抱乐观看法的

例 Many employers are still downsizing because of overly **optimistic** projections, consumers' changing habits, and technological advances such as generative artificial intelligence. 由于过于乐观的预测、消费者习惯的改变，以及生成式人工智能等技术的进步，许多雇主仍在裁员。

派 optimistically / ˌɒptɪ'mɪstɪkli / *adv.* 乐观地

glance / glaːns / ⓿❽❷

释 *v.* 瞥一眼；匆匆一看 *n.* 匆匆一看；一瞥；扫视

搭 glance at/over/through 浏览；粗略地看 ‖ at first glance 乍一看

例 Such an effort at accountability can teach us a lot about the future, as **glancing** backward is often a valuable guide to the path forward. 这种问责努力可以教会我们很多有关未来的东西，因为回顾过去往往是前进道路上的宝贵指南。

call / kɔːl / [0][8][3]

释 *v.* 称呼; 把……叫作; 认为……是; (给……) 打电话; 召唤; 呼唤; 命令; 访问 *n.* 电话; 叫声; 喊声; 要求; 请求; 呼吁

搭 call for 需要 ‖ call up 打电话给; 使回忆起 ‖ call on/upon 邀请; 请求

例 The Food Standards Authority (FSA) has issued a public warning about the risks of a compound **called** acrylamide that forms in some foods cooked at high temperatures. 英国食品标准局 (FSA) 发布了一项公众警告, 称某些经过高温烹饪的食品会产生一种名为丙烯酰胺的化合物, 这种化合物具有一定的风险。(2020年)

cycle / ˈsaɪkl / [0][8][4]

释 *n.* 循环; 周期; 自行车; 摩托车 *v.* 骑自行车

例 Incredibly, this strange sleep **cycle** seems to do the birds no obvious harm, despite the common interpretation that fragmented sleep is bad-quality. 令人难以置信的是, 这种奇怪的睡眠周期似乎对鸟类没有明显的伤害, 尽管人们普遍认为碎片化的睡眠质量很差。

creativity / ˌkriːeɪˈtɪvəti / [0][8][5]

释 *n.* 创造力, 独创性

例 Following the explosion of **creativity** in Florence during the 14th century known as the Renaissance, the modern world saw a departure from what it had once known. 随着14世纪文艺复兴时期佛罗伦萨创造力的爆发, 现代世界见证了它曾经熟知的人与事物的背离。(2020年)

dumb / dʌm / [0][8][6]

释 *adj.* 哑的; 一时说不出话的; 愚蠢的

例 It's hard to imagine that many people are **dumb** enough to want children just because Reese and Angelina make it look so glamorous: most adults understand that a baby is not a haircut. 很难想象有很多人会愚蠢到仅仅因为瑞茜和安吉丽娜让生育孩子看起来光鲜迷人就也想要生孩子: 大多数成年人都明白, 生孩子可不像剪个头发那么简单。(2011年)

派 dumbly / ˈdʌmli / *adv.* 默默地; 无言地 ‖ dumbness / ˈdʌmnəs / *n.* 无言, 沉默

native / ˈneɪtɪv / [0][8][7]

释 *adj.* 本地的; 土著的; 儿时居住地的; 与生俱来的 *n.* 土著; 本地人, 当地人

例 Though **Native** Americans (and later miners and fur trappers) had long recognized the area's riches, most Americans did not. 虽然美洲原住民 (以及后来的矿工和毛皮猎人) 早就认识到了这一地区的财富, 但大多数美国人没有。(2023年)

slow / sləʊ / `088`

釋 *adj.* 缓慢的；慢速的；迟钝的，慢吞吞的 *v.* （使）放慢速度，减缓，松劲

例 With Britain voting to leave the European Union, and GDP already predicted to **slow** as a result, it is now a timely moment to assess what he was referring to. 随着英国公投决定退出欧盟，国内生产总值预计将因此放缓，现在正是评估他所指内容的恰当时机。（2017年）

派 slowness / 'sləʊnəs / *n.* 缓慢；迟钝

boom / buːm / `089`

釋 *n.* （经济的）繁荣，景气；（数量的）增长；（频率的）加快；成功 *v.* （经济的）繁荣，景气

例 The UK is preparing for an economic **boom**. 英国正在为经济繁荣做准备。（2017年）

factor / 'fæktə(r) / `090`

釋 *n.* 因素；要素

例 This suggests the possibility that lifestyle **factors** might help prevent or delay this type of decline. 这表明生活方式因素可能有助于预防或延缓这种衰退。（2021年）

suitable / 'suːtəbl / `091`

釋 *adj.* 合适的；适宜的；适当的

例 To read such books today is to marvel at the fact that their learned contents were once deemed **suitable** for publication in general-circulation dailies. 今天读到这样的书，你会惊讶于这样一个事实：它们博大精深的内容曾被认为适合在大众日报上发表。（2010年）

派 suitability / ˌsuːtə'bɪləti / *n.* 适合；适当；相配

mirror / 'mɪrə(r) / `092`

釋 *n.* 镜子；写照，反映某种情况的事物 *v.* 反映；映照；反射

搭 a mirror of... ……的写照

例 Female participation on corporate boards may not currently **mirror** the percentage of women in the general population, but so what? 目前，女性在公司董事会中的比例可能无法反映女性在总人口中的比例，但那又怎样？（2020年）

近 reflect / rɪ'flekt / *v.* 反映

fierce / fɪəs / `093`

釋 *adj.* 激烈的；凶猛的

例 Such debates reflect **fierce** discussions across the U.S., as researchers, policymakers, teachers and students step up demands for a greater focus on teaching about the facts of climate change in schools. 这样的辩论反映了美国各地的激烈讨论，因为研究人员、政策制定者、教师和学生都进一步要求学校更加关注气候变化事实的教学。（2023年）

organ / ˈɔːɡən /
094

释 *n.* 器官；（政府、集团等的）喉舌，机构；风琴

例 Evidence shows that smoking harms nearly every **organ** of the body. 证据表明，吸烟几乎会损害身体的每一个器官。

prey / preɪ /
095

释 *n.* 猎物；受害者 *v.* 捕食

搭 prey on 捕食

例 Time was when biologists somewhat overworked the evidence that these creatures preserve the health of game by killing the physically weak, or that they **prey** only on "worthless" species. 曾几何时，生物学家们还在费尽心机地寻找证据来证明这些生物通过猎杀弱者来保持种群的健康，或者说，这些生物仅仅捕杀"没有价值的物种"。（2010年）

wing / wɪŋ /
096

释 *n.* 翅膀；机翼；侧厅；翼楼；厢房 *v.* 飞，飞行

搭 spread one's wings 展翅高飞 || on the wing 飞行中的；飞着的

例 Nevertheless every hotel in town seems to be adding a new **wing** or cocktail lounge. 然而，城里的每家酒店似乎都在增加新的翼楼或鸡尾酒吧。（2006年）

lottery / ˈlɒtəri /
097

释 *n.* 彩票抽奖；靠运气的事

例 The man won a $1.35 billion Mega Millions jackpot after purchasing a **lottery** ticket at a gas station. 这名男子在一家加油站买了一张彩票，赢得了13.5亿美元的超级百万大奖。

postpone / pəˈspəʊn /
098

释 *v.* 延迟；延期

例 For these reasons, my doctors have advised me to **postpone** tonight's show. 由于这些原因，我的医生建议我推迟今晚的演出。

近 defer / dɪˈfɜː(r) / *v.* 推迟；延缓

frank / fræŋk /
099

释 *adj.* 坦率的；直率的

搭 to be frank 坦白地说

例 This isn't the first time the famously blunt Osbourne has been **frank** about her appearance, recently addressing her plastic surgery procedures. 这不是以直率著称的奥斯本第一次对自己的外貌直言不讳，最近她谈到了自己的整容手术。

exit / ˈeksɪt /
100

释 *n.* 出口；退场；退出 *v.* 离开；出去；退场；退出（计算机程序）

例 The tech giant recently sent a proposal to Goldman to **exit** from the contract, according to people briefed on the matter. 据知情人士透露，这家科技巨头最近向高盛提出了一项提议，希望退出该合同。

- ☐ ☐ accompany
- ☐ ☐ affirm
- ☐ ☐ agenda
- ☐ ☐ arise
- ☐ ☐ arrest
- ☐ ☐ attempt
- ☐ ☐ betray
- ☐ ☐ boom
- ☐ ☐ call
- ☐ ☐ capable
- ☐ ☐ charge
- ☐ ☐ claim
- ☐ ☐ communicate
- ☐ ☐ complete
- ☐ ☐ counterpart
- ☐ ☐ cover
- ☐ ☐ creativity
- ☐ ☐ cue
- ☐ ☐ cycle
- ☐ ☐ depart
- ☐ ☐ describe
- ☐ ☐ discourage
- ☐ ☐ dumb
- ☐ ☐ edit
- ☐ ☐ effect
- ☐ ☐ efficient
- ☐ ☐ elect
- ☐ ☐ embody
- ☐ ☐ entitle
- ☐ ☐ exclusive
- ☐ ☐ exit

- ☐ ☐ extent
- ☐ ☐ factor
- ☐ ☐ fake
- ☐ ☐ fall
- ☐ ☐ feed
- ☐ ☐ fierce
- ☐ ☐ flourish
- ☐ ☐ foresee
- ☐ ☐ frank
- ☐ ☐ glance
- ☐ ☐ glimpse
- ☐ ☐ glory
- ☐ ☐ handle
- ☐ ☐ hesitate
- ☐ ☐ hygiene
- ☐ ☐ ideal
- ☐ ☐ identical
- ☐ ☐ illusion
- ☐ ☐ implement
- ☐ ☐ instant
- ☐ ☐ intelligent
- ☐ ☐ interview
- ☐ ☐ invisible
- ☐ ☐ lack
- ☐ ☐ limitation
- ☐ ☐ lottery
- ☐ ☐ military
- ☐ ☐ minor
- ☐ ☐ mirror
- ☐ ☐ native
- ☐ ☐ odd

- ☐ ☐ offer
- ☐ ☐ optimistic
- ☐ ☐ organ
- ☐ ☐ package
- ☐ ☐ perceive
- ☐ ☐ perform
- ☐ ☐ postpone
- ☐ ☐ precedent
- ☐ ☐ prepare
- ☐ ☐ prestige
- ☐ ☐ prey
- ☐ ☐ primitive
- ☐ ☐ productivity
- ☐ ☐ profit
- ☐ ☐ progressive
- ☐ ☐ quality
- ☐ ☐ quest
- ☐ ☐ reject
- ☐ ☐ relate
- ☐ ☐ remark
- ☐ ☐ rescue
- ☐ ☐ rival
- ☐ ☐ secure
- ☐ ☐ sentence
- ☐ ☐ slow
- ☐ ☐ solution
- ☐ ☐ suitable
- ☐ ☐ suppose
- ☐ ☐ susceptible
- ☐ ☐ sustain
- ☐ ☐ territory

- ☐ ☐ throughout
- ☐ ☐ trade
- ☐ ☐ universe
- ☐ ☐ urgent
- ☐ ☐ veto
- ☐ ☐ violate
- ☐ ☐ wing

音频

Previous Check

- [ ] tackle
- [ ] utmost
- [ ] intimate
- [ ] erase
- [ ] spectrum
- [ ] coalition
- [ ] convict
- [ ] evident
- [ ] crust
- [ ] parade
- [ ] mock
- [ ] wisdom
- [ ] personality
- [ ] implicit
- [ ] combat
- [ ] negative
- [ ] incentive
- [ ] chief
- [ ] substantial
- [ ] disperse
- [ ] resource
- [ ] advantage
- [ ] fade
- [ ] sector
- [ ] commit
- [ ] positive
- [ ] consume
- [ ] guideline
- [ ] entity
- [ ] shoot
- [ ] economy

- [ ] available
- [ ] lawsuit
- [ ] revolution
- [ ] parcel
- [ ] harness
- [ ] heritage
- [ ] attribute
- [ ] extinct
- [ ] résumé
- [ ] democracy
- [ ] argue
- [ ] prevent
- [ ] broadcast
- [ ] spite
- [ ] volume
- [ ] crude
- [ ] necessity
- [ ] instinct
- [ ] esteem
- [ ] withhold
- [ ] content
- [ ] constitution
- [ ] vote
- [ ] comprise
- [ ] eligible
- [ ] verify
- [ ] climate
- [ ] intensity
- [ ] scarcely
- [ ] attractive
- [ ] demonstrate

- [ ] revive
- [ ] horror
- [ ] critic
- [ ] retain
- [ ] adequate
- [ ] manage
- [ ] design
- [ ] project
- [ ] cope
- [ ] eradicate
- [ ] endure
- [ ] donate
- [ ] field
- [ ] crack
- [ ] shame
- [ ] plastic
- [ ] religious
- [ ] reach
- [ ] spirit
- [ ] modest
- [ ] material
- [ ] position
- [ ] slip
- [ ] enter
- [ ] actual
- [ ] follow
- [ ] update
- [ ] epidemic
- [ ] awkward
- [ ] hope
- [ ] suite

- [ ] rigid
- [ ] trial
- [ ] shrink
- [ ] casual
- [ ] vague
- [ ] personnel
- [ ] household

Writing Models ◎

tackle

utmost

intimate

erase

spectrum

coalition

convict

evident

crust

parade

mock

wisdom

personality

implicit

tackle / ˈtækl /
001

释 *v.* 应付，处理，解决（难题或局面）

例 Despite these factors, many social scientists seem reluctant to **tackle** such problems. 尽管存在这些因素，许多社会科学家似乎不愿意解决这些问题。（2013年）

utmost / ˈʌtməʊst /
002

释 *adj.* 极度的；最大的 *n.* 极限

例 In a diplomatic conversation, the choice of words is of the **utmost** importance. 在外交会谈中，措辞是极为重要的。

intimate
003

释 / ˈɪntɪmət / *adj.* 温馨的；亲密的 *n.* 知己 / ˈɪntɪmeɪt / *v.* 暗示；透露

例 He's been persistent in pushing the song in a way that has fostered a remarkably **intimate** relationship between his audience, himself and the song's lyrics. 他坚持不懈地推广这首歌，在听众、他自己和歌词之间建立了一种非常亲密的关系。

派 intimacy / ˈɪntɪməsi / *n.* 亲密，亲近

erase / ɪˈreɪz /
004

释 *v.* 擦掉（字迹）；抹掉；消除；删除

例 The teacher **erased** the blackboard and began writing math problems on it. 老师将黑板擦干净，然后开始在上面写数学题。

spectrum / ˈspektrəm /
005

释 *n.* 光谱；系列；范围；频谱

例 Avoiding this rather than promoting it should unite the left and right of the political **spectrum**. 避免而不是提倡这种做法应使政治光谱中的左右两派团结起来。（2016年）

coalition / ˌkəʊəˈlɪʃn /
006

释 *n.* 结合体，同盟；结合，联合

例 "We are at a crisis level on the supply of rental housing," said Nick Taylor, executive director of the Workforce Housing **Coalition** of the Greater Seacoast. 大海岸地区劳动力住房联盟执行董事尼克·泰勒说："我们正处于租赁住房供应的危机关头。"（2023年）

convict
007

释 / kənˈvɪkt / *v.* （经审讯）证明……有罪，宣判……有罪 / ˈkɒnvɪkt / *n.* 囚犯

例 Thomas was **convicted** of murder. 托马斯被判谋杀罪。

evident / ˈevɪdənt /
008

释 *adj.* 清楚的；显而易见的；显然的

例 This tendency in the natural sciences has long been **evident** in the social sciences too. 自然科学中的这种倾向在社会科学中也早已体现。（2012年）

crust / krʌst / `009`

释 *n.* （一片）面包皮；硬外皮；外壳；地壳

例 The **crust** of the bread is burnt. 这块面包的外皮烤焦了。

parade / pəˈreɪd / `010`

释 *n.* （庆祝）游行；（检阅时的）游行行列 *v.* 游行；列队行进

搭 on parade 受检阅；在游行

例 On the day of the ceremony, all the guests arrived at the ranch before the beginning of the **parade**. 仪式当天，所有宾客都在游行开始前抵达了牧场。

mock / mɒk / `011`

释 *v.* 嘲笑；（通过模仿）嘲弄；不尊重 *adj.* 模拟的；虚假的 *n.* （英国）模拟考试

例 Meanwhile, many settlers had slighter religious commitments than Dane's, as one clergyman learned in confronting folk along the coast who **mocked** that they had not come to the New World for religion. 与此同时，许多定居者的宗教信仰并不像戴恩那样坚定，正如一位牧师在与沿海居民的争论中所了解到的那样，他们嘲弄自己可不是为了宗教而来到新大陆的。（2009年）

近 ridicule / ˈrɪdɪkjuːl / *v./n.* 嘲笑；嘲弄 ‖ sneer / snɪə(r) / *v./n.* 讥笑；冷笑

wisdom / ˈwɪzdəm / `012`

释 *n.* 智慧；才智；精明；学问

搭 conventional/received wisdom 大多数人的看法；普遍信念

例 It is a wise father that knows his own child, but today a man can boost his paternal (fatherly) **wisdom**—or at least confirm that he's the kid's dad. 了解自己孩子的父亲才是明智的父亲，但今天，一个男人可以提升他的父爱智慧——或者至少确认他是孩子的父亲。（2009年）

personality / ˌpɜːsəˈnæləti / `013`

释 *n.* 性格；个性；（尤指娱乐、广播、体育界）名人

例 **Personality** can affect how a person reacts to eye contact. 性格会影响一个人对眼神交流的反应。（2020年）

近 character / ˈkærəktə(r) / *n.* 性格；特性 ‖ feature / ˈfiːtʃə(r) / *n.* 特征；个性

辨 personality主要指一个人稳定的心理特征；character指对个性或人格所做出的客观评价，常常与道德有关；feature通常指外貌的特征或特别的、有吸引力的东西。

implicit / ɪmˈplɪsɪt / `014`

释 *adj.* 含蓄的，不直接言明的；内含的；无疑问的

例 Her statement is being seen as **implicit** criticism of the research results. 她的话中隐隐约约含有批评研究结果的意味。

反 explicit / ɪkˈsplɪsɪt / *adj.* 毫无隐瞒的；明确的

Writing Models ◎

combat

negative

incentive

chief

substantial

disperse

resource

advantage

fade

sector

commit

positive

consume

combat / 'kɒmbæt /

015

释 *n.* 战斗；搏斗 *v.* 防止；减轻

例 Men go to war and are exposed to **combat** stress. 男人上战场，要承受战斗压力。（2008年）

辨 battle指战争中的一次较全面、时间较长的战斗或个人之间的争斗；fight含义广泛，指战斗、斗争或打斗；struggle 指时间持续长的战斗或奋力斗争；combat 泛指军事行动，尤指小规模的战斗。

negative / 'neɡətɪv /

016

释 *adj.* 负面的；否定的；有害的 *n.* 底片；否定；属阴性（或否定）的结果 *v.* 拒绝；否定……的真实性

例 In the ever-changing 21st century, even the word "habit" carries a **negative** implication. 在瞬息万变的21世纪，甚至连"习惯"一词都带有负面含义。（2009年）

反 positive / 'pɒzətɪv / *adj.* 积极的；（化验结果）阳性的

incentive / ɪn'sentɪv /

017

释 *n.* 动机，刺激，鼓励

例 By the date of his birth Europe was witnessing the passing of the religious drama, and the creation of new forms under the **incentive** of classical tragedy and comedy. 在他出生之前，欧洲正在见证宗教戏剧的消逝，并在古典悲剧和喜剧的激励下创造出新的形式。（2018年）

反 disincentive / ˌdɪsɪn'sentɪv / *n.* 抑制因素

chief / tʃiːf /

018

释 *adj.* 主要的；首席的 *n.* 最高领导人；首领

搭 the chief executive 首席执行官 ‖ editor-in-chief 主编

例 Meanwhile, insurance companies face increasing medical, legal and other operational costs, said Greg McBride, **chief** financial analyst at the website. 那家网站的首席金融分析师格雷格·麦克布莱德说，与此同时，保险公司面临着医疗、法律和其他运营成本的增加。

substantial / səb'stænʃl /

019

释 *adj.* 大量的；很大程度的

例 Genetically speaking, there are advantages to avoiding **substantial** height. 从遗传学角度来说，避免身高过高是有好处的。（2008年）

disperse / dɪ'spɜːs /

020

释 *v.* 使分散，扩散；散开；驱散

例 The crowd **dispersed** quickly. 人群很快散开了。

resource / rɪ'sɔːs /

021

释 *n.* 财力；资源；资料 *v.* 向……提供资金（或设备）

例 What matters is that they will belong to a private monopoly which developed them using public **resources**. 重要的是，它们将属于利用公共资源开发它们的私人垄断企业。（2018年）

advantage / əd'vɑːntɪdʒ /

0 2 2

释 *n.* 有利条件；优势；优点；好处

搭 take advantage of 利用

例 This suggests that dimmer bulbs burn longer, that there is an **advantage** in not being too bright. 这表明，较暗的灯泡燃烧时间更长，不太亮也有好处。（2009年）

fade / feɪd /

0 2 3

释 *v.* （使）变淡，变暗；逐渐消逝；逐渐消失；变得不为人注意；变得无关紧要

搭 fade away（人）衰弱；病重死亡 ‖ fade in/out（画面）淡入/淡出；（声音）渐强/渐弱

例 They are noting that the Victorians suddenly seem to become more human as the hundred-or-so years that separate us **fade** away through our common experience of laughter. 他们注意到，维多利亚人似乎突然变得更有人情味了，因为我们共同的欢笑经历，我们之间一百多年的隔阂逐渐消失了。（2021年）

sector / 'sektə(r) /

0 2 4

释 *n.* （经济的）部门；部分

例 Requiring companies to make gender the primary qualification for board membership will inevitably lead to less experienced private **sector** boards. 要求公司将性别作为董事会成员的首要资格，必然会导致私营部门董事会经验不足。（2020年）

近 department / dɪ'pɑːtmənt / *n.* 部门 ‖ branch / brɑːntʃ / *n.* 分部；分支

commit / kə'mɪt /

0 2 5

释 *v.* 犯（罪）；做（坏事）；承诺，保证；拨出，调配（资金、资源等）；明确表态

例 He keeps delaying his decision because he doesn't want to **commit** himself. 他一直拖延做决定，因为他不想做出承诺。

positive / 'pɒzətɪv /

0 2 6

释 *adj.* 积极乐观的；自信的；表示赞同的；正面的；有把握的；明确的；阳性的；正电的 *n.* 优势；阳性结果（或反应）；正片

例 Jeremy Wright, the culture secretary, should welcome this **positive**, hope-filled proposal, and turn it into action. 文化大臣杰里米·赖特应该欢迎这一积极的、充满希望的建议，并将其付诸行动。（2020年）

consume / kən'sjuːm /

0 2 7

释 *v.* 吃；喝；消耗，耗费（燃料、能源或时间）；烧毁；（使）沉迷

例 There is also an environmental impact with natural lawns, which need mowing and therefore usually **consume** electricity or petrol. 天然草坪也会对环境造成影响，因为草坪需要修剪，因此通常需要消耗电力或汽油。

Writing Models ◎

guideline

entity

shoot

economy

available

lawsuit

revolution

parcel

harness

heritage

attribute

extinct

résumé

guideline / ˈgaɪdlaɪn /   028

释 *n.* 指导方针; 参考

例 Along with Singapore, other governments and mega-corporations are beginning to establish their own **guidelines**. 除了新加坡, 其他国家的政府和大型企业也开始制定自己的指导方针。(2019年)

近 rule / ruːl / *n.* 规则; 条例 ‖ instruction / ɪnˈstrʌkʃn / *n.* 指令; 用法说明

entity / ˈentəti /   029

释 *n.* 实体; 独立存在物

例 Persons and corporations are equivalent **entities** under the law. 依照法律, 个人和企业是对等的实体。

shoot / ʃuːt /   030

释 *v.* 射击; 发射; 拍摄 *n.* 摄影; 狩猎; 嫩芽

例 I want to **shoot** a portrait outdoors in the daytime. 我想在白天拍摄一张户外人像照。

economy / ɪˈkɒnəmi /   031

释 *n.* 经济; 经济状况; 经济体制; 节省

例 As the **economy** picks up, opportunities will abound for aspiring leaders. 随着经济的回暖, 有抱负的领导者将有更多的机会。(2011年)

派 economical / ˌiːkəˈnɒmɪkl / *adj.* 经济的; 省钱的; 节约的

available / əˈveɪləbl /   032

释 *adj.* 可得到的; 有空的

例 Today, we live in a world where GPS systems, digital maps, and other navigation apps are **available** on our smartphones. 如今, 我们生活的世界里, 智能手机上有GPS系统、数字地图和其他导航应用程序。(2019年)

lawsuit / ˈlɔːsuːt /   033

释 *n.* 诉讼案; 诉讼

例 It is the first public-interest **lawsuit** in China related to pollution from automobile exhaust. 这是中国首例与机动车尾气污染有关的公益诉讼案。

revolution / ˌrevəˈluːʃn /   034

释 *n.* 革命; 重大变革

例 We are still at the beginning of this **revolution** and small choices now may turn out to have gigantic consequences later. 我们仍处于这场革命的开端, 现在的微小选择可能会在日后产生巨大的后果。(2018年)

近 reform / rɪˈfɔːm / *n.* 改革

parcel / 'pɑːsl / 035

释 *n.* 包裹；小包 *v.* 包；裹好；打包
搭 part and parcel of 重要部分 ‖ parcel sth. out 把某物分开
例 If the study of law is beginning to establish itself as part and **parcel** of a general education, its aims and methods should appeal directly to journalism educators. 如果法律学习开始确立自己作为通识教育重要组成部分的地位，那么它的目标和方法会直接吸引新闻教育工作者。（2007年）

harness / 'hɑːnɪs / 036

释 *n.* 马具；挽具 *v.* 控制，利用；给（马等）上挽具
搭 in harness (with sb.)（同某人）联手；密切合作
例 And one leading authority says that these intensely powerful mental events can be not only **harnessed** but actually brought under conscious control, to help us sleep and feel better. 一位权威人士说，这些强烈的心理事件不仅可以被利用，而且实际上可以被有意识地控制，从而帮助我们入睡，让我们感觉更好。（2005年）

heritage / 'herɪtɪdʒ / 037

释 *n.* 遗产；继承物；传统
搭 cultural/historical heritage 文化遗产/历史遗产
例 These should be available to them as part of their cultural **heritage** and history and as a source of national pride. 这些都应作为其文化遗产和历史的一部分以及民族自豪感的源泉提供给他们。（2024年）
近 legacy / 'legəsi / *n.* 遗产，遗留之物；遗赠物 ‖ inheritance / ɪn'herɪtəns / *n.* 遗产；继承

attribute 038

释 / ə'trɪbjuːt / *v.* 把……归因于；赋予（某品质或特点）；认为（文章、作品等）出自…… / 'ætrɪbjuːt / *n.* 属性；特征
例 He was searching for tiny engraved seals **attributed** to the ancient Mycenaean culture that dominated Greece from the 1400s to 1200s BC. 他正在寻找公元前15世纪至12世纪期间统治希腊的古迈锡尼文化的微小雕刻印章。（2014年）

extinct / ɪk'stɪŋkt / 039

释 *adj.* 灭绝的；不复存在的；（火山）死的
例 When prehistoric man arrived in new parts of the world, something strange happened to the large animals: they suddenly became **extinct**. 当史前人类来到世界上的新地方时，一些大型动物发生了一些奇怪的事情：它们突然灭绝了。（2006年）
近 vanished / 'vænɪʃt / *adj.* 消失的，不见的

résumé / 'rezjuːmeɪ / 040

释 *n.* 简历，履历
例 I know nothing about her **résumé**. 我对她的履历一无所知。

democracy / dɪˈmɒkrəsi / **041**

释 *n.* 民主精神；民主权利；民主；民主国家；民主政体；民主制度

例 Egalitarian sentiments were often tempered by fears that the mass of the population was unprepared for self-rule and **democracy**. 平等主义情绪往往因担心人民大众没有做好自治和民主的准备而有所缓和。（2007年）

argue / ˈɑːgjuː / **042**

释 *v.* 争吵；争辩；讨论；辩论；主张，认为

例 Many **argue** that it is a flawed concept. It measures things that do not matter and misses things that do. 许多人认为，这是一个有缺陷的概念。它衡量的是不重要的东西，而忽略了重要的东西。（2017年）

prevent / prɪˈvent / **043**

释 *v.* 防止；预防；阻止；阻碍

例 The personal grievance provisions of New Zealand's Employment Relations Act 2000 (ERA) **prevent** an employer from firing an employee without good cause. 新西兰2000年通过的《雇佣关系法》（ERA）中的个人申诉条款禁止雇主在没有正当理由的情况下解雇员工。（2022年）

broadcast / ˈbrɔːdkɑːst / **044**

释 *v.* 传播（信息等）；散布；广播，播送 *n.* 广播节目，电视节目

例 **Broadcasting** his ambition was "very much my decision," McGee says. 麦基说，传播自己的抱负"在很大程度上是我自己的决定"。（2011年）

spite / spaɪt / **045**

释 *n.* 恶意；怨恨 *v.* 刁难；使恼怒

搭 in spite of 不管；尽管 ‖ in spite of oneself 不由自主地

例 In **spite** of "endless talk of difference," American society is an amazing machine for homogenizing people. 尽管"无休止地谈论差异"，但美国社会是一台将人们同质化的神奇机器。（2006年）

volume / ˈvɒljuːm / **046**

释 *n.* 容积，体积；音量；量；额

搭 speak volumes about 充分说明

例 Just as the code-breaking has its wider relevance in the struggle for Spain, so his attempts to make his way up the promotion ladder speak **volumes** about British society. 正如密码破译在争夺西班牙的斗争中具有广泛的意义一样，他在晋升阶梯上的努力也充分说明了英国社会。（2022年）

crude / kruːd /
0 4 7

釋 *n.* 原油，天然的物质 *adj.* 粗糙的，简陋的；粗鲁的；天然的

例 A sacred place of peace, however **crude** it may be, is a distinctly human need, as opposed to shelter, which is a distinctly animal need. 一个安静的圣地，无论多么简陋，都是一种明显的人类需求，而庇护所则是动物特有的需求。（2013年）

necessity / nə'sesəti /
0 4 8

釋 *n.* 必需品；必要；必然

例 Of **necessity**, colonial America was a projection of Europe. 殖民地时期的美国必然是欧洲的投影。（2015年）

instinct / 'ɪnstɪŋkt /
0 4 9

釋 *n.* 本能，天性；直觉

搭 by instinct 出于本能

例 But in Osborneland, your first **instinct** is to fall into dependency—permanent dependency if you can get it—supported by a state only too ready to indulge your falsehood. 但在奥斯本兰，你的第一本能是陷入依赖——如果你能得到的话，永久的依赖——由一个随时准备纵容你的谎言的国家来支持。（2014年）

近 intuition / ˌɪntjuˈɪʃn / *n.* 直觉

esteem / ɪ'stiːm /
0 5 0

釋 *n.* 尊重，敬重 *v.* 尊敬，敬重；把……看作

例 Star watchers were among the most **esteemed** members of Hawaiian society. 观星者是夏威夷社会最受尊敬的成员之一。（2017年）

withhold / wɪð'həʊld /
0 5 1

釋 *v.* 拒给，不给

例 The customer **withheld** payment because of the poor service. 由于服务太差，顾客拒绝付款。

content
0 5 2

釋 / 'kɒntent / *n.* 所容纳之物；所含之物；内容；[pl.]目录；（书、讲话、节目等的）主题，主要内容 / kən'tent / *adj.* 满意的；满足的 *v.* 满足；满意；知足

例 "Ultimately," said Jack Miner, Ohio State University's registrar, "we see students achieve more success because they retake a course and do better in subsequent courses or master the **content** that allows them to graduate on time." 俄亥俄州立大学注册主任杰克·米纳说："最终，我们看到学生取得了更大的成功，因为他们重修了一门课程，并在后续课程中取得了更好的成绩，或者掌握了使他们能够按时毕业的内容。"（2019年）

constitution / ˌkɒnstɪˈtjuːʃn / [053]

释 *n.* 宪法；章程；构造；构成；身体素质；体格

例 New, disruptive technology sometimes demands novel applications of the **Constitution**'s protections. 新的突破性技术有时要求对宪法的保护条例进行全新的应用。（2015年）

派 constitutional / ˌkɒnstɪˈtjuːʃənl / *adj.* 有关宪法的

vote / vəʊt / [054]

释 *v.* 投票；推举 *n.* 投票；选票

例 The state Legislature recently **voted** against a bill that would've made it illegal for towns to create legislation restricting short-term rentals. 州议会最近投票否决了一项法案，该法案认为城镇立法限制短期租赁是非法的。（2023年）

comprise / kəmˈpraɪz / [055]

释 *v.* 包含，包括；组成

搭 be comprised of 由……组成

例 The five volumes **comprise** a single book. 那五册构成一卷书。

eligible / ˈelɪdʒəbl / [056]

释 *adj.* 合格的，有资格的；合适的，合意的

例 Passengers who pass a background check are **eligible** to use expedited screening lanes. 通过背景调查的乘客有资格使用快速安检通道。（2017年）

近 qualified / ˈkwɒlɪfaɪd / *adj.* 有资格的；合格的

反 ineligible / ɪnˈelɪdʒəbl / *adj.* 无入选资格的；不合格的

verify / ˈverɪfaɪ / [057]

释 *v.* 证实，证明

例 The network will require Internet users to **verify** their identity by providing their ID card numbers. 该网站将要求互联网用户提供身份证号码来验证其身份。

climate / ˈklaɪmət / [058]

释 *n.* 气候；风气；思潮；形势；局势

例 It is difficult to find a job in the present economic **climate**. 在目前这种经济形势下很难找到工作。

intensity / ɪnˈtensəti / [059]

释 *n.* 强度；强烈；剧烈；紧张

例 Beethoven's habit of increasing the volume with an extreme **intensity** and then abruptly following it with a sudden soft passage was only rarely used by composers before him. 贝多芬习惯于最大幅度增加音量，然后突然接一个柔和的乐段，这在他之前的作曲家中是很少见的。（2014年）

scarcely / 'skeəsli / `060`

释 adv. 几乎不，简直不；绝不

例 These changes were gradual and at first **scarcely** visible. 这些变化是渐进的，起初几乎看不出来。（2015年）

attractive / ə'træktɪv / `061`

释 adj. 有吸引力的；（人）漂亮的，有魅力的

例 The magazine cover showing an **attractive** mother holding a cute baby is hardly the only Madonna-and-child image on newsstands this week. 杂志封面展示了一位迷人的母亲抱着一个可爱的婴儿，这并不是本周报刊亭里唯一的麦当娜和孩子的照片。（2011年）

demonstrate / 'demənstreɪt / `062`

释 v. 说明；论证；显示；示威；示范

例 Alvarez's experience **demonstrates** the importance of finding ways to diffuse stress before it threatens your health and your ability to function. 阿尔瓦雷斯的经历表明，在压力威胁到你的健康和工作能力之前，找到化解压力的方法非常重要。（2008年）

派 demonstration / ˌdemən'streɪʃn / n. 证明，论证；示威

近 illustrate / 'ɪləstreɪt / v. 说明，阐明 ‖ prove / pruːv / v. 证明，证实

revive / rɪ'vaɪv / `063`

释 v. 使复兴；使复苏；使苏醒；重新使用；重新上演

例 The challenge of coping with automation underlines the need for the U.S. to **revive** its fading business dynamism: Starting new companies must be made easier. 应对自动化带来的挑战凸显了美国需要重振其逐渐衰退的商业活力的必要性：必须让开办新公司变得更容易。（2018年）

派 revival / rɪ'vaɪvl / n. 复活；复兴

horror / 'hɒrə(r) / `064`

释 adj. 内容恐怖的；（经历）非常不愉快的 n. 恐怖；战栗；震惊；憎恶；残酷

搭 shock horror （假装震惊时说）震惊

例 The kids saw the bloody scene in the movie and screamed in **horror**. 孩子们看到电影中的血腥场面，吓得尖叫起来。

critic / 'krɪtɪk / `065`

释 n. 评论员；评论家；批评家；批评者；挑剔的人

例 In those far-off days, it was taken for granted that the **critics** of major papers would write in detail and at length about the events they covered. 在那个遥远的年代，人们理所当然地认为各大报纸的评论员会详细而详尽地评论他们所报道的事件。（2020年）

近 reviewer / rɪ'vjuːə(r) / n. 评论者；审查者

Writing Models ○

retain

adequate

manage

design

project

cope

eradicate

endure

donate

field

crack

shame

retain / rɪ'teɪn / 066

释 v. 保留；保持；继续容纳

例 Half a century of town and country planning has enabled it to **retain** an enviable rural coherence, while still permitting low-density urban living. 半个世纪的城乡规划使其（英国）保留了令人羡慕的乡村连贯性，同时还允许低密度的城市生活。（2016年）

近 keep / kiːp / v. 保持 ‖ preserve / prɪ'zɜːv / v. 保存；维持

adequate / 'ædɪkwət / 067

释 adj. 足够的；合格的；合乎需要的

例 This is an **adequate** amount so long as it is aimed in the right direction. 只要它的目标是正确的，这一金额就足够。（2013年）

manage / 'mænɪdʒ / 068

释 v. 管理；（在某一时间）能办到，能做成；能解决（问题），应付（困难局面等）

例 Not only did they develop such a device but by the turn of the millennium they had also **managed** to embed it in a worldwide system accessed by billions of people every day. 他们不仅开发了这样一种设备，而且在千禧年之交，他们还成功地将其嵌入了每天有数十亿人访问的全球系统中。（2012年）

派 management / 'mænɪdʒmənt / n. 管理；经营

近 administer / əd'mɪnɪstə(r) / v. 管理；治理 ‖ govern / 'gʌvn / v. 统治；管理

design / dɪ'zaɪn / 069

释 v. 设计；（为特定目的）计划；制订 n. 设计；构思；意图

例 The U.S. Supreme Court frowns on sex-based classifications unless they are **designed** to address an "important" policy interest. 美国最高法院不赞成基于性别的分类，除非设计这些分类是为了解决"重要的"政策利益。（2020年）

project 070

释 / 'prɒdʒekt / n. 生产（或研究等）项目；方案；工程；计划 / prə'dʒekt / v. 规划；计划；预计；投射；放映；突出；伸出

例 The alliances are most valuable when scientists and artists have a shared stake in a **project**, are able to jointly design it and can critique each other's work. 当科学家和艺术家在一个项目中拥有共同的利益，能够共同设计项目，并能相互批评对方的工作时，这种联盟就是最有价值的。（2022年）

cope / kəʊp / 071

释 v.（成功地）处理，应付

例 "It's not necessarily that women don't **cope** as well. It's just that they have so much more to **cope** with," says Dr. Yehuda. "这并不一定是说女性不能很好地应对。只是她们要应对的事情太多了。"叶胡达博士说。（2008年）

eradicate / ɪˈrædɪkeɪt / 072

释 v. 消灭; 灭绝; 根除

例 Humanity has the necessary agrotechnological tools to **eradicate** hunger, from genetically engineered crops to artificial fertilizers. 人类有必要的农业技术工具来消灭饥饿, 从转基因作物到人工肥料都有。(2013年)

派 eradication / ɪˌrædɪˈkeɪʃn / n. 根除

endure / ɪnˈdjʊə(r) / 073

释 v. 忍耐; 忍受; 持续; 持久

例 The fossil record shows that many species have **endured** for millions of years—so why shouldn't we? 化石记录显示, 许多物种已经生存了数百万年——那么我们为什么不能呢? (2013年)

派 endurance / ɪnˈdjʊərəns / n. 忍耐力; 耐久力 ‖ endurable / ɪnˈdjʊərəbl / adj. 耐久的

donate / dəʊˈneɪt / 074

释 v. 捐赠, 赠送; 捐献

例 Second, customers may be willing to buy a company's products as an indirect way to **donate** to the good causes it helps. 其次, 消费者可能愿意购买公司的产品, 间接地对企业所资助的慈善事业进行捐赠。(2016年)

派 donation / dəʊˈneɪʃn / n. 捐赠物; 捐赠; 赠送

field / fiːld / 075

释 n. 田; 地; 场地; 学科, 领域; 实地; 战场

例 Kennedy wrote that the rule "limited states' ability to seek long-term prosperity and has prevented market participants from competing on an even playing **field**." 肯尼迪写道, 该规则"限制了各州寻求长期繁荣的能力, 并阻碍了市场参与者在公平的竞争环境中竞争"。(2019年)

crack / kræk / 076

释 v. (使) 破裂; (因压力而) 崩溃; 找到解决 (难题等的) 方法 n. 裂缝

搭 crack down 严厉打击 ‖ crack on (为尽快完成而) 努力干 ‖ crack up 垮掉, 崩溃

例 Across the country, theater owners and studio executives are trying to **crack** the question of what draws moviegoers back to the theater. 在全国范围内, 影院老板和电影公司高管都在努力弄清楚如何能吸引电影观众回到影院这一问题。

shame / ʃeɪm / 077

释 n. 羞愧; 羞耻心; 令人惋惜的事; 耻辱; 丢脸

例 This is a **shame**—the community should be grasping the opportunity to raise its influence in the real world. 这是一件憾事——社会科学界应该抓住这个机会增强其在现实世界中的影响力。(2013年)

Writing Models

plastic

religious

reach

spirit

modest

material

position

slip

enter

actual

follow

update

epidemic

plastic / ˈplæstɪk /   078

释 *n.* 塑料 *adj.* 塑料的；可塑的

例 But some **plastic** materials change over time. They crack and frizzle. They "weep" out additives. They melt into sludge. 但有些塑料材料会随着时间的推移而发生变化。它们会开裂和起毛。它们会"流出"添加剂。它们会融化成污泥。（2022年）

religious / rɪˈlɪdʒəs /   079

释 *adj.* 宗教的；虔诚的

例 Some students at the University of Connecticut who are fearful of their safety are concealing **religious** identifiers to avoid being targeted. 康涅狄格大学的一些学生担心自己的安全，为了避免成为攻击目标，他们隐瞒了自己的宗教标识符号。

reach / riːtʃ /   080

释 *v.* 到达；达到；伸手够到；联系上；延伸；达成 *n.* 手臂展开的长度；波及范围；影响范围

例 For this reason, caravanserais were strategically placed so that they could be **reached** in a day's travel time. 出于这个原因，商队客店的位置很关键，好让他们可以在一天的旅行时间内到达。（2023年）

spirit / ˈspɪrɪt /   081

释 *n.* 精神；心灵；毅力；宗旨

例 When we are deprived of green, of plants, of trees, most of us give in to a demoralization of **spirit** which we usually blame on some psychological conditions, until one day we find ourselves in a garden and feel the oppression vanish as if by magic. 当我们被剥夺了绿色、植物和树木时，我们中的多数人通常把陷入精神萎靡归咎于某些心理疾病，直到有一天我们身处花园时，才忽然发现这种压抑感神奇地消失了。（2013年）

派 spiritual / ˈspɪrɪtʃuəl / *adj.* 精神的

modest / ˈmɒdɪst /   082

释 *adj.* 适度的；（比率等）较小的；谦虚的

例 From then on his sketches, which appeared under the pen name "Boz" in *The Evening Chronicle*, earned him a **modest** reputation. 从那时起，他的小品文以"博兹"的笔名出现在《纪事晚报》上，为他赢得了一定的声誉。（2017年）

material / məˈtɪəriəl /   083

释 *adj.* 物质的，实际的；重要的；必要的 *n.* 材料；原料

例 Anyone with an Internet connection can read the primary source **material**—hundreds of pages of administrative records, letters and meeting minutes. 只要能联网，任何人都可以阅读原始资料——数百页的行政记录、信件和会议记录。

派 materialism / məˈtɪəriəlɪzəm / *n.* 唯物主义；唯物论；物质主义

position / pəˈzɪʃn /
084

释 *n.* 姿态，姿势；处境；地位；状况；观点；态度；职位

例 Now we can understand each other's **positions** and recognize our shared values, since we both care about needy workers. 现在我们可以理解彼此的观点，认识到我们共同的价值观，因为我们都关心贫困的劳动者。（2019年）

slip / slɪp /
085

释 *v.* 滑倒；滑落；下降；溜 *n.* 滑倒；纸条；差错

搭 slip away 消失；消亡；死去 ‖ slip out 无意中说出（或泄露）

例 Don't let the chance to work abroad **slip** through your fingers. 这个出国工作的机会你可不要错过。

enter / ˈentə(r) /
086

释 *v.* 进来；加入；开始从事

搭 enter into 开始讨论；着手处理

例 The chain **entered** the U.S. in 1998 with its first location in California and now has more than 70 nationwide, according to its website. 该连锁店于1998年进入美国，在加利福尼亚州开设了第一家分店，据其网站介绍，目前已在全国开设了70家分店。

actual / ˈæktʃuəl /
087

释 *adj.* 真实的；实际的；真正的

例 The jobseekers' allowance has met their **actual** needs. 求职者津贴已经满足了他们的实际需要。（2014年）

follow / ˈfɒləʊ /
088

释 *v.* 跟随；跟踪；听从；接着……发生；沿着；理解

例 So, if you head downhill, and **follow** any H_2O you find, you should eventually see signs of people. 所以，如果你往山下走，沿着你找到的水源走，你最终会看到有人烟的迹象。（2019年）

update
089

释 / ˌʌpˈdeɪt / *v.* 更新；给……提供最新信息 / ˈʌpdeɪt / *n.* 最新消息；快讯

例 The one thing that she accomplished was raising money to **update** our facilities. 她完成的一件事就是筹集资金来更新我们的设备。

epidemic / ˌepɪˈdemɪk /
090

释 *n.* 流行病；（疾病的）流行，传播；（坏事迅速的）泛滥，蔓延

例 Now utopia has grown unfashionable, as we have gained a deeper appreciation of the range of threats facing us, from asteroid strike to **epidemic** flu and to climate change. 现在，乌托邦已经不再流行，因为我们对自己面临的一系列威胁有了更深刻的认识，从小行星撞击到流感再到气候变化。（2013年）

awkward / ˈɔːkwəd /

091

释 *adj.* 令人尴尬的；笨拙的；不可理喻的；难为情的；难处理的；棘手的

例 **Awkward** or wordy phrasing or unclear sentences and paragraphs should be mercilessly poked and prodded into shape. 对于那些令人费解的、冗长的措辞和表意不明的句子和段落，应该毫不留情地将其挑出，并删改，直至符合要求。（2008年）

hope / həʊp /

092

释 *v./n.* 希望，期望

例 Yet officials also **hope** for a much larger benefit: more long-term decision-making, not only by banks but by all corporations, to build a stronger economy for future generations. 然而，官员们也希望能有更大的好处：不仅是银行，所有企业也都能做出更长远的决策，为子孙后代打造更强大的经济。（2019年）

suite / swiːt /

093

释 *n.* 一套房间；套间；组曲；一套家具

例 At the property, family **suites** include rooms with four bunk beds that sleep up to eight people. 在这家酒店，家庭套房配有四张上下铺的床，最多可住八人。

rigid / ˈrɪdʒɪd /

094

释 *adj.* 过于严格的；刻板的；僵硬的

例 The company's competitors complain that they are hemmed in by **rigid** legal contracts. 该公司的竞争对手们抱怨称，他们受到过于严格的法律合同的限制。

派 rigidity / rɪˈdʒɪdəti / *n.* 严格，刻板；僵化

近 inflexible / ɪnˈfleksəbl / *adj.* 僵化的；死板的；顽固的

trial / ˈtraɪəl /

095

释 *n.* 审讯，审判；试验，试用；考验 *v.* 试验；试用

搭 on trial 在受审中；在考验中

例 In many respects, the dearth of moral purpose frames not only the fact of such widespread phone hacking but the terms on which the **trial** took place. 在许多方面，道德目的的缺失不仅构成了如此广泛的电话窃听的事实，也构成了案件审判所依据的条件。（2015年）

shrink / ʃrɪŋk /

096

释 *v.* （使）缩水，收缩；（使）缩小，减少；退缩

搭 shrink from 畏避，回避（困难等）

例 The center's staff **shrank** to a skeleton crew, and the many ambitious projects came to a halt. 该中心的工作人员缩减到只剩下骨干团队，许多雄心勃勃的项目也戛然而止。

casual / ˈkæʒuəl /
097

释 *adj.* 漫不经心的; 非正式; 随便的; 偶然的; 碰巧的

例 Around half of U.K. employers said that their employees are too **casual** in the office, wearing unacceptable clothing and having unkempt hair. 大约一半的英国雇主表示，他们的员工在办公室过于随意，穿着令人难以接受的衣服，头发蓬乱。

派 casualness / ˈkæʒuəlnəs / *n.* 漫不经心

vague / veɪg /
098

释 *adj.* 含糊的; 不清楚的; 不详细的; 粗略的

例 We could just barely make out the **vague** outline of a plane in the sky. 我们只能勉强辨认出天空中一架飞机的模糊轮廓。

personnel / ˌpɜːsəˈnel /
099

释 *n.* 全体人员，职员; 人事部门

例 The main disadvantage of using AI to respond to customers is that there are concerns about trusting personal interactions to machines, which could lead not only to the subsequent loss of interpersonal connections, but also to a decrease in marketing **personnel**. 使用人工智能来回应客户的主要缺点是人们担心将个人互动托付给机器，这不仅会导致人际关系的丧失，还会导致营销人员的减少。（2023年）

household / ˈhaʊshəʊld /
100

释 *n.* 一家人; 家庭

例 Alvarez's salary barely covered her **household** expenses. 阿尔瓦雷斯的工资几乎不足以支付她的家庭开支。（2008年）

☐ ☐ actual
☐ ☐ adequate
☐ ☐ advantage
☐ ☐ argue
☐ ☐ attractive
☐ ☐ attribute
☐ ☐ available
☐ ☐ awkward
☐ ☐ broadcast
☐ ☐ casual
☐ ☐ chief
☐ ☐ climate
☐ ☐ coalition
☐ ☐ combat
☐ ☐ commit
☐ ☐ comprise
☐ ☐ constitution
☐ ☐ consume
☐ ☐ content
☐ ☐ convict
☐ ☐ cope
☐ ☐ crack
☐ ☐ critic
☐ ☐ crude
☐ ☐ crust
☐ ☐ democracy
☐ ☐ demonstrate
☐ ☐ design
☐ ☐ disperse
☐ ☐ donate
☐ ☐ economy

☐ ☐ eligible
☐ ☐ endure
☐ ☐ enter
☐ ☐ entity
☐ ☐ epidemic
☐ ☐ eradicate
☐ ☐ erase
☐ ☐ esteem
☐ ☐ evident
☐ ☐ extinct
☐ ☐ fade
☐ ☐ field
☐ ☐ follow
☐ ☐ guideline
☐ ☐ harness
☐ ☐ heritage
☐ ☐ hope
☐ ☐ horror
☐ ☐ household
☐ ☐ implicit
☐ ☐ incentive
☐ ☐ instinct
☐ ☐ intensity
☐ ☐ intimate
☐ ☐ lawsuit
☐ ☐ manage
☐ ☐ material
☐ ☐ mock
☐ ☐ modest
☐ ☐ necessity
☐ ☐ negative

☐ ☐ parade
☐ ☐ parcel
☐ ☐ personality
☐ ☐ personnel
☐ ☐ plastic
☐ ☐ position
☐ ☐ positive
☐ ☐ prevent
☐ ☐ project
☐ ☐ reach
☐ ☐ religious
☐ ☐ resource
☐ ☐ résumé
☐ ☐ retain
☐ ☐ revive
☐ ☐ revolution
☐ ☐ rigid
☐ ☐ scarcely
☐ ☐ sector
☐ ☐ shame
☐ ☐ shoot
☐ ☐ shrink
☐ ☐ slip
☐ ☐ spectrum
☐ ☐ spirit
☐ ☐ spite
☐ ☐ substantial
☐ ☐ suite
☐ ☐ tackle
☐ ☐ trial
☐ ☐ update

☐ ☐ utmost
☐ ☐ vague
☐ ☐ verify
☐ ☐ volume
☐ ☐ vote
☐ ☐ wisdom
☐ ☐ withhold

- [ ] produce
- [ ] contribute
- [ ] department
- [ ] minister
- [ ] comprehend
- [ ] shorthand
- [ ] highlight
- [ ] narrative
- [ ] reduce
- [ ] fortune
- [ ] mount
- [ ] analysis
- [ ] undergraduate
- [ ] fund
- [ ] function
- [ ] recruit
- [ ] vehicle
- [ ] sense
- [ ] pattern
- [ ] reform
- [ ] commission
- [ ] cognitive
- [ ] luxury
- [ ] steady
- [ ] qualify
- [ ] liberal
- [ ] prospect
- [ ] valid
- [ ] wrap
- [ ] administer
- [ ] publish

- [ ] vacuum
- [ ] opposite
- [ ] separate
- [ ] characteristic
- [ ] archive
- [ ] insurance
- [ ] present
- [ ] enclose
- [ ] assert
- [ ] hypothesis
- [ ] main
- [ ] induce
- [ ] senate
- [ ] transform
- [ ] pose
- [ ] toil
- [ ] resist
- [ ] plunge
- [ ] refer
- [ ] permanent
- [ ] abolish
- [ ] hunt
- [ ] array
- [ ] attitude
- [ ] assistance
- [ ] deputy
- [ ] dignity
- [ ] vicious
- [ ] inclusive
- [ ] elegant
- [ ] selection

- [ ] enterprise
- [ ] region
- [ ] invention
- [ ] statement
- [ ] data
- [ ] sin
- [ ] bargain
- [ ] offset
- [ ] activate
- [ ] harmony
- [ ] hire
- [ ] dislike
- [ ] representative
- [ ] order
- [ ] infrastructure
- [ ] straight
- [ ] prohibit
- [ ] average
- [ ] cooperative
- [ ] criticize/-ise
- [ ] return
- [ ] taste
- [ ] happen
- [ ] fight
- [ ] heat
- [ ] allowance
- [ ] theme
- [ ] basic
- [ ] distort
- [ ] premier
- [ ] investigation

- [ ] rough
- [ ] point
- [ ] symbol
- [ ] general
- [ ] patient
- [ ] rare
- [ ] cause

001

produce

释 / prə'djuːs / v. 生产; 制造; 生长; 繁育; 引起; 导致; 栽培; 培养; 制作, 拍摄 (电影、戏剧等) / 'prɒdjuːs / n. 产品; (尤指) 农产品

例 We are amazed today at the mere number of plays **produced**, as well as by the number of dramatists writing at the same time for this London of two hundred thousand inhabitants. 如今, 仅仅是戏剧创作的数量就让我们惊讶了, 更不用说同时为拥有20万居民的伦敦写作的剧作家的数量了。(2018年)

002

contribute / kən'trɪbjuːt /

释 v. 贡献, 做出贡献; 捐助; 是 (造成某情况) 的原因

例 Zoos save people trips to wilderness areas and thus **contribute** to wildlife conservation. 动物园省掉了人们前往荒野地区的行程, 从而为保护野生动物做出了贡献。(2022年)

003

department / dɪ'pɑːtmənt /

释 n. 部, 系, 科, 处, 局

例 Boston took things even further, requiring renters to register with the city's Inspectional Services **Department**. 波士顿采取了更进一步的措施, 要求租房者在城市监察服务部登记。(2023年)

004

minister / 'mɪnɪstə(r) /

释 n. 部长; 大臣; 牧师; 公使; 外交使节 v. 照顾; 服侍

例 European **ministers** instantly demanded that the International Accounting Standards Board (IASB) do likewise. 欧洲各国部长立即要求国际会计准则理事会 (IASB) 也这样做。(2010年)

005

comprehend / ˌkɒmprɪ'hend /

释 v. 理解; 领会

例 If you can use a word correctly and effectively, you **comprehend** it. 你如果能正确有效地使用一个单词, 你就理解它了。

006

shorthand / 'ʃɔːthænd /

释 n. 速记 (法)

例 He taught himself **shorthand** to get an even better job later as a court stenographer and as a reporter in Parliament. 他自学速记, 以便日后找到一份更好的工作, 比如法庭速记员和议会记者。(2017年)

007

highlight / 'haɪlaɪt /

释 v. 强调; 使显著, 使突出 n. 最好 (或最精彩、最激动人心) 的部分

例 Those realistic possibilities are **highlighted** in the study presented by David Graddol. 大卫·葛拉多尔提交的研究报告强调了这些现实的可能性。(2017年)

近 emphasize / 'emfəsaɪz / v. 强调; 使突出

narrative / ˈnærətɪv /

释 *adj.* 叙述的; 有故事性的 *n.* 叙述; 记叙文

例 The writer was good at the **narrative** treatment of historical events. 该作家擅长将历史事件做故事化处理。

reduce / rɪˈdjuːs /

释 *v.* 减少; 减小; 减轻; 使沦为, 使陷入; 使简化为

例 As well as making access both in and out of buildings easier for people, the difference in the way many of these doors open helps **reduce** the total area occupied by them. 这些门的不同开启方式不仅方便了人们进出建筑物, 还有助于减少它们占用的总面积。（2024年）

fortune / ˈfɔːtʃuːn /

释 *n.* 机会, 运气; 大笔的钱, 巨款; 发展变化的趋势, 命运

例 That kind of fandom could be fruitful for the film's **fortunes** moving forward. 这种粉丝效应可能会为该影片的未来带来丰厚的回报。

mount / maʊnt /

释 *v.* 组织, 发动; 增加; 增强; 登上; 骑上; 安装 *n.*（用于山名前）山峰; 坐骑

搭 mount up 增加, 上升

例 The soldiers stood beside their horses, waiting for the order to **mount**. 士兵们站在马的旁边, 等待上马的命令。

analysis / əˈnæləsɪs /

释 *n.* 分析; 分析报告

例 The study is a genome-wide **analysis** conducted on 1,932 unique subjects which compared pairs of unrelated friends and unrelated strangers. 这项研究是对1 932名独特的受试者进行的一个全基因组分析, 比较了无血缘关系的朋友和无血缘关系的陌生人。（2015年）

undergraduate / ˌʌndəˈɡrædʒuət /

释 *n.* 大学生; 本科生

例 But now most colleges, save for many selective campuses, allow all **undergraduates**, and even graduate students, to get their low grades forgiven. 但现在, 除了许多名校之外, 大多数大学都允许所有本科生, 甚至是研究生低分豁免。（2019年）

fund / fʌnd /

释 *v.* 拨款给, 为……提供资金 *n.* 资金; 基金

例 To help homeless people toward independence, the government must support job training programs, raise the minimum wage, and **fund** more low-cost housing. 为了帮助无家可归者走向自立, 政府必须支持职业培训计划, 提高最低工资并且拨款建设更多的廉价房。

Writing Models ◎

function

recruit

vehicle

sense

pattern

reform

commission

cognitive

luxury

steady

qualify

liberal

function / 'fʌŋkʃn / `015`

释 *n.* 作用; 功能; 职能; 机能; 社交聚会; 典礼; 函数 *v.* 起作用; 正常工作; 运转

例 But while aging is inevitable, scientists are finding out that certain changes in brain **function** may not be. 不过，虽然衰老是不可避免的，但科学家们发现大脑功能的某些变化可能并非如此。（2021年）

recruit / rɪ'kruːt / `016`

释 *v.* 招募，招收 *n.* 新成员; 新兵

例 You are supposed to write for the Postgraduates' Association a notice to **recruit** volunteers for an international conference on globalization. 你要为研究生协会写一份通知，为全球化国际会议招募志愿者。（2010年）

近 employ / ɪm'plɔɪ / *v.* 雇用

vehicle / 'viːəkl / `017`

释 *n.* 手段; 车辆

搭 autonomous vehicles 无人驾驶汽车

例 The coming use of autonomous **vehicles**, for example, poses thorny ethical questions. 例如，即将付诸使用的无人驾驶汽车就带来了棘手的道德伦理问题。（2019年）

sense / sens / `018`

释 *n.* 感官功能; 感觉，意识; 意义，含义; 判断力 *v.* 感觉到; 意识到; 觉察出; 检测出

搭 make sense 有道理; 有意义; 讲得通

例 But we're going to have questions like that where we have things we're doing that don't make **sense** when the market changes and the world changes. 但我们也会遇到这样的问题，当市场和世界发生变化时，我们正在做的事情就没有意义了。（2016年）

派 sensible / 'sensəbl / *adj.* 明智的 ‖ sensitive / 'sensətɪv / *adj.* 善解人意的; 敏感的; 灵敏的; 有悟性的

pattern / 'pætn / `019`

释 *n.* 模式; 典范; 式样

例 Stemming climate change, for example, is as much about changing consumption **patterns** and promoting tax acceptance as it is about developing clean energy. 例如，遏制气候变化和发展清洁能源有关，也和改变消费模式、提高纳税接受度有关。（2013年）

reform / rɪ'fɔːm / `020`

释 *n.* 改革; 变革; 改良; 改善 *v.* 改革; 改进; 改良; （使）改正，（使）悔改

例 Upcoming **reforms** might bring the price to a more reasonable level. 即将进行的改革可能会使价格达到一个更合理的水平。（2017年）

commission / kəˈmɪʃn /

释 *n.* 委员会；佣金；回扣；委托；服务费；任命 *v.* 正式委托（谱写或制作、创作、完成）；任命……为军官

例 The **commission** was also to consider possible arrangements for the War and Navy Departments. 该委员会还将考虑为陆军部和海军部做出可能的安排。（2018年）

近 appointment / əˈpɔɪntmənt / *n.* 任命

cognitive / ˈkɒgnətɪv /

释 *adj.* 认知的，认识力的

例 To filter out what is unique from what is shared might enable us to understand how complex cultural behaviour arose and what guides it in evolutionary or **cognitive** terms. 从共有的东西中筛选出独特的东西，也许能让我们理解复杂的文化行为是如何产生的，以及在进化或认知方面是什么引导了它。（2012年）

luxury / ˈlʌkʃəri /

释 *n.* 奢侈 *adj.* 奢侈的

搭 luxury goods 奢侈品

例 In the world of capuchins, grapes are **luxury** goods (and much preferable to cucumbers). 在卷尾猴的世界里，葡萄是奢侈品（比黄瓜更受欢迎）。（2005年）

steady / ˈstedi /

释 *adj.* 稳定的；稳固的；稳重的；可靠的 *adv.* 稳定地；持续地；稳固地 *v.* 使平稳；稳定下来

例 Without **steady** education, students can easily fall behind and then perhaps jeopardize their prospects for attending college or getting a job. 如果没有稳定的教育，学生很容易落后，进而可能危及他们上大学或就业的前景。

qualify / ˈkwɒlɪfaɪ /

释 *v.* 取得资格，（使）有资格

搭 qualify for 合格；有……的资格

例 This certificate will **qualify** you for teaching. 这个资格证书让你有资格教学。

liberal / ˈlɪbərəl /

释 *adj.* 开明的；自由的；慷慨的；自由党的 *n.* 自由主义者

例 Regrettably, however, the report's failure to address the true nature of the crisis facing **liberal** education may cause more harm than good. 然而，令人遗憾的是，报告未能正视自由教育所面临危机的真正本质，这可能会弊大于利。（2014年）

近 permissive / pəˈmɪsɪv / *adj.* 宽容的

prospect

027

释 / ˈprɒspekt / *n.* 前景；可能性；[pl.]前途，成功的机会
/ prəˈspekt / *v.* 勘探

例 If everything was going so well, then why did over 17 million people vote for Brexit, despite the warnings about what it could do to their country's economic **prospects**? 如果一切都进展顺利，那么为什么会有1 700多万人投票支持英国脱欧，而不顾英国脱欧可能对其国家经济前景造成何种影响的警告呢？（2017年）

valid / ˈvælɪd /

028

释 *adj.* （法律上）有效的；合理的；（正式）认可的；有根据的；符合逻辑的；系统认可的

例 The evidence had to be economic in order to be **valid**. 证据必须有经济价值，才能有效。（2010年）

wrap / ræp /

029

释 *v.* 裹，缠，卷，包

搭 wrap around 用……包裹，裹身

例 Jeffrey is eating a sandwich which is **wrapped** in wax paper. 杰弗里正在吃一块用蜡纸包着的三明治。

administer / ədˈmɪnɪstə(r) /

030

释 *v.* 管理（公司、组织、机构等）；治理（国家）；执行，实施

例 They have the right to **administer** their own internal affairs. 他们有权管理自己的内部事务。

近 govern / ˈɡʌvn / *v.* 统治；管理 ‖ supervise / ˈsuːpəvaɪz / *v.* 监督，管理

publish / ˈpʌblɪʃ /

031

释 *v.* 出版；发行；发表（作品）；刊登，登载；发布，公布

例 Each year researchers **publish** millions of papers in more than 30,000 journals. 每年，研究人员在三万多种期刊上发表数百万篇论文。（2023年）

vacuum / ˈvækjuːm /

032

释 *n.* 空缺；真空；真空吸尘器 *v.* 用真空吸尘器清扫

搭 in a vacuum 在与世隔绝的状态中

例 His presence should fill the power **vacuum** which has been developing over the past few days. 他的出现将填补过去这几天形成的权力空缺。

opposite / ˈɒpəzɪt /

033

释 *adj.* 对面的；另一边的；相反的；迥然不同的 *n.* 对立的人（或物）；对立面，反面 *prep.* 与……相对；在……对面；与……联袂演出

例 This has resulted in protests from social scientists. But the intention is not to neglect social science; rather, the complete **opposite**. 这引起了社会科学家的抗议，但这样做的目的并不是要忽视社会科学，而是恰恰相反。（2013年）

separate

034

释 / 'seprət / *adj.* 单独的; 独立的; 分开的; 不同的; 不相关的
/ 'sepəreɪt / *v.* (使) 分开, 分离; 分割; 划分; 隔开; 阻隔; 区分, 区别; 分居

搭 go one's separate ways 断绝往来; 分手

例 People suffering from infectious diseases must be **separated** from the other patients. 传染病患者必须同其他病人隔离开来。

characteristic / ˌkærəktə'rɪstɪk /

035

释 *n.* 特征 *adj.* 特有的

例 As fewer such workers enter the country, the **characteristics** of the agricultural workforce are changing. 因为进入美国的这类工人越来越少, 美国农业劳动力的特征正在发生变化。

archive / 'ɑːkaɪv /

036

释 *n.* 档案; 档案馆; 档案室 *v.* 把……存档; 把……归档

例 Finally, there are open-access **archives**, where organizations such as universities or international laboratories support institutional repositories. 最后是开放权限档案模式, 由大学或国际实验室等组织支持机构存储。(2008年)

insurance / ɪn'ʃʊərəns /

037

释 *n.* 保险; 预防措施

例 This "added-worker effect" could support the safety net offered by unemployment **insurance** or disability **insurance** to help families weather bad times. 这种 "新增劳动力效应" 可以补贴由失业保险或伤残保险提供的保障措施, 帮助家庭渡过难关。(2007年)

present

038

释 / prɪ'zent / *v.* 提出; 提交; 呈现; 展现; 表现; 颁发; 上演; 莅临
/ 'preznt / *adj.* 现存的; 当前的; 出席的; 在场的 *n.* 礼物; 目前; 现在

搭 for the present 目前; 暂时 ‖ at present 现在

例 The changes identified by David Graddol all **present** clear and major challenges to the UK's providers of English language teaching to people of other countries and to broader education business sectors. 大卫·葛拉多尔指出的这些变化对向其他国家的人提供英语教学的英国机构以及更广泛的教育商业部门提出了明确而重大的挑战。(2017年)

enclose / ɪn'kləʊz /

039

释 *v.* 围住, 圈起; (随信) 附上

搭 enclose sth. with the letter 随信附上某物

例 The farmer **enclosed** his land and kept cattle away from his crops. 那位农场主把自己的田地圈了起来以防牲畜糟蹋庄稼。

assert / əˈsɜːt /   040

释 v. 断言; 宣称; 维护; 坚持

例 He was willing to **assert** that "I have a fair share of invention, and of common sense or judgment, such as every fairly successful lawyer or doctor must have, but not, I believe, in any higher degree." 他愿意断言: "我有一定的创造力、常识或判断力, 就像每个相当成功的律师或医生都必须具备的那样, 但我认为自己没有更高的水平。"(2008年)

hypothesis / haɪˈpɒθəsɪs /   041

释 n. 假说, 假设; 猜想, 猜测

例 The philosopher constructed a viable **hypothesis** to explain the meaning of life in his speech. 这位哲学家在他的演说中做了一个可行的假设来解释生命的意义。

main / meɪn /   042

释 adj. 主要的; 最重要的 n. 主管道; (水、煤气、电等的)供应系统; 下水道系统

搭 in the main 大体上; 基本上

例 The **main** purpose of this "clawback" rule is to hold bankers accountable for harmful risk-taking and to restore public trust in financial institutions. 这项"奖金延迟支付"规定的主要目的是让银行家为不利的冒险行为负责, 以及恢复公众对金融机构的信任。(2019年)

induce / ɪnˈdjuːs /   043

释 v. 引起, 导致; 诱使; 引产

例 Indeed, the mere presence of a grape in the other chamber (without an actual monkey to eat it) was enough to **induce** resentment in a female capuchin. 事实上, 只要一颗葡萄出现在另一个房间里(哪怕没有猴子来吃它), 就足以引起一只雌性卷尾猴的不满。(2005年)

近 cause / kɔːz / v. 导致, 引起 ‖ lead / liːd / v. 导致; 领导

senate / ˈsenət /   044

释 n. 参议院; 大学理事会

例 Enraged by Entergy's behavior, the Vermont **Senate** voted 26 to 4 last year against allowing an extension. 去年, 佛蒙特州参议院被Entergy公司的行为激怒, 以26比4的投票否决了它的延期申请。(2012年)

transform / trænsˈfɔːm /   045

释 v. 使改变; 使转换; 彻底改变

例 Solar panels had a few niche uses until they became cheap; now they are **transforming** the global energy system. 在太阳能电池板变得廉价之前, 它们只有一些小众用途; 现在, 它们正在改变全球能源系统。(2024年)

pose / pəʊz /   046

释 *v.* 提出；造成（威胁、问题等）；使摆好姿势；伴装，假扮 *n.*（为拍照等摆的）姿势；装腔作势

例 His resignation **poses** the question of whether we now need a deputy manager. 他的辞职引出了一个问题，即我们目前是否需要一个代理经理。

近 propose / prə'pəʊz / *v.* 提议，建议 ‖ suggest / sə'dʒest / *v.* 提出，建议

toil / tɔɪl /   047

释 *v.*（长时间）苦干，辛勤劳作；艰难缓慢地移动；跋涉 *n.* 苦工；劳累的工作

例 Anyone who has **toiled** through CET will testify that test-taking skill also matters, whether it's knowing when to guess or what questions to skip. 任何一个辛苦为CET奋战过的人都可以证实，考试技巧也很重要，不管是知道何时靠猜测，还是哪些问题要跳过。

resist / rɪ'zɪst /   048

释 *v.* 抵抗，抵制；反对；按捺，克制；经得起

例 In other words, religious beliefs can be a source of resilience when people need to persevere and **resist** in the face of injustice. 换句话说，当人们面对不公正需要坚持和抵抗时，宗教信仰可以成为复原力的一种源泉。

plunge / plʌndʒ /   049

释 *v.*（使）投入；突然陷入；将……刺进；骤降；（尤指向水中）一头进入 *n.* 投入，尝试

搭 plunge into（使）投入，陷入 ‖ take the plunge 冒险尝试；采取断然行动

例 After *Pickwick*, Dickens **plunged** into a bleaker world. 在《匹克威克》之后，狄更斯突然陷入了一个更加暗淡的世界。（2017年）

refer / rɪ'fɜː(r) /   050

释 *v.* 谈及；提到，提及；涉及；将……转到（医院就医）；将……转给（专科医生）；查阅，参考（资料）；指引；让……去查询；推荐；介绍

搭 refer to 提到；谈及；涉及；查阅

例 Instead, your doctor can **refer** you to a pain specialist for non-medicine options, such as a physical therapist. 相反，医生可以将你转诊给疼痛专科医生，让你选择非药物治疗，如理疗师。

permanent / 'pɜːmənənt /   051

释 *adj.* 永久的；永恒的；长久的

例 Most of the money would come from a penny-per-letter **permanent** rate increase and from shifting postal retirees into Medicare. 大部分资金将来自每封信一分钱的永久费率上调，以及将邮政退休人员转入医疗保险。（2018年）

abolish / əˈbɒlɪʃ /

释 v. 废除，废止（法律、制度、习俗等）

例 By 1854 slavery had been **abolished** everywhere except Spain's remaining colonies. 到1854年，除了西班牙剩余的殖民地外，其他地方都废除了奴隶制。（2007年）

派 abolition / ˌæbəˈlɪʃn / n. 废除，废止

hunt / hʌnt /

释 v. 搜寻；打猎；追捕 n. 搜寻；打猎；追捕

例 The large, slow-growing animals were easy game, and were quickly **hunted** to extinction. 这种体型庞大、生长缓慢的动物很容易成为猎物，很快就被猎杀殆尽了。（2006年）

array / əˈreɪ /

释 n. 一系列，大量；陈列；数列 v. 排列；配置（兵力）

搭 an array of 大量的

例 People are absorbed into "a culture of consumption" launched by the 19th-century department stores that offered vast **arrays** of goods in an elegant atmosphere. 人们被19世纪百货公司掀起的"消费文化"所吸引，这些公司在优雅的环境中供应大量的商品。（2006年）

attitude / ˈætɪtjuːd /

释 n. 态度；看法；个人风格

搭 negative attitude 消极态度

例 This courageous **attitude** in fact becomes a requirement for the performers of Beethoven's music. 事实上，这种勇敢的态度已成为对弹奏贝多芬音乐的表演者的要求。（2014年）

assistance / əˈsɪstəns /

释 n. 帮助，援助；支持

搭 social assistance programs 社会援助项目

例 Created in 1974, the organization seeks to provide extra **assistance** to society's most vulnerable members, including elderly, blind, and disabled people. 该组织创立于1974年，旨在为社会最弱势成员（包括老年人、盲人和残疾人）提供额外援助。

deputy / ˈdepjuti /

释 adj. 副的；代理的 n. 副手；代理人

例 As the first signs of recovery begin to take hold, **deputy** chiefs may be more willing to make the jump without a net. 随着经济复苏的初步迹象开始显现，副手们可能更愿意在没有限制的情况下跳槽。（2011年）

近 vice / vaɪs / adj. 副的；代替的 ‖ associate / əˈsəʊsiət / adj. 副的；联合的

◎ Study Notes

dignity / 'dɪgnəti / 0 5 8

释 *n.* 庄重; 庄严; 尊严; 自尊; 尊贵, 高贵; 自豪

搭 beneath one's dignity 有失尊严; 有失身份; 有失体面

例 Stealing artifacts from other peoples' cultures is obscene; it robs not only the physical objects, but the **dignity** and spirit of their creators. 从其他民族的文化中窃取文物是下流的行为; 它不仅掠夺了实物, 也掠夺了其创造者的尊严和精神。(2024年)

vicious / 'vɪʃəs / 0 5 9

释 *adj.* 狂暴的; 残酷的; 严厉的; 恶劣的

例 Let go of me, you **vicious** monster! 放开我, 你这可恶的家伙!

近 savage / 'sævɪdʒ / *adj.* 野蛮的; 凶猛的

inclusive / ɪn'kluːsɪv / 0 6 0

释 *adj.* 包容广阔的; 范围广泛的; 包含全部费用在内的

搭 inclusive of 把……包括在内

例 Guided by creative technologists, AI in 2024 will be thoughtful, more **inclusive**, and impact-led. 在创意技术专家的指导下, 2024年的人工智能将会更加深思熟虑、更具包容性、更有影响力。

近 extensive / ɪk'stensɪv / *adj.* 广阔的; 广泛的

elegant / 'elɪgənt / 0 6 1

释 *adj.* (人或物)典雅的, 雅致的, 优美的; 简练的; 简明的

例 He was a fashion designer dressed in theatrical but **elegant** clothes. 他是个时装设计师, 衣着华丽但又不失优雅。

selection / sɪ'lekʃn / 0 6 2

释 *n.* 选择, 挑选; (商店内)可供选择的商品范围

例 That shop has a widest **selection** of cakes. 那家商店提供的蛋糕选择极多。

enterprise / 'entəpraɪz / 0 6 3

释 *n.* 公司; 企业; 事业; 创业; 开创力, 开拓精神

例 Their team were rightly praised for their thrift and **enterprise**. 他们团队因勤俭节约和开创精神而受到了应得的表扬。

region / 'riːdʒən / 0 6 4

释 *n.* 地区, 区域; 行政区; 身体部分

例 And so, the Middle East excepted, Europe is the most monarch-infested **region** in the world, with 10 kingdoms (not counting Vatican City and Andorra). 因此, 除中东外, 欧洲是世界上拥有君主最多的地区, 有十个王国 (梵蒂冈城和安道尔不算在内)。(2015年)

近 district / 'dɪstrɪkt / *n.* 行政区; 区域 ‖ zone / zəʊn / *n.* 区域; 地带

辨 region指较大范围内的区域, 一般按自然条件和自身特点划分; district一般指国家或城市按行政区的划分; zone是个环绕区域, 有严格的边界, 指某一特定的地方或区域, 如经济特区。

invention

statement

data

sin

bargain

offset

activate

harmony

hire

dislike

representative

order

invention / ɪnˈvenʃn /

065

释 *n.* 发明；发明物；虚构

例 After writing two books about the history of **inventions**, one thing I've learnt is that while it is the enchantingly sophisticated technologies that get all the hype, it's the cheap technologies that change the world. 在写了两本关于发明史的书之后，我学到的一点是，虽然那些令人着迷的尖端技术被大肆炒作，但改变世界的却是那些廉价的技术。（2024年）

statement / ˈsteɪtmənt /

066

释 *n.* 陈述；说法；表态；声明；报表；报告；清单；结算单

例 While the **statement** is vague, it represents one starting point. 虽然声明含糊不清，但它代表了一个起点。（2019年）

data / ˈdeɪtə /

067

释 *n.* 数据；资料；材料；（储存在计算机中的）数据资料

例 The researchers looked at **data** that included measurements of lean muscle and abdominal fat from more than 4,000 middle-to-older-aged men and women and compared that **data** to reported changes in fluid intelligence over a six-year period. 研究人员研究了四千多名中老年男性和女性瘦肌肉和腹部脂肪的测量数据，并将这些数据与六年间报告的流体智力的变化进行了比较。（2021年）

派 database / ˈdeɪtəbeɪs / *n.* 数据库

sin / sɪn /

068

释 *n.* 罪恶；罪行；过失 *v.* 犯罪

搭 be/do sth. for one's sins 自作自受

例 Gambling has been a common feature of American life forever, but for a long time it was broadly considered a **sin**, or a social disease. 赌博一直是美国人生活中的常见现象，但在很长一段时间里，人们普遍认为赌博是一种罪行，或者说是一种社会病。（2006年）

bargain / ˈbɑːgən /

069

释 *n.* 交易；契约；特价品；便宜品 *v.* 讨价还价

例 And dead markets partly reflect the paralysis of banks which will not sell assets for fear of booking losses, yet are reluctant to buy all those supposed **bargains**. 死气沉沉的市场在一定程度上反映了银行的瘫痪，它们因担心账面损失而不愿出售资产，但也不愿购买那些所谓的便宜货。（2010年）

offset / ˈɒfset /

070

释 *n./v.* 抵消；补偿 *adj.* 胶印的

例 Prices have risen in order to **offset** the increased cost of materials. 为抵消增加的原料成本，价格被提高了。

activate / 'æktɪveɪt /   071

释 *v.* 激活，激发；使活动

例 You would probably agree that curiosity **activates** creative minds. 你可能会赞同好奇心可以激发创造性思维这一观点。

harmony / 'hɑːməni /   072

释 *n.* 融洽；和睦；和谐；协调

搭 in harmony with 与……和谐相处

例 Human life is regarded as part of nature and, as such, the only way for us to survive is to live in **harmony** with nature. 人的生命被认为是自然的一部分，因此，我们生存的唯一途径就是与自然和谐相处。

hire / 'haɪə(r) /   073

释 *v.* 租用；租借；聘用；录用；雇用

例 Employers need to **hire** new staff. 雇主需要雇用新员工。（2022年）

近 employ / ɪm'plɔɪ / *v.* 雇用；使用

dislike / dɪs'laɪk /   074

释 *v.* 不喜爱；厌恶 *n.* 不喜爱；厌恶；不喜欢的事物

例 They frankly **dislike** the RSC's actors, them with their long hair and beards and sandals and noisiness. 坦率地说，他们不喜欢皇家莎士比亚剧团的演员，他们留着长发和胡子，穿着凉鞋，还吵吵嚷嚷。（2006年）

representative / ˌreprɪ'zentətɪv /   075

释 *n.* 代表；典型人物；代理人；代销人；（美国）众议院议员 *adj.* 有代表性的

例 Weeks after completing the expedition, Hayden collected his team's observations into an extensive report aimed at convincing senators and **representatives**, along with colleagues at government agencies like the Department of the Interior, that Yellowstone ought to be preserved. 在完成探险几周后，海登将他的团队的观察结果汇集成一份详尽的报告，旨在说服参议员和众议员以及内政部等政府机构的同事相信黄石公园应该得到保护。（2003年）

order / 'ɔːdə(r) /   076

释 *n.* 顺序；条理；秩序；命令；订单 *v.* 命令；指挥；要求；订购；点（酒菜等）；整理

搭 in order that/to 为了

例 On Tuesday, the appeals court unanimously upheld the 2017 **order** deregulating broadband providers, citing a Supreme Court ruling from 2005 that upheld a similarly deregulatory move. 本周二，上诉法院援引最高法院2005年的一项支持解除监管举措的类似裁决，一致维持了2017年解除对宽带提供商监管的命令。（2021年）

infrastructure / ˈɪnfrəstrʌktʃə(r) / 　　　077

释 n.（国家或机构的）基础设施，基础建设
例 The sensible place to build new houses, factories and offices is where people are, in cities and towns where **infrastructure** is in place. 建造新房子、工厂和办公室的合理地点是有人的地方，是在基础设施完备的城镇。（2016年）

straight / streɪt / 　　　078

释 adj. 直的；坦诚的；直率的 adv. 直线地，径直地；竖直地；立即，马上
例 Few of us just walk **straight** into the woods without a phone. 很少有人会不带手机就直接走进树林。（2019年）
派 straightness / ˈstreɪtnəs / n. 率直

prohibit / prəˈhɪbɪt / 　　　079

释 v. 禁止；阻止；使不可能
例 Too many workplace policies **prohibit** employees from developing a healthy work-life balance by barring them from taking time off. 太多的工作场所政策禁止员工休假，从而阻碍了员工维持健康的工作与生活平衡。
派 prohibition / ˌprəʊɪˈbɪʃn / n. 禁止；禁令
近 forbid / fəˈbɪd / v. 禁止；不准

average / ˈævərɪdʒ / 　　　080

释 adj. 平均的；正常的；普通的 n. 平均水平；平均数
搭 on average 平均
例 The **average** cost of an electric vehicle is far greater than a similar internal combustion engine vehicle. 电动汽车的平均成本远远高于同类内燃机汽车。

cooperative / kəʊˈɒpərətɪv / 　　　081

释 adj. 合作的；同心协力的；配合的
例 Employees will generally be more **cooperative** if their views are taken seriously. 如果员工们的意见得到认真对待，他们一般都会更加配合。

criticize/-ise / ˈkrɪtɪsaɪz / 　　　082

释 v. 批评
例 It is fair to **criticize** and question the mechanism—that is the culture of research, after all—but it is the prize-givers' money to do with as they please. 批评和质疑这种机制是合理的——毕竟，这就是研究的文化——但这是颁奖人的钱，他们可以随意支配。（2014年）

return / rɪˈtɜːn /

釋 v./n. 返回; 归还; 再现

搭 in return 作为 (对……的) 回报; 作为回应

例 We are hopeful with our shops now open again that normality will **return** and that we will be allowed to buy appropriately. 随着我们的商店重新开业, 我们希望一切将恢复正常, 允许我们适当购买。(2023年)

taste / teɪst /

釋 n. 味觉; 味道; 喜好; 品味 v. 品尝; 体验

例 The danger will come with Charles, who has both an expensive **taste** of lifestyle and a pretty hierarchical view of the world. 查尔斯可能会遇到麻烦, 他不仅喜欢奢华的生活方式, 而且认为这个世界的等级相当分明。(2015年)

happen / ˈhæpən /

釋 v. 发生; 出现; 碰巧; 恰好

搭 happen to 遭到; 遇到

例 Thankfully, there are signs that this is already **happening**, with Generation Z seeking to learn from their millennial predecessors, even if parents and teachers tend to be still set in the degree mindset. 值得庆幸的是, 有迹象表明这种情况已经出现了, Z世代正努力向他们的千禧一代前辈学习, 尽管父母和老师往往仍然停留在注重学位的思维模式中。(2022年)

fight / faɪt /

釋 v. 与……做斗争; 奋斗; 参战; 打架; 吵架 n. 斗争; 奋斗; 战斗; 打架; 吵架

搭 fight back 奋力抵抗; 还击 ‖ fight for 努力争取

例 For example, type in "Wizard with sword and a glowing orb of magic fire **fights** a fierce dragon Greg Rutkowski," and the system will produce something that looks not a million miles away from works in Rutkowski's style. 例如, 输入 "手持宝剑和魔法火球的巫师与凶猛的巨龙搏斗, 格雷格·鲁特科夫斯基", 系统就会生成与鲁特科夫斯基的风格相差无几的作品。(2024年)

heat / hiːt /

釋 n. 热; 温度; 高温天气 v. 加热; 变热; (使) 变暖

搭 heat up 变热; 变暖

例 The weather in Texas may have cooled since the recent extreme **heat**, but the temperature will be high at the State Board of Education meeting in Austin this month as officials debate how climate change is taught in Texas schools. 得克萨斯州的天气自最近的酷暑之后可能有所转凉, 但本月在奥斯汀举行的州教育委员会会议上, 官员们讨论如何在得克萨斯州的学校教授气候变化时, 氛围将会很热烈。(2023年)

Writing Models ◎

allowance

theme

basic

premier

investigation

rough

point

symbol

general

patient

rare

cause

allowance / ə'laʊəns /
[088]

释 n. 补贴; 限额

搭 make allowances for sth. 考虑到某事 ‖ make allowances for sb. 体谅某人

例 There will now be a seven-day wait for the jobseeker's **allowance**. 现在求职者的补贴将有七天的等待期。（2014年）

theme / θiːm /
[089]

释 n. 主题; 中心思想; 主题音乐, 主题曲

例 With its **theme** that "Mind is the master weaver," creating our inner character and outer circumstances, the book *As a Man Thinketh* by James Allen is an in-depth exploration of the central idea of self-help writing. 詹姆斯·艾伦的《思考的人》一书对自助写作的中心思想进行了深入的探索。该书的主题是"心灵是编织大师"，它创造了我们的内在性格和外在环境。（2011年）

basic / 'beɪsɪk /
[090]

释 adj. 基本的; 基础的; 初级的; 必需的

例 One **basic** weakness in a conservation system based wholly on economic motives is that most members of the land community have no economic value. 完全基于经济动机的保护系统的一个基本弱点是, 土地社区的大多数成员都没有经济价值。（2010年）

distort / dɪ'stɔːt /
[091]

释 v. 歪曲; 曲解; 扭曲 n. 毁坏; 破坏; 毁灭

例 They could **distort** the achievement-based system of peer-review-led research. 它们可能会破坏以同行评审为主导的、基于学术成就的研究体系。（2014年）

派 distortion / dɪ'stɔːʃn / n. 歪曲; 曲解

premier / 'premiə(r) /
[092]

释 n. 总理; 首相;（加拿大）省总理 adj. 最好的; 首要的

例 A few **premiers** are suspicious of any federal-provincial deal-making. 一些省总理对任何联邦和省之间的交易都持怀疑态度。（2005年）

investigation / ɪnˌvestɪ'geɪʃn /
[093]

释 n. 调查, 侦查

例 It is under the FCC's **investigation**. 它（该公司）正在接受联邦通信委员会的调查。（2021年）

rough / rʌf /
[094]

释 adj. 粗糙的; 艰难的; 粗略的

例 For snowy weather and **rough** terrain, a good pair of sturdy hiking boots can't be beat. 在下雪的天气和崎岖的地形中, 一双结实的登山靴是必不可少的。

point / pɔɪnt / 095

释 *n.* 论点; 观点; 重点; 时刻; 点; 地点; 得分 *v.* 指向; 朝向

搭 have a point 有道理 ‖ point at 瞄准 ‖ point out 指出

例 Caravanserais served as an informal meeting **point** for the various people who travelled the Silk Road. 商队客店是在丝绸之路上旅行的各种人的非正式聚会点。（2023年）

symbol / 'sɪmbl / 096

释 *n.* 象征; 象征物; 符号

例 Jewelry is often used to mark special occasions, acting as a **symbol** of love and commitment. 珠宝通常用于纪念特殊场合，作为爱和承诺的象征。

派 symbolic / sɪm'bɒlɪk / *adj.* 有象征意义的

general / 'dʒenrəl / 097

释 *adj.* 全体的; 总的; 普遍的; 一般的; 整体的; 全面的; 大体的 *n.* 将军

搭 in general 通常; 大体上; 总的说来; 从总体上看

例 Successive governments have permitted such increases on the grounds that the cost of investing in and running the rail network should be borne by those who use it, rather than the **general** taxpayer. 历届政府都允许这样的涨价，理由是投资和运营铁路网络的成本应该由使用者承担，而不是一般纳税人。（2021年）

派 generally / 'dʒenrəli / *adv.* 一般地; 通常; 大体上

patient / 'peɪʃnt / 098

释 *adj.* 有耐心的 *n.* 病人

例 It failed to pay due attention to **patients**' rights. 它（该协议）未能对患者的权利给予应有的重视。（2015年）

派 patience / 'peɪʃns / *n.* 耐心

rare / reə(r) / 099

释 *adj.* 稀罕的; 珍贵的

例 They are **rare** among photographs of that age. 它们（这些照片）在那个年代的照片中很少见。（2021年）

cause / kɔːz / 100

释 *v.* 造成; 引起; 导致 *n.* 原因, 起因, 理由; 动机; 事业, 目标

例 However, those correlations don't prove **cause** and effect. 然而，这些相关性并不能证明存在因果关系。（2021年）

☐ ☐ abolish
☐ ☐ activate
☐ ☐ administer
☐ ☐ allowance
☐ ☐ analysis
☐ ☐ archive
☐ ☐ array
☐ ☐ assert
☐ ☐ assistance
☐ ☐ attitude
☐ ☐ average
☐ ☐ bargain
☐ ☐ basic
☐ ☐ cause
☐ ☐ characteristic
☐ ☐ cognitive
☐ ☐ commission
☐ ☐ comprehend
☐ ☐ contribute
☐ ☐ cooperative
☐ ☐ criticize/-ise
☐ ☐ data
☐ ☐ department
☐ ☐ deputy
☐ ☐ dignity
☐ ☐ dislike
☐ ☐ distort
☐ ☐ elegant
☐ ☐ enclose
☐ ☐ enterprise
☐ ☐ fight

☐ ☐ fortune
☐ ☐ function
☐ ☐ fund
☐ ☐ general
☐ ☐ happen
☐ ☐ harmony
☐ ☐ heat
☐ ☐ highlight
☐ ☐ hire
☐ ☐ hunt
☐ ☐ hypothesis
☐ ☐ inclusive
☐ ☐ induce
☐ ☐ infrastructure
☐ ☐ insurance
☐ ☐ invention
☐ ☐ investigation
☐ ☐ liberal
☐ ☐ luxury
☐ ☐ main
☐ ☐ minister
☐ ☐ mount
☐ ☐ narrative
☐ ☐ offset
☐ ☐ opposite
☐ ☐ order
☐ ☐ patient
☐ ☐ pattern
☐ ☐ permanent
☐ ☐ plunge
☐ ☐ point

☐ ☐ pose
☐ ☐ premier
☐ ☐ present
☐ ☐ produce
☐ ☐ prohibit
☐ ☐ prospect
☐ ☐ publish
☐ ☐ qualify
☐ ☐ rare
☐ ☐ recruit
☐ ☐ reduce
☐ ☐ refer
☐ ☐ reform
☐ ☐ region
☐ ☐ representative
☐ ☐ resist
☐ ☐ return
☐ ☐ rough
☐ ☐ selection
☐ ☐ senate
☐ ☐ sense
☐ ☐ separate
☐ ☐ shorthand
☐ ☐ sin
☐ ☐ statement
☐ ☐ steady
☐ ☐ straight
☐ ☐ symbol
☐ ☐ taste
☐ ☐ theme
☐ ☐ toil

☐ ☐ transform
☐ ☐ undergradua
☐ ☐ vacuum
☐ ☐ valid
☐ ☐ vehicle
☐ ☐ vicious
☐ ☐ wrap

音频

Previous Check

- [ ] density
- [ ] enclosure
- [ ] undo
- [ ] successive
- [ ] abdomen
- [ ] conservation
- [ ] battle
- [ ] apart
- [ ] infer
- [ ] sort
- [ ] context
- [ ] string
- [ ] provision
- [ ] evade
- [ ] tremble
- [ ] control
- [ ] lobby
- [ ] access
- [ ] harsh
- [ ] object
- [ ] tentative
- [ ] retrospect
- [ ] outlet
- [ ] rein
- [ ] prompt
- [ ] compromise
- [ ] expose
- [ ] repertoire
- [ ] giant
- [ ] revolve
- [ ] strengthen

- [ ] advent
- [ ] elevate
- [ ] hedge
- [ ] switch
- [ ] junk
- [ ] delicate
- [ ] differentiate
- [ ] consolidate
- [ ] reveal
- [ ] keep
- [ ] connect
- [ ] thread
- [ ] share
- [ ] dominate
- [ ] triumph
- [ ] inflation
- [ ] consist
- [ ] correspondence
- [ ] abrupt
- [ ] nevertheless
- [ ] reliable
- [ ] subsequent
- [ ] sensible
- [ ] doubt
- [ ] approval
- [ ] conclusion
- [ ] fundamental
- [ ] desirable
- [ ] complain
- [ ] associate
- [ ] controversy

- [ ] irritate
- [ ] imitate
- [ ] courage
- [ ] navigation
- [ ] approach
- [ ] disappear
- [ ] acclaim
- [ ] erupt
- [ ] prolong
- [ ] key
- [ ] storm
- [ ] polish
- [ ] action
- [ ] sovereign
- [ ] whisper
- [ ] retreat
- [ ] fate
- [ ] platform
- [ ] procedure
- [ ] continuous
- [ ] pause
- [ ] delete
- [ ] prevail
- [ ] eventually
- [ ] float
- [ ] court
- [ ] tension
- [ ] dare
- [ ] depth
- [ ] bind
- [ ] topic

- [ ] curious
- [ ] agent
- [ ] fold
- [ ] dim
- [ ] clause
- [ ] seed
- [ ] digital

001

density / 'densəti /

释 *n.* 密度

例 The resulting settlement maps show how the distribution and **density** of the rural population around the city changed dramatically between AD500 and 850, when Copán collapsed. 由此绘制的定居地图显示了公元500年至850年科潘崩溃期间，城市周围农村人口的分布和密度是如何发生巨大变化的。（2014年）

002

enclosure / ɪnˈkləʊʒə(r) /

释 *n.* （信中的）附件，装入物；圈地；围场

例 This **enclosure** was so vast that the outermost wall could hardly be seen. 这块圈地大得几乎看不见它最外面的围墙。

003

undo / ʌnˈduː /

释 *v.* 松开，解开

例 Bob couldn't **undo** the zipper of his jacket because it was stuck. 鲍勃无法拉开他夹克的拉链，因为它被卡住了。

004

successive / səkˈsesɪv /

释 *adj.* 接连的，连续的；相继的

例 Across the Atlantic came **successive** groups of Englishmen, Frenchmen, Germans, Scots, Irishmen, Dutchmen, Swedes, and many others who attempted to transplant their habits and traditions to the new world. 一批又一批的英国人、法国人、德国人、苏格兰人、爱尔兰人、荷兰人、瑞典人以及其他许多人相继跨越大西洋，试图将他们的习惯和传统移植到新世界。（2015年）

005

abdomen / 'æbdəmən /

释 *n.* 腹部

例 Vaughan got a tattoo on his **abdomen**. 沃恩在腹部刺了个文身。

006

conservation / ˌkɒnsəˈveɪʃn /

释 *n.* （对环境、文物或艺术品的）保护；节约

例 Zoos provide a critical voice for **conservation** and environmental protection. 动物园为自然保护和环境保护发出了重要的声音。（2022年）

007

battle / 'bætl /

释 *n.* 战役；斗争；冲突 *v.* （与……）斗争；与……搏斗；同……作战

例 This lack of growth in recent years means that companies have primarily **battled** for each other's customers rather than hunting for newbies—a zero sum game, according to the analysts. 分析师认为，近年来增长乏力意味着各公司主要在争夺彼此的客户，而不是寻找新客户，这是一种零和游戏。

◎ Study Notes

apart / əˈpɑːt / 〔008〕

释 *adv.* 分开地；分离地；散开地；除……之外；（指空间或时间）相隔

例 Our legal system was designed to set law **apart** from politics precisely because they are so closely tied. 我们的法律制度旨在将法律与政治区分开来，正是因为二者联系如此紧密。（2012年）

infer / ɪnˈfɜː(r) / 〔009〕

释 *v.* 推断，推理；暗示；意指

例 You begin to **infer** a context for the text, for instance, by making decisions about what kind of speech event is involved: Who is making the utterance, to whom, when and where. 例如，你可以通过判断涉及哪种言语事件来开始推断文本的上下文：谁在说话、对谁说话、何时何地说话。（2015年）

派 inference / ˈɪnfərəns / *n.* 推断；推理

近 deduce / dɪˈdjuːs / *v.* 推断；演绎出 ‖ judge / dʒʌdʒ / *v.* 判断

sort / sɔːt / 〔010〕

释 *n.* 排序；分类；种类；品种 *v.* 把……分类；整理；安排妥当

搭 a sort of sth. (表示不十分准确) 近似于某物，有点像是某物

例 At Harvard, Mr Menand notes, "the great books are read because they have been read"—they form a **sort** of social glue. 梅南先生指出，在哈佛，"名著之所以被人阅读，是因为它们曾经被人阅读过"——它们形成了有点像社会黏合剂的东西。（2011年）

context / ˈkɒntekst / 〔011〕

释 *n.* 背景，环境；上下文，语境

例 The **context** of any exhibit is more important to me than whether the object being displayed is 2,000 years old or 2 months old. 对我来说，任何展览的背景都比展出的物品是2 000年前的还是2个月前的更重要。（2024年）

string / strɪŋ / 〔012〕

释 *n.* 一串；一系列；一批 *v.* 系；悬挂；把……连在一起 *adj.* 线的；弦乐器的

例 As a News Feature article in *Nature* discusses, a **string** of lucrative awards for researchers have joined the Nobel Prizes in recent years. 正如《自然》杂志上的一篇新闻专题文章所讨论的那样，近年来，一连串为研究人员设立的丰厚的奖项加入了诺贝尔奖的行列。（2014年）

provision / prəˈvɪʒn / 〔013〕

释 *n.* 提供；准备；（法律文件的）规定，条款；供给

搭 make provision against 预防，预备

例 The personal grievance **provisions** of the ERA are intended to protect the rights of ordinary workers. 《雇佣关系法》的个人申诉条款旨在保护普通工人的权利。（2022年）

evade / ɪˈveɪd /

释 v. 逃脱；躲避；规避；回避（处理或谈论某事）；想不出；（成功、光荣、爱情等）与……无缘

例 What is being called artificial general intelligence, machines that would imitate the way humans think, continues to **evade** scientists. 所谓的人工通用智能，也就是能够模仿人类思维方式的机器，一直让科学家们感到困扰。（2019年）

近 avoid / əˈvɔɪd / v. 避免；躲避 ‖ escape / ɪˈskeɪp / v. 逃避；溜走

tremble / ˈtrembl /

释 v. 颤抖；颤动；哆嗦；恐惧；战栗；抖动；极担心 n. 颤抖；哆嗦；战栗

例 Even he, however, might **tremble** at the thought of what he is about to do. 然而，即使是他，一想到自己将要做的事情，也会不寒而栗。（2008年）

control / kənˈtrəʊl /

释 v. 控制；掌管；操纵 n. 控制权；控制能力；限制

例 By allowing AI to develop content some brand marketers may find that they are losing **control** over the brand narrative. 通过让人工智能开发内容，一些品牌营销人员可能会发现，他们正在失去对品牌叙事的控制。（2023年）

lobby / ˈlɒbi /

释 n. 游说议员的团体；门廊，门厅 v. 对……进行游说

例 Under **lobby** pressure, George Osborne favours rural new-build against urban renovation and renewal. 在游说团体的压力下，乔治·奥斯本倾向于在农村地区新建房屋，而不是进行城市改造和重建。（2016年）

access / ˈækses /

释 v. 使用；存取；接近 n. 进入；使用权；接触的机会或权利

搭 have access to 有权使用，可以使用

例 Ferraro suggests the results may transfer to other parts of Asia, due to commonalities such as the importance of growing rice and market **access**. 费拉罗认为，由于种植水稻和市场准入的重要性等共同点，这些（研究）结果可能会推广到亚洲其他地区。（2021年）

harsh / hɑːʃ /

释 adj. 残酷的，无情的；艰苦的；粗糙的；（声音）刺耳的

例 Steelworkers, airline employees, and now those in the auto industry are joining millions of families who must worry about interest rates, stock market fluctuation, and the **harsh** reality that they may outlive their retirement money. 钢铁工人、航空公司雇员以及现在的汽车行业从业者和数百万家庭一样，必须担心利率、股票市场波动以及养老金可能不够用的残酷现实。（2007年）

object

0 2 0

释 / 'ɒbdʒɪkt / *n.* 物体, 物品; 目标 / əb'dʒekt / *v.* 不同意; 不赞成

例 I make no apology for being obsessed by a particular feature of everyday **objects**: their price. 我对日常物品的一个特殊特征——价格——非常着迷, 对此我并不感到抱歉。(2024年)

tentative / 'tentətɪv /

0 2 1

释 *adj.* 不确定的; 暂定的; 踌躇不决的

例 That is the **tentative** conclusion of a team of astronomers who re-examined images of some 4,000 newborn galaxies observed by Webb. 这是一个天文学家小组得出的初步结论, 他们重新研究了韦伯观测到的大约4 000个新生星系的图像。

retrospect / 'retrəspekt /

0 2 2

释 *n.* 回想, 回顾

搭 in retrospect 回顾往事; 回想起来

例 Jennifer Senior suggests in her article that raising a child can bring happiness in **retrospect**. 詹妮弗·西尼尔在她的文章中提出, 回想起来, 养育孩子可以带来幸福。(2011年)

outlet / 'aʊtlet /

0 2 3

释 *n.* 经销店; 专营店; 折扣店; 发泄途径; 电源插座; 出口

例 Many French politicians and media **outlets** have referred to this as a "GAFA tax," meaning that it is designed to apply primarily to companies such as Google, Apple, Facebook and Amazon—in other words, multinational tech companies based in the United States. 许多法国政治家和媒体端将其称为 "GAFA税", 意指该税种主要适用于谷歌、苹果、脸书和亚马逊等公司, 换句话说, 就是总部设在美国的跨国科技公司。(2020年)

rein / reɪn /

0 2 4

释 *n.* 控制; 缰绳; 掌管; 主宰 *v.* 控制; 驾驭; 勒住

例 At the end of 2018, Governor Charlie Baker of Massachusetts signed a bill to **rein** in those potential investor-buyers. 2018年底, 马萨诸塞州州长查理·贝克签署了一项法案, 以遏制这些潜在的投资者买家。(2023年)

prompt / prɒmpt /

0 2 5

释 *adj.* 敏捷的, 迅速的; 立刻的 *v.* 提示; 促进, 促使 *n.* [计]提示符, 提示; 提示词

搭 prompt response 敏捷的反应

例 His distinctive style is now one of the most commonly used **prompts** in the new open-source AI art generator Stable Diffusion. 他的独特风格现已成为新的开源人工智能艺术生成软件 Stable Diffusion中最常用的提示词之一。(2024年)

026
compromise / ˈkɒmprəmaɪz /
释 *n.* 妥协 *v.* 使陷入危险；（为达成协议而）妥协
例 We neither understand nor respect each other, and we have no basis for **compromise** or cooperation. 我们既不理解对方，也不尊重对方，而且我们也没有妥协或合作的基础。（2019年）

027
expose / ɪkˈspəʊz /
释 *v.* 暴露；显露；曝光；揭露；使面临，使遭受；使接触；使体验
例 In a recent study involving over 400 healthy adults, researchers from Carnegie Mellon University in Pennsylvania examined the effects of perceived social support and the receipt of hugs on the participants' susceptibility to developing the common cold after being **exposed** to the virus. 在最近一项涉及400多名健康成年人的研究中，宾夕法尼亚州卡内基梅隆大学的研究人员研究了感知社会支持和接受拥抱对参与者在接触病毒后患普通感冒的易感性的影响。（2017年）

028
repertoire / ˈrepətwɑː(r) /
释 *n.* （表演者的）全部曲目，可表演项目；全部技能
例 Merely expanding the orchestra's **repertoire** will not be enough. 仅仅增加乐团的曲目是不够的。（2011年）

029
giant / ˈdʒaɪənt /
释 *n.* 巨人；才智超群的人 *adj.* 巨大的
例 He quotes a **giant** of classical economics, Alfred Marshall, in describing this financial impatience as acting like "children who pick the plums out of their pudding to eat them at once" rather than putting them aside to be eaten last. 他引用古典经济学巨匠阿尔弗雷德·马歇尔的话，将这种金融上的急躁描述为"孩子们把李子从布丁里挑出来，然后马上吃掉"，而不是放在一边最后吃。（2019年）

030
revolve / rɪˈvɒlv /
释 *v.* 旋转；环绕；转动
例 Copernicus theorized in 1543 that all of the planets that we knew of **revolved** not around the Earth, but the Sun, a system that was later upheld by Galileo at his own expense. 哥白尼在1543年提出了"我们所知的所有行星不是围绕地球而是围绕太阳旋转"的理论，这是后来伽利略不惜牺牲自己的生命也要坚持的一个理论体系。（2020年）

031
strengthen / ˈstreŋkθn /
释 *v.* 加强；增强；巩固
例 His interventionist approach involves using taxes and government subsidies in a way that **strengthen** the middle class and, in theory, propel the economy into growth. 他的干预方法包括利用税收和政府补贴，以巩固中产阶级，并在理论上推动经济增长的方式。

advent / ˈædvənt / 032

释 *n.* （重大事件、人物、发明等的）出现，到来，来临

例 Even after the **advent** of widespread social media, a pyramid of production remains, with a small number of people uploading material, a slightly larger group commenting on or modifying that content, and a huge percentage remaining content to just consume. 即使在社交媒体普及之后，创造中的金字塔现象依然存在，少数人上传材料，稍多一些人对内容进行评论或修改，还有很大一部分人只是安于消费。（2012年）

近 arrival / əˈraɪvl / *n.* 到达；到来；到达者；引进

elevate / ˈelɪveɪt / 033

释 *v.* 提高；（地位、形象）抬高；举起；提拔

例 Even better would be to help **elevate** notions of beauty beyond the material standards of a particular industry. 更好的做法是帮助提升美的概念，使其超越某个特定行业的物质标准。（2016年）

hedge / hedʒ / 034

释 *n.* 篱笆，树篱；障碍物 *v.* 用树篱笆围住；避免做正面的答复

例 We need to trim away the rough edges on that **hedge**. 我们需要把那个树篱不平整的边缘剪掉。

switch / swɪtʃ / 035

释 *v.* 转换；改变；交换，对调 *n.* 改变，转变；（电路的）开关，闸，转换器

例 This is not to say that there is no point in getting a degree, but rather stress that a degree is not for everyone, that the **switch** from classroom to lecture hall is not an inevitable one and that other options are available. 这并不是说获得学位没有意义，而是强调学位并不适合所有人，从课堂到讲堂的转变并非不可避免，还有其他选择。（2022年）

junk / dʒʌŋk / 036

释 *n.* 废旧物品，垃圾 *v.* 丢弃，抛弃

搭 junk food 垃圾食品

例 Rose bought her furniture in **junk** shops. 罗丝从旧货店买了家具。

delicate / ˈdelɪkət / 037

释 *adj.* 易损的，易碎的；脆弱的；虚弱的；纤弱的；微小的；精美的；精细的，精密的；熟练的；微妙的

例 Parents still have a major role to play, but now it is more **delicate**. They have to be careful not to come across as disappointed in their child. 父母仍然扮演着重要角色，但现在的角色更加微妙。他们必须小心谨慎，避免表现出对孩子失望的样子。（2007年）

differentiate / ˌdɪfəˈrenʃieɪt / 　　038

释 *v.* 区别，区分

搭 differentiate from 与⋯⋯区分

例 A Canadian study found that children as young as 14 months can **differentiate** between a credible person and a dishonest one. 加拿大的一项研究发现，14个月大的儿童就能区分可信的人和不诚实的人。（2018年）

consolidate / kənˈsɒlɪdeɪt / 　　039

释 *v.* 使巩固，使加强；合并，联合

搭 consolidate sth. into sth. 使⋯⋯联合或合并

例 The popularity of these novels **consolidated** Dickens' as a nationally and internationally celebrated man of letters. 这些小说的畅销巩固了狄更斯作为国内和国际知名文学家的地位。（2017年）

reveal / rɪˈviːl / 　　040

释 *v.* 揭示；透露；展示

搭 reveal a secret 泄露一条秘密

例 It listed many documents in code that had been captured from the French Army of Spain, and whose secrets had been **revealed** by the work of one George Scovell, an officer in British headquarters. 它列出了从西班牙法军那里缴获的许多密码文件，这些文件的秘密被英国总部的一名军官乔治·斯科维尔所揭露。（2022年）

近 disclose / dɪsˈkləʊz / *v.* 公开，揭露

keep / kiːp / 　　041

释 *v.* （使）保持；（使）处于；（使）留在；继续；抑制；保留；遵守；存放；储存

例 The use of this little-known practice has accelerated in recent years, as colleges continue to do their utmost to **keep** students in school (and paying tuition) and improve their graduation rates. 近年来，这种鲜为人知的做法越发频繁了，因为各大学继续竭尽全力让学生留在学校（并支付学费），提高他们的毕业率。（2019年）

connect / kəˈnekt / 　　042

释 *v.* （使）连接；使接通（电源、水源等）；与⋯⋯有关系；把⋯⋯联系起来；（使）换乘（飞机或火车）；为（某人）接通电话；（与某人）建立良好关系，沟通

例 At issue is the TMT's planned location on Mauna Kea, a dormant volcano worshiped by some Hawaiians as the piko, that **connects** the Hawaiian Islands to the heavens. 问题的关键在于30米望远镜计划选址在莫纳克亚上，这是一座休眠火山，被一些夏威夷人奉为连接夏威夷群岛和天堂的"piko"。（2017年）

thread / θred /

释 n. （棉、毛、丝等的）线；线索；思路；线状物；贯穿的主线 v. 通过；穿过；给……装入；串在一起；穿成串

例 This initiative, aiming to harness AI's potential while mitigating its risks, **threads** the needle between innovation and moral management. 该倡议旨在利用人工智能的潜力，同时降低其风险，在创新和道德管理之间穿针引线。

share / ʃeə(r) /

释 v. 分享；共有；共享；共同承担；赞同 n. 股份；股票；（若干中的）一份

例 Before you **share** your thoughts, think about what the powerful person cares about—it may be the credibility of their team or getting a project done on time. 在分享你的想法之前，先想想有权势的人关心的是什么——可能是他们的团队信誉，也可能是按时完成项目。

dominate / ˈdɒmɪneɪt /

释 v. 占据支配地位；控制；俯视

例 Third, they now **dominate** left-of-centre politics. 第三，他们现在主导着左翼政治。（2012年）

triumph / ˈtraɪʌmf /

释 n. 胜利，凯旋 v. 获得胜利，战胜

搭 triumph over 战胜……

例 She was confident that she would ultimately **triumph** over adversity. 她相信自己最终能战胜逆境。

inflation / ɪnˈfleɪʃn /

释 n. 通货膨胀；膨胀

例 A report last year pointed out that the costs both of subscriptions and of these "article preparation costs" had been steadily rising at a rate above **inflation**. 去年的一份报告指出，订阅费用和这些"文章准备费用"一直在以高于通胀率的速度稳步上升。（2020年）

consist / kənˈsɪst /

释 v. 由……组成，由……构成；在于，存在于

搭 consist of 由……组成（或构成）‖ consist in 存在于；在于

例 Yet a considerable number of the most significant collections of criticism published in the 20th century **consisted** in large part of newspaper reviews. 然而，在20世纪出版的最重要的评论集中，有相当一部分是由报纸评论组成的。（2010年）

correspondence / ˌkɒrəˈspɒndəns /

释 n. 信件；通信；符合，一致；相似

例 We have been in **correspondence** for many years. 我们一直保持通信联系好多年。

abrupt / əˈbrʌpt / 　　　050

释 *adj.* 生硬的; 突然的; 唐突的; 陡峭的

例 The music is **abrupt** and seemingly disconnected, as in the last piano sonata. 如最后一首钢琴奏鸣曲，音乐生硬，似乎互不关联。（2014年）

nevertheless / ˌnevəðəˈles / 　　　051

释 *adv.* 尽管如此; 然而

例 **Nevertheless**, as any biographer knows, a person's early life and its conditions are often the greatest gift to an individual. 然而，任何传记作家都知道，一个人的早年生活及其状况往往是对他个人最大的馈赠。（2011年）

近 nonetheless / ˌnʌnðəˈles / *adv.* 尽管如此，仍然

reliable / rɪˈlaɪəbl / 　　　052

释 *adj.* 可信赖的; 真实可靠的

例 It has become a grimly **reliable** annual ritual: every January the cost of travelling by train rises, imposing a significant extra burden on those who have no option but to use the rail network to get to work or otherwise. 每年一月，乘火车旅行的费用都会上涨，这已成为一种严峻而可靠的年度惯例，给那些别无选择只能利用铁路上班或做其他事情的人带来了巨大的额外负担。（2021年）

subsequent / ˈsʌbsɪkwənt / 　　　053

释 *adj.* 后来的, 随后的

例 Prior knowledge and interests influence what we experience, what we think our experiences mean, and the **subsequent** actions we take. 先前的知识和兴趣会影响我们的经历、我们对自己的经历的理解以及我们随后采取的行动。（2012年）

近 consequent / ˈkɒnsɪkwənt / *adj.* 随之发生的

sensible / ˈsensəbl / 　　　054

释 *adj.* 明智的, 理智的; 合理的; 敏感的; 灵敏的; 感觉得到的

例 The video does show some more **sensible** uses of the Media Bar, like displaying the name of the car, a red warning sign, or even a birthday greeting. 视频中确实展示了媒体栏的一些更合理的用途，比如显示汽车名称、红色警告标志，甚至生日祝福语。

doubt / daʊt / 　　　055

释 *n.* 疑惑; 疑问; 不确定; 不相信 *v.* 怀疑; 不能肯定; 不确定; 不相信

搭 beyond (any) doubt 无疑; 确实 ‖ no doubt 无疑; 很可能; 确实

例 The ways of reading indicated here are without **doubt** kinds of comprehension. 这里指出的阅读方法无疑是理解的一种。（2015年）

approval / əˈpruːvl / 056

释 *n.* 批准，认可；赞同，同意；赞许，嘉许
例 Its lawmakers gave preliminary **approval** last week to a law that would make it a crime to employ ultra-thin models on runways. 其立法者上周初步批准了一项法律，该法律将把雇用超瘦模特走秀定为犯罪。（2016年）

conclusion / kənˈkluːʒn / 057

释 *n.* 结论；结局；（条约、交易等的）达成；最后
搭 in conclusion 最后；综上所述
例 If your **conclusion** is that the West is better able to preserve these artifacts, think about why you're assuming that to be true. 如果你的结论是西方能更好地保护这些文物，请想一想你为什么认为这是真的。（2024年）

fundamental / ˌfʌndəˈmentl / 058

释 *adj.* 根本的；基础的；基本的 *n.* 基本原理
例 Today the rapid growth of artificial intelligence (AI) raises **fundamental** questions: "What is intelligence, identity, or consciousness? What makes humans humans?" 如今，人工智能（AI）的快速发展引发了一些根本问题："什么是智能、身份或意识？是什么让人类成为人类？"（2019年）

desirable / dɪˈzaɪərəbl / 059

释 *adj.* 理想的；值得拥有的；性感的
例 In his *Case Study House*, Ralph may have mispredicted just how the mechanical revolution would impact everyday life, but his belief that self-sufficiency was both **desirable** and inevitable was widely shared. 在《住宅佳作分析》一书中，拉尔夫可能错误地预测了机械革命对于日常生活的影响，但他所坚持的"自给自足是理想的，也是必然发生的"这一信念得到了广泛的认可。

complain / kəmˈpleɪn / 060

释 *v.* 抱怨；控诉
搭 complain about/of 抱怨某人或某事
例 Social scientists who **complain** about a lack of funding should not expect more in today's economic climate. 在当今的经济环境下，那些抱怨缺乏基金的社会科学家不应该期待更多。（2013年）
派 complaint / kəmˈpleɪnt / *n.* 抱怨；投诉

associate 061

释 / əˈsəʊsieɪt / *v.* 联系；联想；交往 / əˈsəʊsiət / *adj.* 有关联的；非正式的；副的 *n.* 同事；伙伴
例 "We see that the program is **associated** with a 30 percent reduction in deforestation," Ferraro says. 费拉罗说："我们看到，该项目与森林砍伐量减少了30%有关。"（2021年）

controversy / ˈkɒntrəvɜːsi /

0 6 2

释 *n.* 争议；争论，辩论

例 Some blame for the current **controversy** belongs to astronomers. 目前的争议在一定程度上归咎于天文学家。（2017年）

近 argument / ˈɑːgjumənt / *n.* 辩论；争吵 ‖ debate / dɪˈbeɪt / *n.* 辩论，争论

irritate / ˈɪrɪteɪt /

0 6 3

释 *v.* 激怒；刺激；使不适

例 Psychological research backs up the everyday intuition that excuses and denials just **irritate** others. 心理学上的研究证实了我们日常的直觉，借口和否认只会激怒他人。

imitate / ˈɪmɪteɪt /

0 6 4

释 *v.* 模仿，效仿；仿造

例 You shouldn't **imitate** her way of doing things. 你不应该效仿她做事的方式。

派 imitation / ˌɪmɪˈteɪʃn / *n.* 模仿；仿制品

近 copy / ˈkɒpi / *v.* 模仿；复制 ‖ ape / eɪp / *v.* 模仿；学⋯⋯的样子

courage / ˈkʌrɪdʒ /

0 6 5

释 *n.* 勇气

例 His compositions demand the performer to show **courage**, for example in the use of dynamics. 他的作品要求演奏者表现出勇气，例如在力度变化的运用上。（2014年）

派 courageous / kəˈreɪdʒəs / *adj.* 勇敢的

navigation / ˌnævɪˈgeɪʃn /

0 6 6

释 *n.* 导航，领航

例 Today, we live in a world where GPS systems, digital maps, and other **navigation** apps are available on our smartphones. 如今，我们生活在一个智能手机上有GPS系统、数字地图和其他导航应用程序的世界里。（2019年）

approach / əˈprəʊtʃ /

0 6 7

释 *n.* 方式，方法，态度；路径；道路 *v.* 靠近，接近；接洽；建议；要求；（在数额、水平或质量上）接近；对付

例 Such an **approach** can both prompt new research as well as result in powerful art. 这种方法既能促进新的研究，又能产生强大的艺术效果。（2022年）

disappear / ˌdɪsəˈpɪə(r) /

0 6 8

释 *v.* 消失

例 At the beginning of the century songbirds were supposed to be **disappearing**. 21世纪初，人们认为鸣禽正在消失。（2010年）

派 disappearance / ˌdɪsəˈpɪərəns / *n.* 消失

acclaim / əˈkleɪm /   069

释 *v.* 称赞，为……喝彩 *n.* 称赞；欢呼

例 At any rate, this change will ultimately be **acclaimed** by an ever-growing number of both domestic and international consumers, regardless of how long the current consumer pattern will take hold. 无论如何，无论目前的消费模式还能维持多久，这种变化最终都会受到越来越多的国内外消费者的欢迎。（2010年）

近 applaud / əˈplɔːd / *v.* 赞赏，为……喝彩

erupt / ɪˈrʌpt /   070

释 *v.* （火山）爆发，喷发；（冲突、战斗等）突然发生，爆发；（斑疹等）突然出现，冒出；（感情）迸发

例 Protests have **erupted** over construction of the Thirty Meter Telescope (TMT), a giant observatory that promises to revolutionize humanity's view of the cosmos. 30米望远镜（TMT）的建造引发了抗议活动，这座巨型天文台有望彻底改变人类的宇宙观。（2017年）

prolong / prəˈlɒŋ /   071

释 *v.* 延长，拉长

例 I am not eager to **prolong** the agony of the past two weeks. 我再也不想延续过去两周的痛苦了。

key / kiː /   072

释 *n.* 钥匙；关键；答案 *adj.* 主要的；关键的

例 We suddenly can't remember where we put the **keys** just a moment ago, or an old acquaintance's name, or the name of an old band we used to love. 我们突然想不起来刚才把钥匙放在哪里了，或是想不起来一个老熟人的名字，抑或想不起来一个我们曾经喜欢过的老牌乐队的名字。（2014年）

storm / stɔːm /   073

释 *n.* 暴风雨；和风暴有关的恶劣天气；浪潮

例 Many of the ships were lost in **storms**, many passengers died of disease, and infants rarely survived the journey. 许多船只在风暴中沉没，许多乘客死于疾病，婴儿很少能在旅途中幸存下来。（2015年）

polish / ˈpɒlɪʃ /   074

释 *v.* 擦光；磨光；修改；润饰 *n.* 上光剂；亮光剂

例 Executive functioning is being refined and **polished** in the brain for the duration of child and adolescent development, so being unorganized, forgetful, and distracted can be age-appropriate. 在儿童和青少年发育期间，大脑的执行功能正在被完善和打磨，所以无组织、健忘和分心可能是与年龄相适应的。

action / 'ækʃn / [0][7][5]

释 n. 行动；措施；行为；诉讼；情节 adj. 动作（片）的；动作片中的

搭 in action 在运转 ‖ out of action 失去作用；停止运转

例 Congress needs to take **action** to ensure net neutrality. 国会需要采取行动确保网络中立性。（2021年）

sovereign / 'sɒvrɪn / [0][7][6]

释 n. 君主；元首 adj. 有主权的；完全独立的

例 Generally there was a belief that the new nations should be **sovereign** and independent states, large enough to be economically viable and integrated by a common set of laws. 一般来说，人们认为新国家应该是主权独立的国家，其规模应足够大，在经济上具有生存能力，并通过一套共同的法律凝聚为一个整体。（2007年）

whisper / 'wɪspə(r) / [0][7][7]

释 v. 低语；小声说 n. 低语（声）

例 He was having to **whisper** in order to avoid being overheard by their neighbours. 他不得不低声耳语，以免被他们的邻居们听见。

retreat / rɪ'triːt / [0][7][8]

释 n./v. 退却；撤退；离开；退缩

搭 retreat from 逃避……

例 Moreover, the amateur tradition in music criticism has been in headlong **retreat**. 此外，音乐评论的业余传统也在迅速衰退。（2010年）

fate / feɪt / [0][7][9]

释 n. 命运；命运的安排

例 They thought they would never see each other again, but **fate** brought them back together. 他们原以为再也见不到对方了，但命运使他们又走到了一起。

platform / 'plætfɔːm / [0][8][0]

释 n. 站台；讲台；舞台；平台

例 Sellers that use eBay and Etsy, which provide **platforms** for smaller sellers, also haven't been collecting sales tax nationwide. 使用eBay和Etsy（为小型卖家提供平台）的卖家也没有在全球范围内征收销售税。（2019年）

procedure / prə'siːdʒə(r) / [0][8][1]

释 n. 程序；步骤

例 What might be an effect of the ERA's unjustified dismissal **procedures**? 《雇佣关系法》不合理的解雇程序可能会产生什么影响？（2022年）

continuous / kənˈtɪnjuəs / 082

释 *adj.* 不断的; 持续的; 连续的; 反复的

例 Much less is known about its long-term effects, but one theory is that some long COVID patients experience a sort of **continuous** low-grade inflammation that can contribute to tissue and organ damage. 人们对它的长期影响知之甚少, 但有一种理论认为, 一些长期感染冠状病毒的患者会经历一种持续的轻度炎症, 这可能导致组织和器官受损。

pause / pɔːz / 083

释 *v.* 停顿; 暂停 *n.* 停顿; 停顿的时间; 暂停键

例 These **pauses** typically occur at about three per second, and the eyes then jump to another spot, until several important points in the image are registered like a series of snapshots. 这些停顿通常以每秒三次的速度出现, 然后眼睛会跳到另一个点, 直到图像中几个重要的点像一系列快照一样被记录下来。(2020年)

delete / dɪˈliːt / 084

释 *v.* 删除; 划掉

例 Once you have a first draft on paper, you can **delete** material that is unrelated to your thesis and add material necessary to illustrate your points and make your paper convincing. 一旦你的初稿付诸纸上, 你就可以删除与你的论文无关的材料, 并添加必要的材料来证明你的观点, 使你的论文令人信服。(2008年)

派 deletion / dɪˈliːʃn / *n.* 删除

prevail / prɪˈveɪl / 085

释 *v.* 普遍存在; 流行; (思想、观点等) 被接受; 战胜; 压倒; 劝服; 说服

搭 prevail on/upon sb. to do sth. 劝说某人做某事

例 It was an argument in which neither side could **prevail** over the other. 在这个问题上, 谁也不能使对方折服。

派 prevailing / prɪˈveɪlɪŋ / *adj.* 普遍的; 流行的

eventually / ɪˈventʃuəli / 086

释 *adv.* 最后; 终于

例 Coppola lost his studio and was left with debts that **eventually** forced him—and Eleanor—to declare bankruptcy. 科波拉失去了他的工作室, 负债累累, 这最终迫使他和埃莉诺宣布破产。

float / fləʊt / 087

释 *v.* 漂浮; 浮动; 飘然移动

搭 float about/around (思想等) 传播, 流传

例 This means that our noses are limited to perceiving those smells which **float** through the air, missing the majority of smells which stick to surfaces. 这意味着我们的鼻子只能感知空气中飘荡的气味, 而忽略了大多数附着在地面上的气味。(2005年)

Writing Models

court

tension

dare

depth

bind

topic

curious

agent

fold

dim

clause

seed

digital

court / kɔːt / 088

释 *n.* 法院；法庭；全体审判人员

搭 in court 出庭

例 It is welcomed by the Supreme **Court**. 最高法院对此表示欢迎。
（2020年）

tension / 'tenʃn / 089

释 *n.* 紧张局势（或关系、状况）；矛盾；紧张（气氛）；拉伸；张力

例 Global events are intensifying local **tension**, around the workplace water-cooler and our family's dining table. 全球事件加剧了当地的紧张局势，无论是在工作场所的饮水机旁，还是在我们家里的餐桌旁。

dare / deə(r) / 090

释 *v.* 敢于；胆敢

例 "**Dare** to be different, please don't smoke!" pleads one billboard campaign aimed at reducing smoking among teenagers—teenagers, who desire nothing more than fitting in. "敢于与众不同，请不要吸烟！"一个旨在减少青少年吸烟的广告牌广告如此呼吁道，而青少年最想要的是融入群体。（2012年）

depth / depθ / 091

释 *n.* 深（度）；深厚；诚挚；深刻

搭 in depth 全面；深入；详细

例 Students will test the temperature of the water at different **depths**. 学生们将测试不同深度的水的温度。

bind / baɪnd / 092

释 *v.* 捆绑；系；结合；约束

例 Newton's laws of motion and Darwinian evolution each **bind** a host of different phenomena into a single explicatory framework. 牛顿的运动定律和达尔文的进化论都将许多不同的现象纳入一个单一的解释框架之中。（2012年）

topic / 'tɒpɪk / 093

释 *n.* 话题；主题；题目；标题

例 Now that you have developed a **topic** into a tentative thesis, you can assemble your notes and begin to flesh out whatever outline you have made. 既然你已经将一个主题拓展成了一个初步的论题，就可以开始整理要点，充实你已拟好的提纲。（2008年）

curious / 'kjʊəriəs / 094

释 *adj.* 好奇的；求知欲强的；不寻常的；难以理解的

例 In Britain this has had a **curious** result. 这在英国产生了一个不寻常的结果。（2016年）

派 curiosity / ˌkjʊəri'ɒsəti / *n.* 好奇心

agent / 'eɪdʒənt / 　095

释 *n.* 代理商; 代理人, 经纪人; 间谍, 特务

例 The London **agents** Stirling Ackroyd recently identified enough sites for half a million houses in the London area alone, with no intrusion on green belt. 伦敦房地产经纪公司斯特林·阿克罗伊德最近发现, 仅在伦敦地区就有足够建造50万套房屋的地点, 而且不占用绿化带。(2016年)

fold / fəʊld / 　096

释 *v.* 折叠; 交叠 *n.* 折痕; 褶皱

例 The IASB says it does not want to act without overall planning, but the pressure to **fold** when it completes its reconstruction of rules later this year is strong. 国际会计准则委员会表示, 它不想在没有整体规划的情况下采取行动, 但在今年晚些时候完成自身规则重建后, 它将面临很大的压力。(2010年)

反 unfold / ʌn'fəʊld / *v.* 展开; 使(事情等)传开; 逐渐明朗

dim / dɪm / 　097

释 *adj.* 昏暗的; 朦胧的; 模糊的; 悲观的 *v.* (使)变暗淡; (使)变模糊

例 The object looks like a **dim** light moving through the sky just ahead of the fast-moving and much brighter space station. 这个物体看起来就像一束昏暗的灯光, 在天空中移动, 它就在快速移动、明亮得多的空间站的前方。

clause / klɔːz / 　098

释 *n.* 条款; 从句; 分句

例 The southern states would not have signed the Constitution without protections for the "peculiar institution," including a **clause** that counted a slave as three fifths of a man for purposes of congressional representation. 如果没有对这个"特殊制度"的保护, 南方诸州就不会在宪法上签字(其中包括一个条款: 在选举国会代表时, 一个黑奴相当于五分之三个人)。(2008年)

seed / siːd / 　099

释 *n.* 种子; 籽; 起源; 起因

例 More bees dispersed **seeds** across the park, giving life to more types of plants. 更多的蜜蜂在公园里传播种子, 给更多种植物带来了生命。

digital / 'dɪdʒɪtl / 　100

释 *adj.* 数字的; 数码的

例 Instead, the **digital** services tax is part of a much larger trend, with countries over the past few years proposing or putting in place an alphabet soup of new international tax provisions. 相反, 数字服务税是一种更大趋势的一部分, 过去几年, 各国提出或实施了一系列新的国际税收规定。(2020年)

☐ ☐ density
☐ ☐ abdomen
☐ ☐ abrupt
☐ ☐ access
☐ ☐ acclaim
☐ ☐ action
☐ ☐ advent
☐ ☐ agent
☐ ☐ apart
☐ ☐ approach
☐ ☐ approval
☐ ☐ associate
☐ ☐ battle
☐ ☐ bind
☐ ☐ clause
☐ ☐ complain
☐ ☐ compromise
☐ ☐ conclusion
☐ ☐ connect
☐ ☐ conservation
☐ ☐ consist
☐ ☐ consolidate
☐ ☐ context
☐ ☐ continuous
☐ ☐ control
☐ ☐ controversy
☐ ☐ correspondence
☐ ☐ courage
☐ ☐ court
☐ ☐ curious
☐ ☐ dare

☐ ☐ delete
☐ ☐ delicate
☐ ☐ depth
☐ ☐ desirable
☐ ☐ differentiate
☐ ☐ digital
☐ ☐ dim
☐ ☐ disappear
☐ ☐ dominate
☐ ☐ doubt
☐ ☐ elevate
☐ ☐ enclosure
☐ ☐ erupt
☐ ☐ evade
☐ ☐ eventually
☐ ☐ expose
☐ ☐ fate
☐ ☐ float
☐ ☐ fold
☐ ☐ fundamental
☐ ☐ giant
☐ ☐ harsh
☐ ☐ hedge
☐ ☐ imitate
☐ ☐ infer
☐ ☐ inflation
☐ ☐ irritate
☐ ☐ junk
☐ ☐ keep
☐ ☐ key
☐ ☐ lobby

☐ ☐ navigation
☐ ☐ nevertheless
☐ ☐ object
☐ ☐ outlet
☐ ☐ pause
☐ ☐ platform
☐ ☐ polish
☐ ☐ prevail
☐ ☐ procedure
☐ ☐ prolong
☐ ☐ prompt
☐ ☐ provision
☐ ☐ rein
☐ ☐ reliable
☐ ☐ repertoire
☐ ☐ retreat
☐ ☐ retrospect
☐ ☐ reveal
☐ ☐ revolve
☐ ☐ seed
☐ ☐ sensible
☐ ☐ share
☐ ☐ sort
☐ ☐ sovereign
☐ ☐ storm
☐ ☐ strengthen
☐ ☐ string
☐ ☐ subsequent
☐ ☐ successive
☐ ☐ switch
☐ ☐ tension

☐ ☐ tentative
☐ ☐ thread
☐ ☐ topic
☐ ☐ tremble
☐ ☐ triumph
☐ ☐ undo
☐ ☐ whisper

音频

Day **15**

- ☐ leisure
- ☐ collect
- ☐ mysterious
- ☐ outrage
- ☐ discourse
- ☐ withdraw
- ☐ appetite
- ☐ destroy
- ☐ depict
- ☐ pension
- ☐ frustrate
- ☐ celebrity
- ☐ attorney
- ☐ jury
- ☐ preserve
- ☐ diligent
- ☐ logical
- ☐ leak
- ☐ severe
- ☐ equip
- ☐ process
- ☐ damage
- ☐ risk
- ☐ decay
- ☐ refuge
- ☐ despise
- ☐ realize/-ise
- ☐ foundation
- ☐ impose
- ☐ base
- ☐ fabulous

- ☐ scheme
- ☐ insure
- ☐ refuse
- ☐ assembly
- ☐ vary
- ☐ liberate
- ☐ assimilate
- ☐ confront
- ☐ hamper
- ☐ subject
- ☐ resemblance
- ☐ address
- ☐ occasion
- ☐ achieve
- ☐ accuse
- ☐ norm
- ☐ fluctuate
- ☐ originate
- ☐ pledge
- ☐ revenue
- ☐ extend
- ☐ intend
- ☐ item
- ☐ slum
- ☐ suspicious
- ☐ protein
- ☐ stroll
- ☐ sequence
- ☐ applicable
- ☐ attach
- ☐ inject

- ☐ contend
- ☐ assistant
- ☐ prevalent
- ☐ encounter
- ☐ inhibit
- ☐ existence
- ☐ relative
- ☐ tolerate
- ☐ feedback
- ☐ engagement
- ☐ hobby
- ☐ origin
- ☐ constituent
- ☐ knock
- ☐ rude
- ☐ circuit
- ☐ magnificent
- ☐ attack
- ☐ imitation
- ☐ rage
- ☐ wish
- ☐ belt
- ☐ tragedy
- ☐ worm
- ☐ sympathy
- ☐ former
- ☐ period
- ☐ mere
- ☐ pride
- ☐ judg(e)ment
- ☐ chemical

- ☐ cancel
- ☐ pick
- ☐ inherit
- ☐ chain
- ☐ value
- ☐ labo(u)r
- ☐ sow

Writing Models

leisure

collect

mysterious

outrage

discourse

withdraw

appetite

destroy

depict

pension

frustrate

leisure / ˈleʒə(r) / 　　　　　　　　　001

释 *n.* 空闲，闲暇

搭 at leisure 从容地；有空

例 It was specifically to provide city dwellers with spaces for **leisure** where they could experience "a refreshing air." 它专门为城市居民提供休闲空间，在那里他们可以体验"清新的空气"。（2016年）

近 relaxation / ˌriːlækˈseɪʃn / *n.* 休闲；放松

collect / kəˈlekt / 　　　　　　　　　002

释 *v.* 收集；采集；收藏；聚集；汇集；积累；募集；领取；赢得；获得
adj. 对方付通话费的 *adv.* 对方付通话费地

例 We now live in an age of plastic, she says, "and what we decide to **collect** today, what we decide to preserve... will have a strong impact on how in the future we'll be seen." 她说，我们现在生活在一个塑料时代，"我们今天决定收集什么，决定保存什么……将对未来人们如何看待我们产生重大影响"。（2022年）

mysterious / mɪˈstɪəriəs / 　　　　　　003

释 *adj.* 神秘的；可疑的；难以理解的

例 The new contract is written without any **mysterious** terms. 新合同上没有任何难以理解的条款。

outrage / ˈaʊtreɪdʒ / 　　　　　　　　004

释 *n.* 愤怒，愤慨；暴行 *v.* 使震怒，激怒

例 The company, a major energy supplier in New England, provoked **outrage** in Vermont when it announced it was reneging on a longstanding commitment to abide by the strict nuclear regulations. 这家公司是新英格兰的一家主要能源供应商，它宣布其未能兑现严格遵守核能规定的长期承诺，这激起了佛蒙特州民众的愤怒。

派 outrageous / aʊtˈreɪdʒəs / *adj.* 蛮横无理的；过分的 ‖ outraged / ˈaʊtˌreɪdʒd / *adj.* 震惊的；义愤填膺的

近 rage / reɪdʒ / *n.* 狂怒，大怒 *v.* 动怒 ‖ indignation / ˌɪndɪɡˈneɪʃn / *n.* 愤怒；义愤

discourse / ˈdɪskɔːs / 　　　　　　　　005

释 *n.* 语篇；话语；演讲，会话

例 There is "the democratizing uniformity of dress and **discourse**, and the casualness and absence of deference" characteristic of popular culture. 大众文化的特点是"着装和话语的民主化统一性，以及随意性和无敬畏感"。（2006年）

withdraw / wɪðˈdrɔː / 　　　　　　　　006

释 *v.* 撤走；拿走；撤退，撤离；提，取（款）；返回；收回，撤回（所说的话或声明）

例 There are no restrictions on the amount of money you can **withdraw**. 你可以取款的金额没有限制。

appetite / ˈæpɪtaɪt /

007

釋 *n.* 欲望；爱好；食欲

搭 appetite for 对……的爱好

例 Religious associations began, for example, in the desire to secure the favor of overruling powers and to ward off evil influences; family life in the desire to gratify **appetites** and secure family perpetuity; systematic labor, for the most part, because of enslavement to others, etc. 例如，宗教团体的起源是为了获得统治者的青睐和抵御邪恶的影响，家庭生活的起源是为了满足食欲和确保家族的延续，有计划的劳动大多是始于奴役他人，等等。（2009年）

destroy / dɪˈstrɔɪ /

008

釋 *v.* 摧毁，破坏；宰杀

例 Surely it should be obvious to the dimmest executive that trust, that most valuable of economic assets, is easily **destroyed** and hugely expensive to restore—and that few things are more likely to **destroy** trust than a company letting sensitive personal data get into the wrong hands. 想必连最愚蠢的高管也明白，信任是最有价值的经济资产，它很容易被破坏，恢复成本高昂，而且很少有什么事情比公司让敏感的个人数据落入坏人之手更容易破坏信任。（2007年）

depict / dɪˈpɪkt /

009

釋 *v.* 描写，描绘

例 In the movies and on television, artificial intelligence (AI) is typically **depicted** as something sinister that will upend our way of life. 在电影和电视中，人工智能（AI）通常被描绘成一种邪恶的东西，它会颠覆我们的生活方式。（2021年）

pension / ˈpenʃn /

010

釋 *n.* 养老金；退休金；抚恤金；（尤指法国的）廉价小旅店 *v.* 准许或强迫某人退休（并发给养老金）

例 Politicians have repeatedly "backloaded" public-sector pay deals, keeping the pay increases modest but adding to holidays and especially **pensions** that are already generous. 政客们一再"变相地提高"公共部门的薪资待遇，薪资涨幅不大，但增加了假期，尤其是增加了本已丰厚的养老金。（2012年）

frustrate / ˈfrʌstreɪt /

011

釋 *v.* 使懊恼，使沮丧；挫败

例 Some physicians—**frustrated** by their inability to cure the disease and fearing loss of hope in the patient—too often offer aggressive treatment far beyond what is scientifically justified. 一些医生因为无法治愈这种疾病而感到沮丧，又担心病人失去希望，所以常常采用激进的治疗方法，这些方法远远超出了科学能够认同的范围。

celebrity

attorney

jury

preserve

diligent

logical

leak

severe

equip

process

damage

risk

---

celebrity / sə'lebrəti /　　　　　　012

释 *n.* 名人；名望

例 Having children contributes little to the glamour of **celebrity** moms. 生儿育女对明星妈妈的魅力贡献不大。（2011年）

---

attorney / ə'tɜːni /　　　　　　013

释 *n.* 律师；代理人

例 The judges on the Federal Circuit are "reacting to the anti-patent trend at the Supreme Court," says Harold C. Wegner, a patent **attorney** and professor at George Washington University Law School. 乔治·华盛顿大学法学院教授、专利律师哈罗德·C. 韦格纳说，联邦巡回法院的法官们正在"对最高法院的反专利趋势做出反应"。（2010年）

近 lawyer / 'lɔɪjə(r) / *n.* 律师 ‖ counsel / 'kaʊnsl / *n.* 律师

辨 attorney、lawyer和counsel都有"律师"的意思。attorney主要在美国使用，有时可与lawyer通用，泛指辩护律师；lawyer为普通用词，指精通法律规则并有权以法律代理人或顾问身份为委托人服务的人；counsel指单独或集体为当事人提供咨询或出庭处理案件的法律顾问或律师。

---

jury / 'dʒʊəri /　　　　　　014

释 *n.* 陪审团；评审委员会

搭 jury box 陪审团席位

例 The high court's decision said the judge in Mr. McDonnell's trial failed to tell a **jury** that it must look only at his "official acts", or the former governor's decisions on "specific" and "unsettled" issues related to his duties. 高等法院的裁决称，审判麦克唐奈尔先生的法官没有告诉陪审团必须只审查他的"官方行为"，或这位前州长就与其职责相关的"具体"和"未决"问题做出的决定。（2017年）

---

preserve / prɪ'zɜːv /　　　　　　015

释 *v.* 维护；保护；贮存 *n.* 保护区；[pl.]果酱；独揽之事，专门领域

例 What was more, many original French dispatches had been **preserved** in this collection, which, I realized, was priceless. 更重要的是，许多原始的法文电报都保存在这本集子里，我意识到这是无价之宝。（2022年）

近 conserve / kən'sɜːv / *v.* 保存 ‖ protect / prə'tekt / *v.* 保护

---

diligent / 'dɪlɪdʒənt /　　　　　　016

释 *adj.* 勤奋的，勤勉的

例 Workers tended to be **diligent** for the first few days of the week in any case, before hitting a plateau and then slackening off. 在任何情况下，工人们在一周的头几天往往都很勤奋，继而进入一个稳定期，然后就会松懈下来。（2010年）

派 diligence / 'dɪlɪdʒəns / *n.* 勤奋

近 industrious / ɪn'dʌstriəs / *adj.* 勤勉的

logical / ˈlɒdʒɪkl / 017

释 *adj.* 合逻辑的，合理的；逻辑学的

例 **Logical** thinking is not necessarily related to the way we talk. 逻辑思维与我们说话的方式没有必然联系。（2005年）

派 logically / ˈlɒdʒɪkli / *adv.* 逻辑上，理论上

leak / liːk / 018

释 *v.* 漏；泄漏 *n.* 漏洞；泄露

例 The roof has a **leak**, and the rain is **leaking** in. 屋顶有个漏洞，雨水正漏进来。

severe / sɪˈvɪə(r) / 019

释 *adj.* 严重的；严厉的；苛刻的

例 In Indonesia, the program has provided enough food and medicine to substantially reduce **severe** growth problems among children. 在印度尼西亚，该计划提供了足够的食物和药品，大大减少了儿童严重的生长问题。（2021年）

equip / ɪˈkwɪp / 020

释 *v.* 装备；配备；使有能力；使有所准备；训练

例 Emergency physicians are highly **equipped** to handle situations that need immediate attention: various wounds, shattered bones, heart attacks. 急诊科医生有很强的能力处理需要立即关注的情况：各种伤口、骨折、心脏病发作。

process 021

释 / ˈprəʊses / *n.* 过程；步骤；手续 *v.* 对……加工处理；审阅
/ prəˈses / *v.* 列队行进；缓缓前进

搭 in the process of 在……过程中

例 There has been a kind of inflationary **process** at work: nowadays anyone applying for a research post has to have published twice the number of papers that would have been required for the same post only 10 years ago. 有一种通货膨胀过程在起作用：如今，任何申请研究职位的人所发表的论文数量必须是十年前申请同一职位所需的论文数量的两倍。（2019年）

damage / ˈdæmɪdʒ / 022

释 *v.* 破坏，损坏；损害；伤害 *n.* 损坏；损害；伤害；[pl.]损害赔偿金

例 While studies have shown that acrylamide can cause neurological **damage** in mice, there is no conclusive evidence that it causes cancer in humans. 虽然研究表明丙烯酰胺会对小鼠造成神经损伤，但并没有确凿证据表明丙烯酰胺会对人类致癌。（2020年）

risk / rɪsk / 023

释 *n.* 风险；会带来风险的事物 *v.* 冒险（做某事）；冒着……的风险

例 When education becomes one-size-fits-all, it **risks** overlooking a nation's diversity of gifts. 当教育变得一刀切的时候，就会存在忽视一个国家人才多样化的风险。

decay / dɪ'keɪ /

024

释 *v.* (使)腐烂; 衰败;(力量、影响等)衰退, 衰减 *n.* 腐烂; 衰败

例 The development of the Elizabethan drama for the next twenty-five years is of exceptional interest to students of literary history, for in this brief period we may trace the beginning, growth, blossoming, and **decay** of many kinds of plays, and of many great careers. 研究文学史的学生对伊丽莎白时代戏剧在此后25年的发展格外感兴趣, 因为在这段短暂的时间里, 我们可以追溯到许多剧种和许多伟大事业的开端、成长、绽放和衰落。(2018年)

近 decline / dɪ'klaɪn / *v./n.* 衰落; 降低

refuge / 'refjuːdʒ /

025

释 *n.* 避难; 避难所

搭 take/seek refuge (in sth.)(在……中)避难

例 During the frequent air-raids, people took **refuge** in their cellars. 在频繁的空袭期间, 人们在地窖中避难。

despise / dɪ'spaɪz /

026

释 *v.* 鄙视, 看不起; 不喜欢

例 Animals **despise** being captives in zoos. 动物不喜欢被囚禁在动物园里。(2022年)

realize/-ise / 'riːəlaɪz /

027

释 *v.* 意识到; 认识到; 使成为现实; 理解

例 Think of those fleeting moments when you look out of an aeroplane window and **realise** that you are flying, higher than a bird. 想一想, 当你从飞机窗口向外望去, 意识到自己正在飞翔, 飞得比鸟儿还高时, 那种一闪而过的瞬间。(2012年)

派 realization / ˌriːəlaɪ'zeɪʃn / *n.* 实现

foundation / faʊn'deɪʃn /

028

释 *n.* 基础, 根本; 根据, 依据; 创办; 基金会; 粉底

搭 on the foundation of 在……的基础上

例 "Elephants never forget"—or so they say—and that piece of folklore seems to have some **foundation**. "大象永远不会忘记"——他们是这么说的, 而且这个民间传说似乎有一定的依据。(2024年)

impose / ɪm'pəʊz /

029

释 *v.* 把……强加于; 使接受, 使意识到; 推行, 采用(规章制度); 迫使; 强制实行; 勉强(某人做某事); 使(别人)接受自己的意见

搭 impose a restriction on sth. 对某事实行限制

例 Financial regulators in Britain have **imposed** a rather unusual rule on the bosses of big banks. 英国的金融监管机构对大银行的老板们实施了一项非同寻常的规定。(2019年)

派 imposing / ɪm'pəʊzɪŋ / *adj.* 壮观的; 使人印象深刻的 ‖ imposition / ˌɪmpə'zɪʃn / *n.* 实施; 征收

base / beɪs /
`030`

🟠 *n.* 基础; 基数; 基底; 基地 *v.* 以⋯⋯为基础（或根据）; 把基地设在⋯⋯

🟠 The earliest films often bore little resemblance to the musicals in which they were **based**. 最早的电影往往与它们所改编的音乐剧几乎毫无相似之处。

🟠 basic / 'beɪsɪk / *adj.* 基本的 ‖ basis / 'beɪsɪs / *n.* 基础; 缘由

🟠 foundation / faʊn'deɪʃn / *n.* 地基; 基金会; 基础;（机构或组织的）创建

fabulous / 'fæbjələs /
`031`

🟠 *adj.* 极好的, 绝妙的; 难以置信的

🟠 The second half of the 20th century saw a collection of geniuses, warriors, entrepreneurs and visionaries labour to create a **fabulous** machine that could function as a typewriter and printing press, studio and theatre, paintbrush and gallery, piano and radio, the mail as well as the mail carrier. 20 世纪下半叶, 一批天才、勇士、企业家和远见卓识者努力创造出一台绝妙的机器: 它既是打字机, 又是印刷机; 既是工作室, 又是剧院; 既是画笔, 又是画廊; 既是钢琴, 又是收音机; 既是邮件, 又是邮递员。（2012年）

scheme / skiːm /
`032`

🟠 *n.*（政府或其他机构的）大规模计划; 计划 *v.* 密谋

🟠 In order to "change lives for the better" and reduce "dependency," George Osborne, Chancellor of the Exchequer, introduced the "upfront work search" **scheme**. 为了"改善生活", 减少"依赖", 英国财政大臣乔治·奥斯本推出了"前期工作搜索"计划。（2014年）

insure / ɪn'ʃʊə(r) /
`033`

🟠 *v.* 承保; 确保; 投保

🟠 And this has actually implicated the interests directly of well over a dozen countries, with crews from all sorts of different places, ships registered and **insured** in different places. 这实际上直接牵涉到十几个国家的利益, 船员来自不同的地方, 船只在不同的地方注册和投保。

refuse
`034`

🟠 / rɪ'fjuːz / *v.* 拒绝; 回绝 / 'refjuːs / *n.* 废物; 垃圾

🟠 They **refused** to back to the work unless certain conditions were met. 除非某些条件得到满足, 否则他们拒绝回去工作。

assembly / ə'sembli /
`035`

🟠 *n.* 议会; 立法机构; 装配, 组装; 集合, 集会

🟠 The national **assembly** has voted to adopt the budget. 国民议会已表决通过预算。

🟠 congress / 'kɒŋgres / *n.* 国会; 会议 ‖ council / 'kaʊnsl / *n.* 会议

vary / 'veri / ⓪③⑥

释 *v.* 各不相同；（使）变化

搭 vary with 随……而变化 ‖ vary from 不同于 ‖ vary in 在……方面有差异

例 Although the figure may **vary**, analysts do agree on another matter: that the number of the homeless is increasing. 尽管数字可能会有所不同，但分析家们在另一个问题上确实达成了一致：无家可归者的人数正在增加。（2006年）

liberate / 'lɪbəreɪt / ⓪③⑦

释 *v.* 解放；释放；使自由

例 Bolivar had received aid from Haiti and had promised in return to abolish slavery in the areas he **liberated**. 玻利瓦尔接受了海地的援助，作为回报，他承诺在他解放的地区废除奴隶制。（2007年）

派 liberation / ˌlɪbə'reɪʃn / *n.* 解放；释放

近 discharge / dɪs'tʃɑːdʒ / *v.* 允许……离开；释放 *n.* 排出；释放

assimilate / ə'sɪməleɪt / ⓪③⑧

释 *v.* （使或被）同化；（被）吸收，（被）消化

例 Some of these languages have vanished, as the nations who spoke them died out or became **assimilated** and lost their native languages. 这些语言中有一些已经不复存在了，这是由于说这些语言的民族消亡了或者被同化了，从而丧失了自己的本族语言。

派 assimilation / əˌsɪmə'leɪʃn / *n.* 消化；同化，同化作用

近 absorb / əb'zɔːb / *v.* 吸收 ‖ digest / daɪ'dʒest / *v.* 消化

confront / kən'frʌnt / ⓪③⑨

释 *v.* 面临（问题、任务、困难等）；正视；面对；与（某人）对峙（尤指准备打斗、争论或竞争）；与（某人）对质

搭 be confronted with sth. 面临……

例 We may infer from the second paragraph that in its early days the U.S. was **confronted** with delicate situations. 我们可以从第二段中推断出，美国在成立初期面临着微妙的局面。（2008年）

近 encounter / ɪn'kaʊntə(r) / *v.* 遭遇；遇到 ‖ meet / miːt / *v.* 遇见；对付

hamper / 'hæmpə(r) / ⓪④⓪

释 *v.* 束缚；妨碍 *n.* 带盖的大篮子

例 More than anything, the historians say, the founders were **hampered** by the culture of their time. 历史学家们说，创始人受制于当时的文化，这比什么都重要。（2008年）

近 hinder / 'hɪndə(r) / *v.* 阻碍；打扰 ‖ obstruct / əb'strʌkt / *v.* 阻碍；阻塞

subject

释 / 'sʌbdʒɪkt / *n.* 话题; 主题; 科目; 题材; 主语; 实验对象; 研究对象 *adj.* 受·····支配的; 受······影响的 / səb'dʒekt / *v.* 使遭受

例 Although one of the most popular toys ever, Barbie was the **subject** of intense controversy, seen both as a symbol of female empowerment and as an impossible standard of beauty and femininity. 尽管芭比娃娃是有史以来最受欢迎的玩具之一, 但却是引起激烈争议的一个对象, 它既被视为女性赋权的象征, 又被视为不可能达到的美丽和女性气质的标准。

resemblance / rɪ'zembləns /

释 *n.* 相似, 相似处

例 The **resemblance** between the two signatures was remarkable. 两个签名的相似之处很明显。

address / ə'dres /

释 *n.* 地址, 住址; 演讲, 演说; 称呼 *v.* 演讲; 称呼 (某人); 致函; 设法解决; 向·····说话; 写 (收信人) 姓名地址

例 The threat of nationalisation may have been seen off for now, but it will return with a vengeance if the justified anger of passengers is not **addressed** in short order. 国有化的威胁可能暂时被抛诸脑后, 但如果乘客的合理愤怒不能在短期内得到解决, 这种威胁就会卷土重来。 (2021年)

occasion / ə'keɪʒn /

释 *n.* 场合; 时机

搭 on occasion 有时; 不时

例 I can't find clothes proper for the **occasion**. 我找不到适合这种场合穿的衣服。

achieve / ə'tʃiːv /

释 *v.* (经努力) 完成; 达到; 获得

例 The Gutenberg printing press transformed civilisation not by changing the nature of writing but by changing its cost—and it would have **achieved** little without a parallel collapse in the price of surfaces to write on, thanks to an often-overlooked technology called paper. 古腾堡印刷机不是通过改变书写的性质, 而是通过改变书写的成本改变了人类文明, 如果书写表面的价格没有同步大幅下降, 那么它就不会取得什么成就, 这要归功于一种经常被忽视的技术——纸张。 (2024年)

accuse / ə'kjuːz /

释 *v.* 控告, 指控; 谴责; 归咎于

例 Of course, many discussions are not so successful. Still, we need to be careful not to **accuse** opponents of bad arguments too quickly. 当然, 许多讨论并不那么成功。不过, 我们还是要小心, 不要过早地指责对手的论点不正确。 (2019年)

norm

fluctuate

originate

pledge

revenue

extend

intend

item

slum

suspicious

protein

stroll

norm / nɔːm / 〔047〕

释 *n.* 标准；准则；惯例，常规

搭 norms of conduct 行为准则

例 You must obey the **norms** of the society you live in. 你一定要遵守你所生活的社会中的准则。

近 regulation / ˌreɡjuˈleɪʃn / *n.* 规章，规则 ‖ rule / ruːl / *n.* 规则；条例

fluctuate / ˈflʌktʃueɪt / 〔048〕

释 *v.* 波动，起伏

例 However, because these connections are made through effort and practice, scientists believe that intelligence can expand and **fluctuate** according to mental effort. 然而，由于这些联系是通过努力和练习建立起来的，科学家们认为，智力可以根据脑力劳动而扩展和波动。（2014年）

originate / əˈrɪdʒɪneɪt / 〔049〕

释 *v.* 起源于；来自

搭 originate from/in 来自；起源于

例 Soon after *Sketches by Boz* appeared, a publishing firm approached Dickens to write a story in monthly installments, as a backdrop for a series of woodcuts by the then-famous artist Robert Seymour, who had **originated** the idea for the story. 在《博兹札记》出版后不久，一家出版公司找到狄更斯，希望他以每月一期的形式写一个故事，作为当时著名艺术家罗伯特·西摩的一系列木刻画的背景，西摩为该故事的创作提出想法。（2017年）

pledge / pledʒ / 〔050〕

释 *n.* 誓言；保证 *v.* 保证（做某事）；承诺支付；抵押

搭 fulfill one's pledge 履行诺言

例 It also **pledged** not to deploy AI whose use would violate international laws or human rights. 它（谷歌）还保证不会部署使用会违反国际法或侵犯人权的人工智能。（2019年）

revenue / ˈrevənjuː / 〔051〕

释 *n.* 税收；收入

例 These unilateral developments differ in their specifics, but they are all designed to tax multinationals on income and **revenue** that countries believe they should have a right to tax, even if international tax rules do not grant them that right. 这些单边发展的具体内容各不相同，但其目的都是对跨国公司的收入征税，这些国家认为它们应该有权征税，即使国际税收规则没有赋予它们这一权利。（2020年）

近 income / ˈɪnkʌm / *n.* 收入

辨 revenue专指国家或企业的收入，税收主要指国家的；income主要指个人收入。

extend / ɪk'stend / 052

释 *v.* 延长；延伸；伸出；持续；包括，涉及

例 They started out as a novelty feature, but as their use has grown, their benefits have **extended** within our technologically advanced world. 起初，它们只是一种新奇的功能，但随着使用范围的不断扩大，它们的好处也在我们这个技术先进的世界里得到了延伸。（2024年）

intend / ɪn'tend / 053

释 *v.* 打算，计划；想要

例 I **intend** to apply for the job vacancy of the manager's secretary. 我打算应聘经理秘书这个空缺职位。

派 intended / ɪn'tendɪd / *adj.* 有意的；故意的 ‖ intention / ɪn'tenʃn / *n.* 意图；目的

item / 'aɪtəm / 054

释 *n.* 项目；条款；一件商品（或物品）；一条（新闻）

例 Americans, she finds, buy roughly 20 billion garments a year—about 64 **items** per person—and no matter how much they give away, this excess leads to waste. 她发现，美国人每年大约购买200亿件服装，每人大约购买64件，无论他们送出多少，这些过剩的服装都会造成浪费。（2013年）

slum / slʌm / 055

释 *n.* 贫民窟，贫民区

例 According to the UN, it has one of the higher densities of **slum** dwellers in the world. 根据联合国的数据，这里是世界上贫民窟居民最密集的地方之一。

suspicious / sə'spɪʃəs / 056

释 *adj.* 怀疑的；可疑的

例 In 2016, researchers developed an algorithm to recognize **suspicious** citation patterns, including groups of authors that disproportionately cite one another and groups of journals that cite each other frequently to increase the impact factors of their publications. 2016年，研究人员开发了一种算法来识别可疑的引用模式，包括不成比例地相互引用的作者群体，以及为提高出版物影响因子而频繁相互引用的期刊群体。（2023年）

protein / 'prəʊtiːn / 057

释 *n.* 蛋白质

例 Fish was a major source of **protein** for the working man in that island. 鱼肉曾是那个岛屿的劳动者的主要蛋白质来源。

stroll / strəʊl / 058

释 *n./v.* 漫步，闲逛

例 He **strolls** in and out as he pleases. 他随心所欲地来回闲逛。

近 wander / 'wɒndə(r) / *v.* 漫步，徘徊 *n.* 漫游

sequence / ˈsiːkwəns /   059

释 n. 先后; 次序; 一系列 v. 按顺序排列; 测定……的序列

搭 a sequence of 一系列

例 The book contains a **sequence** of carefully arranged lessons in computer programming. 此书包括一系列精心编写的有关计算机编程的课程。

applicable / əˈplɪkəbl /   060

释 adj. 可适用的; 合适的; 适当的; 可实施的

例 This section of the law is **applicable** only to corporations. 这部分法律只适用于大公司。

attach / əˈtætʃ /   061

释 v. 把……固定, 把……附在……上; 认为有重要性(或意义、价值、分量等); 重视; 与……有关联

例 According to the standard history of American philosophy, nowhere else in colonial America was "so much importance **attached** to intellectual pursuits." 根据标准的美国哲学史, 在殖民时期的美国, 没有任何其他地方"如此重视智力追求"。(2009年)

inject / ɪnˈdʒekt /   062

释 v. 注射; 增加; 投入(资金)

搭 inject sb. with sth. 给某人注射某物

例 They reimagined the 300-year-old score by **injecting** the latest climate prediction data for each season—provided by Monash University's Climate Change Communication Research Hub. 他们将莫纳什大学气候变化交流研究中心提供的每个季节的最新气候预测数据注入其中, 重新演绎了这首已有300年历史的乐曲。(2022年)

contend / kənˈtend /   063

释 v. (尤指在争论中)声称, 主张; 竞争, 争夺; 处理

例 He **contends** that unemployment is our most serious social evil. 他认为失业是我们社会最为严重的弊病。

近 announce / əˈnaʊns / v. 宣布, 声称 ‖ proclaim / prəˈkleɪm / v. 声明, 宣告

assistant / əˈsɪstənt /   064

释 n. 助理; 助手; 助教 adj. 助理的; 副的

例 In the 2006 film version of *The Devil Wears Prada*, Miranda Priestly, played by Meryl Streep, scolds her unattractive **assistant** for imagining that high fashion doesn't affect her. 在2006年电影版《穿普拉达的女王》中, 由梅丽尔·斯特里普饰演的米兰达·普利斯特里斥责她那不漂亮的助理, 说她以为高级时装不会影响她。(2013年)

prevalent / ˈprevələnt /
　0 6 5
释 *adj.* 流行的，普遍存在的
例 The **prevalent** opinion is in favor of reform. 舆论普遍都支持改革。
近 popular / ˈpɒpjələ(r) / *adj.* 流行的；通俗的

encounter / ɪnˈkaʊntə(r) /
　0 6 6
释 *v.* 遭遇；邂逅 *n.* 邂逅；特殊经历
例 After a bruising **encounter** with Congress, America's Financial Accounting Standards Board (FASB) rushed through rule changes. 在与国会激烈交锋之后，美国财务会计准则委员会（FASB）匆忙通过了规则变更。（2010年）

inhibit / ɪnˈhɪbɪt /
　0 6 7
释 *v.* 阻止，妨碍；抑制
搭 inhibit from 禁止；抑制
例 Childhood viral infections will **inhibit** the development of brain cells. 童年时期感染的病毒将会抑制脑细胞的发育。

existence / ɪgˈzɪstəns /
　0 6 8
释 *n.* 存在；生活方式
例 To be sure, the future is not all rosy. But we are now knowledgeable enough to reduce many of the risks that threatened the **existence** of earlier humans, and to improve the lot of those to come. 可以肯定的是，未来并不都是美好的。但我们现在的知识足以减少威胁早期人类生存的许多风险，并改善未来人类的命运。（2013年）

relative / ˈrelətɪv /
　0 6 9
释 *adj.* 相对的；比较的；关于……的；相关联的 *n.* 亲戚；亲属；同类事物
例 This doesn't, however, make interpretation merely **relative** or even pointless. 然而，这并不会使理解变得相对化，甚至毫无意义。（2015年）

tolerate / ˈtɒləreɪt /
　0 7 0
释 *v.* 容许，允许；忍受；包容；（对药物）有耐受性；能经受（困难条件）
例 "Their capacity for **tolerating** stress may even be greater than men's," she observes, "it's just that they're dealing with so many more things that they become worn out from it more visibly and sooner." "她们承受压力的能力甚至可能比男性更强，"她评论道，"只是她们要处理的事情太多了，以至于她们会更明显、更快地因此而疲惫不堪。"（2008年）

feedback / ˈfiːdbæk /
　0 7 1
释 *n.* 反馈；反馈的意见（或信息）；（电器的）反馈噪音
例 The program keeps track of your progress and provides detailed **feedback** on your performance and improvement. 程序会跟踪你的进度，并就你的表现和进步提供详细反馈。（2014年）

engagement / ɪnˈɡeɪdʒmənt / 072

释 *n.* 约会; 订婚; 约定; 聘用

例 Arron and Cynthia announced their **engagement** in February 2024 after three years of dating. 阿伦和辛西娅在约会三年后于2024年2月宣布订婚。

hobby / ˈhɒbi / 073

释 *n.* 业余爱好

例 Supporting your children's **hobbies** encourages them to pursue their interests. 支持孩子的业余爱好可以鼓励他们追求自己的兴趣。

origin / ˈɒrɪdʒɪn / 074

释 *n.* 起源; 源头; 起因; 身世; 出身

例 It is clear that the countries of **origin** have never been compensated for the stolen artifacts. 显然, 原属国从未因被盗文物而获得赔偿。（2024年）

派 original / əˈrɪdʒənl / *adj.* 原来的; 起初的; 原作的 *n.* 原件, 原作 ‖ originate / əˈrɪdʒɪneɪt / *v.* 起源; 发源; 发端于

constituent / kənˈstɪtʃuənt / 075

释 *adj.* 组成的; 构成的 *n.* 选民, 选举人; 成分; 构成要素

例 It's meant to quantify the consciousness that exists in any system, based on the total information that is brought together by its **constituent** parts. 它的目的是根据系统各组成部分所汇集的全部信息, 对任何系统中存在的意识进行量化。

knock / nɒk / 076

释 *v.* 敲; 击; 碰, 撞; 打掉; 敲动; 打破 *n.* 敲击声; 敲击; 撞击

搭 knock down 打倒; 推倒; 降价 ‖ knock off 停止; 中断; 下班; 减少; 偷

例 England had been **knocked** out of the World Cup. 英格兰队已被淘汰出世界杯赛。

rude / ruːd / 077

释 *adj.* 粗鲁的; 无礼的

例 Too much eye contact is instinctively felt to be **rude**. 过多的眼神接触会让人本能地觉得不礼貌。（2020年）

派 rudeness / ˈruːdnəs / *n.* 粗野; 无礼

circuit / ˈsɜːkɪt / 078

释 *n.* 电路; 线路; 巡回; 巡游

例 The movie was a hit on the festival **circuit** in 2022 and took home an award at the prestigious Berlin International Film Festival. 这部电影在2022年的电影节上大受欢迎, 并在久负盛名的柏林国际电影节上获得了奖项。

magnificent / mæɡˈnɪfɪsnt /

079

释 *adj.* 宏伟的；壮丽的；令人印象深刻的

例 When visiting the Baltimore Museum of Art, I came across a **magnificent** 15th-century Chinese sculpture. It inspired me to learn more about the culture that it represented. 在参观巴尔的摩艺术博物馆时，我看到了一件15世纪的令人印象深刻的中国雕塑。它激发了我更多地了解它所代表的文化的兴趣。（2024年）

attack / əˈtæk /

080

释 *v./n.* 袭击；攻击；抨击

例 And now Climate Change agitators are **attacking** publicly displayed works in European museums. 现在，气候变化煽动者正在抨击欧洲博物馆公开展出的作品。（2024年）

imitation / ˌɪmɪˈteɪʃn /

081

释 *n.* 仿制品；模仿；效仿

例 Social change, after all, is driven by **imitation**, not exclusion. 毕竟，推动社会变革的是模仿，而不是排斥。

rage / reɪdʒ /

082

释 *n.* 暴怒；狂怒；风靡一时；非常流行；肆虐 *v.* 发怒；怒斥；迅速蔓延

例 DNA testing is also the latest **rage** among passionate genealogists—and supports businesses that offer to search for a family's geographic roots. DNA检测最近在热衷于研究家谱的学者中十分流行，并且也为提供家族寻根服务的公司提供了支持。（2009年）

wish / wɪʃ /

083

释 *v.* 希望；想要；祝愿 *n.* 愿望

例 In this as in much else, those who **wish** to influence the future must prepare for it. 在这方面上，和其他许多方面一样，那些希望影响未来的人必须为此做好准备。（2017年）

belt / belt /

084

释 *n.* 腰带；皮带；传送带；地带；地区

例 Hill's pressure later led to the creation of national parks and green **belts**. 希尔的压力后来促成了国家公园和绿化带的建立。（2016年）

tragedy / ˈtrædʒədi /

085

释 *n.* 悲惨的事；不幸；悲剧；悲剧作品

例 To fail to act, and watch this number increase, would be more than a **tragedy**. 如果不采取行动，眼睁睁地看着这个数字增加，那将不仅仅是一场悲剧。

worm / wɜːm /

086

释 *n.* 蠕虫；幼虫；懦夫；可怜虫 *v.* 蠕动，曲折前进

例 A major portion of their diet comes from nuts, berries, **worms**, and even grasses and insects. 它们的主要食物是坚果、浆果、蠕虫，甚至是草和昆虫。

sympathy / 'sɪmpəθi / 087

释 *n.* 同情; 赞同; 支持

搭 feel sympathy for sb. 对某人感到同情 ‖ in sympathy with sb. 赞同或支持某人

例 There is a growing proportion of people that have **sympathy** with the innocent civilians there. 越来越多的人同情那里的无辜平民。

派 sympathize/-ise / 'sɪmpəθaɪz / *v.* 同情; 赞同; 支持

former / 'fɔːmə(r) / 088

释 *adj.* 以前的; 前者的 *n.* 前者

例 In the **former** case the education is incidental; it is natural and important, but it is not the express reason of the association. 在前一种情况下, 教育是附带的, 它自然发生, 也很重要, 但却不是与人交往的确切原因。(2009年)

period / 'pɪəriəd / 089

释 *n.* 一段时间; 阶段, 时期, 时代

例 It was also, and this is unknown even to many people well read about the **period**, a battle between those who made codes and those who broke them. 同时, 这也是一场编码者和破解者之间的战争, 甚至很多熟读当时历史的人都不知道这一点。(2022年)

mere / mɪə(r) / 090

释 *adj.* 仅仅的; 只不过; 单的（用来指某事虽小却有重要影响）

例 We don't consider our customers to be **mere** consumers; we consider them to be our friends. 我们不认为我们的客户仅仅是消费者, 我们把他们当作朋友。

pride / praɪd / 091

释 *n.* 自豪; 尊严; 自尊心; 傲慢; 引以为傲的人（或事物）*v.* 以……而自豪

搭 swallow one's pride 放下自尊; 忍气吞声; 放下架子

例 They needed help, but their **pride** wouldn't let them ask for it. 他们需要帮助, 但他们的自尊心不允许他们开口求助。

judg(e)ment / 'dʒʌdʒmənt / 092

释 *n.* 判断力; 看法; 判决

例 That kind of activity makes it less likely that the court's decisions will be accepted as impartial **judgments**. 这种行为使得法院的判决不太可能被人们视为公正的判决。(2012年)

chemical / 'kemɪkl / 093

释 *adj.* 化学的; 与化学有关的 *n.* 化学制品

例 Van Oosten calls those **chemicals** "sunscreens" because their goal was to prevent further light damage and rebuild worn polymer fibers. 凡·奥斯腾称这些化学制品为"防晒霜", 因为它们的目的是防止进一步的晒伤并修复受损的聚合物纤维。(2022年)

cancel / ˈkænsl /　　094

释 v. 取消; 撤销; 废除

搭 cancel out 抵消

例 He has **canceled** a trip to a climate conference in Dubai. 他取消了前往迪拜参加气候会议的行程。

pick / pɪk /　　095

释 v. 选择; 挑选; 采; 摘 n. 选择; 精华; 精英

搭 pick out 精心挑选 ‖ pick up 拿起; 学会; 接电话; (开车)接人

例 And people are **picking** it for good reason—the city is home to great restaurants, bars, and some of the best entertainment options in the nation. 人们选择这座城市是有理由的——这里有一流的餐厅、酒吧和一些全国最好的娱乐项目。

inherit / ɪnˈherɪt /　　096

释 v. 继承; 接手; 接任; 经遗传而获得(特征、品质等)

例 To a certain extent, our ability to excel in making the connections that drive intelligence is **inherited**. 在某种程度上,我们擅长建立驱动智力的联系的能力是遗传的。(2014年)

chain / tʃeɪn /　　097

释 n. 链子; 锁链; 一系列; 连锁店 v. 用锁链拴住(或束缚、固定)

例 The sporting goods **chain** is opening 13 locations around the metro immediately after the game. 比赛结束后,这家体育用品连锁店将立即在地铁周围开设13家分店。

value / ˈvæljuː /　　098

释 n. 价值; 好处; 价值观; 值 v. 重视; 珍视

例 Our research provides strong support for the **value** of zoos in connecting people with animals and with nature. 我们的研究为动物园在连接人与动物和人与自然方面的价值上提供了强有力的支持。(2022年)

labo(u)r / ˈleɪbə(r) /　　099

释 n. 劳动; 工人; 劳动力 v. 干苦力活; 努力做

例 There are fewer and fewer young people who want to do hard physical **labor**. 想从事重体力劳动的年轻人越来越少了。

sow / səʊ /　　100

释 v. 播种; 灌输; 激起; 散布

例 Artists are trying to **sow** the seeds of compassion and nurture blooms of culture. 艺术家们正在努力播下同情的种子,培育文化的花朵。

☐ ☐ accuse
☐ ☐ achieve
☐ ☐ address
☐ ☐ appetite
☐ ☐ applicable
☐ ☐ assembly
☐ ☐ assimilate
☐ ☐ assistant
☐ ☐ attach
☐ ☐ attack
☐ ☐ attorney
☐ ☐ base
☐ ☐ belt
☐ ☐ cancel
☐ ☐ celebrity
☐ ☐ chain
☐ ☐ chemical
☐ ☐ circuit
☐ ☐ collect
☐ ☐ confront
☐ ☐ constituent
☐ ☐ contend
☐ ☐ damage
☐ ☐ decay
☐ ☐ depict
☐ ☐ despise
☐ ☐ destroy
☐ ☐ diligent
☐ ☐ discourse
☐ ☐ encounter
☐ ☐ engagement

☐ ☐ equip
☐ ☐ existence
☐ ☐ extend
☐ ☐ fabulous
☐ ☐ feedback
☐ ☐ fluctuate
☐ ☐ former
☐ ☐ foundation
☐ ☐ frustrate
☐ ☐ hamper
☐ ☐ hobby
☐ ☐ imitation
☐ ☐ impose
☐ ☐ inherit
☐ ☐ inhibit
☐ ☐ inject
☐ ☐ insure
☐ ☐ intend
☐ ☐ item
☐ ☐ judg(e)ment
☐ ☐ jury
☐ ☐ knock
☐ ☐ labo(u)r
☐ ☐ leak
☐ ☐ leisure
☐ ☐ liberate
☐ ☐ logical
☐ ☐ magnificent
☐ ☐ mere
☐ ☐ mysterious
☐ ☐ norm

☐ ☐ occasion
☐ ☐ origin
☐ ☐ originate
☐ ☐ outrage
☐ ☐ pension
☐ ☐ period
☐ ☐ pick
☐ ☐ pledge
☐ ☐ preserve
☐ ☐ prevalent
☐ ☐ pride
☐ ☐ process
☐ ☐ protein
☐ ☐ rage
☐ ☐ realize/-ise
☐ ☐ refuge
☐ ☐ refuse
☐ ☐ relative
☐ ☐ resemblance
☐ ☐ revenue
☐ ☐ risk
☐ ☐ rude
☐ ☐ scheme
☐ ☐ sequence
☐ ☐ severe
☐ ☐ slum
☐ ☐ sow
☐ ☐ stroll
☐ ☐ subject
☐ ☐ suspicious
☐ ☐ sympathy

☐ ☐ tolerate
☐ ☐ tragedy
☐ ☐ value
☐ ☐ vary
☐ ☐ wish
☐ ☐ withdraw
☐ ☐ worm

音频

Previous Check

- [ ] confident
- [ ] portable
- [ ] occurrence
- [ ] tribute
- [ ] talent
- [ ] expansion
- [ ] consultant
- [ ] research
- [ ] preface
- [ ] academy
- [ ] blaze
- [ ] suffer
- [ ] robust
- [ ] outlook
- [ ] identify
- [ ] reluctant
- [ ] practical
- [ ] detail
- [ ] idle
- [ ] clarity
- [ ] inevitable
- [ ] immigrant
- [ ] jealous
- [ ] thrive
- [ ] prosecute
- [ ] linguistic
- [ ] interrupt
- [ ] usage
- [ ] cable
- [ ] minority
- [ ] strive

- [ ] issue
- [ ] adjust
- [ ] royal
- [ ] suspicion
- [ ] implication
- [ ] dependent
- [ ] sophisticated
- [ ] sculpture
- [ ] ownership
- [ ] captive
- [ ] survival
- [ ] substitute
- [ ] exceed
- [ ] exert
- [ ] serve
- [ ] merit
- [ ] belief
- [ ] instance
- [ ] debt
- [ ] participate
- [ ] strategy
- [ ] retire
- [ ] certificate
- [ ] aspect
- [ ] forge
- [ ] deliberate
- [ ] proceed
- [ ] survive
- [ ] prone
- [ ] strain
- [ ] option

- [ ] classification
- [ ] anticipate
- [ ] normal
- [ ] subsidy
- [ ] service
- [ ] response
- [ ] evaluate
- [ ] illegal
- [ ] protect
- [ ] sight
- [ ] enjoy
- [ ] pronounce
- [ ] epic
- [ ] horizon
- [ ] hug
- [ ] monarch
- [ ] foolish
- [ ] fortunate
- [ ] alive
- [ ] rail
- [ ] monotonous
- [ ] guard
- [ ] knit
- [ ] sweep
- [ ] quantitative
- [ ] belong
- [ ] suggestion
- [ ] mature
- [ ] emergency
- [ ] bill
- [ ] sharp

- [ ] annual
- [ ] amiable
- [ ] export
- [ ] relation
- [ ] track
- [ ] peace
- [ ] colleague

confident / ˈkɒnfɪdənt /　　001

释 *adj.* 确信的，自信的，有信心的

搭 be confident of/in 对……有信心

例 Edward Dolman, Christie's chief executive, says: "I'm pretty **confident** we're not at the bottom." 克里斯蒂跨国公司的首席执行官爱德华·多尔曼说："我坚信我们没有处于谷底。"

portable / ˈpɔːtəbl /　　002

释 *adj.* 便携式的；手提的；轻便的 *n.* 便携机；手提电脑；便携式电视机

例 As a professional stylist, Diva swears by a **portable** steamer that is lightweight and easy to travel with. 作为一名专业造型师，迪瓦信赖那种重量轻、携带方便的便携式蒸汽熨斗。

occurrence / əˈkʌrəns /　　003

释 *n.* 发生；出现；存在；发生的事情；存在的事物

例 As the brain fades, we refer to these **occurrences** as "senior moments." 随着大脑的衰退，我们将这些发生的事情称为"高龄时刻"。（2014年）

tribute / ˈtrɪbjuːt /　　004

释 *n.* 贡品，贡金；致敬，悼念；体现，显示

例 Many conquered nations then had to pay **tribute** to the rulers of ancient Rome. 那时许多被征服的国家必须向古罗马的统治者朝贡。

talent / ˈtælənt /　　005

释 *n.* 人才；天赋；天才

搭 tech talents 科技人才

例 Their work makes a rather startling assertion: the trait we commonly call **talent** is highly overrated. 他们的研究提出了一个相当惊人的论断：我们通常称之为天赋的特质被严重高估了。（2007年）

expansion / ɪkˈspænʃn /　　006

释 *n.* 扩张；膨胀

例 Most leading retailers have already tried e-commerce, with limited success, and **expansion** abroad. 大多数领先的零售商已经尝试过电子商务，但成效有限，此外还尝试向海外扩张。（2010年）

consultant / kənˈsʌltənt /　　007

释 *n.* 顾问；会诊医师；高级顾问医师

例 In one example, an individual—acting as author, editor, and **consultant**—was able to use at least 15 journals as citation providers to articles published by five scientists at three universities. 在一个例子中，一个人既是作者，又是编辑和顾问，他能够使用至少15种期刊作为三所大学的五位科学家所发表文章的引文提供者。（2023年）

research / rɪ'sɜːtʃ /

008

释 *v.* 研究 *n.* 研究；研究员

例 Neither one of them actually participated in any contributions to animal **research** or conservation. 他们两人实际上都没有为任何动物研究或保护做出过贡献。（2022年）

preface / 'prefəs /

009

释 *n.* 序言，引言，前言 *v.* 为……写序；以……为开端

例 He has written a fine **preface** to the play. 他为这个剧本写了一篇精彩的引言。

近 foreword / 'fɔːwɜːd / *n.* 序；前言 ‖ introduction / ˌɪntrə'dʌkʃn / *n.* 前言，引言

academy / ə'kædəmi /

010

释 *n.* 学院；研究院；学会；专科院校

搭 the American Academy of Arts and Sciences 美国人文与科学院

例 In response, the American **Academy** formed the Commission on the Humanities and Social Sciences. 为此，美国科学院成立了人文和社会科学委员会。（2014年）

blaze / bleɪz /

011

释 *n.* 火焰，火光；闪光，光辉 *v.* 燃烧；发光；怒视；大肆宣扬

搭 a blaze of 大量的

例 On New Year's eve, every main street was a **blaze** of light. 新年之夜，每条主干道都灯火辉煌。

suffer / 'sʌfə(r) /

012

释 *v.* 受苦，受难，受折磨；蒙受；变差，变糟

例 But I believe that well-run zoos, and the heroic animals that **suffer** their captivity, do serve a higher purpose. 但我相信，经营良好的动物园和那些在囚禁中受苦的英雄动物，确实有更高的意义。（2022年）

robust / rəʊ'bʌst /

013

释 *adj.* 健壮的；强壮的；坚固的，结实的

例 The only major objection came from Justice Antonin Scalia, who offered an even more **robust** defense of state privileges going back to the Alien and Sedition Acts. 唯一主要的反对意见来自大法官安东宁·斯卡利亚，他为可以追溯到《外侨与叛乱法》的州级特权提供了更为有力的辩护。（2013年）

outlook / 'aʊtlʊk /

014

释 *n.* 前景；观点；景色，景致

例 The town planning commission said that their financial **outlook** for the next year was optimistic. 城镇规划委员会曾表示说，他们来年的财政前景非常乐观。

identify / aɪˈdentɪfaɪ / 　　　015

释 v. 识别；确认；找到，发现；理解；认同

搭 identify sb./sth. with sth. 把某人视为；把某物等同于

例 Vaux says that *Science*'s idea to pass some papers to statisticians "has some merit, but a weakness is that it relies on the board of reviewing editors to **identify** 'the papers that need scrutiny' in the first place". 沃克斯说，《科学》杂志将一些论文交给统计学家的想法"有一定的可取之处，但不足之处在于它得首先依赖审稿编辑委员会来确定'需要审查的论文'"。（2015年）

reluctant / rɪˈlʌktənt / 　　　016

释 adj. 不情愿的，勉强的

搭 reluctant to do sth. 不想做某事

例 He is still **reluctant** to admit he was wrong. 他仍然不愿承认自己有错。

practical / ˈpræktɪkl / 　　　017

释 adj. 实际的；实践性的；客观存在的；适用的 n. 实习课

例 When social scientists do tackle **practical** issues, their scope is often local: Belgium is interested mainly in the effects of poverty on Belgium, for example. 当社会科学家确实在处理实际问题时，他们的研究范围往往在当地：例如，比利时主要关注贫困对比利时的影响。（2013年）

反 impractical / ɪmˈpræktɪkl / adj. 不切实际的；缺乏实际能力的

detail / ˈdiːteɪl / 　　　018

释 n. 详情，全部细节；特遣队 v. 详述；分遣

搭 in detail 详细地

例 The **details** may be unknowable, but the independence of standard-setters, essential to the proper functioning of capital markets, is being compromised. 具体细节可能不得而知，但对资本市场正常运作至关重要的标准制定者的独立性正在受到损害。（2010年）

idle / ˈaɪdl / 　　　019

释 adj. 空闲的；闲置的；无用的，无效的；懈怠的；闲散的 v. 闲荡，无所事事

搭 idle capital 游资；闲置资本

例 It's **idle** to expect help from Paul, for he is just a troublemaker. 指望保罗帮忙是没用的，因为他是个只会捣乱的家伙。

clarity / ˈklærəti / 　　　020

释 n. 清楚，明晰；（思路或轮廓的）清晰；清澈

例 As many people hit middle age, they often start to notice that their memory and mental **clarity** are not what they used to be. 许多人步入中年后，他们往往会开始发现自己的记忆力和头脑清晰度大不如前。（2014年）

inevitable / ɪnˈevɪtəbl /
0221

释 *adj.* 不可避免的; 惯常的

例 Some people seem to think that this result is **inevitable**. 有些人似乎认为这种结果是不可避免的。

近 unavoidable / ˌʌnəˈvɔɪdəbl / *adj.* 不可避免的

immigrant / ˈɪmɪɡrənt /
0222

释 *n.* 移民; 侨民

例 By 1996 foreign-born **immigrants** who had arrived before 1970 had a home ownership rate of 75.6 percent, higher than the 69.8 percent rate among native-born Americans. 截止到1996年, 生于国外且在1970年之前抵达美国的移民的住房拥有率为75.6%, 高于本土出生的美国人的69.8%的比例。(2006年)

jealous / ˈdʒeləs /
0223

释 *adj.* 妒忌的, 羡慕的; 珍惜的, 悉心守护的

例 He was **jealous** of Tom's success. 他妒忌汤姆的成功。

派 jealousy / ˈdʒeləsi / *n.* 妒忌; 猜忌

近 envious / ˈenviəs / *adj.* 羡慕的, 嫉妒的

thrive / θraɪv /
0224

释 *v.* 兴旺发达; 欣欣向荣

例 Over the past century, all kinds of unfairness and discrimination have been condemned or made illegal. But one insidious form continues to **thrive**: alphabetism. 在过去的一个世纪里, 各种各样的不公和歧视遭到了谴责或被定为非法。但是有一种隐蔽的不公平形式仍在盛行, 那就是按字母表顺序排名。

近 prosper / ˈprɒspə(r) / *v.* 繁荣 ‖ flourish / ˈflʌrɪʃ / *v.* 繁荣

prosecute / ˈprɒsɪkjuːt /
0225

释 *v.* 起诉; 告发, 检举

例 The study found that, among **prosecuted** firms, those with the most comprehensive CSR programmes tended to get more lenient penalties. 研究发现, 在被起诉的企业中, 那些实施了最全面的企业社会责任计划的企业受到的处罚往往会更宽松。(2016年)

linguistic / lɪŋˈɡwɪstɪk /
0226

释 *adj.* 语言的; 语言学的

例 The ability to write is a supreme test of **linguistic** competence. 写作能力是对语言能力的最高形式的测试。

interrupt / ˌɪntəˈrʌpt /
0227

释 *v.* 插嘴; 打扰; 打岔; 使暂停; 使中断; 遮挡; 阻断

例 At stroke onset, a clot or broken blood vessel **interrupts** blood flow to the brain. 中风发病时, 血栓或破裂的血管会阻断血液流向大脑。

usage / ˈjuːsɪdʒ / 028

释 *n.* 使用；（词的）意义，用法

例 Complex international, economic, technological and cultural changes could start to diminish the leading position of English as the language of the world market, and UK interests which enjoy advantage from the breadth of English **usage** would consequently face new pressures. 复杂的国际、经济、技术和文化变化可能会开始削弱英语作为世界市场语言的领先地位，因此，因英语使用的广泛性而享有优势的英国利益集团将面临新的压力。（2017年）

cable / ˈkeɪbl / 029

释 *n.* 缆绳；电缆；（海底）电报；有线电视 *v.* 发电报

例 From the early days of broadband, advocates for consumers and web-based companies worried that the **cable** and phone companies selling broadband connections had the power and incentive to favor affiliated websites over their rivals'. 在宽带发展初期，消费者和网络公司的拥护者就担心，销售宽带连接的有线电视和电话公司有能力和动机偏袒其附属网站而不是竞争对手的网站。（2021年）

minority / maɪˈnɒrəti / 030

释 *n.* 少数；少数派；少数人；少数民族

搭 in a/the minority 占少数

例 In his book *The Tipping Point*, Malcolm Gladwell argues that "social epidemics" are driven in large part by the actions of a tiny **minority** of special individuals, often called influentials, who are unusually informed, persuasive, or well connected. 马尔科姆·格拉德威尔在其著作《引爆点》中指出，"社会流行病"在很大程度上是由极少数特殊个体的行为所驱动的，这些个体通常被称为"有影响力的人"，他们见多识广、说服力强或人脉广。（2010年）

strive / straɪv / 031

释 *v.* 努力，奋斗

例 The most successful monarchies **strive** to abandon or hide their old aristocratic ways. 最成功的君主国都在努力摒弃或掩盖其旧有的贵族作风。（2015年）

近 endeavor / ɪnˈdevə(r) / *v.* 努力，尽力 ‖ struggle / ˈstrʌgl / *v./n.* 奋斗，努力

issue / ˈɪʃuː / 032

释 *v.* 公布，发表；发行；流出 *n.* 问题；发行（物）；报刊期号

搭 at issue 讨论或争议中的（问题、争论点等）

例 Short-term rentals themselves are not the crux of the **issue**, said Keren Horn, an expert on affordable housing policy. 经济适用房政策专家克伦·霍恩说，短期租赁本身并不是问题的关键。（2023年）

近 problem / ˈprɒbləm / *n.* 问题 ‖ publicize / ˈpʌblɪsaɪz / *v.* 公布

adjust / ə'dʒʌst /

033

释 *v.* 改变（行为或观点）以适应；调节；整理（衣服）；校正，校准（机器）

例 Fundamentally, the USPS is in a historic squeeze between technological change that has permanently decreased demand for its bread-and-butter product, first-class mail, and a regulatory structure that denies management the flexibility to **adjust** its operations to the new reality. 从根本上说，美国邮政正处于一个历史性挤压中，一方面，技术变革永久性地减少了对其看家产品（即一类邮件）的需求，另一方面，监管结构剥夺了管理层根据新的现状调整运营的灵活性。（2018年）

royal / 'rɔɪəl /

034

释 *adj.* 皇家的；王室的；高贵的

例 While polls show Britons rate "the countryside" alongside the **royal** family, Shakespeare and the National Health Service (NHS) as what makes them proudest of their country, this has limited political support. 尽管民意调查显示，英国人将"乡村"与王室、莎士比亚和英国国家医疗服务体系（NHS）并列视为他们对自己国家最感到自豪的事情，但这一观点在政治上得到的支持十分有限。（2016年）

派 royalty / 'rɔɪəlti / *n.* 版税；王室成员

suspicion / sə'spɪʃn /

035

释 *n.* 怀疑，猜疑；少量，些许

例 **Suspicions** were first aroused when questions from local residents remained unanswered. 当地居民的疑问没有得到解答，人们就开始起疑心了。

派 suspicious / sə'spɪʃəs / *adj.* 多疑的；可疑的

近 distrust / dɪs'trʌst / *n.* 不信任，怀疑 ‖ doubt / daʊt / *n.* 怀疑，不确定

implication / ˌɪmplɪ'keɪʃn /

036

释 *n.* 含意，暗指；可能的影响（或结果）

搭 by implication 言下之意；暗示地

例 The **implication** is that Millennials prefer news from the White House to be filtered through other sources, not a president's social media platform. 这意味着千禧一代更喜欢通过其他渠道，而不是总统的社交媒体平台来筛选来自白宫的新闻。（2018年）

dependent / dɪ'pendənt /

037

释 *adj.* 依赖的，依靠的；受……的影响 *n.* （=dependant）家眷；受抚养者；随从，侍从

例 While few craftsmen or farmers, let alone **dependents** and servants, left literary compositions to be analyzed, it is obvious that their views were less fully intellectualized. 虽然很少有工匠或农场主能留下可供分析的文学作品，更不用说随从和仆人了，但他们的观点显然没有那么理性。（2009年）

038
sophisticated / səˈfɪstɪkeɪtɪd /

释 *adj.* 巧妙的，精心的；先进的，尖端的；复杂的

例 AI "vision" today is not nearly as **sophisticated** as that of humans. 如今，人工智能的"视觉"远没有人类那么复杂。（2019年）

近 complicated / ˈkɒmplɪkeɪtɪd / *adj.* 复杂的

039
sculpture / ˈskʌlptʃə(r) /

释 *n.* 雕像，雕塑品；雕刻术

例 She is proud that several **sculptures** have even gone on display again, albeit sometimes beneath protective cases. 令她自豪的是，有几件雕塑作品甚至再次展出，尽管有时是在保护箱里。（2022年）

近 carving / ˈkɑːvɪŋ / *n.* 雕刻；雕刻品 ‖ statuette / ˌstætʃuˈet / *n.* 小雕像

040
ownership / ˈəʊnəʃɪp /

释 *n.* 所有权；产权

搭 ownership of property 财产所有权

例 The other reason why costs are so high is the restrictive guild-like **ownership** structure of the business. 费用如此之高的另一个原因是限制性的行会式企业所有权结构。（2014年）

041
captive / ˈkæptɪv /

释 *adj.* 被监禁的；被圈养的；受控制的 *n.* 战俘，俘虏；囚徒

搭 be captive to sth. 受控于……

例 Our committee should not be **captive** to the mistakes of the past. 委员会不应该受制于过去的错误。

042
survival / səˈvaɪvl /

释 *n.* 幸存；生存

例 He argued that human evolution was characterized by a struggle he called the "**survival** of the fittest," in which weaker races and societies must eventually be replaced by stronger, more advanced races and societies. 他认为，人类进化的特点是一场他称之为"适者生存"的斗争，在这场斗争中，较弱的种族和社会最终一定会被更强大、更先进的种族和社会所取代。（2009年）

043
substitute / ˈsʌbstɪtjuːt /

释 *n.* 代替者；代替物；替补运动员 *v.* 代替，取代

例 If you cannot go yourself, try to find someone to **substitute** for you. 你要是自己不能去，可以找个人来代替你去。

044
exceed / ɪkˈsiːd /

释 *v.* 超过，胜过

例 The price of the new product will not **exceed** $100. 这款新产品的价格不会超过100美元。

exert / ɪgˈzɜːt / 　045

释 *v.* 施加（压力等）；竭力，努力

搭 exert... on... 对……施加……‖ exert oneself to do sth. 竭力做某事

例 And interest groups ranging from postal unions to greeting-card makers **exert** self-interested pressure on the USPS's ultimate overseer—Congress—insisting that whatever else happens to the Postal Service, aspects of the status quo they depend on get protected. 从邮政工会到贺卡制造商，各种利益集团对美国邮政的最终监管者——国会——施加利己的压力，要求无论邮政局发生什么变化，他们所依赖的现状的各个方面都要得到保护。（2018年）

派 exertion / ɪgˈzɜːʃn / *n.* 尽力；行使

serve / sɜːv / 　046

释 *v.* 接待；服务；能满足……的需要；提供；供应；可用作；任期为；担任（职务）；服（刑）；发（球）*n.* 发球

例 They **serve** no purpose in a museum in the United States or elsewhere except as curious objects. 在美国或其他地方的博物馆中，它们除了作为奇特的物品外，没有任何用途。（2024年）

merit / ˈmerɪt / 　047

释 *n.* 优点；价值；功绩；长处；美德；值得赞扬（或奖励、钦佩）的特点 *v.* 应得；值得

例 In seminars, my classmates and I listened to old and new compositions, followed by sometimes raucous discussions about their **merits**. 在研讨会上，我和同学们一起聆听新老作品，有时还会就作品的优点展开热烈讨论。

belief / bɪˈliːf / 　048

释 *n.* 信仰；信念；相信；看法

例 As a result, these structures became important centres for cultural exchange and interaction, with travellers sharing their cultures, ideas and **beliefs**, as well as taking knowledge with them, greatly influencing the development of several civilisations. 因此，这些建筑成了文化交流和互动的重要中心，旅行者们在这里分享他们的文化、思想和信仰，并带走知识，这极大地影响了多个文明的发展。（2023年）

instance / ˈɪnstəns / 　049

释 *n.* 例子；实例；事例 *v.* 举……为例

例 Can you quote me an **instance**? 你能给我举例说明一下吗？

debt / det / 　050

释 *n.* 债务；负债情况；人情债

例 Students who do not need the extra training could cut their **debt** mountain by a third. 不需要额外培训的学生可以减少三分之一的债务。（2014年）

Writing Models ◉

participate

strategy

retire

certificate

aspect

forge

deliberate

proceed

survive

prone

strain

option

participate / pɑːˈtɪsɪpeɪt /
释 *v.* 参加，参与；分享
搭 participate in 参加
例 In contrast, only five of the 30 children paired with the "unreliable" tester **participated** in a follow-up activity. 相比之下，与"不可靠"测试者配对的30名儿童中，只有5人参加了后续活动。（2018年）

strategy / ˈstrætədʒi /
释 *n.* 战略，策略
例 Merrill Lynch got legal protection for an asset allocation **strategy**. 美林证券的资产配置策略获得了法律保护。（2010年）
近 tactic / ˈtæktɪk / *n.* 策略，战略
辨 strategy和tactic都有"策略"的意思。strategy指全局性的前线战略部署，也可指为达到某种目的而采取的策略；tactic指在战场或军事行动中指导如何用兵的具体战术，也指为完成某计划而采取的策略或手段。

retire / rɪˈtaɪə(r) /
释 *v.* 退休；（因伤）退出（比赛等）；退役；（令）退职；撤离，撤退
例 It's not just a financial decision, but an emotional one. Many people believe they can't **retire**. 这不仅是一个财务决定，也是一个情感决定。很多人认为他们不能退休。

certificate
释 / səˈtɪfɪkət / *n.* 证明；证明书；合格证书；文凭 / səˈtɪfɪkeɪt / *v.* 发给结业证书
例 If you were to examine the birth **certificates** of every soccer player in 2006's World Cup tournament, you would most likely find a noteworthy quirk: elite soccer players are more likely to have been born in the earlier months of the year than in the later months. 如果你要检查2006年世界杯足球赛中每个足球运动员的出生证明，你很可能会发现一个值得注意的怪现象：精英足球运动员更有可能出生在一年中较早的月份，而不是较晚的月份。（2007年）

aspect / ˈæspekt /
释 *n.* 方面；外表
搭 in all aspects 在所有方面；在各个方面
例 First, scientific work tends to focus on some **aspect** of prevailing knowledge that is viewed as incomplete or incorrect. 首先，科学工作倾向于关注主流知识中被视为不完整或不正确的某些方面。（2012年）

forge / fɔːdʒ /
释 *v.* 努力地缔造，建立；伪造；锻造（金属）
搭 forge a treaty 缔结条约
例 They agreed to **forge** closer economic ties. 他们同意建立更加紧密的经济联系。

deliberate 057

释 / dɪˈlɪbərət / *adj.* 故意的; 深思熟虑的 / dɪˈlɪbəreɪt / *v.* 仔细考虑, 深思熟虑

例 There is a marked difference between the education which every one gets from living with others and the **deliberate** educating of the young. 每个人从与他人相处中获得的教育与刻意对年轻人进行的教育有着明显的不同。(2009年)

派 deliberation / dɪˌlɪbəˈreɪʃn / *n.* 细想; 审慎

proceed / prəˈsiːd / 058

释 *v.* 继续进行

搭 proceed to do sth. (做完某事之后)接着(做另一事) ‖ proceed with 继续进行

例 In court, government lawyers suggested none of those moves was sufficient to allow the takeover to **proceed**. 在法庭上, 政府律师表示, 这些举措都不足以让收购继续进行。

survive / səˈvaɪv / 059

释 *v.* 存活; 挺过; 幸存; 比⋯⋯活得长

例 During their six- to twelve-week voyage, they **survived** on barely enough food allotted to them. 在长达六到十二周的航行中, 他们仅靠勉强足够的食物配给生存。(2015年)

prone / prəʊn / 060

释 *adj.* 易于⋯⋯的, 有⋯⋯倾向的; 俯卧的

搭 be prone to 易于⋯⋯的, 有⋯⋯倾向的

例 She is **prone** to lose her temper when people disagree with her. 别人一不同意她的意见, 她就发脾气。

近 apt / æpt / *adj.* 有⋯⋯倾向的; 恰当的 ‖ liable / ˈlaɪəbl / *adj.* 有⋯⋯倾向的; 有责任的

strain / streɪn / 061

释 *n.* 重负, 压力; 扭伤 *v.* 扭伤; 使受到压力

例 Most women today are coping with a lot of obligations, with few breaks, and feeling the **strain**. 如今, 大多数女性都背负着很多责任, 几乎没有休息时间, 并且感觉有压力。

近 stress / stres / *n.* 压力; 紧张

option / ˈɒpʃn / 062

释 *n.* 供选择的东西; 选择权; 购买权; 选修课

例 Another **option**: Climb high and look for signs of human habitation. 另一种选择: 爬到高处, 寻找人类居住的痕迹。(2019年)

派 optional / ˈɒpʃənl / *adj.* 任选的

近 alternative / ɔːlˈtɜːnətɪv / *n.* 可供选择的事物 *adj.* 可供选择的 ‖ choice / tʃɔɪs / *n.* 选择

classification / ˌklæsɪfɪˈkeɪʃn / 　　063

释 *n.* 分类; 类别; 编目

例 He is quite interested in the **classification** of plants. 他对植物分类十分感兴趣。

anticipate / ænˈtɪsɪpeɪt / 　　064

释 *v.* 预期; 预料; 预计; 先于……行动

例 We need someone who can **anticipate** and respond to changes in the fashion industry. 我们需要一个能够预测和应对时尚行业变化的人。

normal / ˈnɔːml / 　　065

释 *adj.* 正常的, 平常的; 身心正常的 *n.* 常态; 通常标准

例 In today's world, it has become **normal** that well-paid executives should not be accountable for what happens in the organizations that they run. 在当今世界, 高薪聘请的高管不应对其所管理的组织发生的一切负责已成为一种常态。(2015年)

近 ordinary / ˈɔːdnri / *adj.* 普通的; 平常的 ‖ regular / ˈreɡjələ(r) / *adj.* 定期的; 有规律的

辨 ordinary强调一般性和普通性, 不含突出的意味; regular指有规律或定期的; normal指不超过某种限度、符合某种标准或常规的。

subsidy / ˈsʌbsədi / 　　066

释 *n.* 补贴, 津贴

例 Anyway, the townsfolk can't understand why the Royal Shakespeare Company needs a **subsidy**. 总之, 乡亲们不明白为什么皇家莎士比亚剧团需要补贴。(2006年)

service / ˈsɜːvɪs / 　　067

释 *n.* 服务; 使用; 检修; 发球 *v.* 维修; 提供服务; 保养; 检修

例 "A lot of workers are **servicing** the tourist industry, and the tourism industry is **serviced** by those people coming in short term," Castle said, "and so it's a cyclical effect." 卡塞尔说: "很多工人是为旅游业服务的, 而旅游业又是由这些短期来访者服务的, 因此这是一种周期性效应。"(2023年)

response / rɪˈspɒns / 　　068

释 *n.* 反应; 响应; 回答, 答复

搭 in response to 响应; 回答

例 One possible **response** is for classical performers to program attractive new music that is not yet available on record. 一种可能的回应是, 古典表演者可以录制尚未录制的、有吸引力的新音乐。(2011年)

派 responsible / rɪˈspɒnsəbl / *adj.* 负责的

evaluate / ɪˈvæljueɪt / 069

释 v. 评价; 评估
例 In a statement provided by email, the spokeswoman for the company said that Amazon is constantly **evaluating** emerging technologies. 该公司发言人在通过电子邮件提供的一份声明中说, 亚马逊正在不断评估新兴技术。

illegal / ɪˈliːgl / 070

释 adj. 不合法的; 非法的; 违法的 n. 非法移民; 非法劳工
例 In this state, it is **illegal** for anyone under the age of 21 to drink alcohol. 在这个州, 任何未满21岁的人饮酒都是违法的。

protect / prəˈtekt / 071

释 v. 保护; 防护
例 Lucky for us, we also have a sixth sense for dishonesty that may **protect** us. 幸运的是, 我们对不诚实也有第六感, 这可能会保护我们。(2018年)
派 protection / prəˈtekʃn / n. 保护; 防护 ‖ protective / prəˈtektɪv / adj. 保护的; 防护的; 呵护的

sight / saɪt / 072

释 n. 视力; 视觉; 看见 v. 突然看见
搭 at the sight of 一看见……就 ‖ in sight 在视野内, 可以看见
例 They sometimes travel more than sixty miles to find food or water, and are very good at working out where other elephants are—even when they are out of **sight**. 它们有时要走60多英里才能找到食物或水, 而且非常善于找出其他大象的位置——即使它们不在视线范围内。(2024年)

enjoy / ɪnˈdʒɔɪ / 073

释 v. 享受……的乐趣; 欣赏; 喜爱
搭 enjoy oneself 玩得痛快; 得到乐趣
例 Even Mark Twain, a man who **enjoyed** a hearty laugh, said that when it came to photographic portraits there could be "nothing more damning than a silly, foolish smile fixed forever". 就连喜欢开怀大笑的马克·吐温也说过, 在摄影肖像中, "没有什么比永远摆着一个愚蠢的微笑更可恶的了"。(2021年)
派 enjoyable / ɪnˈdʒɔɪəbl / adj. 令人愉快的 ‖ enjoyment / ɪnˈdʒɔɪmənt / n. 愉快; 乐趣

pronounce / prəˈnaʊns / 074

释 v. 发音; 正式宣布
例 The kid learned new words slowly and struggled to **pronounce** them correctly, mixing up similar-sounding words. 这个孩子学习新单词的速度很慢, 而且很难正确发音, 还会混淆发音相似的单词。
派 pronunciation / prəˌnʌnsiˈeɪʃn / n. 发音; 读音

Writing Models ◎

epic

horizon

hug

monarch

foolish

fortunate

alive

rail

monotonous

guard

knit

sweep

quantitative

epic / ˈepɪk / 075
释 *n.* 叙事诗; 史诗; 史诗般的电影（或书籍）*adj.* 史诗般的; 宏大的
例 An **epic** novel follows three generations of a family in southern India from 1900 through 1977. 这部史诗小说讲述了印度南部一个家庭从1900年到1977年间的三代人的故事。

horizon / həˈraɪzn / 076
释 *n.* 地平线; 范围; 眼界; 见识
搭 on the horizon 很可能即将发生; 已露端倪
例 In addition, the study finds that TikTok functions to expand its users' musical **horizons**. 此外, 该研究还发现, TikTok的功能是开阔用户的音乐眼界。
派 horizontal / ˌhɒrɪˈzɒntl / *adj.* 水平的; 与地面平行的

hug / hʌg / 077
释 *v.* 拥抱; 抱紧 *n.* 拥抱
例 **Hugging** "is a marker of intimacy and helps generate the feeling that others are there to help in the face of difficulty". 拥抱 "是亲密的标志, 有助于产生在困难面前别人会伸出援手的感觉"。（2017年）
近 embrace / ɪmˈbreɪs / *v.* 拥抱; 欣然接受

monarch / ˈmɒnək / 078
释 *n.* 君主; 帝王
例 "The ancient Hawaiians were astronomers," wrote Queen Liliuokalani, Hawaii's last reigning **monarch**, in 1897. "古代夏威夷人都是天文学家", 1897年, 夏威夷最后一位执政君主利留卡拉尼女王写道。（2017年）
派 monarchy / ˈmɒnəki / *n.* 君主制; 君主国

foolish / ˈfuːlɪʃ / 079
释 *adj.* 愚蠢的; 傻的
例 It would be **foolish** to raise hopes unnecessarily. 无缘无故地寄予希望是愚蠢的。
近 silly / ˈsɪli / *adj.* 愚蠢的; 荒唐的 ‖ stupid / ˈstjuːpɪd / *adj.* 笨的

fortunate / ˈfɔːtʃənət / 080
释 *adj.* 幸运的; 吉利的
例 Hoffman's modern counterparts are not so **fortunate**. 霍夫曼的现代同行就没那么幸运了。

alive / əˈlaɪv / 081
释 *adj.* 活着的; 有活力的
搭 come alive 生动起来; 有精神起来
例 If the trade unionist Jimmy Hoffa were **alive** today, he would probably represent civil servants. 如果工会成员吉米·霍法今天还活着, 他可能会代表公务员。（2012年）

rail / reɪl / 082

释 *n.* 栏杆; 铁轨 *v.* 怒斥, 责骂

搭 get back on the rails 恢复常轨; 东山再起 ‖ go off the rails 失去控制; 无法正常运行

例 However, over the past 12 months, those commuters have also experienced some of the worst **rail** strikes in years. 然而, 在过去的12个月里, 这些通勤者也经历了多年来最严重的铁路罢工。（2021年）

monotonous / məˈnɒtənəs / 083

释 *adj.* 单调乏味的

例 Critics and audiences felt cheated by the title and grew bored with the repetitive and **monotonous** film. 影评人和观众都觉得被片名欺骗了, 厌倦了这部重复而单调的电影。

guard / ɡɑːd / 084

释 *n.* 卫兵; 警卫员; 看守 *v.* 警卫; 守卫; 保卫; 保护; 看守

搭 be on one's guard 警惕; 提防; 警戒

例 Personal grievance procedures were designed to **guard** the jobs of ordinary workers from "unjustified dismissals". 个人申诉程序旨在保护普通工人的工作, 使其免遭 "不合理解雇"。（2022年）

派 guardian / ˈɡɑːdiən / *n.* 监护人 ‖ guardianship / ˈɡɑːdiənʃɪp / *n.* 监护权

knit / nɪt / 085

释 *v.* 编织;（使）紧密结合 *n.* 针织衫; 编织的衣服

例 For H&M to offer a $5.95 **knit** miniskirt in all its 2,300-plus stores around the world, it must rely on low-wage overseas labor, order in volumes that strain natural resources, and use massive amounts of harmful chemicals. H&M要想在全球2 300多家门店销售5.95美元的针织迷你裙, 就必须依靠廉价的海外劳动力, 必须要大量订购, 而这将使自然资源紧张, 并使用大量有害的化学物质。（2013年）

sweep / swiːp / 086

释 *v.* 打扫; 清扫; 猛烈吹过; 掠过; 席卷; 扫视 *n.* 清扫; 挥动; 搜查

搭 sweep out 打扫干净

例 Lower-cost laptops have **swept** into American schools and some homes. 售价低廉的笔记本电脑已经席卷了美国的学校和一些家庭。

quantitative / ˈkwɒntɪtətɪv / 087

释 *adj.* 数量的; 量化的; 定量性的

例 Unfortunately, the long-term costs of using simple **quantitative** metrics to assess researcher merit are likely to be quite great. 不幸的是, 使用简单的定量指标来评估研究人员价值的长期成本可能相当高。（2019年）

Writing Models

belong

suggestion

mature

emergency

bill

sharp

annual

amiable

export

relation

track

peace

colleague

belong / bɪˈlɒŋ /   088

释 *v.* 应在（某处）；适应；合得来

搭 belong to 属于某人；是（俱乐部、组织等）的成员；是（某族类或纲目）的一部分；属于

例 The administration in both cases says immigration enforcement authority **belongs** with the federal government, not the states. 在这两个案例中，政府都表示移民执法权属于联邦政府，而非各州。

suggestion / səˈdʒestʃən /   089

释 *n.* 建议；提议；暗示；迹象

例 Those **suggestions** have grown ever the more imperative now that the recent strikes affect a sizable chunk of the local workforce. 鉴于最近的罢工影响了相当一部分当地劳动力，这些建议变得更加迫切。

mature / məˈtʃʊə(r) /   090

释 *adj.* 成熟的；发育完全的 *v.* 成熟；长成

例 But it takes collective scrutiny and acceptance to transform a discovery claim into a **mature** discovery. 但是，要将一项发现声明转变为一项成熟的发现，需要集体的审查和接受。（2012年）

emergency / ɪˈmɜːdʒənsi /   091

释 *n.* 突发事件；紧急情况

例 The brain finds it best to keep smell receptors available for unfamiliar and **emergency** signals such as the smell of smoke, which might indicate the danger of fire. 大脑发现，最好让嗅觉感受器能随时用于接收不熟悉的、紧急事件的信号，比如烟味，因为这可能预示着有发生火灾的危险。（2005年）

bill / bɪl /   092

释 *n.* 账单；议案，法案 *v.* 给（某人）开账单

搭 fill/fit the bill 符合要求；合格

例 Energy companies can use AI to help customers reduce their electricity **bills**, saving them money while helping the environment. 能源公司可以利用人工智能帮助客户减少电费账单，在为客户省钱的同时也为环境做出贡献。（2021年）

sharp / ʃɑːp /   093

释 *adj.* 锋利的；尖锐的；剧烈的，猛烈的；急剧的；骤然的；敏锐的；锐利的；鲜明的 *adv.*（用于表时间的词语后，表示准时）整

例 The **sharp** hit to growth predicted around the world and in the UK could lead to a decline in the everyday services we depend on for our well-being and for growth. 全球和英国的经济增长预计将遭到重创，这可能导致我们维持幸福感和经济增长所依赖的日常服务水平下降。（2017年）

派 sharply / ˈʃɑːpli / *adv.* 尖刻地；急剧地 ‖ sharpen / ˈʃɑːpən / *v.* 使尖锐；使明朗

annual / ˈænjuəl /   094

释 *adj.* 一年一次的；年度的

例 The **annual** base salary in the district starts at roughly $50,000. 该地区的基本年薪大约是5万美元起。

amiable / ˈeɪmiəbl /   095

释 *adj.* 亲切友好的；和蔼可亲的

例 We have a very **amiable** companionship. 我们之间是一种非常亲切友好的伙伴关系。

近 affable / ˈæfəbl / *adj.* 和蔼可亲的

export / ˈekspɔːt /   096

释 / ɪkˈspɔːt / *v.* 出口；输出 ˈekspɔːt / *n.* 出口；输出；出口产品

例 This will be the first time Galileo satellites, which are used for both civilian and military purposes, have been **exported** outside of European territory. 这将是用于民用目的和军事目的的伽利略卫星首次出口到欧洲领土以外。

反 import / ˈɪmpɔːt / *n.* 进口；输入；引进 / ɪmˈpɔːt / *v.* 进口；引进

relation / rɪˈleɪʃn /   097

释 *n.* 关系；联系；关联；亲属

例 Composure is a state of mind made possible by the structuring of one's **relation** to one's environment. 沉着是一种心态，当一个人与其所处的环境建立起联系时，才能拥有。（2013年）

track / træk /   098

释 *n.* 轨道；（移动的）路线，方向；跑道；音轨，声道；足迹，踪迹；滑轨，滑道；车辙；小径 *v.* 追踪；跟踪

搭 back on track 恢复正常 ‖ keep/lose track of 了解/不了解……的动态；与……保持/失去联系

例 Trail blazes, tire **tracks**, and other features can lead you to civilization. 树上用来指路的刻痕、车辙和其他特征可以引导你到达文明社会。（2019年）

peace / piːs /   099

释 *n.* 和平；平静；宁静

搭 at peace 处于平静、安宁的状态

例 One of these urges has to do with creating a state of **peace** in the midst of turbulence, a "still point of the turning world," to borrow a phrase from T. S. Eliot. 其中一种冲动与在动荡中创造一种和平状态有关，借用 T. S. 艾略特的话来说，这是"转动世界的静止点"。（2013年）

colleague / ˈkɒliːg /   100

释 *n.* 同事

例 So van Oosten and her **colleagues** worked to preserve Gilardi's sculptures. 因此，凡·奥斯腾和她的同事们致力于保护吉拉尔迪的雕塑。（2022年）

☐ ☐ academy
☐ ☐ adjust
☐ ☐ alive
☐ ☐ amiable
☐ ☐ annual
☐ ☐ anticipate
☐ ☐ aspect
☐ ☐ belief
☐ ☐ belong
☐ ☐ bill
☐ ☐ blaze
☐ ☐ cable
☐ ☐ captive
☐ ☐ certificate
☐ ☐ clarity
☐ ☐ classification
☐ ☐ colleague
☐ ☐ confident
☐ ☐ consultant
☐ ☐ debt
☐ ☐ deliberate
☐ ☐ dependent
☐ ☐ detail
☐ ☐ emergency
☐ ☐ enjoy
☐ ☐ epic
☐ ☐ evaluate
☐ ☐ exceed
☐ ☐ exert
☐ ☐ expansion
☐ ☐ export

☐ ☐ foolish
☐ ☐ forge
☐ ☐ fortunate
☐ ☐ guard
☐ ☐ horizon
☐ ☐ hug
☐ ☐ identify
☐ ☐ idle
☐ ☐ illegal
☐ ☐ immigrant
☐ ☐ implication
☐ ☐ inevitable
☐ ☐ instance
☐ ☐ interrupt
☐ ☐ issue
☐ ☐ jealous
☐ ☐ knit
☐ ☐ linguistic
☐ ☐ mature
☐ ☐ merit
☐ ☐ minority
☐ ☐ monarch
☐ ☐ monotonous
☐ ☐ normal
☐ ☐ occurrence
☐ ☐ option
☐ ☐ outlook
☐ ☐ ownership
☐ ☐ participate
☐ ☐ peace
☐ ☐ portable

☐ ☐ practical
☐ ☐ preface
☐ ☐ proceed
☐ ☐ prone
☐ ☐ pronounce
☐ ☐ prosecute
☐ ☐ protect
☐ ☐ quantitative
☐ ☐ rail
☐ ☐ relation
☐ ☐ reluctant
☐ ☐ research
☐ ☐ response
☐ ☐ retire
☐ ☐ robust
☐ ☐ royal
☐ ☐ sculpture
☐ ☐ serve
☐ ☐ service
☐ ☐ sharp
☐ ☐ sight
☐ ☐ sophisticated
☐ ☐ strain
☐ ☐ strategy
☐ ☐ strive
☐ ☐ subsidy
☐ ☐ substitute
☐ ☐ suffer
☐ ☐ suggestion
☐ ☐ survival
☐ ☐ survive

☐ ☐ suspicion
☐ ☐ sweep
☐ ☐ talent
☐ ☐ thrive
☐ ☐ track
☐ ☐ tribute
☐ ☐ usage

音频

- exemplify
- propose
- economic
- spiritual
- application
- imperative
- generous
- conduct
- submit
- moral
- scold
- dilemma
- command
- condemn
- poke
- district
- desire
- visible
- glow
- nasty
- gross
- proposal
- dispute
- collective
- trivial
- prior
- temper
- capacity
- divert
- editorial
- swamp

- prefer
- expand
- threat
- solve
- numerous
- entertain
- critical
- effective
- orient
- mystery
- caution
- section
- review
- calculate
- fulfil(l)
- accelerate
- inhabitant
- association
- recall
- powerful
- retail
- principal
- distinction
- formal
- appropriate
- current
- startle
- enhance
- shelter
- exist
- profitable

- beam
- supervise
- extension
- comply
- genuine
- suspend
- authority
- poverty
- toxic
- sheet
- regardless
- journal
- hijack
- objective
- corrupt
- tough
- vain
- appointment
- copy
- jog
- efficiency
- emphasize
- rush
- rest
- empirical
- raise
- mask
- admit
- shake
- secondary
- witness

- possession
- anxious
- lip
- drop
- bond
- introduce
- headline

Writing Models ◎

exemplify

propose

economic

spiritual

application

imperative

generous

conduct

submit

moral

scold

dilemma

exemplify / ɪɡˈzemplɪfaɪ / 001

释 *v.* 举例证明；是……的榜样
例 All these recipes **exemplify** my cooking: healthy, delicious and quick. 所有这些食谱是我的饭菜既健康、美味又快捷的例证。

propose / prəˈpəʊz / 002

释 *v.* 提议，建议；求婚
搭 propose doing sth. 提议做某事 ‖ propose a toast 敬酒；举杯
例 This year, it was **proposed** that the system be changed: Horizon 2020, a new program to be enacted in 2014, would not have such a category. 今年，有人建议改变这一制度：将于2014年颁布的新计划"地平线2020"将不设这一类别。（2013年）

economic / ˌiːkəˈnɒmɪk / 003

释 *adj.* 经济的；盈利的
例 In response to these many unilateral measures, the Organization for **Economic** Cooperation and Development (OECD) is currently working with 131 countries to reach a consensus by the end of 2020 on an international solution. 针对这么多单边措施，经济合作与发展组织（OECD）目前正与131个国家合作，争取在2020年底前就一项国际解决方案达成共识。（2020年）
派 economics / ˌiːkəˈnɒmɪks / *n.* 经济学；经济状况

spiritual / ˈspɪrɪtʃuəl / 004

释 *adj.* 精神的；宗教的；心灵的
例 The ancient **spiritual** practice, which first originated in India, ultimately aims to achieve self-discovery and liberation through movements, meditation, and breathing techniques. 最早起源于印度的古代精神修行，最终旨在通过运动、冥想和呼吸技巧实现自我发现和解放。

application / ˌæplɪˈkeɪʃn / 005

释 *n.* 申请；申请书；应用，运用；应用程序
例 The creation of the "statistics board" was motivated by concerns broadly with the **application** of statistics and data analysis in scientific research and is part of *Science*'s overall drive to increase reproducibility in the research we publish. 成立"统计委员会"是出于对统计和数据分析在科学研究中的应用的广泛关注，也是《科学》杂志为提高我们所发表的研究成果的可复制性而做出的全面努力的一部分。（2015年）

imperative / ɪmˈperətɪv / 006

释 *adj.* 重要的；紧急的，迫切的 *n.* 紧急的事；必要的事
例 Kevin said it was an **imperative** that he must speak with you right away. 凯文说那是一件他必须立刻和你谈的紧急事。

◎ Study Notes

007

generous / ˈdʒenərəs /

釋 *adj.* 丰厚的；慷慨的

例 Instead, the claimant receives a time-limited "allowance," conditional on actively seeking a job; no entitlement and no insurance, at £71.70 a week, one of the least **generous** in the EU. 取而代之的是，申请人只能领取一个有时间限制的"津贴"，条件是必须积极寻找工作；没有政府津贴，也没有保险，每周71.70英镑，是欧盟最不慷慨的津贴之一。（2014年）

008

conduct

釋 / kənˈdʌkt / *v.* 组织并实施；表现；传导（热、电）；指挥
/ ˈkɒndʌkt / *n.* 实施；行为方式

例 A 2014 survey **conducted** in Australia, Britain, and the United States by the University of Wisconsin-Madison found that young people's reliance on social media led to greater political engagement. 2014年，威斯康星大学麦迪逊分校在澳大利亚、英国和美国进行的一项调查发现，年轻人对社交媒体的依赖导致了更多的政治参与。（2018年）

009

submit / səbˈmɪt /

釋 *v.* 提交，呈递；顺从；屈服；投降；不得已接受；主张

例 At the same time, Dickens, who had a reporter's eye for transcribing the life around him, especially anything comic or odd, **submitted** short sketches to obscure magazines. 与此同时，狄更斯以记者的眼光记录身边的生活，尤其是滑稽或古怪的任何事情，向一些不知名的杂志投稿幽默短剧。（2017年）

010

moral / ˈmɒrəl /

釋 *adj.* 道德的；精神上的；品行端正的 *n.* 寓意；道德

搭 moral norms 道德准则

例 He was not interested in daily politics, but concerned with questions of **moral** behavior and the larger questions of right and wrong affecting the entire society. 他对日常政治不感兴趣，而是关注道德行为问题以及影响整个社会的大是大非问题。（2014年）

近 ethical / ˈeθɪkl / *adj.* 道德的；伦理的 ‖ virtue / ˈvɜːtʃuː / *n.* 美德；优点，优势

011

scold / skəʊld /

釋 *v.* 训斥；责骂

例 Don't **scold** your children every time they don't listen to you. 小孩不听你的话，不要一味训斥他们。

012

dilemma / dɪˈlemə /

釋 *n.* 困境；（进退两难的）窘境

例 The logic behind his answer was based on the prisoner's **dilemma**, a concept in game theory. 他的答案背后的逻辑是基于博弈论中的"囚徒困境"的概念。

command / kə'mɑːnd / [013]

释 v. 命令；指挥；控制；掌管；应得 n. 指令；命令；控制；指挥；指挥部，司令部

搭 at one's command 可自由使用；可支配

例 If you are working on a word processor, you can take advantage of its capacity to make additions and deletions as well as move entire paragraphs by making just a few simple keyboard **commands**. 如果你使用的是文字处理软件，只需执行几个简单的键盘命令，你就可以利用它的功能进行添加和删除，以及移动整个段落。（2008年）

condemn / kən'dem / [014]

释 v. 谴责；责备；判（某人某罪）；迫使（陷于不幸的境地）

例 It claims that the former president watched the violence unfold on that day but did nothing to **condemn** it. 它声称，前总统目睹了当天暴力事件的发生，但却没有采取任何行动对此予以谴责。

poke / pəʊk / [015]

释 v. 捅，戳；露出，探出；搜查 n. 捅，戳；探究，打探

搭 poke out of/through 伸出；露出

例 Awkward or wordy phrasing or unclear sentences and paragraphs should be **poked** and prodded into shape. 别扭或冗长的措辞，以及表意不明的句子和段落应该被揪出来，并进行删改。

近 stick / stɪk / v. 刺；坚持 ‖ stab / stæb / v. 刺；戳

district / 'dɪstrɪkt / [016]

释 n. 地区；区域；行政区

例 I drive through the business **district** every morning. 我每天早晨都开车穿过商业区。

desire / dɪ'zaɪə(r) / [017]

释 n. 渴望；愿望；欲望 v. 渴望；想要

例 It has been estimated that this generation, due to the pressures of technology, the wish for personal fulfilment and **desire** for diversity, will work for 17 different employers over the course of their working life and have five different careers. 据估计，由于技术的压力，出于对个人成就感的愿望和多样性的渴望，这一代人在其职业生涯中将为17个不同的雇主工作，以及会从事五种不同的职业。（2022年）

visible / 'vɪzəbl / [018]

释 adj. 明显的；看得见的，可见的

例 What is more, they can be detected even when they are not actually **visible**. 更重要的是，即使它们实际上不可见，也能被检测到。（2024年）

派 invisible / ɪn'vɪzəbl / adj. 看不见的；无形的

◎ Study Notes

---

glow / gləʊ / `019`

释 v. 发光；泛光；发出暗淡的光；容光焕发；洋溢着 n. 微弱稳定的光；满面红光；红晕

搭 sunset glow 晚霞

例 A cigarette end **glowed** red in the darkness. 一个烟头在黑暗中发着微弱的红光。

---

nasty / 'nɑːsti / `020`

释 adj. 令人讨厌的；严重的；恶意的；无礼的

例 The court did suggest that accepting favors in return for opening doors is "distasteful" and "**nasty**". 法院确实认为，接受好处并以为他人开后门作为回报是"令人反感"和"讨厌的"。（2017年）

近 disgusting / dɪsˈɡʌstɪŋ / adj. 令人厌恶的，使人反感的

---

gross / ɡrəʊs / `021`

释 adj.（钱）总的，毛的；显而易见的；粗俗的；严重的，让人恶心的

搭 gross income 总收入

例 I can't bear such **gross** behavior. 我无法忍受这种粗俗的行为。

---

proposal / prəˈpəʊzl / `022`

释 n. 提议，建议；求婚

例 The Education Department is holding a key public hearing later this week to evaluate **proposals** to provide debt relief based on hardship. 教育部将于本周晚些时候举行一次重要的公开听证会，评估根据困难程度提供债务减免的提议。

---

dispute / dɪˈspjuːt / `023`

释 v. 反驳；争夺 n. 争论

例 Another factor may be that more people are trying to overpack their carry-on bags to avoid checked-baggage fees, though the airlines strongly **dispute** this. 另一个因素可能是越来越多的人试图将随身行李装得过满，以逃避托运行李费，尽管航空公司对此强烈反对。（2017年）

---

collective / kəˈlektɪv / `024`

释 adj. 集体的；共同的；总体的 n. 企业集团；合作农场

例 They kept **collective** silence. 他们全都保持沉默。

---

trivial / 'trɪviəl / `025`

释 adj. 琐碎的；不重要的

例 I suggest we stop discussing **trivial** details and get to the point. 我建议咱们别再谈琐碎细节了，切入正题吧。

---

prior / 'praɪə(r) / `026`

释 adj. 优先的；在前的

搭 prior to 在……之前

例 Constitution is **prior** to all other laws. 宪法高于一切其他法律。

temper / ˈtempə(r) /
| 027

释 *n.* 情绪；易怒的性情 *v.* 使缓和，使温和
搭 in a temper 在发脾气中 ‖ lose one's temper 发脾气
例 We should not **temper** justice with mercy. 我们不能用仁慈来调和正义。
近 alleviate / əˈliːvieɪt / *v.* 减轻

capacity / kəˈpæsəti /
| 028

释 *n.* 能力，才能；生产量，生产（或运输）能力；可容纳人数；职责，职位 *adj.* 充满的，达到最大限度的；座无虚席的
例 At the end of adolescence, however, the brain shuts down half of that **capacity**, preserving only those modes of thought that have seemed most valuable during the first decade or so of life. 然而，在青春期结束时，大脑会关闭一半的能力，只保留那些在生命最初的十年左右时间里看起来最有价值的思维模式。（2009年）

divert / daɪˈvɜːt /
| 029

释 *v.* 使转向；改变（资金等）的用途；使分心
例 The TSA cannot continue **diverting** resources into underused PreCheck lanes while most of the traveling public suffers in unnecessary lines. 运输安全管理局不能继续将资源转移到使用率不高的预检通道上，而让大多数出行民众在不必要的排队中受苦。（2017年）

editorial / ˌedɪˈtɔːriəl /
| 030

释 *adj.* 编辑的，编者的；社论的 *n.* （报刊的）社论；（美国电台或电视台的）评论
例 "Readers must have confidence in the conclusions published in our journal," writes McNutt in an **editorial**. 麦克纳特在一篇社论中写道："读者一定会对本刊发表的结论有信心。"（2015年）

swamp / swɒmp /
| 031

释 *v.* 淹没；使不堪承受 *n.* 沼泽地
搭 swamp sb. with sth. 使某人疲于应对某事
例 In other words, whatever inborn differences two people may exhibit in their abilities to memorize, those differences are **swamped** by how well each person "encodes" the information. 换句话说，无论两个人在记忆能力上存在怎样的先天差异，那些差异都会被个人的信息"编码"能力好坏所淹没。（2007年）
近 overwhelm / ˌəʊvəˈwelm / *v.* 淹没；压倒 ‖ flood / flʌd / *v.* 淹没

prefer / prɪˈfɜː(r) /
| 032

释 *v.* 更喜欢，较喜欢，喜欢……多于……
例 Some students may **prefer** to be at home talking online rather than socializing with a classmate sitting next to them. 有些学生可能更喜欢在家上网聊天，而不是与坐在旁边的同学社交。

expand / ɪk'spænd /

释 v. 扩充；扩大；增加；发展；扩展

搭 expand on/upon 详述；充分叙述；详细阐明

例 But even as the number of English speakers **expands** further there are signs that the global predominance of the language may fade within the foreseeable future. 但是，即使讲英语的人数进一步增加，也有迹象表明，在可预见的未来，英语在全球的主导地位可能会逐渐消失。（2017年）

threat / θret /

释 n. 威胁；恐吓

例 Listed as Least Concern as the species is very widely distributed, adaptable, currently increasing, and there are no major **threats** resulting in an overall population decline. 由于该物种分布非常广泛，适应性强，目前数量正在增加，并且没有导致其总体数量下降的重大威胁，因此它被列为"低关注度物种"。（2013年）

solve / sɔːlv /

释 v. 解决；解答

例 Fluid intelligence is the type of intelligence that has to do with short-term memory and the ability to think quickly, logically, and abstractly in order to **solve** new problems. 流体智力是一种与短期记忆有关的智力，是一种为解决新问题而进行快速、逻辑和抽象思考的能力。（2021年）

近 resolve / rɪ'zɒlv / v. 解决

辨 solve是普通用词，含义广泛，指为有一定难度的问题找到满意的解决方案；resolve主要指对问题进行细致地分析或思索，以得出结论或解决方法。

numerous / 'nuːmərəs /

释 adj. 众多的，许多的

例 The interviewers had rated applicants on a scale of one to five. This scale took **numerous** factors into consideration. 面试官按照1~5的等级对申请人进行评分。这个评分标准考虑了许多因素。（2013年）

entertain / ˌentə'teɪn /

释 v. 使娱乐，使欢乐；招待，款待

例 The entertainment venue has introduced an army of robots to assist with various tasks, including offering directions, **entertaining** guests and participating in conversations. 这家娱乐场所引进了一支机器人大军，协助完成各种任务，包括指路、招待客人和参与对话。

critical / 'krɪtɪkl /

释 adj. 批判性的；危急的；病危的；关键的

搭 be critical of 对……不满

例 We are at a **critical** time in our history. 我们正处于历史的紧要关头。

effective / ɪˈfektɪv /

039

释 *adj.* 有效的; 生效的; 实际的

例 Kids need plenty of practice delaying gratification and deploying **effective** organizational skills, such as managing time and setting priorities. 孩子们需要在延迟满足和运用有效的组织技能方面做大量的练习, 比如管理时间和设置优先事项。(2007年)

orient / ˈɔːrient /

040

释 *v.* 朝向; 确定方向; 熟悉; 适应 *n.* [O-]东方

例 It could be that we are evolving two communities of social scientists: one that is discipline-**oriented** and publishing in highly specialized journals, and one that is problem-**oriented** and publishing elsewhere, such as policy briefs. 我们可能正在形成两个社会科学家群体: 一个以学科为导向, 在高度专业化的期刊上发表文章; 另一个以问题为导向, 在诸如政策简报等其他地方发表文章。(2013年)

mystery / ˈmɪstri /

041

释 *n.* 不可理解之事, 神秘; 神秘小说, 侦探小说

例 The **mystery** is that this should come as a surprise to any boss. 令人费解的是, 这对任何一个老板来说都应该是个惊喜。(2007年)

caution / ˈkɔːʃn /

042

释 *n.* 警告; 告诫; 谨慎 *v.* 警告; 告诫

例 But for all the reasons there are to celebrate the computer, we must also act with **caution**. 但是, 尽管有各种理由庆祝计算机的诞生, 我们也必须谨慎行事。(2012年)

section / ˈsekʃn /

043

释 *n.* 部分; (文件、书等的)节, 段; 区, 区域; 部门

释 The trade magazine *The Bookseller* reported that Waterstones branch managers were being told to remove PRH books from prominent areas such as tables, display spaces and windows, and were "quietly retiring them to their relevant **sections**". 据行业杂志《书商》报道, 水石书店的分店经理被告知要将企鹅兰登的书籍从桌面、展示空间和橱窗等显眼的地方移走, 并"悄悄地将它们放回到其相关的区域"。(2023年)

review / rɪˈvjuː /

044

释 *n.* 评审, 审查; 检查, 检讨; 报告; 回顾; 评论; 温习, 复习 *v.* 回顾; 温习, 复习; 复查; 检阅(部队); 写评论; 校阅

例 "I think that, for the majority of scientific papers nowadays, statistical **review** is more essential than expert **review**," he says. 他说: "我认为, 对于现在的大多数科学论文来说, 统计审查比专家审查更必要。"(2015年)

calculate / 'kælkjuleɪt /   045

释 *v.* 计算；估计；推测

例 People who perceived greater social support were less likely to come down with a cold, and the researchers **calculated** that the stress-reducing effects of hugging explained about 32 percent of that beneficial effect. 感受到更多社会支持的人患感冒的可能性较小，研究人员计算出，拥抱的减压效果大约能解释这种有益效果的32%。（2017年）

fulfil(l) / fʊl'fɪl /   046

释 *v.* 履行，执行；实现

搭 fulfill a duty/an obligation/a promise 履行职责/义务/承诺

例 It is writers' duty to **fulfill** journalistic goals. 实现新闻目标是作家的职责。（2010年）

accelerate / ək'seləreɪt /   047

释 *v.* 使加快，使增速；加速；促进

例 In order to catch up with and surpass the advanced world levels we'll have to **accelerate** our speed. 要赶超世界先进水平，我们还得快马加鞭。

inhabitant / ɪn'hæbɪtənt /   048

释 *n.* 居民，住户

例 The roughly 20 million **inhabitants** of these nations looked hopefully to the future. 这些国家中约有两千万居民满怀希望地展望未来。（2007年）

近 citizen / 'sɪtɪzn / *n.* 公民 ‖ resident / 'rezɪdənt / *n.* 居民；住宿者

辨 inhabitant为最普通用词，一般指常住居民；citizen指拥有某国国籍或有某地区合法身份的人，即公民；resident多指长期居住或暂时居住的居民，有时也指旅居者。

association / ə,səʊʃi'eɪʃn /   049

释 *n.* 联系；协会；联盟；交往

例 However, short-term rentals also provide housing for tourists, pointed out Ryan Castle, CEO of a local **association** of realtors. 然而，当地房地产经纪人协会首席执行官荣恩·卡索指出，短期租赁也为游客提供了住房。（2023年）

recall / rɪ'kɔːl /   050

释 *v.* 回忆起；召回（某人/产品）*n.* 召回；记忆力

例 "With the first subject, after about 20 hours of training, his digit span had risen from 7 to 20," Ericsson **recalls**. 埃里克森回忆说："在对第一名受试者进行了约20个小时的训练后，他（能记住）的数字范围从7位数增加到了20位数。"（2007年）

Writing Models ◎

powerful

retail

principal

distinction

formal

appropriate

current

startle

enhance

shelter

exist

profitable

beam

powerful / ˈpaʊəfl /

051

释 *adj.* 有权势的；有影响力的；强壮的

例 Discussing the issue in private will make the **powerful** person feel less threatened. 私下讨论这个问题会减少有权人士的受威胁感。

retail / ˈriːteɪl /

052

释 *n.* 零售 *v.* （按某种价格）零售

例 The losers, said **retail** analyst Neil Saunders, are online-only retailers, especially smaller ones. 零售业分析师尼尔·桑德斯说，输家是只做线上的零售商，尤其是小型零售商。（2019年）

派 retailer / ˈriːteɪlə(r) / *n.* 零售商

principal / ˈprɪnsəpl /

053

释 *adj.* 首要的，最重要的 *n.* 校长；本金；委托人，当事人

例 They found that the **principal** requirement for what is called "global cascades"—the widespread propagation of influence through networks—is the presence not of a few influentials but, rather, of a critical mass of easily influenced people. 他们发现，所谓"全球级联"——影响力通过网络广泛传播——的首要条件不是有几个有影响力的人，而是有足够多的容易受影响的人。（2010年）

distinction / dɪˈstɪŋkʃn /

054

释 *n.* 差别；区分；荣誉；卓越；特质

例 Plays aiming at literary **distinction** were written for schools or court, or for the choir boys of St. Paul's and the royal chapel, who, however, gave plays in public as well as at court. 旨在获得文学荣誉的戏剧是为学校或宫廷创作的，或者是为圣保罗教堂和皇家小教堂的唱诗班男孩创作的，虽然男孩们在公共场合和宫廷中表演。（2018年）

formal / ˈfɔːml /

055

释 *adj.* 正式的；正规的

例 Millennials, it seems, face the paradox of being the least **formal** generation yet the most conscious of style and personal branding. 千禧一代似乎面临着这样一个矛盾：他们是最不拘小节的一代，然而也是最注重风格和个人品牌的一代。（2016年）

appropriate

056

释 / əˈprəʊpriət / *adj.* 合适的，恰当的 / əˈprəʊprieɪt / *v.* 挪用；拨款

例 Data can be gathered on where the customer can be engaged, such as location, devices used, website interactions, and sites visited, to display marketing messages in **appropriate** forms, including emails, social media posts, pop-up advertisements, and banners at an **appropriate** frequency. 可以收集有关客户参与地点的数据，如位置、使用的设备、网站互动和访问过的网站，从而以适当的形式展示营销信息，形式包括电子邮件、社交媒体帖子、弹出式广告和以适当频率发布的横幅广告。（2023年）

current / ˈkʌrənt /

[057]

释 *adj.* 流行的；当前的，现在的；通用的 *n.* 水流；气流；思潮

搭 current affairs 时事

例 It says that the problem is not merely that people do bad science, but that our **current** system of career advancement positively encourages it. 它说，问题不仅仅在于人们研究的科学质量低下，而是我们目前的职业晋升制度积极地鼓励了这种行为。（2019年）

startle / ˈstɑːtl /

[058]

释 *v.* 使惊吓；使震惊

例 The sudden noise in the bushes **startled** her horse. 灌木丛中突如其来的响声使她的马受到了惊吓。

enhance / ɪnˈhɑːns /

[059]

释 *v.* 提高，增进，增加

例 "Artists help scientists reach a broader audience and make emotional connections that **enhance** learning," one respondent said. 一位受访者说："艺术家帮助科学家接触到更广泛的受众，建立能提高学习的情感联系。"（2022年）

shelter / ˈʃeltə(r) /

[060]

释 *n.* 住处；（躲避恶劣天气或危险的）遮蔽物，庇护处；遮蔽，庇护；收容所 *v.* 保护；掩蔽

例 Even when homeless individuals manage to find a **shelter** that will give them three meals a day and a place to sleep at night, a good number still spend the bulk of each day wandering the street. 无家可归者即使设法找到了可以为他们提供一日三餐和夜晚住宿的收容所，但还是会有很多人每天大部分时间都在街头游荡。（2006年）

exist / ɪgˈzɪst /

[061]

释 *v.* 存在；生存

例 Citation cartels, where journals, authors, and institutions conspire to inflate citation numbers, have **existed** for a long time. 期刊、作者和机构合谋抬高引用次数的引用卡特尔存在已久。（2023年）

派 existence / ɪgˈzɪstəns / *n.* 存在；生活方式

profitable / ˈprɒfɪtəbl /

[062]

释 *adj.* 有利可图的，赚钱的；有益的

例 The concept of sustainable development has been defined as **profitable**. 可持续发展的概念被定义为有利可图。（2016年）

beam / biːm /

[063]

释 *v.* 照射；发射（电波）；笑容满面；射出光（或热）；播送 *n.* （建筑物的）梁；（粒子的）束；（电波的）波束；光线；笑容

例 Our magazines feature **beaming** celebrities and happy families in perfect homes. 我们的杂志刊登了笑容满面的名人和完美家园中的幸福家庭。（2006年）

supervise / ˈsuːpəvaɪz /

0 6 4

释 *v.* 管理；监督

例 In 1924 America's National Research Council sent two engineers to **supervise** a series of experiments at a telephone-parts factory called the Hawthorne Plant near Chicago. 1924年，美国国家研究委员会派遣两名工程师去监督在芝加哥附近一家名为霍桑工厂的电话配件厂进行的一系列实验。（2010年）

派 supervisor / ˈsuːpəvaɪzə(r) / *n.* 管理者；监督者

extension / ɪkˈstenʃn /

0 6 5

释 *n.* 延期；扩大；扩建部分

例 In 2006, the state went a step further, requiring that any **extension** of the plant's license be subject to the Vermont legislature's approval. 2006年，佛蒙特州更进一步，要求该工厂许可证的任何延期都必须获得佛蒙特州立法机构的批准。（2012年）

comply / kəmˈplaɪ /

0 6 6

释 *v.* 遵从，依从，服从

搭 comply with 遵守；服从

例 After all, it has an ad business too, which it says will **comply** with DNT requests, though it is still working out how. 毕竟，该公司也有广告业务，它表示将遵守DNT要求，但仍在研究如何遵守。（2013年）

genuine / ˈdʒenjuɪn /

0 6 7

释 *adj.* 真正的；名副其实的；诚实的

例 But a **genuine** partnership must be a two-way street. 但真正的伙伴关系必须是双向的。（2022年）

suspend / səˈspend /

0 6 8

释 *v.* 暂停；搁置；悬挂；使暂时停职

例 In dreams, a window opens into a world where logic is **suspended** and dead people speak. 在梦中，一扇窗户打开了一个世界，在那里逻辑暂停，死人会说话。（2005年）

派 suspension / səˈspenʃn / *n.* 暂停；悬挂

authority / ɔːˈθɒrəti /

0 6 9

释 *n.* 授权；当局；权力；权威；专家；当权（地位）

例 Specifically, a 5–4 majority decided that wetlands protected by the EPA under its Clean Water Act **authority** must have a "continuous surface connection" to bodies of water. 具体而言，5比4的多数票决定，环保局根据《清洁水法》的授权保护的湿地必须与水体有"连续的表面联系"。（2024年）

poverty / 'pɒvəti /   070

释 *n.* 贫穷，贫困；缺少

例 Even if this program didn't reduce **poverty**, Ferraro says, "the value of the avoided deforestation just for carbon dioxide emissions alone is more than the program costs." 费拉罗说，即使这项计划不能减少贫困，但"仅就二氧化碳排放而言，避免毁林的价值就超过了计划的成本"。（2021年）

反 wealth / welθ / *n.* 富有；财富 ‖ richness / 'rɪtʃnəs / *n.* 富裕；丰富

toxic / 'tɒksɪk /   071

释 *adj.* 有毒的，引起中毒的

例 When spilled into the sea, oil can be **toxic** to marine plants and animals. 石油泄漏到海洋里可能会引起海洋动植物中毒。

近 poisonous / 'pɔɪzənəs / *adj.* 有毒的

sheet / ʃiːt /   072

释 *n.* 床单；被单；一张（纸）；简要记录；纪要；一大片（覆盖物）

例 Once the decision is reached, he can date and sign the **sheet**. 一旦做出决定，他就可以在那张纸上注明日期并签名。

regardless / rɪ'ɡɑːdləs /   073

释 *adv.* 不顾；不加理会

搭 regardless of 不管；无论

例 And **regardless** of transferability, the study shows that what's good for people may also be good for the environment. 抛开可转移性不谈，这项研究表明，对人类有益的东西可能对环境也有益。（2021年）

journal / 'dʒɜːnl /   074

释 *n.* 报纸，刊物，杂志；日记

例 The advent of electronic publishing and authors' need to find outlets for their papers resulted in thousands of new **journals**. 电子出版的出现和作者需要为他们的论文寻找发表途径导致了成千上万的新期刊的诞生。（2023年）

hijack / 'haɪdʒæk /   075

释 *v.* 劫持；操纵 *n.* 劫持；敲诈；威逼

例 Members of social networks, for instance, are learning that they can **hijack** media to apply pressure on the businesses that originally created them. 例如，社交网络的成员正在认识到，他们可以操纵媒体，向最初创建这些媒体的企业施加压力。（2011年）

objective / əb'dʒektɪv /   076

释 *n.* 目标 *adj.* 客观的

例 **Objective** knowledge is the goal, not the starting point. 客观知识是目标，而不是起点。（2012年）

corrupt / kəˈrʌpt / 077

释 v. 使腐化; 使堕落; 破坏, 损坏 adj. 贪污的; 受贿的; 腐败的

例 There is no doubt of the alternative—the **corrupted** landscapes of southern Portugal, Spain or Ireland. 无疑还有另外一种结果——葡萄牙南部、西班牙和爱尔兰的自然风光遭到破坏。(2016年)

派 corruption / kəˈrʌpʃn / n. 腐败; 贪污; 贿赂; 受贿

tough / tʌf / 078

释 adj. 艰难的; 强硬的; 严厉的; 艰苦的; 坚强的; 棘手的; 能吃苦耐劳的; 健壮的

例 I have a **tough** constitution, and my profession taught me how to compete against long odds and big obstacles. 我有健壮的体格, 我的职业教会了我如何克服重重困难和巨大的障碍。

vain / veɪn / 079

释 adj. 徒劳的; 枉然的

搭 in vain 徒劳无益; 白费力气

例 But his efforts were not in **vain**, and the comedian who stands just over 5 feet tall, has certainly achieved a larger-than-life status. 但他的努力并没有白费, 这位身高五英尺多一点的喜剧演员无疑获得了具有传奇意义的地位。

appointment / əˈpɔɪntmənt / 080

释 n. 任命; 委任; 约会; 预约; 约定

搭 make an appointment 预约

例 One of the reasons why the **appointment** came as such a surprise, however, is that Gilbert is comparatively little known. 然而, 这项任命之所以如此出人意料, 其中一个原因是吉尔伯特相对来说不太出名。

copy / ˈkɒpi / 081

释 n. 复印件, 副本, 复制品; 一册; 一份 v. 复制; 复印; 仿造; 模仿; 抄袭

例 He asked Jackson to print out large **copies** and distributed them, along with reproductions of Moran's paintings, to each member of Congress. 他请杰克逊打印了大量副本, 连同莫兰画作的复制品一起分发给每位国会议员。(2023年)

jog / dʒɒg / 082

释 v./n. 慢跑

例 But because hard laughter is difficult to sustain, a good laugh is unlikely to have measurable benefits the way, say, a walk or a **jog** does. 但因为开怀大笑很难持续, 所以欢笑不太可能像散步或慢跑那样带来显著的好处。

efficiency / ɪˈfɪʃnsi / 083

释 *n.* 效率；功效

例 The words that have mattered are **efficiency**, flexibility, shareholder value, business-friendly, wealth generation, sales, impact and, in newspapers, circulation. 效率、变通、股东价值、商业友好、创造财富、销售额、影响力以及报纸的发行量都是重要的词。（2015年）

emphasize / ˈemfəsaɪz / 084

释 *v.* 强调；重读；着重；重视；使突出；使明显

例 College officials tend to **emphasize** that the goal of grade forgiveness is less about the grade itself and more about encouraging students to retake courses critical to their degree program and graduation without incurring a big penalty. 大学官员倾向于强调，分数宽恕的目的与分数本身无关，更多的是为了鼓励学生重修对他们的学位项目至关重要的课程，毕业时不会招致太重的不利后果。（2019年）

rush / rʌʃ / 085

释 *v.* （使）匆忙行事；急促 *n.* 匆忙；仓促

例 Part of the issue is that the government did not anticipate the steep increase in airline travel, so the TSA is now **rushing** to get new screeners on the line. 部分原因是政府没有预料到航空旅行的急剧增加，所以运输安全管理局现在正匆忙在安检队伍前安装新的设备。（2017年）

rest / rest / 086

释 *v.* 休息；安息，长眠；被搁置；放松；（使）倚靠 *n.* 其他；休息时间；剩余部分；其余的人

搭 have/take a rest 休息一下 ‖ rest on 依靠，依赖；基于

例 At the very least, the court should make itself subject to the code of conduct that applies to the **rest** of the federal judiciary. 至少，法院自己应该遵守适用于联邦司法机构其他部门的行为准则。（2012年）

empirical / ɪmˈpɪrɪkl / 087

释 *adj.* 以实验（或经验）为依据的；经验主义的

例 The second, by Joshua Greenberg, takes a more **empirical** approach to universality, identifying traits (particularly in word order) shared by many languages, which are considered to represent biases that result from cognitive constraints. 由乔舒亚·格林堡做的第二次尝试采用了更为经验主义的方法来研究（语言的）普遍性，确定了多种语言（尤其在词序方面）的共有特征，而人们认为这些特征代表了由认知限制产生的偏好。（2012年）

raise / reɪz /

088

释 v. 举起；提起；增加，提高；征集；引起；养育

例 And anything that **raises** GPAs will likely make students—who, at the end of the day, are paying the bill—feel they've gotten a better value for their tuition dollars, which is another big concern for colleges. 任何提高平均学分绩点的措施都可能会让学生们——他们最终还是要为此付费——觉得他们的学费花得物有所值，这是各大学的另一个重大关切。（2019年）

mask / mɑːsk /

089

释 n. 面具；面罩；面膜；伪装 v. 掩饰；掩藏

例 The eye **mask** is made of cashmere, which may be uncomfortable for some travelers. 这个眼罩是用羊绒制成的，这对于一些旅行者来说可能会不舒服。

admit / ədˈmɪt /

090

释 v. 承认；招认；准许……进入；准许……加入（俱乐部、组织）

例 A large part of evaluation is calling out bad arguments, but we also need to **admit** good arguments by opponents and to apply the same critical standards to ourselves. 评估的很大一部分是指出不好的论点，但我们也需要承认对手的好论点，并将同样的批评标准应用到我们自己身上。（2019年）

派 admission / ədˈmɪʃn / n. 承认；加入权；入场费

shake / ʃeɪk /

091

释 v. 摇；（与某人）握手；摇动；摇头；动摇；颤抖；抖（掉）n. 抖动；摇动；颤抖；颤动；哆嗦；战栗

搭 shake one's hand（与某人）握手

例 Explosions sound in the distance, violently **shaking** the walls. 远处传来爆炸声，墙壁剧烈地摇晃着。

secondary / ˈsekəndri /

092

释 adj. 次要的；从属的；中学的

例 For the most passionate researchers, money is a **secondary** consideration to the question of how more powerful AI is to be developed and deployed. 对于最热情的研究人员来说，如何开发和部署更强大的人工智能，金钱是次要考虑的问题。

witness / ˈwɪtnəs /

093

释 n. 目击者；见证；证人 v. 见证；当场看到，目击；是……的迹象；（摆证据）就是证据，看……就知道

搭 be (a) witness to sth. 目击，看见（某事发生）

例 Thinking they wouldn't be noticed, the two of them went to watch a game play out, only to **witness** a remarkable reaction. 以为不会被注意到，他们两个人就去看了一场比赛，结果却目睹了一场非同寻常的反应。

possession / pə'zeʃn /

094

释 *n.* 具有; 拥有; 个人财产; 私人物品

搭 in possession of 拥有

例 But this distinction misses the point that it is processing and aggregation, not the mere **possession** of bits, that gives the data value. 但这种区分忽略了一点, 即赋予数据价值的是处理和汇总, 而不仅仅是拥有数字。(2018年)

anxious / 'æŋkʃəs /

095

释 *adj.* 焦虑的; 担心的; 渴望的

例 Meanwhile, as the recession is looming large, people are getting **anxious**. 与此同时, 由于经济衰退迫在眉睫, 人们开始焦虑起来。(2010年)

lip / lɪp /

096

释 *n.* 嘴唇; 边沿

例 "Nature gave us **lips** to conceal our teeth," ran one popular Victorian saying, alluding to the fact that before the birth of proper dentistry, mouths were often in a shocking state of hygiene. 维多利亚时代流行着这样一句话: "大自然给我们嘴唇, 是为了掩盖我们的牙齿。"这句话暗指在适当的牙科技术诞生之前, 口腔的卫生状况往往令人震惊。(2021年)

drop / drɒp /

097

释 *n.* 下降; 滴; 减少 *v.* (使)降低, 减少; 落下, 掉下; 中途卸客

搭 drop by 短暂、随意地拜访 ‖ drop out 不再参加; 退出

例 Not surprisingly, up to half of all doctoral students in English **drop** out before getting their degrees. 毫不奇怪, 多达一半的英语专业博士生在获得学位之前就辍学了。(2011年)

bond / bɒnd /

098

释 *n.* 纽带; 联系 *v.* 使牢固结合

例 The couple have been regulars on the New York City running circuit, **bonding** over their love of racing. 这对夫妇一直是纽约市跑步赛场上的常客, 他们因热爱赛车而结缘。

introduce / ˌɪntrə'djuːs /

099

释 *v.* 把……介绍(给); 推行; 实施; 采用

例 Sixty toddlers were each **introduced** to an adult tester holding a plastic container. 60名幼儿被分别介绍给一个拿着塑料容器的成年测试者。(2018年)

headline / 'hedlaɪn /

100

释 *n.* (报纸的)大字标题 *v.* 给(报道、文章)加标题; 是(音乐会或演出的)主角

例 She only had time to scan the **headlines** before she had to rush out the door. 她冲出门之前, 只有扫一眼标题的时间。

☐ ☐ accelerate
☐ ☐ admit
☐ ☐ anxious
☐ ☐ application
☐ ☐ appointment
☐ ☐ appropriate
☐ ☐ association
☐ ☐ authority
☐ ☐ beam
☐ ☐ bond
☐ ☐ calculate
☐ ☐ capacity
☐ ☐ caution
☐ ☐ collective
☐ ☐ command
☐ ☐ comply
☐ ☐ condemn
☐ ☐ conduct
☐ ☐ copy
☐ ☐ corrupt
☐ ☐ critical
☐ ☐ current
☐ ☐ desire
☐ ☐ dilemma
☐ ☐ dispute
☐ ☐ distinction
☐ ☐ district
☐ ☐ divert
☐ ☐ drop
☐ ☐ economic
☐ ☐ editorial

☐ ☐ effective
☐ ☐ efficiency
☐ ☐ emphasize
☐ ☐ empirical
☐ ☐ enhance
☐ ☐ entertain
☐ ☐ exemplify
☐ ☐ exist
☐ ☐ expand
☐ ☐ extension
☐ ☐ formal
☐ ☐ fulfil(l)
☐ ☐ generous
☐ ☐ genuine
☐ ☐ glow
☐ ☐ gross
☐ ☐ headline
☐ ☐ hijack
☐ ☐ imperative
☐ ☐ inhabitant
☐ ☐ introduce
☐ ☐ jog
☐ ☐ journal
☐ ☐ lip
☐ ☐ mask
☐ ☐ moral
☐ ☐ mystery
☐ ☐ nasty
☐ ☐ numerous
☐ ☐ objective
☐ ☐ orient

☐ ☐ poke
☐ ☐ possession
☐ ☐ poverty
☐ ☐ powerful
☐ ☐ prefer
☐ ☐ principal
☐ ☐ prior
☐ ☐ profitable
☐ ☐ proposal
☐ ☐ propose
☐ ☐ raise
☐ ☐ recall
☐ ☐ regardless
☐ ☐ rest
☐ ☐ retail
☐ ☐ review
☐ ☐ rush
☐ ☐ scold
☐ ☐ secondary
☐ ☐ section
☐ ☐ shake
☐ ☐ sheet
☐ ☐ shelter
☐ ☐ solve
☐ ☐ spiritual
☐ ☐ startle
☐ ☐ submit
☐ ☐ supervise
☐ ☐ suspend
☐ ☐ swamp
☐ ☐ temper

☐ ☐ threat
☐ ☐ tough
☐ ☐ toxic
☐ ☐ trivial
☐ ☐ vain
☐ ☐ visible
☐ ☐ witness

音频

Previous Check

- profession
- statute
- wake
- award
- blame
- keen
- commute
- physiology
- dismiss
- inform
- exclude
- code
- enable
- accuracy
- shatter
- ingredient
- commercial
- recommend
- sympathetic
- superior
- intellectual
- ethnic
- initial
- deed
- fit
- denote
- represent
- contrast
- economics
- grasp
- resistant

- foster
- condition
- extreme
- financial
- ornament
- complement
- suspect
- opportunity
- barrier
- strike
- system
- measure
- reward
- reduction
- emphasis
- motivate
- weight
- include
- depend
- management
- allege
- miserable
- confirm
- marginal
- layout
- disorder
- extensive
- cultivate
- fame
- original
- universal

- replace
- overall
- departure
- curve
- facility
- necessitate
- signal
- delay
- progress
- income
- boundary
- favo(u)r
- nurture
- march
- surface
- communication
- squeeze
- relationship
- comic
- contradict
- title
- enthusiastic
- aid
- atmosphere
- feasible
- pupil
- direction
- various
- discard
- plus
- dubious

- diet
- delight
- spare
- alarm
- parallel
- draw
- breath

profession / prəˈfeʃn /

001

释 *n.* 职业

例 All around the world, lawyers generate more hostility than the members of any other **profession**—with the possible exception of journalism. 在全世界范围内，律师比其他任何职业的成员都更容易招致敌意——新闻业可能是个例外。（2014年）

statute / ˈstætʃuːt /

002

释 *n.* 法规，章程，规则

搭 guardian by statute 法定监护人

例 Two of the three objecting Justice—Samuel Alito and Clarence Thomas—agreed with this Constitutional logic but disagreed about which Arizona rules conflicted with the federal **statute**. 提出异议的三位大法官中的两位——塞缪尔·阿利托和克拉伦斯·托马斯——在宪法这一逻辑上意见一致，但在亚利桑那州的哪些规则与联邦法规相冲突的问题上存在分歧。（2013年）

wake / weɪk /

003

释 *v.* 醒来；唤起

搭 wake up 醒来；唤醒

例 She fell asleep immediately but **woke** an hour later. 她马上睡着了，但一小时后又醒了。

award / əˈwɔːd /

004

释 *v.* 授予；奖励；判给 *n.* 奖；奖品；奖金；奖状；奖学金；助学金；（毕业证书等的）授予

例 The proposal is that it should sit alongside the existing city of culture title, which was held by Hull in 2017, and has been **awarded** to Coventry for 2021. 该提议认为，它应与现有的文化城市称号并列，该称号在2017年由赫尔市获得，并在2021年授予考文垂市。（2020年）

blame / bleɪm /

005

释 *v.* 把……归咎于 *n.*（坏事或错事）责任

搭 shoulder the blame 承担责任

例 Some **blame** for the current controversy belongs to astronomers. 当前的争议一部分责任归咎于天文学家。（2017年）

keen / kiːn /

006

释 *adj.* 热情的，渴望的；激烈的；敏锐的；锋利的

搭 be keen on 喜爱…… ‖ be keen to do sth. 热切地想做某事

例 **Keen** to read more, I was surprised to find that Oman's appendix, published in 1914, was the only considered thing that had been written about this secret war. 渴望阅读更多，我惊讶地发现，1914年出版的阿曼附录是关于这场秘密战争的唯一经过深思熟虑的内容。（2022年）

commute / kəˈmjuːt /

释 *v.* 上班往返两地；减刑；代偿 *n.* 上下班路程

例 I live within **commuting** distance of Dublin. 我住在离都柏林上下班可通勤的地方。

派 commuter / kəˈmjuːtə(r) / *n.* 上下班往返的人

physiology / ˌfɪziˈɒlədʒi /

释 *n.* 生理学；生理机能

例 He was awarded the Nobel Prize for achievements in **physiology**. 他因生理学方面的建树而被授予诺贝尔奖。

dismiss / dɪsˈmɪs /

释 *v.* 不予考虑；解雇；驳回；免职；去除，消除，摒除（思想、感情等），摒弃

搭 dismiss ... as ... 把……轻视为；对……不屑一提

例 Rather than **dismissing** ourselves as unchangeable creatures of habit, we can instead direct our own change by consciously developing new habits. 与其把自己轻视为无法改变的习惯性动物，相反，我们可以通过有意识地培养新习惯来引导自己改变。（2009年）

派 dismissal / dɪsˈmɪsl / *n.* 解雇；不予考虑

近 discharge / dɪsˈtʃɑːdʒ / *v.* 解雇；卸下 ‖ fire / ˈfaɪə(r) / *v.* 解雇，开除

inform / ɪnˈfɔːm /

释 *v.* 通知；告诉；报告；检举；赋（思想或特质）于；渗透入

例 Ideally, different kinds of reading **inform** each other, and act as useful reference points for and counterbalances to one another. 理想的情况是，不同类型的阅读相互借鉴，互为有用的参考，以及相互制衡。（2015年）

exclude / ɪkˈskluːd /

释 *v.* 把……排除在外；排斥，拒绝

例 I have **excluded** him because, while his accomplishments may contribute to the solution of moral problems, he has not been charged with the task of approaching any but the factual aspects of those problems. 我把他排除在外，是因为尽管他的成就可能有助于道德问题的解决，但他承担的任务只是研究这些问题的事实方面。（2006年）

近 eliminate / ɪˈlɪmɪneɪt / *v.* 剔除，排除 ‖ abolish / əˈbɒlɪʃ / *v.* 废除

反 include / ɪnˈkluːd / *v.* 包括

code / kəʊd /

释 *n.* 道德准则，行为规范；密码；编码 *v.* 将……译成密码；编程序

例 Native American languages are indeed different, so that Navajo could be used by the U.S. military as a **code** during World War II to send secret messages. 美洲土著语言的确是不同的，以至于在二战期间，纳瓦霍语被美军当作密码用来发送秘密电报。

enable / ɪ'neɪbl / ⓪₁₃

释 *v.* 使能够；使成为可能

例 Their well-developed hippocampal structures may **enable** elephants, like rats and people, to construct cognitive maps. 大象发达的海马体结构可能使它们能够像老鼠和人一样构建认知地图。（2024年）

accuracy / 'ækjərəsi / ⓪₁₄

释 *n.* 准确（性）；精确（度）

例 What is in question is not the retrieval of an absolute, fixed or "true" meaning that can be read off and checked for **accuracy**, or some timeless relation of the text to the world. 问题的关键不在于读取一个绝对的、固定的或"真实的"意义，可以读出并检查其准确性，也不在于文本与世界的某种永恒关系。（2015年）

shatter / 'ʃætə(r) / ⓪₁₅

释 *v.* （使）粉碎；（使）破灭；被破坏；给予极大打击 *n.* 碎片

例 The accident **shattered** John's collarbone. 这次事故致使约翰的锁骨粉碎。

ingredient / ɪn'griːdiənt / ⓪₁₆

释 *n.* 成分，原料；要素，因素

例 Depending on the restaurant's preferences, its menu could show you nutritional information, **ingredients** lists and photographs of the dishes. 根据餐厅偏好不同，它的菜单可能会向你展示其菜品的营养信息、原料列表和图片。

commercial / kə'mɜːʃl / ⓪₁₇

释 *adj.* 商业化的；商业的 *n.* （电台或电视播放的）广告

例 Each company is fighting to protect its own **commercial** interests. 每家公司都在奋力保护自己的商业利益。

recommend / ˌrekə'mend / ⓪₁₈

释 *v.* 推荐；建议；介绍；劝告；使受欢迎；使有优势

例 The two highly **recommended** lifestyle approaches are maintaining or increasing your level of aerobic exercise and following a Mediterranean-style diet that is high in fiber and eliminates highly processed foods. 强烈推荐的两种生活方式是：保持或增加有氧运动量，以及采用高纤维、杜绝高度加工食品的地中海式饮食习惯。（2021年）

sympathetic / ˌsɪmpə'θetɪk / ⓪₁₉

释 *adj.* 同情的，有同情心的；赞同的

搭 sympathetic to/towards sb. 同情某人

例 I did not feel **sympathetic** at all towards Kate. 我一点也不同情凯特。

◉ Study Notes

superior / suːˈpɪəriə(r) /   ⓪②⓪

🈂 *adj.* 比……好的；有优越感的；上级的；（人数）占优势的 *n.* 上级；较好的人或事物

🈂 superior to 优于……

🈂 He adds humbly that perhaps he was "**superior** to the common run of men in noticing things which easily escape attention, and in observing them carefully." 他还谦虚地补充说，也许他"比一般人更善于注意那些容易被忽视的事物，并仔细观察它们"。（2008年）

🈂 inferior / ɪnˈfɪəriə(r) / *adj.* 次等的；下级的

intellectual / ˌɪntəˈlektʃuəl /   ⓪②①

🈂 *adj.* 智力的；理智的；有才智的 *n.* 知识分子，脑力劳动者

🈂 intellectual curiosity 求知欲

🈂 Teachers need to be aware of the emotional, **intellectual** and physical changes that young adults experience. 教师需要了解青少年所经历的情绪、智力和身体上的变化。

ethnic / ˈeθnɪk /   ⓪②②

🈂 *adj.* 种族的；少数民族的；有民族特色的

🈂 The experts have different research focuses in the study of **ethnic** issues. 这些专家研究种族问题的侧重点不同。

initial / ɪˈnɪʃl /   ⓪②③

🈂 *adj.* 开始的，最初的 *n.* 首字母 *v.* 用姓名的首字母做标记（或签名）于

🈂 The **initial** letter of the word is m. 这个单词的首字母是m。

deed / diːd /   ⓪②④

🈂 *n.* 行为，行动；[律]契约，证书；杰出成就，功绩

🈂 We need actual **deeds** and not flowery language. 我们需要的是实际行动，而不是花哨的辞藻。

fit / fɪt /   ⓪②⑤

🈂 *v.* 合身；适合；相配，符合；使胜任（任务、角色）*adj.* 健壮的；健康的；适合的；胜任的 *n.* 适合；胜任

🈂 fit in (with sb./sth.)（与……）合得来；适应 ‖ the survival of the fittest 适者生存

🈂 The sort of portable power bank that **fits** in a bag is great when you're stuck at the airport or in a conference room without outlets. 当你被困在机场或处在没有插座的会议室里时，这种适合装在包里的便携式充电宝就非常有用。

denote / dɪˈnəʊt /   ⓪②⑥

🈂 *v.* 表示；标志；意指；象征；预示

🈂 Her title has been used by the monarchy since the 14th century to **denote** the wife of the Prince of Wales. 自14世纪以来，王室一直使用她的头衔来意指威尔士亲王的妻子。

represent / ˌreprɪˈzent / 027

释 v. 代表; 象征; 描述

例 His story of self-improvement and hard work would make a fascinating biography in its own right, but **represents** something more than that. 他自强不息、艰苦奋斗的故事本身就是一部引人入胜的传记，但他所代表的意义远不止于此。（2022年）

contrast 028

释 / kənˈtrɑːst / v. 形成对比; 对比, 对照 / ˈkɒntrɑːst / n. 对比, 对照; 反差

例 An infant born to a hunter-gatherer society could have more than ten caregivers—this **contrasts** starkly to nursery settings in the UK where regulations call for a ratio of one carer to four children aged two to three. 在狩猎采集社会出生的婴儿可能有十多个照顾者——这与英国托儿所的规定形成鲜明对比，在英国，规定要求一位看护人要照顾四个两岁到三岁的孩子。（2024年）

近 comparison / kəmˈpærɪsn / n. 比较

economics / ˌiːkəˈnɒmɪks / 029

释 n. 经济学; 经济因素; 经济情况; 经济意义

例 In just one generation, millions of mothers have gone to work, transforming basic family **economics**. 在短短一代人的时间里，数百万母亲走上了工作岗位，改变了基本的家庭经济状况。（2007年）

grasp / grɑːsp / 030

释 v. 抓紧; 抓牢; 理解; 领悟; 明白 n. 紧抓; 控制; 理解（力）; 领会; 能力所及

搭 grasp at 抓住某物; 抓住机会 ‖ grasp at straws（在危难中）抓住救命稻草

例 It is also the reason why when we try to describe music with words, all we can do is articulate our reactions to it, and not **grasp** music itself. 这也是为什么当我们试图用语言来描述音乐时，我们所能做的只是阐明我们对音乐的感受，而不是领悟音乐本身。（2014年）

resistant / rɪˈzɪstənt / 031

释 adj. 抵抗的, 有抵抗力的; 抵制的, 阻止的; 抗……的, 耐……的

搭 be resistant to 对……有抵抗力; 抵制的

例 Elderly people are not always **resistant** to change. 上了年纪的人并不总是会抵制变革。

近 stubborn / ˈstʌbən / adj. 固执的 ‖ rebellious / rɪˈbeljəs / adj. 反抗的

foster / ˈfɒstə(r) / 032

释 v. 培养; 助长; 收养; 抚育 adj. 领养的, 代养的

搭 foster mother/father 养母/养父

例 His job is to detect and **foster** artistic talent. 他的工作是发现并培养艺术人才。

condition / kənˈdɪʃn /   ⓪③③

释 *n.* 状态, 状况; 环境; 条件

搭 under certain conditions 在特定条件下

例 They are profitable institutions whose bottom line is much more important than the **condition** of the animals. 它们（动物园）是营利机构, 其最终赢利比动物的状态重要得多。（2022年）

派 conditional / kənˈdɪʃənl / *adj.* 附带条件的

extreme / ɪkˈstriːm /   ⓪③④

释 *n.* 极端; 极度; 极限; 完全相反的事物; 极端不同的感情（或境况、行为方式等）*adj.* 极端的; 极度的; 严重的; 极大的; 偏激的; 过分的; 严厉的; 异乎寻常的; 远离中心的

例 The parliament also agreed to ban websites that "incite excessive thinness" by promoting **extreme** dieting. 议会还同意封禁那些通过宣传极端节食来"煽动过度瘦身"的网站。（2016年）

financial / faɪˈnænʃl /   ⓪③⑤

释 *adj.* 财政的; 财务的; 金融的

搭 financial crisis 金融危机 ‖ financial assistance 经济援助

例 Times of national turmoil generally roil a country's **financial** markets. 在国家动荡不安时期, 该国的金融市场一般都会出现混乱。

近 economic / ˌiːkəˈnɒmɪk / *adj.* 经济的; 经济学的 ‖ fiscal / ˈfɪskl / *adj.* 财政上的; 国库的

ornament   ⓪③⑥

释 / ˈɔːnəmənt / *n.* 装饰; 装饰物; 为……增添光彩的人（或物）
/ ˈɔːnəment / *v.* 装饰; 点缀

例 Some families make a special **ornament** each Spring Festival and mark the happy day. 有些家庭会在每年春节做一些特别的装饰以庆祝这一快乐的日子。

complement   ⓪③⑦

释 / ˈkɒmplɪment / *v.* 衬托; 补充 / ˈkɒmplɪmənt / *n.* 衬托物; 补充物

例 This wine **complements** the food perfectly. 这种葡萄酒完美衬托了这种食物的味道。

suspect   ⓪③⑧

释 / səˈspekt / *v.* 怀疑; 认为 / ˈsʌspekt / *n.* 嫌疑人 *adj.* 可疑的; 不可靠的, 不可信的

例 Now researchers **suspect** that dreams are part of the mind's emotional thermostat, regulating moods while the brain is "off-line". 现在, 研究人员怀疑梦是大脑情绪恒温器的一部分, 在大脑"离线"时调节情绪。（2005年）

opportunity

barrier

strike

system

measure

reward

reduction

emphasis

motivate

weight

include

039

opportunity / ˌɒpəˈtjuːnəti /

释 *n.* 机会；时机

例 But almost all have ignored the big, profitable **opportunity** in their own backyard: the wholesale food and drink trade, which appears to be just the kind of market retailers need. 但几乎所有人都忽视了自己后院的巨大盈利机会：食品和饮料批发贸易，这似乎正是零售商所需要的市场。（2010年）

辨 opportunity和chance都有"机会"的意思。opportunity侧重指有利或适合于采取行动，以达到某一目的或实现某种愿望的最佳时机或机会；chance侧重指偶然或意外的机会，有时也指正常或好的机会。

040

barrier / ˈbæriə(r) /

释 *n.* 屏障，障碍物；阻力；关卡；隔阂；分界线

例 There was no real **barrier** between reality and fantasy in his works. 在他的作品中，现实与幻想之间并没有真正的分界线。

041

strike / straɪk /

释 *v.* 罢工；打；击；突然想到；（疾病、灾难等）侵袭，爆发；突击；撞；碰；给……印象；摆出（姿态）；表现出（态度）；删去，划掉 *n.* 罢工；（军事）打击；击球末中；击；意外发现

搭 strike out 开辟新路；（使）三击不中出局；愤怒地打，生气地说 ‖ strike up (with sb.)（和某人）建立友谊，开始来往，交谈起来

例 Continuing **strikes** are beginning to play havoc with the national economy. 持续的罢工开始严重破坏国家经济。

042

system / ˈsɪstəm /

释 *n.* 系统；体制

例 Children may face serious difficulties in coping with significant moves, especially if it removes them from their current school or support **system**. 孩子们在应对重大变迁时可能会面临严重的困难，尤其是如果让他们离开目前就读的学校或支持系统的话。

派 systematic / ˌsɪstəˈmætɪk / *adj.* 系统的；有计划的

043

measure / ˈmeʒə(r) /

释 *v.* 测量；度量；估量，判定（重要性、价值或影响等） *n.* 措施，方法；尺度，标准；程度；判断；衡量；计量工具

搭 measure up to 符合（标准）；达到（期望）‖ beyond measure 不可估量；极其

例 The **measure** targeted animal rights activists who for years decried lack of any legal accountability for people who mistreated or abandoned their pets, or failed to chip or neuter them. 这项措施针对的是动物权利活动家，他们多年来一直谴责那些虐待或遗弃宠物，没有为宠物植入芯片或绝育的人缺乏任何法律责任。

reward / rɪ'wɔːd / 0|4|4

释 v. 奖励; 给予报酬 n. 奖励; 报酬; 悬赏金

例 Bankers' fat pay packets have attracted much criticism, but a public-sector system that does not **reward** high achievers may be a much bigger problem for America. 银行家们丰厚的薪酬已经招致了许多批评，但公共部门系统不奖励高成就者对美国来说可能是一个更大的问题。（2012年）

近 award / ə'wɔːd / v. 授予; 奖给

reduction / rɪ'dʌkʃn / 0|4|5

释 n. 减少; 缩小; 缩图; 缩版; 减价, 折扣

例 Supporters of the new railway systems argue that these mergers will allow for substantial cost **reductions** and better coordinated service. 支持新的铁路系统的人认为，这些合并将带来大幅度的成本降低和更好的协调服务。

近 decrease / dɪ'kriːs / n. 减少 ‖ decline / dɪ'klaɪn / n. 下降

反 increase / ɪn'kriːs / n. 增加

emphasis / 'emfəsɪs / 0|4|6

释 n. 重点; 强调; 重读

例 One reason for this change was the increasing **emphasis** given to the historical approach to man. 这一变化出现的一个原因是人们越来越重视用历史的方法研究人类。

motivate / 'məʊtɪveɪt / 0|4|7

释 v. 成为……的动机; 是……的原因; 激励

搭 be motivated by 被……所激励

例 To do that, you need to **motivate** them, listen to them, connect with them, and support them when they need it. 要做到那一点，你需要激励他们，倾听他们的心声，与他们保持联络，并且在他们有需要时支持他们。

近 trigger / 'trɪɡə(r) / v. 引发; 触发

weight / weɪt / 0|4|8

释 n. 重量; 分量; 重要性; 重任 v. 在……上加重量 v. 使加权;（用重物）固定; 使负重; 在……上加重量

搭 weight loss 体重减轻

例 Symbols and metaphors also hold significant **weight** in my visual storytelling. 象征和隐喻在我的视觉故事中也占有重要地位。

include / ɪn'kluːd / 0|4|9

释 v. 包括; 包容

例 The team **included** a meteorologist, a zoologist, a mineralogist, and an agricultural statistician. 团队成员包括一名气象学家、一名动物学家、一名矿物学家和一名农业统计学家。（2023年）

Writing Models ◉ ┄┄┄┄┄┄

depend

management

allege

miserable

confirm

marginal

layout

disorder

extensive

cultivate

fame

original

depend / dɪ'pend / 0050

释 *v.* 依靠，依赖；取决于；指望

搭 depend on 取决于

例 The careers of scientists and the reputation of their institutions **depend** on the number and prestige of the papers they produce, but even more so on the citations attracted by these papers. 科学家的职业生涯及其所在机构的声誉取决于他们所发表论文的数量和声望，但更取决于这些论文所吸引的引用次数。（2023年）

派 dependency / dɪ'pendənsi / *n.* 依赖 ‖ dependent / dɪ'pendənt / *adj.* 依赖的；取决于……的

management / 'mænɪdʒmənt / 0051

释 *n.* 管理人员；管理

搭 quality management 质量管理

例 Yet bank shares rose and the changes enhance what one lobbying group politely calls "the use of judgment by **management**." 然而，银行股价却上涨了，而且这些变化增强了一个游说团体礼貌地称之为"管理层对判断力的应用"的说法。（2010年）

allege / ə'ledʒ / 0052

释 *v.* （在未提出证据的情况下）断言，指控，声称

搭 It is alleged that... 据说……

例 This suggests that the **alleged** "Hawthorne effect" is hard to pin down. 这表明，所谓的"霍桑效应"难以确定。（2010年）

派 allegedly / ə'ledʒɪdli / *adv.* 据说

近 assert / ə'sɜːt / *v.* 声称，断言 ‖ affirm / ə'fɜːm / *v.* 断言，肯定

辨 allege多指在无真凭实据的情况下断言或宣称；assert主观意味强，指自认为某事就是如此，而不管事实如何；declare指正式且清楚明白地宣称某事；affirm强调在做出断言时表现出的坚定与不可动摇的态度。

miserable / 'mɪzrəbl / 0053

释 *adj.* 痛苦的；可怜的；使不舒服的；乖戾的；少得可怜的

例 The accident made her life **miserable**. 那场事故让她的生活很痛苦。

近 painful / 'peɪnfl / *adj.* 痛苦的；不愉快的；艰难的

confirm / kən'fɜːm / 0054

释 *v.* 证实，证明，确认；使确信；认可

例 The system compares a traveler's appearance to their photo on a valid ID while **confirming** their possession of a legitimate boarding pass. 该系统将旅客的外貌与其有效身份证件上的照片进行比对，同时确认旅客持有合法的登机牌。

marginal / 'mɑːdʒɪnl / 0055

释 *adj.* 不重要的；边缘的；小的；微不足道的；微小的；末端的

例 This makes it harder for the **marginal** manager to gain employment. 这使得不重要的管理人员更难就业。（2022年）

layout / ˈleɪaʊt / ⁰⁵⁶

释 *n.* 布局；安排；设计

例 They are making some alterations to the office **layout**. 他们在对办公室的布局做一些改变。

disorder / dɪsˈɔːdə(r) / ⁰⁵⁷

释 *n.* 失调，紊乱；疾病；混乱，杂乱，凌乱

例 And a significant number of the homeless have serious mental **disorders**. 无家可归者中有相当一部分人患有严重的精神疾病。（2006年）

派 disordered / dɪsˈɔːdəd / *adj.* 混乱的，杂乱的；紊乱的，失调的

extensive / ɪkˈstensɪv / ⁰⁵⁸

释 *adj.* 广泛的；大量的；广阔的；广大的；广博的

例 Studying Scovell's papers at the Public Record Office, London, I found that he had left an **extensive** journal and copious notes about his work in the Peninsula. 在伦敦公共档案局研究斯科威尔的文件时，我发现他留下了关于他在半岛工作的大量日记和笔记。（2022年）

近 immense / ɪˈmens / *adj.* 极广大的 ‖ universal / ˌjuːnɪˈvɜːsl / *adj.* 普遍的

反 limited / ˈlɪmɪtɪd / *adj.* 有限的

cultivate / ˈkʌltɪveɪt / ⁰⁵⁹

释 *v.* 培养（态度、技巧等）；耕作，种植；建立（友谊）；获得（支持）；逐渐形成（某种态度、谈话或举止方式等）

例 They gave justices permanent positions so they would be free to upset those in power and have no need to **cultivate** political support. 他们给予大法官永久职位，这样他们就可以自由地惹恼当权者，而无须获得政治支持。（2012年）

派 cultivation / kʌltɪˈveɪʃn / *n.* 培养；种植

fame / feɪm / ⁰⁶⁰

释 *n.* 名誉，名声

例 The runaway success of *The Pickwick Papers*, as it is generally known today, secured Dickens's **fame**. 众所周知，《匹克威克外传》的巨大成功为狄更斯赢得了名誉。（2017年）

original / əˈrɪdʒənl / ⁰⁶¹

释 *adj.* 最初的；原来的；首创的；原作的 *n.* 原件，原作

搭 in the original 用原著的语言；未经翻译

例 The **original** interview notes were subsequently lost. 后来，采访记录原稿丢失了。

近 primary / ˈpraɪməri / *adj.* 初始的；首要的

Writing Models ◎

universal

replace

overall

departure

curve

facility

necessitate

signal

delay

progress

income

boundary

favo(u)r

---

universal / ˌjuːnɪˈvɜːsl /

释 *adj.* 普遍的; 宇宙的; 全世界的 *n.* 普遍原则; 通用原理

例 Neither of these patterns is borne out by the analysis, suggesting that the structures of the languages are lineage-specific and not governed by **universals**. 这两种模式都没有在分析中得到证实，这表明语言结构是世系特有的，不受普遍原则的制约。（2012年）

replace / rɪˈpleɪs /

释 *v.* 代替; 取代; 以……取代; 以……接替; 更新; 把……换回原处

例 Part of the increase comes from drugs being used to **replace** other kinds of treatments. 增加的部分原因是药物被用来替代其他种类的治疗。（2005年）

overall

释 / ˌəʊvəˈrɔːl / *adj.* 全面的; 总体的; 结合的 *adv.* 全部; 一般来说 / ˈəʊvərɔːl / *n.* 外套; 工作服

例 And whether the community's work contributes much to an **overall** accumulation of knowledge is doubtful. 至于社区的工作是否对知识的整体积累有很大贡献，则难说。（2013年）

近 whole / həʊl / *adj.* 全部的，完整的 ‖ complete / kəmˈpliːt / *adj.* 完整的

反 partial / ˈpɑːʃl / *adj.* 部分的

departure / dɪˈpɑːtʃə(r) /

释 *n.* 出发，离开; 背离，违反

例 It might be hard for airlines to co-ordinate the **departure** times and destinations of passenger aircraft in a way that would allow them to gain from formation flight. 航空公司可能很难协调每架客机的起飞时间与目的地，使它们能从编队飞行中获益。

反 arrival / əˈraɪvl / *n.* 到达; 到达者

curve / kɜːv /

释 *n.* 曲线 *v.* 使弯曲 *adj.* 弯曲的

例 In such a case, the company's response may not be sufficiently quick or thoughtful, and the learning **curve** has been steep. 在这种情况下，公司的反应可能不够迅速或周到，而且学习曲线也很坎坷。（2011年）

近 arch / ɑːtʃ / *n.* 弧形; 拱形 ‖ bend / bend / *v.* 使弯曲

facility / fəˈsɪləti /

释 *n.* [pl.]设施

搭 local facilities 本地设施

例 The museum has special **facilities** for blind and partially sighted visitors. 博物馆有专门设备供失明和视力有缺陷的参观者使用。

necessitate / nəˈsesɪteɪt /

释 v. 需要；（使）成为必要

例 In 1866, the construction of the North Wing of the Treasury Building **necessitated** the demolition of the State Department building. 1866年，财政部大楼北翼的修建使国务院大楼不得不拆除。（2018年）

signal / ˈsɪɡnəl /

释 n. 信号；标志；信号灯 v. 示意；表明

例 Each automatic door system analyses the light, sound, weight or movement in their vicinity as a **signal** to open. 每个自动门系统都会分析其附近的光线、声音、压力或移动，以此作为开门信号。（2024年）

delay / dɪˈleɪ /

释 v. 推迟，延期；延误，耽搁；拖延 n. 延期；延误

例 It's also a good idea to **delay** the conversation if you're in a meeting room or other public space. 如果你们在会议室或在其他公共场所，推迟谈话也是一个好主意。

progress

释 / ˈprəʊɡres / n. 进展，进步；前进 / prəˈɡres / v. 进展；行进；使……发展

搭 in progress 在进行中

例 We have made great **progress** in controlling inflation. 我们在控制通货膨胀方面取得了巨大进展。

派 progression / prəˈɡreʃn / n. 发展；前进

近 advance / ədˈvɑːns / v. 前进 ‖ proceed / prəˈsiːd / v. 行进；前进

income / ˈɪnkʌm /

释 n. 收入，收益，所得

例 Losing a job is hurting: you don't skip down to the jobcentre with a song in your heart, delighted at the prospect of doubling your **income** from the generous state. 失去工作是一种伤害：你不会心里唱着歌，跑去就业中心，为从慷慨的政府那里获得双倍收入而高兴。（2014年）

boundary / ˈbaʊndri /

释 n. 边界；界限；分界线

例 The fence marked the **boundary** between my property and hers. 那道篱笆曾是我的房子和她的房子的地界。

favo(u)r / ˈfeɪvə(r) /

释 n. 喜爱；支持；恩惠 v. 更喜欢；偏袒

搭 in favor of 支持；有利于 ‖ out of favor 失宠；失去……的支持

例 Retailers that the upper middle class often **favors** have experienced a fall in sales over the past three months. 中上阶层经常青睐的零售商在过去三个月的销售额出现下滑。

Writing Models ◎

nurture

march

surface

communication

squeeze

relationship

comic

contradict

title

enthusiastic

aid

atmosphere

075

nurture / ˈnɜːtʃə(r) /

释 *v.* 培养; 养育 *n.* 培育

例 His mother **nurtured** his artistic side, buying him his first film camera. 他的母亲培养了他艺术的一面, 给他买了第一台胶片照相机。

076

march / mɑːtʃ /

释 *v.* 前进; 行军 *n.* 行进; 行军; 游行

搭 march on 继续行进; 快速经过 ‖ on the march 在行进中; 在进展中

例 Police said 300,000 supporters **marched** peacefully in London, the largest such event there since the war started. 警方表示, 30万名支持者在伦敦和平游行, 这是伦敦自战争爆发以来规模最大的一次游行。

077

surface / ˈsɜːfɪs /

释 *n.* 表面, 外表, 外观

搭 on the surface 表面上; 从外表看; 乍一看

例 How do archaeologists know where to find what they are looking for when there is nothing visible on the **surface** of the ground? 当地面上什么都看不见的时候, 考古学家怎么知道在哪里找到他们要找的东西呢?(2014年)

078

communication / kəˌmjuːnɪˈkeɪʃn /

释 *n.* 表达; 交流, 交际; 通信

例 Curriculums—from grammar school to college—should evolve to focus less on memorizing facts and more on creativity and complex **communication**. 从文法学校到大学的课程设置都应该逐渐减少对记忆事实的关注, 而更多地关注创造力和复杂的交流。(2018年)

079

squeeze / skwiːz /

释 *v.* 紧捏; 挤压; 压榨; 塞进; 挤进

例 About half of U.S. jobs are at high risk of being automated, according to a University of Oxford study, with the middle class disproportionately **squeezed**. 牛津大学的一项研究显示, 美国大约一半的工作岗位面临着被自动化的高风险, 中产阶级受到的挤压尤为严重。(2018年)

080

relationship / rɪˈleɪʃnʃɪp /

释 *n.* 关系; 联系

例 In some instances, there is absolutely no **relationship** between the content of the article and the citations. 在某些情况下, 文章的内容和引用的内容完全没有关系。(2023年)

comic / ˈkɒmɪk /

释 *adj.* 喜剧的; 滑稽的 *n.* 喜剧演员; 连环画杂志

例 The **comic** novel, *The Posthumous Papers of the Pickwick Club*, appeared serially in 1836 and 1837 and was first published in book form in 1837. 喜剧小说《匹克威克外传》在1836年和1837年连载, 并于1837年首次以书的形式出版。(2017年)

contradict / ˌkɒntrəˈdɪkt /

释 *v.* 反驳, 驳斥; 相矛盾

搭 contradict oneself 自相矛盾

例 Sometimes her recollections **contradicted** her mom's. 有时她的回忆与她母亲的相矛盾。

title / ˈtaɪtl /

释 *n.* 名称; 标题; 题目; 称号; 头衔; 职称 *v.* (给书籍、乐曲等)加标题, 定题目

例 It's taken almost two decades, but Shah is now sitting firmly on the company's leadership team and holds the **title** of global president of Mars Food & Nutrition. 虽然历时近20年, 但沙阿如今已稳居公司领导层, 并担任玛氏食品与营养全球总裁一职。

enthusiastic / ɪnˌθjuːziˈæstɪk /

释 *adj.* 热心的; 满腔热情的

搭 be enthusiastic about (doing) sth. 对(做)某事满腔热忱

例 The Faroese are so **enthusiastic** about music that the islands, despite having a population of just 56,000, have a music school in the capital of Torshavn and a full symphony orchestra. 法罗人对音乐是如此的热情, 以至于尽管这个岛上只有56 000的人口, 却在首都托尔港有一所音乐学校和一个完整的交响乐团。

aid / eɪd /

释 *n.* 援助; 救援物 *v.* 帮助

搭 in aid of sth./sb. 为了帮助某事物/某人

例 Here are a few ways AI is **aiding** companies without replacing employees. 以下是人工智能在不取代员工的情况下帮助公司的几种方式。(2021年)

atmosphere / ˈætməsfɪə(r) /

释 *n.* 大气, 大气层; 气氛; 氛围

例 The latest was a panel from the National Academy of Sciences, enlisted by the White House, to tell us that the Earth's **atmosphere** is definitely warming and that the problem is largely man-made. 最近的一次是由白宫邀请的美国国家科学院的一个专家小组, 他们告诉我们地球大气层确实在变暖, 而这个问题主要是人为造成的。(2005年)

feasible / ˈfiːzəbl / 　　　　　087

释 *adj.* 可行的；行得通的；做得到的

例 This includes permitting creative thinking and establishing a framework where experimentation is **feasible** and failures are seen as learning opportunities. 这包括允许创造性思维和建立一个框架，在这个框架中，实验是可行的，失败被视为学习的机会。

派 feasibility / ˌfiːzəˈbɪləti / *n.* 可行性

pupil / ˈpjuːpl / 　　　　　088

释 *n.* 学生，（尤指）小学生；弟子，门生

例 Teachers and principals warn that social apps have become a major distraction, prompting some **pupils** to keep messaging their friends during class. 教师和校长们警告说，社交应用程序成了主要的分心因素，促使一些学生在上课时不断给朋友发信息。

direction / dəˈrekʃn / 　　　　　089

释 *n.* 方向，方位；（发展）方向，趋势，倾向；指示，说明；导演

例 While firms of all sizes cut staff and overhead, chairman Bold sped in the opposite **direction**. 尽管各种规模的公司都在削减员工和日常开支，但董事长博尔德却在相反的方向加速前行。

various / ˈveəriəs / 　　　　　090

释 *adj.* 各种各样的；多姿多彩的

例 Those retailers may face headaches complying with **various** state sales tax laws. 这些零售商可能会面临遵守各州销售税法的难题。（2019年）

discard / dɪˈskɑːd / 　　　　　091

释 *v.* 丢弃；抛弃 *n.* 被抛弃的人（或物）

例 On a larger scale, over 50 billion garments are **discarded** within a year of being made. 在更大的范围内，超过500亿件衣服在被制成后的一年内被丢弃。

plus / plʌs / 　　　　　092

释 *conj.* 此外；而且，况且 *prep.* [数]加；和；也 *n.* [数]加号；优势，好处

例 **Plus**, whatever image we present is magnified by social-media services like LinkedIn. 此外，我们展示的任何形象都会被像领英这样的社交媒体放大。（2016年）

dubious / ˈdjuːbiəs / 　　　　　093

释 *adj.* 有疑虑的；可疑的；不太可靠的

例 Back then the market was still **dubious** of EVs: Tesla had only just started building its first car, the Roadster—and the Model S was still four years away. 当时市场对电动汽车仍有疑虑：特斯拉刚刚开始生产其首款汽车Roadster，而Model S的诞生还需要四年时间。

diet / ˈdaɪət /
094

释 *n.* 日常饮食；（因减肥而吃的）规定饮食 *v.* 节食 *adj.* 低热量的

例 But as **diet** and health improved, children and adolescents have, on average, increased in height by about an inch and a half every 20 years, a pattern known as the secular trend in height. 但随着饮食和健康状况的改善，儿童和青春期少年的身高平均每20年增加1.5英寸，这种模式被称为身高的长期趋势。（2008年）

delight / dɪˈlaɪt /
095

释 *n.* 高兴，愉快；令人高兴的事 *v.* 使高兴

搭 delight in (doing) sth. 以（做）某事为乐

例 Formerly, too, pictures had given him considerable, and music very great, **delight**. 以前，绘画也曾给他带来过极大的乐趣，音乐更是如此。（2008年）

spare / speə(r) /
096

释 *adj.* 不用的，闲置的；备用的 *v.* 留出，匀出；省得，免去

例 In eight months, the space station will have no deliveries of food, fuel, **spare** parts, or anything else. 在之后的八个月，空间站将没有食物、燃料、备用物品或其他任何东西送达。

alarm / əˈlɑːm /
097

释 *n.* 惊恐；惊慌；恐慌 *v.* 使惊恐；使害怕；使担心

例 The rapid spread of the disease has **alarmed** many people. 这种疾病的迅速蔓延使许多人感到害怕。

parallel / ˈpærəlel /
098

释 *adj.* 平行的；极相似的；同时发生的 *v.* 与……媲美，比得上；与……相似；与……同时发生

例 Arizona had attempted to fashion state policies that ran **parallel** to the existing federal ones. 亚利桑那州曾试图制定与现有联邦政策相似的州政策。

draw / drɔː /
099

释 *v.* 画，描绘；拖，拉；吸引

搭 draw back 退缩；撤销 ‖ draw on 凭借；利用

例 Clearly you try to comprehend, in the sense of identifying meanings for individual words and working out relationships between them, **drawing** on your implicit knowledge of English grammar. 显然，你设法理解文章，从某种意义上，利用你的英语语法的隐性知识识别每个单词的意思以及单词与单词之间的关系。（2015年）

breath / breθ /
100

释 *n.* 呼气；呼吸

搭 out of breath 喘不过气

例 It's a message even more bitter than a clove cigarette, yet, somehow, a **breath** of fresh air. 这是一种比丁香香烟还苦涩的信息，然而，不知何故，它也是一股新鲜的空气。（2006年）

☐ ☐ accuracy	☐ ☐ dismiss	☐ ☐ measure
☐ ☐ aid	☐ ☐ disorder	☐ ☐ miserable
☐ ☐ alarm	☐ ☐ draw	☐ ☐ motivate
☐ ☐ allege	☐ ☐ dubious	☐ ☐ necessitate
☐ ☐ atmosphere	☐ ☐ economics	☐ ☐ nurture
☐ ☐ award	☐ ☐ emphasis	☐ ☐ opportunity
☐ ☐ barrier	☐ ☐ enable	☐ ☐ original
☐ ☐ blame	☐ ☐ enthusiastic	☐ ☐ ornament
☐ ☐ boundary	☐ ☐ ethnic	☐ ☐ overall
☐ ☐ breath	☐ ☐ exclude	☐ ☐ parallel
☐ ☐ code	☐ ☐ extensive	☐ ☐ physiology
☐ ☐ comic	☐ ☐ extreme	☐ ☐ plus
☐ ☐ commercial	☐ ☐ facility	☐ ☐ profession
☐ ☐ communication	☐ ☐ fame	☐ ☐ progress
☐ ☐ commute	☐ ☐ favo(u)r	☐ ☐ pupil
☐ ☐ complement	☐ ☐ feasible	☐ ☐ recommend
☐ ☐ condition	☐ ☐ financial	☐ ☐ reduction
☐ ☐ confirm	☐ ☐ fit	☐ ☐ relationship
☐ ☐ contradict	☐ ☐ foster	☐ ☐ replace
☐ ☐ contrast	☐ ☐ grasp	☐ ☐ represent
☐ ☐ cultivate	☐ ☐ include	☐ ☐ resistant
☐ ☐ curve	☐ ☐ income	☐ ☐ reward
☐ ☐ deed	☐ ☐ inform	☐ ☐ shatter
☐ ☐ delay	☐ ☐ ingredient	☐ ☐ signal
☐ ☐ delight	☐ ☐ initial	☐ ☐ spare
☐ ☐ denote	☐ ☐ intellectual	☐ ☐ squeeze
☐ ☐ departure	☐ ☐ keen	☐ ☐ statute
☐ ☐ depend	☐ ☐ layout	☐ ☐ strike
☐ ☐ diet	☐ ☐ management	☐ ☐ superior
☐ ☐ direction	☐ ☐ march	☐ ☐ surface
☐ ☐ discard	☐ ☐ marginal	☐ ☐ suspect

☐ ☐ sympathetic
☐ ☐ system
☐ ☐ title
☐ ☐ universal
☐ ☐ various
☐ ☐ wake
☐ ☐ weight

音频

☐ concede	☐ stay	☐ exchange	☐ ahead
☐ excessive	☐ formulate	☐ cherish	☐ literary
☐ change	☐ bubble	☐ devil	☐ adolescent
☐ precision	☐ isolate	☐ expression	☐ comedy
☐ deprive	☐ refrain	☐ significant	☐ seldom
☐ capture	☐ deserve	☐ viewpoint	☐ channel
☐ proof	☐ expense	☐ duplicate	☐ stable
☐ property	☐ rise	☐ stir	
☐ sensitive	☐ emotion	☐ split	
☐ inventory	☐ embark	☐ magnify	
☐ hinder	☐ derive	☐ exceptional	
☐ dense	☐ reliance	☐ shape	
☐ arrogant	☐ administration	☐ behavio(u)ral	
☐ sheer	☐ cloak	☐ propagate	
☐ apply	☐ logic	☐ fancy	
☐ artificial	☐ consult	☐ fond	
☐ bait	☐ regret	☐ version	
☐ wit	☐ threaten	☐ send	
☐ inhale	☐ source	☐ react	
☐ ignorant	☐ alert	☐ lame	
☐ faith	☐ contribution	☐ passive	
☐ formation	☐ lead	☐ aggressive	
☐ remove	☐ instantaneous	☐ instrument	
☐ invest	☐ opponent	☐ lie	
☐ perpetual	☐ suit	☐ success	
☐ prime	☐ worthwhile	☐ fix	
☐ cite	☐ veteran	☐ proper	
☐ guidance	☐ reap	☐ occupation	
☐ gather	☐ poll	☐ bright	
☐ solidarity	☐ enrich	☐ stuff	
☐ vision	☐ mechanical	☐ shut	

Writing Models ◎

0001
concede / kən'siːd /

- 释 v. (不情愿地) 承认; 让予; 让步, 认输
- 搭 concede sth. to sb. 在某事上对某人让步
- 例 After being defeated in the war, the country **conceded** a portion of the land to its neighboring country. 战败后, 该国将一部分土地割让给了邻国。

0002
excessive / ɪk'sesɪv /

- 释 adj. 过多的; 过分的
- 例 Society also suffers from **excessive** employment protections. 过度的就业保护也会使社会蒙受损失。(2022年)

0003
change / tʃeɪndʒ /

- 释 n. 变化 v. 改变; 变换
- 例 But the force of geographic conditions peculiar to America, the interplay of the varied national groups upon one another, and the sheer difficulty of maintaining old-world ways in a raw, new continent caused significant **changes**. 但是, 美洲特有的地理条件的自然力、不同民族群体之间的相互影响, 以及在一个原始的新大陆上保持旧世界的方式所面临的巨大困难, 都导致了重大的变化。(2015年)

0004
precision / prɪ'sɪʒn /

- 释 n. 精确; 准确
- 例 Not all artistic works need this degree of **precision**. 并不是所有的艺术作品都需要这种程度的精确。
- 近 accuracy / 'ækjərəsi / n. 准确 ‖ exactness / ɪg'zæktnəs / n. 正确; 精确

0005
deprive / dɪ'praɪv /

- 释 v. 剥夺; 使丧失
- 搭 deprive sb. of sth. 使某人不能拥有某物
- 例 A lot of children from war-torn areas have been **deprived** of a normal life. 来自战乱地区的许多孩子被剥夺了正常的生活。
- 近 rob / rɒb / v. 抢劫 ‖ steal / stiːl / v. 偷窃; 窃取

0006
capture / 'kæptʃə(r) /

- 释 v. 捕获, 俘获; 拍摄; 吸引 n. 俘获; 占领
- 搭 capture one's attention/interest 引起某人的注意/兴趣
- 例 The images were **captured** outside the base by the TV crews. 这些影像是剧组人员在外景地拍摄的。
- 近 seize / siːz / v. 抓住 ‖ snatch / snætʃ / v. 抢夺, 夺走

0007
proof / pruːf /

- 释 n. 证明, 证据; 检验, 证实 adj. (构成合成词) 防……的, 抗……的
- 搭 proof of identity 身份证明
- 例 Can you provide any **proof** of identity? 你能提供什么身份证明吗?

property / ˈprɒpəti /

释 *n.* 所有物, 财产; 性质, 性能

搭 Each spouse retains whatever **property** he or she brought into the marriage, and jointly-acquired **property** is divided equally. 配偶双方均可保留其带进婚姻中的任何财产, 而共同财产则平分。(2016年)

sensitive / ˈsensətɪv /

释 *adj.* 敏感的; 有感知力的; 机密的; 灵敏的; 棘手的

例 Americans should take steps to protect their digital privacy. But keeping **sensitive** information on these devices is increasingly a requirement of normal life. 美国人应该采取措施保护自己的数字信息隐私。但是, 在这些设备上保存敏感信息越来越成为正常生活的需要。(2015年)

inventory / ˈɪnvəntri /

释 *n.* 库存; (商店的) 存货; (建筑物里的物品、家具等的) 清单; 财产清单

例 Quicker turnarounds mean less wasted **inventory**, more frequent releases, and more profit. 更快的周转意味着更少的库存浪费、更频繁的发布和更多的利润。(2013年)

hinder / ˈhɪndə(r) /

释 *v.* 阻止, 妨碍

搭 hinder sb. from doing sth. 阻止或阻碍某人做某事

例 The policy will promote rather than **hinder** reform. 这项政策将促进而不是妨碍改革。

近 inhibit / ɪnˈhɪbɪt / *v.* 抑制; 禁止

反 promote / prəˈməʊt / *v.* 促进; 提升

dense / dens /

释 *adj.* 密集的, 稠密的; (烟、雾等) 浓重的; 密度大的

搭 dense fog 浓雾

例 The temple lay deep within the **dense** forest. 那座寺庙坐落在密林深处。

arrogant / ˈærəgənt /

释 *adj.* 傲慢的, 自大的; 嚣张的

例 An **arrogant** person will act as though he is better than others. 傲慢的人总表现得好像高人一等。

近 proud / praʊd / *adj.* 自豪的; 高傲的 ‖ haughty / ˈhɔːti / *adj.* 傲慢的; 目中无人的

反 modest / ˈmɒdɪst / *adj.* 谦逊的 ‖ humble / ˈhʌmbl / *adj.* 谦逊的

sheer / ʃɪə(r) / 014

释 *adj.* 纯粹的; 十足的, 全然的

搭 by sheer chance 完全出于偶然

例 Mary won the skating competition by **sheer** luck. 玛丽能赢得这次滑冰比赛纯属运气好。

apply / ə'plaɪ / 015

释 *v.* 应用, 实施; 申请, 请求; 涂上; 施用

搭 apply to 适用; 应用 ‖ apply for 向……申请

例 This pesticide can be diluted with water and **applied** directly to the fields. 这种杀虫剂用水稀释便可直接施用在农田里。

artificial / ˌɑːtɪ'fɪʃl / 016

释 *adj.* 人造的, 人工的; 人为的

例 The debate is not about **artificial** intelligence but about **artificial** consciousness. 争论的焦点不是人工智能, 而是人工意识。

bait / beɪt / 017

释 *v.* 下诱饵; 故意激怒 *n.* 饵; 用作诱饵的人

例 The fish snapped at the **bait**. 那条鱼咬住了鱼饵。

wit / wɪt / 018

释 *n.* 才智, 智慧; 悟性

搭 at one's wits' end 智穷技尽

例 He hasn't the **wits** to realize the danger. 他悟性差, 没有意识到危险。

近 intelligence / ɪn'telɪdʒəns / *n.* 智力 ‖ wisdom / 'wɪzdəm / *n.* 智慧

辨 wit指先天的智力、悟性等, 隐含小聪明的意味; intelligence指处理或应对问题或情况的特殊才智; wisdom较文雅, 也可指明智的言行。

inhale / ɪn'heɪl / 019

释 *v.* 吸入; 吸气

例 Jack closed his eyes and **inhaled** deeply before diving. 杰克潜水前闭上眼, 深深地吸了一口气。

派 inhalation / ˌɪnhə'leɪʃn / *n.* 吸气; 吸入药

ignorant / 'ɪɡnərənt / 020

释 *adj.* 无知的; 愚昧的

搭 be ignorant of 对……不了解, 不知道

例 You will be happy to convince people with bad arguments. You can call their views stupid, or joke about how **ignorant** they are. 你会乐于用糟糕的论据说服别人。你可以说他们的观点是愚蠢的, 也可以对他们如此的无知开玩笑。(2019年)

○ Study Notes

faith / feɪθ /

释 n. 信心；信任；宗教信仰

例 While most leaders sought to maintain Catholicism as the official religion of the new states, some sought to end the exclusion of other **faiths**. 虽然大多数领导人都试图维持天主教作为新州的官方宗教，但也有一些人试图结束对其他宗教信仰的排斥。（2007年）

formation / fɔːˈmeɪʃn /

释 n. 建造；形成；养成；建立；编队，队形；组成物

搭 formation flying 编队飞行

例 Brain researchers have discovered that the **formation** of new habits can be guided. 大脑研究人员发现，新习惯的养成是可以引导的。（2009年）

remove / rɪˈmuːv /

释 v. 移开；去除

例 Companies are using artificial intelligence to **remove** some of the unconscious bias from hiring decisions. 公司正在利用人工智能去除招聘决策中的一些无意识偏见。（2021年）

invest / ɪnˈvest /

释 v.（把资金）投入；投资；投入（时间、精力等）

例 Now it is a good time to **invest** in the property market. 现在是对房地产市场投资的好时机。

perpetual / pəˈpetʃuəl /

释 adj. 持续的，长久的；一再重复的

例 The **perpetual** noise of traffic almost drives me crazy. 不绝于耳的交通噪音几乎把我逼疯了。

近 endless / ˈendləs / adj. 无止境的；连续的

prime / praɪm /

释 n. 全盛时期；初期；青年 adj. 首要的，主要的；最佳的 v. 使准备好；填装

搭 Prime Minister 首相 ‖ in the prime of life 盛年

例 When Hoffa's Teamsters were in their **prime** in 1960, only one in ten American government workers belonged to a union; now 36% do. 1960 年，当霍法的卡车司机工会处于全盛时期时，每10名美国政府工作人员中只有1人加入工会，而现在有 36% 的人加入了工会。（2012年）

cite / saɪt /

释 v. 引证，引用；举例；召唤，传讯；指控

例 The author **cited** a passage from Shakespeare. 作者引用了莎士比亚的一段文字。

近 adduce / əˈdjuːs / v. 引证；举出 ‖ quote / kwəʊt / v. 引用；引证

Writing Models ⊚ ....

guidance

gather

solidarity

vision

stay

formulate

bubble

isolate

refrain

deserve

expense

rise

emotion

guidance / 'gaɪdns /   028

释 *n.* 指导；引导；（火箭等的）制导，导航；咨询

例 This **guidance** can be used as a compass, directing us towards confident and purposeful strides in achieving our 2024 career goals. 这种指导可以作为指南针，指引我们在实现2024年职业目标上充满信心、目标明确地大步前进。

gather / 'ɡæðə(r) /   029

释 *v.* 聚集；召集；收集；积聚；认为；猜想

例 They **gather** all the data they can, not just performance statistics and biographical details but also the results of their own laboratory experiments with high achievers. 他们收集一切可以收集到的数据，不仅包括成绩统计数据和履历详情，还包括他们自己与成绩优异者进行实验室实验的结果。（2007年）

solidarity / ˌsɒlɪ'dærəti /   030

释 *n.* 团结，一致

例 A world of peace and **solidarity** can only be accomplished by acknowledging and celebrating the diversity. 只有承认和颂扬多样性才能实现一个和平与团结的世界。

vision / 'vɪʒn /   031

释 *n.* 憧憬；远见卓识；视力，视野；幻象；画面

例 Up until a few decades ago, our **visions** of the future were largely—though by no means uniformly—glowingly positive. 直到几十年前，我们对未来的憧憬在很大程度上——尽管丝毫不一致——是极其乐观的。（2013年）

stay / steɪ /   032

释 *v.* 保持；停留；待；逗留；暂住 *n.* 停留，逗留

搭 stay up 深夜不睡；熬夜 ‖ stay out 待在户外；不在家

例 We're doing these things because we know they help people **stay** off benefits and help those on benefits get into work faster. 我们正在做这些事情，因为我们知道它们能帮助人们远离救济金，并帮助那些领取救济金的人更快地找到工作。（2014年）

formulate / 'fɔːmjuleɪt /   033

释 *v.* 制订；规划；构想；准备；确切表达，认真阐述

例 Next time you state your position, **formulate** an argument for what you claim and honestly ask yourself whether your argument is any good. 下次你表明立场时，请为自己的主张准备论据，并诚实地问问自己，你的论据是否有道理。（2019年）

bubble / 'bʌbl /   034

释 *n.* 泡沫；气泡 *v.* 冒泡；沸腾；继续发生

例 The stock **bubble** harms the healthy development of economic entities. 股市泡沫对实体经济的健康发展有害。

◎ Study Notes

isolate / ˈaɪsəleɪt / 035

释 *v.* 分离；（使）孤立，隔绝

搭 isolate... from... 使……与……分离

例 Patients will be **isolated** from other people for between one week and one month after treatment. 治疗之后，患者将会被与他人隔离一周到一个月的时间不等。

refrain / rɪˈfreɪn / 036

释 *v.* 抑制，克制；节制；避免

例 California has asked the justices to **refrain** from a sweeping ruling, particularly one that upsets the old assumptions that authorities may search through the possessions of suspects at the time of their arrest. 加利福尼亚已经要求法官们避免做出一刀切的裁决，尤其是推翻有关当局可以在嫌疑人被捕时搜查其财产的旧有假设的裁决。（2015年）

deserve / dɪˈzɜːv / 037

释 *v.* 值得；应得；应受

例 While animals in captivity **deserve** sympathy, zoos play a significant role in starting young people down the path of related sciences. 虽然被囚禁的动物值得同情，但动物园在启蒙青少年走上相关科学道路方面发挥着重要作用。（2022年）

expense / ɪkˈspens / 038

释 *n.* 费用；花销，业务费；价钱；花钱的东西 *v.* 向……收取费用

搭 at the expense of 在牺牲（或损害）……的情况下 ‖ at sb.'s expense 由某人付钱

例 There seems to be a predominance of short-term thinking at the **expense** of long-term investing. 以牺牲长期投资为代价的短期思维似乎占据了主导地位。（2019年）

rise / raɪz / 039

释 *v.* 上升；（数量）增加，增长；提高；升起；站起来；起床；起义；起源 *n.* 上升；（数量或水平的）增加，提高；增强；加薪

例 When work started again on Monday, output duly **rose** compared with the previous Saturday and continued to **rise** for the next couple of days. 周一重新开工后，产量比上周六适当增加了，并在接下来的几天里持续上升。（2010年）

emotion / ɪˈməʊʃn / 040

释 *n.* 情感；情绪；激情；强烈的感情

例 According to one classical theory of **emotion**, our feelings are partially rooted in physical reactions. 根据一个经典的情感理论，我们的情感部分源于生理反应。（2011年）

派 emotional / ɪˈməʊʃənl / *adj.* 情感上的；情绪的；易情绪激动的

embark / ɪmˈbɑːk /

释 v. 登（船），上（船）；开始从事
搭 embark on 着手，开始做
例 Although more than half of Harvard undergraduates end up in law, medicine or business, future doctors and lawyers must study a non-specialist liberal-arts degree before **embarking** on a professional qualification. 尽管超过半数的哈佛本科生最终就读法律、医学或商业专业，但未来的医生和律师在着手获得专业资格前必须学习一个非专科的人文学科学位。

derive / dɪˈraɪv /

释 v. 源自，源于；得到，获得（优势或愉快的感受）
搭 derive from 由……而来，源自
例 The supposed importance of influentials **derives** from a plausible-sounding but largely untested theory called the "two-step flow of communication": Information flows from the media to the influentials and from them to everyone else. 有影响力者的所谓重要性来自一个听起来似乎很有道理但却基本上未经验证的理论，即"两级传播理论"：信息从媒体流向有影响力的人，再从他们流向其他人。（2010年）
派 derivation / ˌderɪˈveɪʃn / n. 起源；派生
近 secure / sɪˈkjʊə(r) / v. 获得，获取
辨 derive常指自然获得某结果，指客观过程；secure侧重表达获得事物和维持事物的困难性。

reliance / rɪˈlaɪəns /

释 n. 依靠，依赖
搭 reliance on/upon 对……的依靠、依赖
例 While the quality of legal journalism varies greatly, there is an undue **reliance** amongst many journalists on interpretations supplied to them by lawyers. 虽然法律新闻的质量参差不齐，但在许多记者中存在对律师提供给他们的解释的过分依赖。（2007年）

administration / ədˌmɪnɪˈstreɪʃn /

释 n. 管理；行政；（尤指美国）政府；执行；行政部门；管理部门；施行
例 It is as though 20 years of ever-tougher reforms of the job search and benefit **administration** system never happened. 就好像20年来对求职和福利管理制度进行的越来越严厉的改革从未发生过一样。（2014年）
派 administrative / ədˈmɪnɪstrətɪv / adj. 管理的；行政的

cloak / kləʊk /

释 v. 遮蔽，掩盖 n. 斗篷，披风；遮盖物
例 The talk was **cloaked** in secrecy. 会谈是秘密进行的。

logic / ˈlɒdʒɪk /

释 n. 逻辑; 逻辑性; 条理性; (做某事的) 道理; 思维方式

例 Humanity's relationship with machines became disappointed, not just at work—where efficiency, automation, and quantity dominated values—but also with this **logic** spilling into consumer experiences. 人类与机器的关系变得令人失望, 这不仅体现在工作中——效率、自动化和数量 (在工作中) 主导了价值观, 还体现在这种思维方式渗透到了消费者体验中。

consult / kənˈsʌlt /

释 v. 咨询; 请教; (与某人) 商议, 商量 (以得到许可或帮助决策); 查阅; 查询; 参看

例 Our team **consulted** multiple experts, including a physical therapist, and some fitness and health editors, and also viewed thousands of expert reviews to find the very best options available online. 我们的团队咨询了多位专家, 包括一名理疗师以及一些健身健康编辑, 还浏览查看了数千条专家评论, 以找到网上可用的最佳选择。

regret / rɪˈgret /

释 n. 悔恨; 失望; 后悔; 遗憾 v. 对……感到后悔或抱歉; 因……遗憾

例 It doesn't seem quite fair, then, to compare the **regrets** of parents to the **regrets** of the childless. 因此, 将为人父母者的遗憾与无子女者的遗憾相提并论似乎不太公平。(2011年)

threaten / ˈθretn /

释 v. 威胁; 危及; 恐吓; 对……构成威胁; 扬言要; 有……危险; 预示凶兆

例 More Americans are opting to work well into retirement, a growing trend that **threatens** to upend the old workforce model. 越来越多的美国人选择一直工作到退休, 这一日益增长的趋势对颠覆旧的劳动力模式构成了威胁。

source / sɔːs /

释 n. 来源, 出处; 根源, 起源 v. (从……) 获得

搭 at source 在源头; 在发源地; 从一开始

例 Candidates are required to publish the **sources** of their campaign funds. 候选人被要求公布其竞选经费的来源。

近 origin / ˈɒrɪdʒɪn / n. 起源 ‖ root / ruːt / n. 根源

alert / əˈlɜːt /

释 n. 提示; 警报 v. 使警觉, 使警惕 adj. 警惕的; 戒备的

搭 be alert to 对……保持警惕

例 He wanted to **alert** people to the activities of the group. 他想警告人们注意这个组织的行动。

contribution / ˌkɒntrɪˈbjuːʃn /　　　052

㊾ *n.* 贡献；促成作用；捐款

㊭ make contribution to 为……做贡献

㊀ His **contribution** is to offer the most readable overview of the science to date. 他的贡献是提供了迄今最具可读性的科学综述。

lead / liːd /　　　053

㊾ *v.* 引领；通往；领先；过……的生活；导致，致使；引导 *n.* 领先；铅；主角

㊀ Such practices can **lead** an article to accrue more than 150 citations in the same year that it was published. 这种做法可能导致一篇文章在发表当年就被引用超过150次。（2023年）

instantaneous / ˌɪnstənˈteɪniəs /　　　054

㊾ *adj.* 瞬间的，即刻的

㊀ We live in an age when information is pretty much **instantaneous**. 我们生活在一个信息瞬息万变的时代。

opponent / əˈpəʊnənt /　　　055

㊾ *n.* 反对者；对手，竞争者；阻止者

㊀ Pairs of **opponents** hit the ball back and forth until one winner emerges from all who entered. 多组竞争者来回击球，直到所有参赛者中产生一名获胜者。（2019年）

㊚ rival / ˈraɪvl / *n.* 对手；可匹敌者 ‖ competitor / kəmˈpetɪtə(r) / *n.* 竞争者，对手

㊫ ally / ˈælaɪ / *n.* 同盟者；支持者

suit / suːt /　　　056

㊾ *v.* 适合；适宜；相配；有利于；合身；满足（某人）需要；对（某人）方便 *n.* 诉讼；套装；西服

㊀ It's not obvious how the capacity to visualize objects and to figure out numerical patterns **suits** one to answer questions that have eluded some of the best poets and philosophers. 将物体可视化和计算数字模式的能力是如何有利于一个人回答一些连最优秀的诗人和哲学家都无法回答的问题的，这一点我们尚不清楚。（2007年）

㊙ suitable / ˈsuːtəbl / *adj.* 合适的

worthwhile / ˌwɜːθˈwaɪl /　　　057

㊾ *adj.* 值得的；重要的；值得花时间（或花钱、努力等）；令人愉快的

㊀ As always there will be some in-house candidates as well as some **worthwhile** names to look at around college football. 与往常一样，会有一些内部候选人以及一些值得大学橄榄球赛事关注的名字。

veteran / ˈvetərən / 058

释 *n.* 经验丰富的人；退伍军人；老手；老兵 *adj.*（尤指军事方面）老练的；资格老的

例 The **veteran** worker ranks high in public love and esteem. 那位老工人深受大伙的爱戴。

reap / riːp / 059

释 *v.* 收获，获得；收割

搭 You reap what you sow. 一分耕耘，一分收获。

例 The modest receive benefit, while the conceited **reap** failure. 谦受益，满招损。

近 gain / geɪn / *v.* 获得，赢得

poll / pəʊl / 060

释 *n.* 民意测验，民意调查；选举投票，计票 *v.* 做民意调查

搭 carry out/conduct a poll 进行民意测验

例 From the online **poll**, at the time of writing, only 30% of users had been able to upgrade, or do a clean install, without any problems. 截止到写这篇文章的时候，从线上调查来看，只有30%的用户能够顺利升级或者进行简洁安装。

enrich / ɪnˈrɪtʃ / 061

释 *v.* 充实；使丰富；使富有

例 Most breakfast cereals are **enriched** with vitamins. 多数谷物早餐都富含维生素。

mechanical / məˈkænɪkl / 062

释 *adj.* 机械的，机动的；呆头呆脑的

例 For example, the Long Now Foundation has as its flagship project a **mechanical** clock that is designed to still be marking time thousands of years hence. 例如，Long Now 基金会将一个机械钟表作为其旗舰项目，其设计目的是在几千年后仍能显示时间。（2013年）

exchange / ɪksˈtʃeɪndʒ / 063

释 *n.* 交换；交流；交易所；兑换；对话 *v.* 交换；交流；交易；更换

例 The conference is a good place to share information and **exchange** ideas. 研讨会是互通信息、交流思想的好场合。

cherish / ˈtʃerɪʃ / 064

释 *v.* 珍惜；重视；维护；爱护；怀念

例 It was a wonderful occasion which we will **cherish** for many years to come. 那是一个美好的时刻，我们将在未来的许多年中倍加怀念。

devil / ˈdevl / 065

释 *n.*（尤指基督教中的）魔鬼

例 The cartoon represented the president as a **devil**. 这幅漫画把那位总统画成了一个魔鬼。

expression

significant

viewpoint

duplicate

stir

split

magnify

exceptional

shape

behavio(u)ral

propagate

fancy

fond

expression / ɪkˈspreʃn /

066

释 *n.* 表达；表情；表达方式

例 The statement could serve as a reminder to business leaders about the value of free **expression**. 该声明可以作为企业领导人注意言论自由的价值的一个提醒。

significant / sɪgˈnɪfɪkənt /

067

释 *adj.* 有重大意义的；显著的；意味深长的；重大的

例 The building has housed some of the nation's most **significant** diplomats and politicians and has been the scene of many historic events. 这座建筑曾接待过一些国家最重要的外交官和政治家，也是许多历史事件的发生地。（2018年）

viewpoint / ˈvjuːpɔɪnt /

068

释 *n.* 观点；看法；视角

例 He explained his **viewpoint** that taxes should be increased. 他解释了他认为税收应该增加的观点。

duplicate

069

释 / ˈdjuːplɪkət / *n.* 复制品；副本 *adj.* 复制的；副本的
/ ˈdjuːplɪkeɪt / *v.* 复写；复制；复印

例 Is this a **duplicate** or the original? 这是复制品还是原件？

派 duplication / ˌdjuːplɪˈkeɪʃn / *n.* 复制；重复

近 copy / ˈkɒpi / *n.* 复制品 *v.* 复制

stir / stɜː(r) /

070

释 *v.* 搅动，搅拌；引发，激起；（使）微动 *n.* 搅动；轰动；纷乱，骚乱

例 I've found quite a few, and—since I started posting them on Twitter—they have been causing quite a **stir**. 我发现了不少，自从我开始把它们发布到推特上，它们就引起了不小的轰动。（2021年）

split / splɪt /

071

释 *v.* 分开；分裂；分手，断绝关系 *n.* 分裂；分离；划分；分别；分歧；裂缝

例 "Carry a book with you at all times" can work if time can be evenly **split** for reading and working. 如果阅读和工作的时间可以平均分配的话，随身携带一本书会很有帮助。

近 apart / əˈpɑːt / *adv.* 相距；分离；成碎片；（指所说的不包括在内）除外

magnify / ˈmægnɪfaɪ /

072

释 *v.* 放大；增大；夸大

例 These challenges can be **magnified** for smaller studios with limited resources. 对于资源有限的小型工作室来说，这些挑战可能会被放大。

派 magnification / ˌmægnɪfɪˈkeɪʃn / *n.* 放大；放大倍数

073

exceptional / ɪkˈsepʃənl /

释 *adj.* 非凡的，卓越的；例外的

例 Your team should be composed of individuals who share your passion for the industry and who have the skills and expertise to provide **exceptional** service to your clients. 你的团队应该由那些与你一样对这个行业充满热情，并具备为客户提供卓越服务的技能和专业知识的人组成。

074

shape / ʃeɪp /

释 *v.* 决定……的形成；塑造 *n.* 形状；状况；情况

搭 out of shape 变形的；走样的 ‖ take shape 成形；有了模样

例 This is because the networked computer has sparked a secret war between downloading and uploading—between passive consumption and active creation—whose outcome will **shape** our collective future in ways we can only begin to imagine. 这是因为联网的计算机在下载和上传之间——在被动消费和主动创造之间——引发了一场秘密战争，其结果将以我们才刚刚开始想象的方式塑造我们共同的未来。（2012年）

075

behavio(u)ral / bɪˈheɪvjərəl /

释 *adj.* 行为方面的；行为科学的

例 These issues all have root causes in human behavior: all require **behavioral** change and social innovations, as well as technological development. 这些问题都有人类行为的根源：都需要行为改变和社会创新，以及技术发展。（2013年）

076

propagate / ˈprɒpəgeɪt /

释 *v.* 传播；宣传；繁殖

例 Television advertising **propagates** a false image of the ideal family. 电视广告传播着理想家庭的一种假象。

派 propagation / ˌprɒpəˈgeɪʃn / *n.* 宣传

077

fancy / ˈfænsi /

释 *v.* 想要；认为；设想；自负；爱慕；自认为是；自命不凡 *n.* 想象（力）；爱好；想象的事物 *adj.* 花哨的；精致的；绚丽的

搭 catch/take sb.'s fancy 吸引某人；中某人的意

例 He started to chat to me and I could tell that he really **fancied** himself. 他和我聊起天来，我看得出他确实自以为了不起。

078

fond / fɒnd /

释 *adj.* 喜爱的；深情的

搭 be fond of 喜欢

例 The closure announcement sparked some to recall **fond** memories of the platform. 关闭公告引发了一些人回想起关于该平台的美好回忆。

Writing Models ◎ ·············

version

send

react

lame

passive

aggressive

instrument

lie

success

fix

proper

occupation

version / 'vɜːʃn /

079

释 *n.* 版本; 变体; 说法

例 It said that Internet Explorer 10, the **version** due to appear with Windows 8, would have DNT as a default. 它表示, Internet Explorer 10（将随Windows 8一起发布的版本）将把DNT作为默认设置。（2013年）

send / send /

080

释 *v.* 邮寄; 发送; 转达; 派遣; 使作出（某种反应）; 告知

搭 send for sb. 请某人来（帮忙等）‖ send out 分发; 散发

例 Under the ruling Thursday, states can pass laws requiring out-of-state sellers to collect the state's sales tax from customers and **send** it to the state. 根据周四的裁决, 各州可以通过法规, 要求州外卖家向客户收取州销售税并将其上缴到该州。（2019年）

react / ri'ækt /

081

释 *v.* 回应;（对……）作出反应; 起化学反应

搭 react against 反对; 反抗

例 As to how a team should **react** to a game like this, James didn't have answers. 至于一支球队应该如何对这样一场比赛做出反应, 詹姆斯没有答案。

派 reaction / ri'ækʃn / *n.* 反应; 回应

lame / leɪm /

082

释 *adj.* 瘸的; 跛的; 站不住脚的; 无说服力的

例 He was aware that she was **lame** in one leg. 他知道她有一条腿是瘸的。

passive / 'pæsɪv /

083

释 *adj.* 消极的; 被动的; 被动语态的

例 And hours of watching TV shows with canned laughter only teaches kids to process information in a **passive** way. 看几个小时有预录笑声的电视节目只会教会孩子以被动的方式处理信息。

aggressive / ə'gresɪv /

084

释 *adj.* 好斗的; 挑衅的; 侵略的; 积极进取的

例 In those situations, it's better to be more **aggressive** than less **aggressive**. 在这种情况下, 积极一点总比消极一点好。（2016年）

instrument / 'ɪnstrəmənt /

085

释 *n.* 仪器; 器具; 乐器; 受利用（或控制）的人; 工具

例 If you want to play an **instrument** well, you've got to stick at it. 要想练好一种乐器, 你必须持之以恒。

派 instrumental / ˌɪnstrə'mentl / *adj.* 用乐器演奏的; 起重要作用的

086

lie / laɪ /

释 v. 躺；平躺；平卧；处于；位于；在于；说谎 n. 说谎；谎言

搭 lie in 在于

例 The miracle of the Chesapeake Bay **lies** not in its depths, but in the complexity of its natural construction, the interaction of fresh and saline waters, and the mix of land and water. 切萨皮克湾的奇迹不在于它的深度，而在于其复杂的自然构造、淡水和盐水的相互作用以及水陆交融。（2024年）

087

success / sək'ses /

释 n. 成功；胜利；发财；成名；成功的人（或事物）

例 Despite **success** stories like van Oosten's, preservation of plastics will likely get harder. 尽管有像凡·奥斯腾这样的成功故事，但塑料的保存可能会变得越来越困难。（2022年）

派 successful / sək'sesfl / adj. 获得成功的；有成效的

088

fix / fɪks /

释 v. 使固定；安装；确定；安排；修理，维修；处理，解决；收拾 n. 解决方案（措施）

搭 fix up 修理

例 Now comes word that everyone involved—Democrats, Republicans, the Postal Service, the unions and the system's heaviest users—has finally agreed on a plan to **fix** the system. 现在有消息称，所有相关方——民主党人、共和党人、邮政服务局、工会和该系统最重要的用户——终于就一项维修该系统的计划达成了一致。（2018年）

089

proper / 'prɒpə(r) /

释 adj. 适宜的；合适的；适当的；正确的；恰当的；得体的；符合规则的

例 Millions of people who live in informal settlements in Kenya lack access to **proper** nutrition, adequate sanitation, and quality health care, leaving them vulnerable to preventable diseases. 在肯尼亚，数百万生活在非正式住区的人无法获得适当的营养、达标的卫生设施和高质量的医疗保健，这使他们容易感染本可预防的疾病。

090

occupation / ˌɒkju'peɪʃn /

释 n. 工作；职业

例 Certain industries will be impacted by AI automation, including industries that are not of a scientific and technological nature, such as managerial, economic, and legal **occupations**. 某些行业将受到人工智能自动化的影响，包括不具有科学和技术性质的行业，如管理、经济和法律职业。

派 occupational / ˌɒkju'peɪʃənl / adj. 职业的

Writing Models ◎

bright

stuff

shut

ahead

literary

adolescent

comedy

seldom

channel

stable

bright / braɪt /

091

释 *adj.* 明亮的; 聪明的; 有希望的; 鲜艳的

例 In the 1960s, the Italian artist Piero Gilardi began to create hundreds of **bright**, colorful foam pieces. 20世纪60年代, 意大利艺术家皮耶罗·吉拉迪开始创造数百件色彩鲜艳的泡沫制品。(2022年)

stuff / stʌf /

092

释 *n.* 东西, 物品

例 But that hasn't stopped a myriad of start-ups from selling the **stuff** to customers with the hopes of expanding their lifespans and managing their weight. 但这并没有阻止无数的初创企业向希望能延年益寿、控制体重的客户销售这种东西。

shut / ʃʌt /

093

释 *v.* 关闭; 关上; (使)停止营业

搭 shut down 关张; 停业 ‖ shut off 关闭; 关上; 停止运转 ‖ shut up 住口, 闭嘴

例 First, they can **shut** things down without suffering much in the way of consequences. 首先, 他们可以在不承担太多后果的情况下关闭一切。(2012年)

ahead / əˈhed /

094

释 *adv.* 向前面, 在前面; 提前; 在将来 *prep.* 在……前面; 将要发生; 领先于, 超过; 提前

搭 ahead of 在……前面; 领先于

例 But improved regulation will not be the only key to the wider adoption of anti-drone technologies in the years **ahead**. 但在未来几年, 改善监管并不是反无人机技术得到更广泛采用的唯一关键。

literary / ˈlɪtərəri /

095

释 *adj.* 文学的; 文学上的; 书面的

例 Scandinavia is renowned for its rich culture, including its Viking history, modern design, and a strong **literary** tradition. 斯堪的纳维亚以其丰富的文化而闻名, 包括维京人的历史、现代设计和强大的文学传统。

adolescent / ˌædəˈlesnt /

096

释 *adj.* 青春期的 *n.* 青春期少年

例 UNICEF estimates that one in seven children and **adolescents** between the ages of 10 and 19 is living with a mental disorder. 联合国儿童基金会估计, 每七个10至19岁的儿童和青春期少年中就有一个有精神障碍。

派 adolescence / ˌædəˈlesns / *n.* 青春期

comedy / ˈkɒmədi /

097

释 *n.* 喜剧; 喜剧片; 滑稽; 幽默; 诙谐

例 Basically, the movie blends elements of fantasy, **comedy**, and drama to tell the story of a woman's quest for freedom. 总的来说，这部电影融合了幻想、喜剧和戏剧性元素，讲述了一个女人追求自由的故事。

seldom / ˈseldəm /

098

释 *adv.* 不常; 难得; 很少

例 Public-sector unions **seldom** get in trouble for their actions. 公共部门的工会很少因为他们的行为而惹上麻烦。（2012年）

channel / ˈtʃænl /

099

释 *n.* 电视频道; 渠道; 途径; 海峡; 方式, 方法

例 Authors welcome the new **channel** for publication. 作者们欢迎这种新的出版方式。

stable / ˈsteɪbl /

100

释 *adj.* 稳定的; 沉稳的

例 His analysis should therefore end any self-contentedness among those who may believe that the global position of English is so **stable** that the young generations of the United Kingdom do not need additional language capabilities. 因此，他的分析应该终结一些人的自满情绪，这些人可能认为英语的全球地位如此稳定，以至于英国的年轻一代不需要额外的语言能力。（2017年）

派 stability / stəˈbɪləti / *n.* 稳定（性）

- ☐ ☐ administration
- ☐ ☐ adolescent
- ☐ ☐ aggressive
- ☐ ☐ ahead
- ☐ ☐ alert
- ☐ ☐ apply
- ☐ ☐ arrogant
- ☐ ☐ artificial
- ☐ ☐ bait
- ☐ ☐ behavio(u)ral
- ☐ ☐ bright
- ☐ ☐ bubble
- ☐ ☐ capture
- ☐ ☐ change
- ☐ ☐ channel
- ☐ ☐ cherish
- ☐ ☐ cite
- ☐ ☐ cloak
- ☐ ☐ comedy
- ☐ ☐ concede
- ☐ ☐ consult
- ☐ ☐ contribution
- ☐ ☐ dense
- ☐ ☐ deprive
- ☐ ☐ derive
- ☐ ☐ deserve
- ☐ ☐ devil
- ☐ ☐ duplicate
- ☐ ☐ embark
- ☐ ☐ emotion
- ☐ ☐ enrich

- ☐ ☐ exceptional
- ☐ ☐ excessive
- ☐ ☐ exchange
- ☐ ☐ expense
- ☐ ☐ expression
- ☐ ☐ faith
- ☐ ☐ fancy
- ☐ ☐ fix
- ☐ ☐ fond
- ☐ ☐ formation
- ☐ ☐ formulate
- ☐ ☐ gather
- ☐ ☐ guidance
- ☐ ☐ hinder
- ☐ ☐ ignorant
- ☐ ☐ inhale
- ☐ ☐ instantaneous
- ☐ ☐ instrument
- ☐ ☐ inventory
- ☐ ☐ invest
- ☐ ☐ isolate
- ☐ ☐ lame
- ☐ ☐ lead
- ☐ ☐ lie
- ☐ ☐ literary
- ☐ ☐ logic
- ☐ ☐ magnify
- ☐ ☐ mechanical
- ☐ ☐ occupation
- ☐ ☐ opponent
- ☐ ☐ passive

- ☐ ☐ perpetual
- ☐ ☐ poll
- ☐ ☐ precision
- ☐ ☐ prime
- ☐ ☐ proof
- ☐ ☐ propagate
- ☐ ☐ proper
- ☐ ☐ property
- ☐ ☐ react
- ☐ ☐ reap
- ☐ ☐ refrain
- ☐ ☐ regret
- ☐ ☐ reliance
- ☐ ☐ remove
- ☐ ☐ rise
- ☐ ☐ seldom
- ☐ ☐ send
- ☐ ☐ sensitive
- ☐ ☐ shape
- ☐ ☐ sheer
- ☐ ☐ shut
- ☐ ☐ significant
- ☐ ☐ solidarity
- ☐ ☐ source
- ☐ ☐ split
- ☐ ☐ stable
- ☐ ☐ stay
- ☐ ☐ stir
- ☐ ☐ stuff
- ☐ ☐ success
- ☐ ☐ suit

- ☐ ☐ threaten
- ☐ ☐ version
- ☐ ☐ veteran
- ☐ ☐ viewpoint
- ☐ ☐ vision
- ☐ ☐ wit
- ☐ ☐ worthwhile

音频

- [ ] imagination
- [ ] gasp
- [ ] bribe
- [ ] label
- [ ] inspire
- [ ] collapse
- [ ] intricate
- [ ] formula
- [ ] immerse
- [ ] hint
- [ ] obtain
- [ ] blunder
- [ ] attain
- [ ] colonial
- [ ] elite
- [ ] deceive
- [ ] identity
- [ ] payment
- [ ] explore
- [ ] flight
- [ ] insist
- [ ] express
- [ ] recovery
- [ ] organize/-ise
- [ ] simulate
- [ ] sanction
- [ ] continue
- [ ] concept
- [ ] initiative
- [ ] imply
- [ ] core

- [ ] clarify
- [ ] additional
- [ ] privilege
- [ ] vanish
- [ ] expectation
- [ ] expect
- [ ] fossil
- [ ] envy
- [ ] indulge
- [ ] count
- [ ] persuade
- [ ] slogan
- [ ] domestic
- [ ] apparent
- [ ] consequently
- [ ] bypass
- [ ] beneficial
- [ ] parliament
- [ ] permit
- [ ] appreciate
- [ ] motion
- [ ] concrete
- [ ] emigrate
- [ ] paradox
- [ ] republican
- [ ] exhibit
- [ ] liability
- [ ] state
- [ ] equation
- [ ] subtle
- [ ] likewise

- [ ] excess
- [ ] interpret
- [ ] obligation
- [ ] forecast
- [ ] note
- [ ] exclaim
- [ ] abandon
- [ ] prosperity
- [ ] terrific
- [ ] setback
- [ ] moderate
- [ ] join
- [ ] decide
- [ ] fresh
- [ ] bottom
- [ ] prize
- [ ] trail
- [ ] literacy
- [ ] activity
- [ ] trap
- [ ] wealth
- [ ] anxiety
- [ ] tolerance
- [ ] choice
- [ ] exception
- [ ] interference
- [ ] freedom
- [ ] doctrine
- [ ] comprehensive
- [ ] bear
- [ ] staff

- [ ] bloody
- [ ] hate
- [ ] edge
- [ ] run
- [ ] surprise
- [ ] arbitrary
- [ ] excel

imagination / ɪˌmædʒɪ'neɪʃn /

释 *n.* 想象力；想象；幻想物；创造力
例 These novels still have a great attraction for young readers of today because of their bold **imagination** and scientific accuracy. 因为这些小说大胆的想象和科学方面的准确性，它们对于今天的年轻读者来说仍然有极大的吸引力。

001

gasp / gæsp /

释 *n.* 喘气，喘息；倒吸气 *v.* 倒吸气
搭 the last gasp 最后时刻 ‖ gasp for breath 上气不接下气
例 After running a marathon, my breath came in short, quick **gasps**. 跑完马拉松后，我呼吸短促，气喘吁吁。

002

bribe / braɪb /

释 *n./v.* 贿赂
例 The senator damaged his image by accepting the **bribe**. 那位参议员因收受贿赂而损害了自己的形象。

003

label / 'leɪbl /

释 *n.* 标记；标签；外号；叫法；唱片公司 *v.* 贴标签于；（尤指不公正地）把……称为
例 Stick a **label** on your suitcase. 贴一个标签在你的手提箱上。

004

inspire / ɪn'spaɪə(r) /

释 *v.* 激励；鼓舞；赋予灵感；启发思考；引起联想
例 Artifacts in museums have the power to **inspire**, and perhaps spark that need to learn and understand the nature of their creators. 博物馆中的手工艺品具有激发灵感的力量，或许能激发人们学习和了解其创造者本质的需求。（2024年）

005

collapse / kə'læps /

释 *n./v.* 倒塌，瓦解；突然失败；贬值；暴跌
例 The emerging consensus around the bill is a sign that legislators are getting frightened about a politically embarrassing short-term **collapse** at the USPS. 围绕该法案逐渐形成的共识表明，立法者们开始恐惧美国邮政会在政治上出现令人尴尬的短期崩溃。（2018年）

006

intricate / 'ɪntrɪkət /

释 *adj.* 错综复杂的；难以理解的
例 She likes reading novels with **intricate** plots. 她喜欢看情节错综复杂的小说。
近 complex / 'kɒmpleks / *adj.* 复杂的 ‖ complicated / 'kɒmplɪkeɪtɪd / *adj.* 复杂的；难懂的

007

formula / 'fɔ:mjələ / 008

释 *n.* 公式，方程式；准则，方案；分子式

例 What is the **formula** for water? 水的分子式是什么？

派 formulate / 'fɔ:mjuleɪt / *v.* 制定，规划；确切表达，认真阐述 ‖ formulation / ˌfɔ:mju'leɪʃn / *n.* 规划；制定

immerse / ɪ'mɜ:s / 009

释 *v.* 使浸没于；（使）深陷于，沉浸在，专心于

搭 immerse sb./sth. in 使沉浸在，使专注于

例 Artists and scientists alike are **immersed** in discovery and invention, and challenge and critique are core to both, too. 艺术家和科学家都沉浸在发现和发明之中，而挑战和批评也是两者的核心工作。（2022年）

hint / hɪnt / 010

释 *n.* 暗示；提示；线索；秘诀 *v.* 暗示；示意

搭 give a hint 给出提示 ‖ take the hint 领会到暗示/提示/线索

例 And perhaps faintly, they **hint** that people should look to intangible qualities like character and intellect rather than dieting their way to size zero or wasp-waist physiques. 也许它们（禁令）隐隐约约地暗示了人们应该注重品格和智力等无形的品质，而不是通过节食来达到零号身材或黄蜂腰体型。（2016年）

obtain / əb'teɪn / 011

释 *v.* 获得，赢得；（规则、制度、习俗等）存在；流行；沿袭

例 Parenting tips **obtained** from hunter-gatherers in Africa may be the key to bringing up more contented children, researchers have suggested. 研究人员认为，从非洲狩猎采集者那里获得的育儿诀窍可能是培养出更满意的孩子的关键。（2024年）

blunder / 'blʌndə(r) / 012

释 *v.* 犯愚蠢错误；跌跌跄跄地走；误入（危险或困境）*n.* 愚蠢的错误

搭 blunder about/around 跌跌跄跄地走

例 The travelers **blundered** about the dark forest. 旅行者们在黑暗的森林中跄跄前行。

attain / ə'teɪn / 013

释 *v.* 获得，得到；达到

例 You have much more skills to **attain** so don't let imaginary limits hinder your growth. 你还有很多要去获得的技能，所以不要让那些虚构的限制阻碍了你的成长。

colonial / kə'ləʊniəl / 014

释 *adj.* 殖民的；殖民国家的；殖民主义的 *n.* 生活在殖民地的宗主国居民

例 Tunisia achieved independence from France **colonial** rule in 1956. 突尼斯于1956年从法国的殖民统治下获得了独立。

elite / eɪ'liːt / 〔0 1 5〕

释 *n.* 精英 *adj.* 精英的；最优秀的

例 Instead of intimate shops catering to a knowledgeable **elite** these were stores anyone could enter, regardless of class or background. 这些商店不再是为知识精英服务的私密商店，而是任何人都可以进入的商店，无论其社会阶级或背景如何。（2006年）

deceive / dɪ'siːv / 〔0 1 6〕

释 *v.* 欺骗；误导

搭 deceive oneself 自欺

例 He was foiled in his attempt to **deceive** us. 他企图欺骗我们，但没有得逞。

identity / aɪ'dentəti / 〔0 1 7〕

释 *n.* 身份；本身；本体；同一性；一致；特有的感觉（或信仰）

例 Their names of this article have been changed for the purposes to protect their **identities**. 出于保护他们的身份的目的，本文对他们的姓名进行了改动。

payment / 'peɪmənt / 〔0 1 8〕

释 *n.* 付款额；支付；报酬，报答

例 It's the hardest thing to take care of a teenager, have a job, pay the rent, pay the car **payment**, and pay the debt. 既要照顾青少年，又要工作、交房租、付车费、还债，这是最困难的事情。（2008年）

explore / ɪk'splɔː(r) / 〔0 1 9〕

释 *v.* 勘探；勘查；探索；考察；探究；调查研究；探讨

例 Chaudhary said that Britain should **explore** the possibility that older siblings helping their parents "might also enhance their own social development". 乔杜里说，英国应探讨哥哥姐姐帮助父母"也可能促进其自身社交发展"的可能性。（2024年）

flight / flaɪt / 〔0 2 0〕

释 *n.* 航班，班机；航行，航程；（物体的）飞行，飞行方向；一段楼梯；（一起飞行的）鸟群（或机群）

例 Have you noticed that you can leave on a **flight** an hour late but still arrive on time? 你有没有注意到，你可能晚了一个小时起飞，但航班仍然准时抵达了？

insist / ɪn'sɪst / 〔0 2 1〕

释 *v.* 坚决要求；坚持；坚持说；固执己见

搭 insist on/upon 坚决要求

例 King Juan Carlos of Spain once **insisted** "kings don't abdicate, they die in their sleep." 西班牙国王胡安·卡洛斯曾坚称"国王不会退位，他们会在睡梦中死去"。（2015年）

express / ɪkˈspres /

释 v. 表示；表达；（想法、情感）流露；呈现 adj. 特快的；快速的；快递的；明白表示的 n. 快速列车；快递服务；快运服务

例 Teenagers are paradoxical. That's a mild and detached way of saying something that parents often **express** with stronger language. 青少年是自相矛盾的。这是一种温和且客观的说法，而父母们往往用更强硬的语言来表达这种说法。

recovery / rɪˈkʌvəri /

释 n. 痊愈；复原，恢复；复苏，好转；取回

搭 recovery from 从……中恢复

例 Improved consumer confidence is crucial to an economic **recovery**. 消费者信心的提升对经济的复苏至关重要。

近 restoration / ˌrestəˈreɪʃn / n. 恢复

organize/-ise / ˈɔːɡənaɪz /

释 v. 组织；安排

例 Mies's signature phrase "less is more" means that less decoration, properly **organized**, has more impact than a lot. 米斯的惯用语"少即多"的意思是：合理安排的情况下，较少的装饰比过多的装饰效果更好。

近 arrange / əˈreɪndʒ / v. 安排，筹备

simulate / ˈsɪmjuleɪt /

释 v. 假装，冒充；模仿

例 The professor showed us some insects that **simulated** dead leaves. 教授向我们展示了一些伪装成枯叶的昆虫。

sanction / ˈsæŋkʃn /

释 n. 制裁；批准；许可 v. 批准；许可

例 The basic point is that **sanctions** cannot be counted on to produce a sure result. 最重要的一点是，制裁并不一定能带来一个确定的结果。

continue / kənˈtɪnjuː /

释 v. 持续；继续存在；继续做；（停顿后）再开始

例 The value of work is also driving folks to **continue** working past retirement. 工作的价值也促使人们在退休后继续工作。

concept / ˈkɒnsept /

释 n. 概念；观念

例 Privacy law builds on the **concept** of damage to an individual from identifiable knowledge about them. 隐私法建立在因可识别的个人身份信息对其本人造成损害的概念之上。（2018年）

Writing Models

initiative

imply

core

clarify

additional

privilege

vanish

expectation

expect

fossil

envy

indulge

count

persuade

initiative / ɪˈnɪʃətɪv / 029

释 *n.* 新动议，倡议；主动性，主动权；首创精神

例 If the Administration won't take the legislative **initiative**, Congress should help to begin fashioning conservation measures. 如果政府不采取立法行动，国会应该帮助开启制定保护措施。（2005年）

imply / ɪmˈplaɪ / 030

释 *v.* 暗示；含有……的意思；说明

例 Are there tragedies? Of course. But they are the exception, not the norm that Ms. Marris **implies**. 有悲剧吗？当然有。但它们只是例外，而不是马里斯女士所暗示的常态。（2022年）

近 suggest / səˈdʒest / *v.* 暗示；建议

core / kɔː(r) / 031

释 *adj.* 核心的 *n.* 核心，要点；果核

例 In America, the **core** scientific publishing market is estimated at between $7 billion and $11 billion. 在美国，核心科学出版市场估计在70亿至110亿美元之间。（2008年）

近 principal / ˈprɪnsəpl / *adj.* 主要的，首要的 ‖ primary / ˈpraɪməri / *adj.* 主要的

反 marginal / ˈmaːdʒɪnl / *adj.* 边际的；末端的；微小的

clarify / ˈklærəfaɪ / 032

释 *v.* 澄清；阐明；纯净，净化；使更清晰易懂

例 You should go through the paper many times—and then again—working to substantiate and **clarify** your ideas. 你应该多次通读论文，然后再次通读，努力证实和阐明你的观点。（2008年）

additional / əˈdɪʃənl / 033

释 *adj.* 附加的，额外的

例 The government is expected to lay an **additional** tax on us by the end of the year. 年底，政府估计要向我们征收一项附加税。

近 extra / ˈekstrə / *adj.* 额外的

privilege / ˈprɪvəlɪdʒ / 034

释 *n.* （有钱有势者的）特权，特殊待遇；特殊利益

例 Health care is a **privilege** in Kenya, especially for residents of informal settlements who often get into debt to receive some of the most basic health care services. 在肯尼亚，医疗保健是一种特权，特别是对于非正规住区的居民来说，他们常常为了获得一些最基本的医疗保健服务而负债累累。

vanish / ˈvænɪʃ / 035

释 *v.* 突然消失；消亡

例 With a wave of his hand, the magician made the rabbit **vanish**. 魔术师手一挥就把兔子变没了。

近 disappear / ˌdɪsəˈpɪə(r) / *v.* 消失；失踪

expectation / ˌekspek'teɪʃn /

释 *n.* 预期；期望，期盼

搭 against/contrary to (all) expectations 出乎意料；意想不到

例 Indeed, grade forgiveness is just another way that universities are responding to consumers' **expectations** for higher education. 事实上，成绩豁免只是大学满足消费者对高等教育期望的另一种方式。（2019年）

近 hope / həʊp / *n.* 希望，期望 ‖ outlook / 'aʊtlʊk / *n.* 展望

036

expect / ɪk'spekt /

释 *v.* 预期；预计；期待；要求；指望；猜想

例 Citizens still have a right to **expect** private documents to remain private and protected by the Constitution's prohibition on unreasonable searches. 公民仍然有权要求私人文件保持私密性，并受到《宪法》关于禁止无理搜查规定的保护。（2015年）

037

fossil / 'fɒsl /

释 *n.* 化石；（尤指）老顽固

搭 living fossil 活化石

例 The **fossil** record shows that many species have endured for millions of years—so why shouldn't we? 化石记录表明，许多物种已经存活了数百万年，那么为什么我们不能呢？（2013年）

038

envy / 'envi /

释 *v.* 羡慕；忌妒 *n.* 羡慕；忌妒；羡慕的对象；令人忌妒的特征

例 All these abilities are the **envy** of scientists, who have spent a lot of time and money designing robots. 所有这些能力都是花费大量的时间和金钱设计机器人的科学家们忌妒的对象。

039

indulge / ɪn'dʌldʒ /

释 *v.* 纵容；（使）沉溺；放纵；满足

搭 indulge in 沉溺，纵容

例 The British welfare system **indulges** jobseekers' laziness. 英国的福利制度纵容了求职者的懒惰。（2014年）

040

count / kaʊnt /

释 *v.* 数数；有价值；认为；把……算入 *n.* 总数

例 Grade forgiveness allows students to retake a course in which they received a low grade, and the most recent grade or the highest grade is the only one that **counts** in calculating a student's overall GPA. 成绩豁免允许学生重修成绩较低的课程，在计算学生的总平均学分绩点时，只把最近的成绩或最高成绩计算在内。（2019年）

041

persuade / pə'sweɪd /

释 *v.* 说服；劝说；使相信

例 I allowed myself to be **persuaded** into entering the conference. 我被说服参加了会议。

042

Writing Models

slogan

domestic

apparent

consequently

bypass

beneficial

parliament

permit

appreciate

motion

concrete

emigrate

slogan / ˈsləʊɡən / 0453

释 *n.* 标语，口号

例 In dealing with a challenge on such a scale, it is no exaggeration to say, "United we stand, divided we fall"—and if I had to choose a **slogan** it would be "Unity in our diversity." 在应对如此大规模的挑战时，可以毫不夸张地说，"团结则存，分裂则亡"——如果让我选择一个口号的话，那就是"在我们的多样性中求团结"。（2005年）

近 banner / ˈbænə(r) / *n.* 横幅；标语

domestic / dəˈmestɪk / 0454

释 *adj.* 国内的；家庭的；家用的；家务的；驯养的

例 The kinds of interpersonal violence that women are exposed to tend to be in **domestic** situations, by, unfortunately, parents or other family members, and they tend not to be one-shot deals. 不幸的是，女性遭受的人际暴力往往发生在家庭环境中，由父母或其他家庭成员造成，而且往往不是一次性的。（2008年）

apparent / əˈpærənt / 0455

释 *adj.* 显然的；显而易见的；表面上的；貌似的

搭 for no apparent reason 莫名其妙地

例 Other artists besides Rutkowski have been surprised by the **apparent** popularity of their work in text-to-image generators—and some are now fighting back. 除了鲁特科夫斯基，其他艺术家也对自己的作品在文本到图像生成器中的明显人气感到惊讶——有些人现在正在进行反击。（2024年）

consequently / ˈkɒnsɪkwəntli / 0456

释 *adv.* 因此，因而

例 This will pose a threat to agriculture and the food chain, and **consequently** to human health. 这会对农业和食物链造成威胁，并因此危害人类健康。

bypass / ˈbaɪpɑːs / 0457

释 *v.* 绕过，避开；不顾 *n.* 心脏搭桥手术；（绕过城镇中心的）旁道

例 Instead, the new habits we deliberately press into ourselves create parallel pathways that can **bypass** those old roads. 相反，我们刻意让自己养成的新习惯会创造出平行的道路，可以绕过那些旧路。（2009年）

beneficial / ˌbenɪˈfɪʃl / 0458

释 *adj.* 有益的，有利的；可帮助的

例 Certain decisions were made that seemed meaningful and necessary at the time, but in retrospect, we know that some of them are not as **beneficial** as the creators then believed. 做出某些决策在当时似乎是有意义且必要的，但回顾一下，我们就会发现其中有些决策并不像创建者当时认为的那样有益。

parliament / ˈpɑːləmənt /

释 *n.* 议会; 国会; 一届议会

例 He suggested that the **parliament** should give legislative drafters more time to prepare bills. 他建议, 议会应该给法律文件起草人更多的时间来准备提案。

permit

释 / ˈpɜːmɪt / *n.* 许可; 许可证 / pəˈmɪt / *v.* 允许; 使成为可能, 成为可能

例 An inspector filed a complaint with the municipal government because the building did not acquire a **permit** for the work. 由于这栋建筑没有获得施工许可, 一名检查员向市政府提出了投诉。

appreciate / əˈpriːʃieɪt /

释 *v.* 欣赏; 理解; 感激; 升值

例 Sometimes years are required for truly novel discovery claims to be accepted and **appreciated**. 有时, 真正新颖的发现声明需要数年时间才能被接受和理解。(2012年)

motion / ˈməʊʃn /

释 *n.* 运动; 提议, 动议 *v.* 示意; 做动作

搭 in motion 在运转中

例 For example, a busy street might not suit a **motion**-sensored door, as it would constantly be opening for passers-by. 例如, 在一条繁忙的街道上可能不适合使用运动感应门, 因为它会不断地为路人开门。(2024年)

派 motionless / ˈməʊʃnləs / *adj.* 不动的, 静止的

concrete / ˈkɒŋkriːt /

释 *adj.* 有形的; 实在的; 确实的, 具体的; 混凝土制的 *n.* 混凝土

例 **Concrete** is a mixture of sand and cement. 混凝土是沙和水泥的混合物。

emigrate / ˈemɪɡreɪt /

释 *v.* 移居国外; 移居

搭 emigrate from ... to ... 从……移民到……

例 A tailor named John Dane, who **emigrated** in the late 1630s, left an account of his reasons for leaving England that is filled with signs. 一位名叫约翰·戴恩的裁缝在17世纪30年代末移居国外, 他留下了关于他离开英国原因的记录, 上面写满了标语。(2009年)

派 emigrant / ˈemɪɡrənt / *n.* 从本国移往他国的移民; 侨民 ‖ emigration / ˌemɪˈɡreɪʃn / *n.* 移居外国, 迁移出境

反 immigrate / ˈɪmɪɡreɪt / *v.* 移入, 移居入境

paradox / 'pærədɒks / 〔055〕

释 *n.* 自相矛盾；悖论；似非而是的论点

例 The **paradox** is that the region's most dynamic economies have the most primitive financial systems. 自相矛盾的是，该地区最具活力的经济体制有着最原始的金融体系。

近 contradiction / ˌkɒntrə'dɪkʃn / *n.* 矛盾；反驳

republican / rɪ'pʌblɪkən / 〔056〕

释 *n.* 共和党员；共和主义者 *adj.* 共和国的；共和政体的

例 But embarrassing scandals and the popularity of the **republican** left in the recent Euro-elections have forced him to eat his words and stand down. 但是，令人尴尬的丑闻和共和党左翼在最近欧洲议会选举中的受欢迎程度迫使他不得不食言并下台。（2015年）

exhibit / ɪg'zɪbɪt / 〔057〕

释 *v.* 展览；展出；表现，显出（感情、品质或能力）*n.*（一件）展览品，陈列品；物证

例 She **exhibits** the idealism common to many advocates of sustainability, be it in food or in energy. 她表现出许多可持续发展倡导者所共有的理想主义，无论是在食品还是能源方面。（2013年）

liability / ˌlaɪə'bɪləti / 〔058〕

释 *n.* 责任；[pl.]负债，债务；累赘

例 Meanwhile, it has more than \$120 billion in unfunded **liabilities**, mostly for employee health and retirement costs. 同时，它还有超过1 200 亿美元的负债资金没有着落，主要是员工的医疗和退休费用。（2018年）

state / steɪt / 〔059〕

释 *n.* 状态；状况；国家；州；邦；政府 *v.* 陈述；说明；声明；规定；公布 *adj.* 国家提供（或控制）的；州的；邦的

例 In Maryland, the good news is that there are many **state** laws in place that provide wetlands protections. 在马里兰州，好消息是有许多州法律提供湿地保护。（2024年）

equation / ɪ'kweɪʒn / 〔060〕

释 *n.* 方程式，公式；平衡；综合体

例 What does Y represent in this **equation**? 这个方程式中的Y代表什么？

subtle / 'sʌtl / 〔061〕

释 *adj.* 不易察觉或描述的，微妙的；巧妙的；灵敏的

例 The **subtle** and intelligent little book *The Marketplace of Ideas: Reform and Resistance in the American University* should be read by every student thinking of applying to take a doctoral degree.《思想的市场：美国大学的改革与反抗》这本小书精妙而睿智，每一个打算申请博士学位的学生都应该读一读这本书。（2011年）

近 delicate / 'delɪkət / *adj.* 微妙的；精细的

likewise / ˈlaɪkwaɪz /

释 *adv.* 同样地；又，也，而且

例 Some have little power to do good, and they have **likewise** little strength to resist evil. 一些人没有能力去做善事，同样他们也没有力量抵制邪恶。

excess

释 / ˈekses / *adj.* 过量的，额外的 / ɪkˈses / *n.* 过量，过剩

搭 in excess 过度地，过分

例 For women, the association may be attributable to changes in immunity that resulted from **excess** abdominal fat; in men, the immune system did not appear to be involved. 对于女性来说，这种关联可能是由于腹部脂肪过多导致免疫力发生变化；而对于男性来说，免疫系统似乎与此无关。（2021年）

interpret / ɪnˈtɜːprət /

释 *v.* 解释；口译

例 One could **interpret** much of the work of Beethoven by saying that suffering is inevitable, but the courage to fight it renders life worth living. 贝多芬的许多作品都可以这样解释：苦难是不可避免的，但与苦难抗争的勇气使生命更有价值。（2014年）

派 interpretation / ɪnˌtɜːprəˈteɪʃn / *n.* 解释；口译 ‖ interpreter / ɪnˈtɜːprətə(r) / *n.* 口译者；解释者

obligation / ˌɒblɪˈgeɪʃn /

释 *n.* 责任；义务

例 Whoever has done the damage is under **obligation** to pay for it. 凡造成损坏的人均有赔偿的责任。

近 responsibility / rɪˌspɒnsəˈbɪləti / *n.* 责任；义务 ‖ duty / ˈdjuːti / *n.* 责任；义务

辨 obligation、responsibility和duty都有"义务"的意思。obligation指道义上或法律上对他人的义务，强调强制性，也指因做出承诺而被迫履行的某种义务；responsibility指根据任何义务或职责应尽的本分，强调对他人的责任；duty指一个人按道德和法律的标准要尽的义务，强调自觉性。

forecast / ˈfɔːkɑːst /

释 *n./v.* 预测；预报

例 But policymakers who refocus efforts on improving well-being rather than simply worrying about GDP figures could avoid the **forecasted** doom and may even see progress. 但是，如果政策制定者能够重新将工作重点放在改善福祉上，而不是简单地担心国内生产总值数字，就可以避免预测的厄运，甚至可能看到进步。（2017年）

note / nəut / `067`

释 v. 提到; 注意到 n. 证明; 记录; 笔记
例 I'll make a **note** of our next meeting in my diary. 我将把下次会议的事在我的记事簿上做个记录。

exclaim / ɪkˈskleɪm / `068`

释 v. 呼喊, 惊叫; 大声说
搭 exclaim at 对……惊叫; 斥责
例 The frightened girl started shivering and **exclaiming**. 那个受惊的女孩开始颤抖并惊叫起来。

abandon / əˈbændən / `069`

释 v. 遗弃、抛弃; 放弃 n. 放任, 放纵
例 The baby had been **abandoned** by her mother. 这个婴儿被其母亲遗弃了。

prosperity / prɒˈsperəti / `070`

释 n. 繁荣; 成功
例 Today, policy-makers must choose with respect to AI: freedom or technocracy, **prosperity** or economic insignificance. 今天, 政策制定者们必须在人工智能方面做出选择: 自由还是技术统治, 繁荣还是经济无足轻重。

terrific / təˈrɪfɪk / `071`

释 adj. 极好的, 了不起的; 很大的, 巨大的
例 My sister is a **terrific** jazz singer. 我姐姐是个很棒的爵士乐歌手。
近 wonderful / ˈwʌndəfl / adj. 极好的; 精彩的 ‖ superb / suːˈpɜːb / adj. 极好的; 超凡的

setback / ˈsetbæk / `072`

释 n. 阻碍; 挫折
例 He had suffered a **setback** in his career. 他曾经在事业上遭遇过挫折。

moderate `073`

释 / ˈmɒdəreɪt / v. 使缓和, 使适中 / ˈmɒdərət / adj. (数量或程度) 适中的; 温和的; (变化) 不大的 n. 温和派 (尤指政见)
例 Such bodily reaction might conceivably help **moderate** the effects of psychological stress. 可以想象, 这种身体反应可能有助于缓和心理压力的影响。(2011年)
近 mild / maɪld / adj. 温和的; 轻微的

join / dʒɔɪn / `074`

释 v. 连接; 结合; 加入
搭 join in 加入, 参加 ‖ join up 入伍; 联合
例 I've had my doubts about his work since he **joined** the firm. 自从他加入公司以来, 我对他的工作一直有怀疑。

decide / dɪ'saɪd / 075

释 *v.* 决定；裁决；成为（某人）做某事的原因

搭 decide on/upon 决定；选定

例 The Nobels were, of course, themselves set up by a very rich individual who had **decided** what he wanted to do with his own money. 当然，诺贝尔奖本身是由一个非常富有的人设立的，他决定了他想用自己的钱做什么。（2014年）

派 decision / dɪ'sɪʒn / *n.* 决定

fresh / freʃ / 076

释 *adj.* 新鲜的；新产的；清新的；精力充沛的；刚从……来；新近出现的

例 When a faculty or department grows from, say, 5 to 20 members within three or four years, and when the new staff are predominantly young men and women **fresh** from postgraduate study, they largely define the norms of academic life in that faculty. 比如说，当一个学院或部门在三到四年内从5人增加到20人，当新员工主要是刚从研究生院毕业的年轻男女时，他们在很大程度上决定了该院系的学术生活规范。

bottom / 'bɒtəm / 077

释 *n.* 底部；最下部 *adj.* 底部的；最后的；尽头的

搭 at bottom 归根结底；本质上；实际上

例 At the **bottom** of the leaderboard was Alyson and Sasha with a 51/60. 选手积分榜上排名垫底的是艾莉森和萨沙，积分分别为51和60。

prize / praɪz / 078

释 *n.* 奖；奖赏；奖励；难能可贵的事物

例 First, most researchers would accept such a **prize** if they were offered one. 首先，如果给大多数研究人员一个这样的奖励，他们会接受的。（2014年）

trail / treɪl / 079

释 *n.* 痕迹，踪迹；（乡间的）小路

例 When you find yourself off a **trail**, but not in a completely unfamiliar area of land, you have to answer two questions: Which way is downhill, in this particular area? And where is the nearest water source? 当你发现自己偏了一条小路，但并不是在一个完全陌生的地方，你必须回答两个问题：在这个特定区域，哪条路是下坡？还有最近的水源在哪里？（2019年）

literacy / 'lɪtərəsi / 080

释 *n.* 读写能力；识字；有文化

例 For this essay, Laura spoke with librarians and **literacy** experts to determine the best books for toddlers. 为了写这篇文章，劳拉与图书管理员和扫盲专家进行了交谈，以确定最适合幼儿阅读的书籍。

activity / æk'tɪvəti /

释 *n.* 活动; 活跃状况

例 So, what Kennedy was referring to was that while GDP has been the most common method for measuring the economic **activity** of nations, as a measure, it is no longer enough. 所以, 肯尼迪所指的是, 虽然GDP一直是衡量国家经济活动的最常用方法, 但作为一种衡量标准, 它已经不够充分了。(2017年)

081

trap / træp /

释 *n.* 陷阱; 诡计; 困境, 牢笼 *v.* 使陷入困境; 卡住

搭 trap sb. into (doing) sth. 使某人陷入圈套而做某事

例 Thus poor countries might not be able to escape their poverty **traps** without changes that may be possible only with broader formal education. 因此, 如果没有变革, 贫穷国家可能无法摆脱自身的贫困陷阱, 而这种变革只有通过更广泛的正规教育才能实现。

082

wealth / welθ /

释 *n.* 钱财; 财产; 财物; 财富

搭 wealth of 大量; 众多

例 This type of integrity requires well-enforced laws in government transparency, such as records of official meetings, rules on lobbying, and information about each elected leader's source of **wealth**. 这种廉正要求有关政府透明度方面的法律得到严格执行, 如官方会议记录、游说规则以及每位当选领导人的财产来源信息。(2017年)

083

anxiety / æŋ'zaɪəti /

释 *n.* 焦虑; 忧虑; 担心; 渴望

例 A more direct finding is that people who scored high for negative emotions like **anxiety** looked at others for shorter periods of time and reported more comfortable feelings when others did not look directly at them. 一个更直接的发现是, 像是焦虑这种负面情绪得分高的人看别人的时间更短, 而且他们说当别人不直视他们时, 他们感觉更自在。(2020年)

084

tolerance / 'tɒlərəns /

释 *n.* 忍受; 宽容; 忍耐力; 耐力

例 They are talking **tolerance**, but few take action. 他们都在谈论宽容, 但很少有人采取行动。

085

choice / tʃɔɪs /

释 *n.* 选择; 选择权; 供选择的品种; 可选的范围

搭 by choice 出于自己的选择

例 They then set up a "food station" experiment, in which they gave the elephants a series of **choices** based only on smell. 然后, 他们设置了一个"食物站"实验, 实验中, 他们让大象仅根据气味做出一系列选择。(2024年)

近 option / 'ɒpʃn / *n.* 可选的事物; 选择

086

exception / ɪk'sepʃn /

087

释 *n.* 例外；例外的事物

搭 make an exception 让……成为例外 ‖ without exception 一律；无一例外

例 But those **exceptions** have been nearly inaccessible in all but the most extreme cases. 但是，除了最极端的情况外，这些例外几乎都无法实现。

派 exceptional / ɪk'sepʃənl / *adj.* 特别的；杰出的

interference / ˌɪntə'fɪərəns /

088

释 *n.* 干涉；干预；介入；干扰

例 The number of women on corporate boards has been steadily increasing without government **interference**. 在没有政府干预的情况下，公司董事会中的女性人数一直在稳步增长。（2020年）

freedom / 'friːdəm /

089

释 *n.* 自由

例 Especially significant was his view of **freedom**, which, for him, was associated with the rights and responsibilities of the individual: he advocated **freedom** of thought and of personal expression. 特别重要的是他的自由观，在他看来自由关系到个人的权利和责任；他主张思想自由和个人表达自由。（2014年）

doctrine / 'dɒktrɪn /

090

释 *n.* 教义；主义；学说；信条

例 For a generation, the collective **doctrine** has been that the sorting mechanism of society should be profit. 一代人以来，集体主义一直认为，社会的分类机制应该是利润。（2015年）

comprehensive / ˌkɒmprɪ'hensɪv /

091

释 *adj.* 全部的；（几乎）无所不包的；综合性的

例 A smartphone may contain an arrestee's reading history, financial history, medical history and **comprehensive** records of recent correspondence. 智能手机可能包含被捕者的阅读记录、财务记录、医疗史和近期通信的综合记录。（2015年）

派 comprehensiveness / ˌkɒmprɪ'hensɪvnəs / *n.* 综合；详尽

bear / beə(r) /

092

释 *v.* 承受；忍受；承担责任；显示；生育 *n.* 熊

搭 bear with 耐心对待；容忍

例 Who will **bear** the blame for this tragedy? 谁将为这场悲剧承担责任？

staff / staːf /

093

释 *n.* 全体职员；员工 *v.* 任职于；为……配备职员

例 We advertised for **staff** in a local newspaper. 我们在一份地方报纸上登了广告招聘员工。

Writing Models ⊙

bloody

hate

edge

run

surprise

arbitrary

excel

bloody / ˈblʌdi /　094

🈂 *adj.* 流血的; 血腥的 *v.* 使流血

🈐 Thousands of people died in this **bloody** war. 成千上万人在这场血腥的战争中丧生。

hate / heɪt /　095

🈂 *v.* 厌恶, 讨厌; 不愿, 不想

🈐 Networkers get most of their motivation from building relationships with colleagues and are more likely to **hate** working from home. 社交型员工的工作动力主要来自与同事建立关系, 他们更可能讨厌在家办公。

edge / edʒ /　096

🈂 *n.* 边缘; 边线; 边沿; 优势

🈳 on the edge of 在……的边缘; 濒临 ‖ be on edge 紧张不安的

🈐 They're relying on him to give the team a cutting **edge**. 他们指望他给这个队伍带来优势。

run / rʌn /　097

🈂 *v.* 跑; 运行; 经营 *n.* 跑步; 竞选

🈳 run for 竞选 ‖ in the long/short run 从长/短期来看

🈐 Plants can't **run** away from danger, so investing energy in a body system which recognizes a threat and can feel pain would be a very poor evolutionary strategy, according to the article. 这篇文章说, 植物不能逃避危险, 所以把能量投入到一个能识别威胁并能感受到疼痛的身体系统中是一种非常糟糕的进化策略。（2022年）

surprise / səˈpraɪz /　098

🈂 *n.* 意外; 惊讶; 意想不到（或突然）的事 *adj.* 令人惊奇的; 出乎意料的 *v.* 使吃惊; 使惊喜

🈐 The game proved to be a **surprise** hit with critics and received numerous gaming awards nominations. 事实证明, 这款游戏出人意料地受到了评论界的青睐, 并获得了众多游戏奖项的提名。

arbitrary / ˈɑːbɪtrəri /　099

🈂 *adj.* 随意的; 任意的; 武断的; 随心所欲的; 专横的

🈐 I don't know why I chose that one; it was a completely **arbitrary** decision. 我不知道我为什么选择了这个; 这完全是一个随意的决定。

excel / ɪkˈsel /　100

🈂 *v.* 擅长; 善于; 突出

🈳 excel in/at 擅长

🈐 Cardona discussed the Department of Education's priorities, including providing students with training needed to **excel** in their careers. 卡多纳讨论了教育部的优先事项, 包括为学生们提供在职业生涯中脱颖而出所需的培训。

Review

□ □ abandon
□ □ activity
□ □ additional
□ □ anxiety
□ □ apparent
□ □ appreciate
□ □ arbitrary
□ □ attain
□ □ bear
□ □ beneficial
□ □ bloody
□ □ blunder
□ □ bottom
□ □ bribe
□ □ bypass
□ □ choice
□ □ clarify
□ □ collapse
□ □ colonial
□ □ comprehensive
□ □ concept
□ □ concrete
□ □ consequently
□ □ continue
□ □ core
□ □ count
□ □ deceive
□ □ decide
□ □ doctrine
□ □ domestic
□ □ edge

□ □ elite
□ □ emigrate
□ □ envy
□ □ equation
□ □ excel
□ □ exception
□ □ excess
□ □ exclaim
□ □ exhibit
□ □ expect
□ □ expectation
□ □ explore
□ □ express
□ □ flight
□ □ forecast
□ □ formula
□ □ fossil
□ □ freedom
□ □ fresh
□ □ gasp
□ □ hate
□ □ hint
□ □ identity
□ □ imagination
□ □ immerse
□ □ imply
□ □ indulge
□ □ initiative
□ □ insist
□ □ inspire
□ □ interference

□ □ interpret
□ □ intricate
□ □ join
□ □ label
□ □ liability
□ □ likewise
□ □ literacy
□ □ moderate
□ □ motion
□ □ note
□ □ obligation
□ □ obtain
□ □ organize/-ise
□ □ paradox
□ □ parliament
□ □ payment
□ □ permit
□ □ persuade
□ □ privilege
□ □ prize
□ □ prosperity
□ □ recovery
□ □ republican
□ □ run
□ □ sanction
□ □ setback
□ □ simulate
□ □ slogan
□ □ staff
□ □ state
□ □ subtle

□ □ surprise
□ □ terrific
□ □ tolerance
□ □ trail
□ □ trap
□ □ vanish
□ □ wealth

图书在版编目(CIP)数据

20天背完考研英语（一）核心词汇 / 新东方考试研
究中心编著. -- 杭州：浙江教育出版社，2024.4
ISBN 978-7-5722-7720-7

Ⅰ.①2… Ⅱ.①新… Ⅲ.①英语－词汇－研究生－
入学考试－自学参考资料 Ⅳ.①H319.34

中国国家版本馆CIP数据核字(2024)第072011号

20天背完考研英语（一）核心词汇
20 TIAN BEI WAN KAOYAN YINGYU (YI) HEXIN CIHUI
新东方考试研究中心　编著

责任编辑	赵清刚
美术编辑	韩　波
责任校对	马立改
责任印务	时小娟
文字编辑	张瑞琪
封面设计	申海风
出版发行	浙江教育出版社
	地址：杭州市天目山路40号
	邮编：310013
	电话：（0571）85170300－80928
	邮箱：dywh@xdf.cn
印　　刷	三河市良远印务有限公司
开　　本	710mm×960mm　1/16
成品尺寸	168mm×230mm
印　　张	23.5
字　　数	424 000
版　　次	2024年4月第1版
印　　次	2024年4月第1次印刷
标准书号	ISBN 978-7-5722-7720-7
定　　价	48.00元